LATINO HIGH SCHOOL GRADUATION
Defying the Odds

THE HOGG FOUNDATION MONOGRAPH SERIES
Charles M. Bonjean, Editor

LATINO HIGH SCHOOL GRADUATION

Defying the Odds

HARRIETT D. ROMO AND TONI FALBO

UNIVERSITY OF TEXAS PRESS, AUSTIN

Requests for permission to reproduce material from this work should be sent to Permissions, University of Texas Press, Box 7819, Austin, TX 78713-7819.

⊗ The paper used in this publication meets the minimum requirements of American National Standard for Information Sciences—Permanence of Paper for Printed Library Materials, ANSI Z39.48-1984.

LIBRARY OF CONGRESS CATALOGING IN PUBLICATION DATA

Romo, Harriett.

    Latino high school graduation : defying the odds / Harriett D. Romo and Toni Falbo. — 1st ed.
        p.   cm. — (The Hogg Foundation research series)
    Includes bibliographical references and index.
    ISBN 0-292-72494-2 (cloth : alk. paper). — ISBN 0-292-72495-0 (pbk. : alk. paper)
    1. Mexican-American students—Social conditions—Case studies. 2. High school dropouts—United States—Case studies. 3. High school graduates—United States—Case studies. 4. Socially handicapped students—Education (Secondary)—United States—Case studies. I. Falbo, Toni. II. Title. III. Series.
LC2683.4.R65   1996
371.97′6872073—dc20   95-16645

TO OUR OWN FAMILIES

AND TO THE FAMILIES WHO SHARED THEIR LIVES WITH US.

CONTENTS

FOREWORD

The Hogg Foundation for Mental Health was established in 1940 to develop and conduct "... a broad mental health program of great benefit to the people of Texas" (Miss Ima Hogg, 1939). Unique as a permanent endowment given to a state university, its grantmaking activities and staff-operated programs seek to (1) improve the quality, scope, and delivery of mental health services; (2) increase public understanding of mental health issues; (3) advance training in mental health; and (4) contribute to that body of scientific knowledge related to mental health.

The Foundation's monograph series was established in 1958 primarily to strengthen its mental health research and education functions. Over the years, the publications in this series have helped to achieve *all* of the goals listed above, but seldom in a single publication. *Latino High School Graduation: Defying the Odds* may be an exception since it has the potential to make a contribution in all of these areas.

Harriett Romo and Toni Falbo offer new information and fresh ideas about those factors contributing to a serious problem in our nation's schools and communities—the *decline* in high school graduation rates for Hispanics at the same time those rates are *improving* for Anglos and African Americans. Their research findings are presented in a way that will be appreciated by academics and easily understood by mental health and educational policymakers, professionals, advocates, and students. Their bold and creative policy recommendations directly target the barriers they identify which make it difficult or impossible for many Latino students to cope effectively with personal, social, and academic demands. If adopted, their suggestions could go a long way toward improving the training and activities of those who directly affect the mental health of minority students during most of their waking hours—school administrators and teachers.

At the outset of this project, the Foundation's executive staff members had confidence in and high expectations for the study's potential. We were impressed with Romo and Falbo's innovative and positive approach to the problem, which sought to identify strategies associated with *success*, rather than just those factors related to failure. We felt that their use of both ethnographic and quantitative data and analysis could yield insights that might be missed by using only a single approach. Their topic combined two mental health areas of sustained central concern to the Foundation—children and youth, and minority mental health. And finally, we thought their findings would have important implications for both family practice and public policy. As the three-year study of one hundred students (designated "at risk" by their schools) and their families proceeded, its scope was also expanded. Early on it appeared that family attitudes and behavior were indeed related to students' progress, but so were poverty, negative self-images, alcoholism, peer group pressure (including gangs), teachers, schools and their policies—especially tracking, and a long history of institutional discrimination.

How these factors affect Latino students and their families are vividly described in the words of the students and their parents and are convincingly explained through analyses of the interview data and discussions with school personnel, examinations of school policies and records, and the use of state educational data and policies.

Even before their research was completed, Romo and Falbo were asked by many groups to discuss their preliminary findings and to offer suggestions based on them. The news about their research spread, and parts of their study and some of their ideas appeared in major metropolitan papers and in the August 19, 1991, issue of *Newsweek*. About the same time they were thinking about writing this book, they had to decide whether to orient it primarily to academics or to a wider audience. We were delighted when they opted to take a more applied and humanistic approach and believe that the result will appeal to both academics and many others with special interests in mental health, Latinos, and/or our educational system. Readers will appreciate the strikingly direct and human way in which the successes and failures of these students are spelled out. They will also learn that the most significant problems lie not with students themselves or their parents, but rather in their communities and especially their schools. Adopting Romo and Falbo's policy recommendations could make a major contribution to the future of our society by giving Latino students and their families new hopes and greater opportunities to succeed in their schools and their lives.

CHARLES M. BONJEAN, EDITOR

THE HOGG FOUNDATION MONOGRAPH SERIES

PREFACE

We acknowledge from the outset that our own personal histories influenced the contents of this book. Our own strong beliefs in education as a tool for personal and social advancement drove us to begin the research project that is the basis of this book. Our backgrounds had an effect on the observations we made as we studied the "at risk" youth and families participating in our research project. No doubt, our personal histories influenced the conclusions we drew from these observations. The fact that we recognize this influence is not a weakness, but a strength. All researchers are influenced by their own personal histories. We will briefly describe ours here so that the readers of this book can understand our perspective.

STATEMENT BY HARRIETT D. ROMO

In their perceptions of education, my parents were very much like the parents I interviewed for this book. My family valued education, but it did not have much of a practical impact on their lives. My father was killed in World War II shortly before I was born. As a struggling single parent, my mother had to move in with her mother in Louisiana to make ends meet. She had a high school diploma, but had acquired few skills that would allow her to get a job. She remarried when I was five and moved to Texas where my stepfather worked in a chemical refinery as an operator. The town I grew up in had an active Ku Klux Klan organization and clauses in real estate deeds that prohibited African Americans or Mexicans from owning property in the subdivisions. A small group of Mexican Americans attended my high school, which was on the outskirts of the town, but they did not socialize with the Anglo students.

Growing up, I never met anyone with a college education except my teachers and the family physician. When I discovered that a World War II Veteran's

Orphan benefits program would pay my way to college, I was determined to attend and become a teacher. Having no role models of women who worked or went to college, my family did not understand why I would want to leave home to go to school or why I would want to work. My mother's advice when I began my freshman year at the University of Texas in Austin was "Don't get involved in a career and let marriage pass you by." While they were proud of my academic achievements, they had little understanding of the importance of education and themselves had not received any practical benefits from a high school diploma. My mother was always interested in what I was doing, but was embarrassed to come to the school to talk with my teachers.

At the university, I became interested in Latino issues and met my future husband, a Mexican American, participating in an exchange program for Latino students from Chile. I decided to teach for a year in Nicaragua to learn Spanish.

After returning from Nicaragua, my first public school assignment was in an inner-city school in Los Angeles, the September after the Watts riots. The personnel director for the school district was so surprised that I requested an inner-city school that he called the University of Texas long-distance and had my transcripts verified over the phone. He hired me on the spot. My assignment was a fifth-grade classroom of 40 students. None of my charges read above the third-grade level. I was the only Anglo in the classroom. Many of the students were immigrants from Mexico who spoke no English. All were from low-income families.

My experiences that year, and the next five years, in which I taught English as a Second Language, organized a remedial math and reading program, and wrote proposals to start a bilingual program, shaped my interest in Latino youth and their families and provided the impetus of my desires to learn how to make schooling more rewarding for Latino students. Realizing that I could make few changes at the classroom level, I took a job at a National Origin Desegregation Center. In that position I traveled to school districts through-out California to help administrators and teachers plan programs for limited-English-speaking students.

I returned to graduate school in sociology hoping to find answers to the achievement problems I saw Latino students encounter. My dissertation re-search focused on Mexican immigrant children. I did fieldwork with undocu-mented immigrant families who had very little formal education. I was im-pressed with the parents' ability to cut to the heart of issues affecting their children, with their insights into their experiences in the U.S., and with their ability to articulate their feelings about education. As newcomers to the U.S., they valued education highly and saw it as a way to improve the lives of their children. When I began the project described in this book, I was eager to interview the Latino high school students that the school district had identified as "at risk of dropping out of school." I hoped the ethnographic component of the present study would provide an opportunity to expand my dissertation research and allow me to delve more deeply into Latino families' experiences with schooling.

I was not disappointed. The interviews were poignant; I often left a home feeling deeply depressed and angry about what had happened to the family in the schools. I shared their disappointments and their frustrations when a child dropped out of school. I also felt their sense of achievement when their child received that high school diploma. I had not anticipated the intensity of emotion that this fieldwork would generate. My interviews with these families left me with worries about my own teenagers' school experiences and a sense of guilt because I had the educational and financial resources to make the system work for my children.

Several things surprised me from the fieldwork. I was unprepared for the sense of failure that lingered long after an individual dropped out of school. Parents who had dropped out as adolescents themselves still felt a deep anger, remorse, and defeat associated with school. Their sense of failure was intensified as they tried to help their own children stay in school. The same sense of failure was evident in the interviews of the youths, some of whom told us as we tried to schedule the last interviews, "You don't want to talk to me, I dropped out." Others blamed themselves for their school failures. Many of the parents and youth dealt with these failures by developing alternatives to school achievement—career alternatives, self-esteem alternatives, and success alternatives. One family celebrated their son's passing of the GED exam, once the parents realized the high school diploma was not a possibility. Another mother aspired for her son to graduate from high school and go to college, but resolved that she was happy that he had finally settled down with his girlfriend and started a family. Dropping out of school was so common among family members, friends, and neighbors that while it came as a disappointment, it was not unexpected.

Although I was well aware of the serious problems facing public schools, having taught in Los Angeles in the late 1960s, I had expected more progress when we began our work in the schools in 1988. I was surprised by the discrepancies in what the school district reported they were doing for "at risk" students and what the parents and students told us was lacking. The district we studied voiced a strong commitment to reduce the dropout rate, but the variety of programs listed for "at risk" students and the policies that stated the district's commitment to this problem did not address the deep sense of alienation and powerlessness that we encountered among the students and parents. I talked with students who did not know the names of their teachers. Students preferred dead-end jobs to school because "at work they care if you show up." Students told us they avoided talking to their teachers because they anticipated reprimands for poor achievement. Students told us they wanted to be doctors and lawyers, but by age 20 they had earned only a fraction of the credits required to earn a high school diploma. Not only did gangs affect those who were active members and involved in violent and illegal acts, but gang members also threatened those who tried to do well in school and intimidated others from attending. Peer culture promoted truancy, negative school attitudes, and disrespect for academic achievement. The programs that seemed to help students stay in school and graduate had long waiting lists or were not available at the schools our students attended.

We began the present study at a pivotal point, just when school districts in Texas were required for the first time to identify students who were "at risk of dropping out of school." I worried about the negative effects of this labeling, but I knew I could use the skills I had acquired in my graduate studies and teaching of sociology to place these students' experiences in a larger social context. Public schools have provided me with social and economic mobility and an intellectually satisfying career. I remain convinced that the same could happen for "at risk" students.

STATEMENT BY TONI FALBO

I have always believed that education was essential for human progress. My parents were deeply committed to my own education, making it the centerpiece of their lives for two decades. One of the reasons why they were so dedicated to my education was that my parents had suffered from deprivation, as children and youth, and they wanted to do all they could to prevent this from happening to me. They told me countless times that getting an education was the most important thing I could do to prevent bad things from happening to me. I share their values. Like most people of the American middle class, I assumed that all parents were like my parents and that all students graduated from high school.

I grew up in the Washington, D.C., area during a time when there was no significant Hispanic community there. The first time I remember seeing a Mexican American was at a Texas festival on the grounds of the Smithsonian Institution. On a stage surrounded by vendors selling sausage and Texas barbecue was a mariachi band. They wore tight black pants and jackets. The seams of their costumes were outlined with white embroidery and beans were sewn along their pant legs. They wore gigantic straw hats. They sang their hearts out, and I loved the passion, the humor, the liveliness of their music.

About one year later, I left D.C. to go to graduate school in Los Angeles. I lived where other graduate students lived, on the beach. Other than frequent visits to Mexican restaurants, I had no daily contact with Mexican Americans. There were very few Mexican Americans among my graduate student peers. I didn't think much about this at the time. None of my peers did either, then.

As a graduate student in social psychology, I worked on a project about school desegregation. I learned how to analyze on a computer the numerical data about student achievement. One of the things I learned from this project was that the people in the southwestern part of the U.S. were divided into three categories: Mexican Americans, Blacks, and Anglos. I was an Anglo. I also learned that Mexican American students on the average did not do well in school.

I got my Ph.D. and joined the graduate faculty at the University of Texas. By this time I was very aware of the large proportion of the population that was of Mexican origin in California and Texas. I expected Mexican American students to show up in my graduate seminars, and I looked forward to working with them on trying to discover ways of improving the scholastic performance of Mexican Americans. I took Spanish classes. I waited.

After almost 20 years of teaching graduate school in Texas, I can count on one hand the number of Mexican American students I have taught. Over 90% of the American students in my graduate seminars have been Anglos.

It became clear to me that I would never have more than a handful of Mexican American graduate students unless I worked with public schools to improve the high school graduation rates of Mexican American students. Because so many Mexican American students never graduate from high school, there are relatively few eligible to go to college. And graduate school selects among those who have graduated from college. It is a wonder I have had any Mexican American graduate students at all!

In the long process of working on this project, I made many personal discoveries. One of the most painful was the way that many of my colleagues defended the status quo. As I explained my research to my colleagues, I uncovered attitudes that helped explain why Mexican Americans, and other minority groups, have remained in poverty. One colleague predicted that at the end of my research I would discover that "the smart ones will graduate"—in other words, that ability would explain it all. Another told me that the problem was in "the low quality of their family environments"—essentially, that the lack of education among Mexican-origin parents was responsible for their children's dropping out of school. Both of these explanations support the status quo in education because they blame Hispanics for their own school failures.

Few of my colleagues suspected that the problem was largely in the schools. Indeed, I became aware of how much some of my colleagues benefit from the status quo in public education and, consequently, had no desire to change it. One colleague complained to me about changes in local school policies that allowed any student to take an honors course in high school. This professor was certain that this would "water down" the standards and prevent his "gifted" children from getting the education they deserved.

I have resigned myself to the fact that some parents will fight the changes that we propose in the schools because they realize that our recommendations would radically shift the school's resources to serving the needs of the majority of students, not just the few who qualify to be in the elite programs.

I was delighted by the prospect of working with Harriett Romo on this topic for two reasons. First, Harriett was as motivated as I was to find ways of improving the high school graduation rates of Mexican American students. Second, Harriett was trained as an ethnographer and had done extensive fieldwork with Mexican-origin families. I was trained to combine statistical information with case studies. Over the course of my career, I have refined my ability to integrate quantitative skills with my skills in the analysis of qualitative information. Harriett and I realized that if we combined our methodological skills, we would be more likely to develop a deeper understanding of the educational problems of Latino youths.

OUR STATEMENT

Our position is that the goal of public education should be to educate *all students* so that they can be productive adults and good citizens. At present, most public schools in the U.S. are not doing this because they have been rewarded for focusing their attention on the needs of students from the middle class. While some of the students we studied could have obtained bachelor's degrees, none of them succeeded in four-year universities after high school graduation. This underachievement was due in part to the schools' tracking of Mexican American students into general or vocational coursework that did not train them to have the skills they needed to get a bachelor's degree or a job that offered future mobility. Most of our students did not even make it to community college. Indeed, some very bright students we studied were unable to graduate from high school because school policies were not responsive to their needs, as children of uneducated Mexicans.

Our collective failure to educate Mexican-origin students up to the levels that will make them eligible for good jobs will cost us dearly. Not only will we be losing the quality work that they could have done, but also we will be preventing several generations from full participation in the mainstream economy.

We learned from the families we studied that parents of "at risk" students were reluctant to demand that the schools take action to prevent school failure for their children. Most of the parents were demoralized by their feelings that they had failed in public schools. They also believed that they were powerless to make the schools work for their children. The majority of the parents were grateful for our attention to their children's school problems and thanked us for interviewing them and for listening to their experiences.

As we wrote this book, we incorporated the words of the parents and adolescents directly from the transcribed interviews. We wanted to capture the tone and intensity of their reflections. We have tried to represent their experiences as they presented them to us. We hope that these stories motivate people to make the changes needed in our schools and communities to assure that all students can be successful.

ACKNOWLEDGMENTS

We are grateful to the Hogg Foundation for Mental Health for providing most of the funds needed to conduct this research. Dr. Charles M. Bonjean, now Executive Director of the Hogg Foundation, encouraged us to seek funding from the Foundation and guided us in the formulation of the project. He also gave us useful feedback as we wrote and revised each chapter of this book.

We are also grateful for the collaboration of the Austin Independent School District, particularly Dr. Linda Frazer and the Office of Research and Evaluation.

Many students and staff helped us collect, transcribe, code, and statistically analyze the data we collected during our research. We wish to thank the following people for their help: Jana Swedo, Kathy Sowards, Rosa Campos, Diana Cornelius, Mary Dorst, Allison Frank, Miguel Guajardo, Yetilu Baessa, Rich Ann Roche, Jang-Young Lee, Susa Bohey, Reymundo Guzman, Betty Milstead, Mary Maggi, Melinda Farmer, Stacie Schauer, Debbie Vargas, and Cindy Russell. Joy Touchstone, Alissa Friedman-Torres, and Lillian Ramirez were funded by the National Science Foundation's Research Experience for Minority Undergraduates to work on our project during the summers.

H.D.R.

T.F.

ONE

The Goals
and Methods
of This Book

The purpose of this book is to describe how "at risk" Hispanic youth defy the odds and stay in school to earn a high school diploma. We have focused on the success stories—the stories of students who graduated from high school, against the odds. We hope that these case studies and our analyses of them will aid other students, parents, and schools in keeping "at risk" students in school and on the pathway toward high school completion.

Such information is needed because Hispanic youth drop out of school at about twice the rate of non-Hispanic Whites;[1] many leave school before completing the ninth grade. These low levels of educational attainment limit the youths' ability to obtain good jobs and become successful citizens of their state and nation. A good job is one that generates an income above the poverty level for a 40-hour work week. It is also one which is satisfying, includes on-the-job training, and provides opportunities for advancement.[2]

Recent research on American dropouts by the U.S. Department of Education indicates that while the proportion of American youth earning high school diplomas has improved overall since 1972, the proportion of Hispanic youth who have not completed high school remains high. In 1991, 35.3% of Hispanics ages 16–24 were not in school and had not received a high school diploma, about the same percentage as in 1972. In contrast, the dropout rates for Whites and African Americans have shown steady improvement over the same period. For non-Hispanic Whites in 1972, 12.3% were not in school and had not graduated, and in 1991, this percentage had dropped to 8.9%; for African Americans, this shift was from 21.3% to 13.6%.[3]

THE SPECIAL FOCUS OF THIS BOOK

Our book is based on the results of a four-year, longitudinal study of 100 Hispanic youth whom their school district had designated as "at risk" of dropping out of school. The students were 15 years old when we first interviewed them and their families. We followed them through the next four years in order to observe the pathways they took to complete high school or to drop out.

The high number of students leaving school before graduation is regarded as a major national problem. Therefore, at first glance, a book based on a study of 100 students from a single school district may seem unimportant. Nonetheless, it is widely acknowledged that most of the solutions to the dropout problem must come from individual school districts dealing with individual students. By focusing on a typical urban school district and individual students, we will explore the nature of the problem and its possible solutions. In this way, we believe that our findings can help to improve graduation rates nationwide.

Most studies of the educational attainment of Mexican-origin youth "at risk" of dropping out focus on the characteristics of dropouts[4] or the demographic nature and extent of the dropout problem.[5] This book is special because it explains how a group of "at risk" youth overcame their academic difficulties to graduate from high school. The book emphasizes the strategies the youth, their parents, and their schools used to bring about high school graduation.

We gathered information about our "at risk" students from a wide range of sources, including their families, their schools, and the youth themselves. Most studies of high school dropouts are based on data solely from institutional sources[6] or students.[7] We combine information from the school district with information from the students and their parents, along with our own observations, to create a deeper understanding of each youth's school successes and failures.

We followed our sample over four years, during an age span (15–19) when young people are expected to be completing high school. Many studies of dropouts use cross-sectional data, that is, data collected at one point in time, to examine the correlates of school success and failure. Because we collected information about these youth throughout this four-year span, we were able to create a chronology of events leading up to high school completion or dropping out for individual youth.

Some of our data are numeric (i.e., quantitative) and some are statements individuals made during interviews (i.e., qualitative). We combine information from both types of data in each chapter of this book. The quantitative information comes both from such sources as the school district and from the questionnaires we administered to parents and students at the beginning of the study. Examples of quantitative information include whether the student qualified for free, reduced-price, or full-price lunch, and standardized test scores (e.g., grade equivalents on the Iowa Test of Basic Skills). We analyze the quantitative data statistically and the results of such analyses are reported throughout the book.

The qualitative information comes from structured, open-ended interviews with the "at risk" youth and their parents, as well as interviews with relevant others, such as teachers, high school vice principals, and police officers. We tape-recorded the student and parent interviews and transcribed the recordings. Fieldwork in places frequented by the youths and their families during the fall of 1989 and the summers of 1989, 1991, and 1992 enabled us to collect information about the social and physical environments they lived and worked in. The researchers and research assistants visited summer schools and observed and conducted informal interviews with Hispanic youth at clubs, arcades, malls, and apartment complexes. One research assistant tutored students who had not passed the state exit-level exam; another worked in a "Communities in Schools" program. We accompanied one of the school district dropout coordinators on his home visits and talked with other community leaders and school district personnel about the dropout problem. We compared these field notes with comments of parents and students in the open-ended interviews to help us better understand the experiences of the students participating in our study.

In short, the longitudinal data collection and the combination of qualitative and quantitative data are strengths of this study that are seldom, if ever, found in studies of high school students.

The seven chapters at the core of this book are focused on specific aspects of the problem. The key problems we selected were those which emerged from our qualitative and quantitative analyses as critical in determining the student's success or failure at obtaining a diploma. Specifically, one chapter is focused on each of the following: the tracking of students, grade retention and high standards, gang involvement, teen motherhood, the special needs of immigrant families, the GED, and administrative glitches and punitive school policies.

We start each of these chapters with the stories of individual students and then analyze their stories in terms of the causes of their successes and failures. On the basis of what we have learned from these cases, we make recommendations for changes in school policies that will improve the outcomes for similar students in the future.

In order to protect the identities of the students and their families, we assigned fictitious names to the individuals described and, in some cases, gave the parents different occupations. We assigned Spanish-language names to individuals whose real names were of Spanish origin and we assigned average American names to individuals whose real names were common American ones. For example, we would assign the name Pedro to someone named Jaime and we would assign the name Robert to someone named Richard.

THE CONTEXT OF OUR STUDY

The State

Texas ranked 42d nationally in the percentage of its youth who graduated from high school in the late 1980s; at that time, almost one third of all Texas youth were beginning adult life without a high school diploma.[8] Nonetheless, when educational issues began to be a concern for Texas politicians during the early 1980s, they were more interested in raising academic standards than in reducing dropout rates. In 1984 the Texas 68th Legislature, Second Called Session, passed House Bill No. 72, Chapter 28, which radically reformed education (*See General and Special Laws of Texas, Book 1*, 68th Legislature, Second Called Session, 1984, pp. 117–192). Specifically, the number of courses required for graduation was increased; a program of minimum-competency tests was established, which students had to pass in order to graduate; the attendance requirements for receiving course credit were strengthened; and the "no pass/no play" rule was instituted, which meant that students who failed a course were unable to participate in extracurricular activities.

After 1984, school districts complained about the impact of the new education laws on dropout rates. They argued that many students were giving up rather than knuckling down to meet the new standards, and consequently, dropout rates were increasing. In response, the Texas Legislature enacted a dropout law in 1987. Among other things, the law required school districts to report dropout rates according to a common statewide definition, to create a dropout prevention plan, and to designate someone in the district as dropout coordinator. In addition, the law required each district to identify students "at risk" of dropping out according to the common statewide definition and notify the students' parents of their status and of the programs and/or services which could help the "at risk" student.

The City

Our sample of 100 students lived in the Austin metropolitan area in 1988, and almost all of them continued to live in Austin during the period of our study.

Austin, the state capital, has one of the youngest (one half of the adults are under 35) and best-educated (37% have college degrees) metropolitan populations in the U.S. Overall, the metropolitan area is predominantly non-Hispanic White (70%). Approximately 20% of the area's population is Hispanic. African Americans are the second largest minority, representing about 10% of the population.

Austinites are a geographically mobile group with about 40% of all adults having lived in the area less than five years. Part of this mobility is caused by the fact that Austin is the home of the University of Texas, which enrolls about 50,000 students annually. The presence of the university and the state capitol means that a high proportion of the area's citizens are government employees. Other major employers include manufacturers, particularly high-tech industries.[9]

Employment forecasts for Austin suggest that the city will continue to attract industries involved in the development and manufacturing of high technology and specialized instruments. Research and development for high technology manufacturing, computer programming, and business services are expected to expand. Computers and related products and microelectronics manufacturing jobs are expected to account for over 61% of the total manufacturing employment in Austin by the year 2000.[10]

The East Side

Austin is divided into East and West by an interstate highway. Traditionally, the residents of East Austin have been African Americans or Mexican Americans. As families of these minorities improved their financial situation, they moved out of the inner core of East Austin to the northern or southern suburbs usually east of the interstate. The residents of West Austin have been predominantly middle- or upper-middle-class non-Hispanic Whites.

Most of the families in our study lived east of the interstate, particularly in the inner-city East Austin area. During the time of our study, the poverty rate for this area was in excess of 40%.[11] According to census information, the Eastside barrios had very high percentages of adults with less than a ninth-grade education.[12]

The School District

We worked with the Austin Independent School District (AISD), one of the eight major urban school districts in Texas. Although the district is relatively large (the enrollment in AISD during the period of our study was around

71,000 students), it does not encompass all of the Austin metropolitan area. Surrounding the AISD are suburban school districts which have experienced great growth during the last 15 years. During the time of our study, AISD had 13 high schools, 15 junior high or middle schools, and 63 elementary schools. AISD was one of the largest employers in Austin.

The average amount of money that the district spent on each student during the time of our study ranged from $3,641 in the 1988–89 school year to $3,952 in the 1990–1991 school year. This level of spending was about average for Texas school districts.[13]

Since 1980, the district's enrollment has become increasingly minority, and demographic projections indicate that this trend will continue. In 1980, 19% of the students were African Americans, 27% were Hispanic Americans, and the remainder (54%) were non-Hispanic White Americans (and Others). By 1990, 20% were African Americans, 33% were Hispanics, and 47% were categorized as non-Hispanic Whites (and Others). Thus, during our study, the combined number of Hispanic and African American students became greater than the number of non-Hispanic Whites. Furthermore, an increasing number of students have been coming from low-income homes, and demographic projections indicate that the future growth in enrollment for the district will be from such homes.[14]

The district's attention to the dropout problem preceded the state reforms, and consequently, it has made some progress in reducing the dropout rate. In fact, the desire to improve graduation rates motivated AISD to work with us on this research project. Still, the dropout rate remains unacceptably high. According to the Texas Education Agency,[15] the estimated longitudinal dropout rate for AISD for the 1990–91 school year was 36.6%, among the highest rates for all districts in the state. Some of the other large school districts with higher rates included Laredo Independent School District, along the Texas-Mexican border, with an estimated longitudinal dropout rate of 38.7%, and Houston Independent School District, the largest district in the state, with a 39.3% rate.

According to AISD records, the dropout rate for Hispanic students has been twice that of non-Hispanic White students. For example, during the 1988–89 school year, 7.6% of the White high school students dropped out, while 14.8% of the Hispanic high school students did. Similarly, for the 1989–90 school year, the percentage of White high school students who dropped out fell to 6.3%, while that of the Hispanic high school students was down only slightly, to 14.5%.[16]

Like the other urban districts in Texas, AISD attempted to solve the dropout problem with "programs" aimed at helping "at risk" youth. Unfortunately, over half of the "at risk" students during the years of our project were not served by any yearlong program for "at risk" students. Most notably, no programs existed for students under the age of 16 who had excessive absences and wanted to begin earning credits toward graduation.

While the district maintained a long list of programs that were thought to reduce the dropout rate, only a few were proven to be effective, as judged by the district's own evaluation staff. These same internal evaluations indicated that the students enrolled in the ineffective programs actually were more likely to drop out than were comparable students.[17]

THE STUDY

Our Sample

All of our sample of Hispanic youth were of Mexican origin. Because of the shared heritage of the Mexican Americans and Mexicans in our sample, we chose to use the term *Mexican origin* to describe both groups. Most of the Mexican-origin population in the United States resides in two states, California and Texas. According to the results of the 1990 Census, people of Mexican origin comprised about 64% of all those designated as Hispanic in the U.S. In Texas, about 94% of all Hispanics were of Mexican origin.[18]

All of our students had been designated as *"at risk"* of dropping out of school, according to guidelines found in House Bill 1010 passed in the 70th Legislature, Regular Session, in 1987.[19] In order to be designated as "at risk," a student had to possess at least one of the following characteristics:

- Retained at least one grade.
- Scored two or more years below grade level in reading or mathematics, according to norm-referenced standardized tests.
- Failed at least two courses in one semester and was therefore unlikely to graduate in four years since beginning the ninth grade.
- Failed at least one section of the statewide standardized test designed to ensure that all high school graduates have basic skills.

During the three years of our study, the percentage of students designated as "at risk" of dropping out ranged from 41% to 46% of all seventh to twelfth graders in the school district. A greater proportion of the Hispanic (54%–60%) and African American (59%–61%) students were identified as "at risk" than were Asian American (34%–40%) or White American (25%–31%) students.

In the early part of the 1988–89 school year, the school district mailed letters to the parents of all seventh to twelfth grade students identified as "at risk" according to the state criteria, described above. Each letter was personalized, in that it described the reason why the specified child was thought to be "having academic difficulties." The letters were placed on the letterhead of the school that the student attended, and each letter indicated that it had been sent by the school's principal.

By prearrangement with the school district, we mailed our letters inviting the parents and students to volunteer for our study within two days of the notification letters from each school. We invited all Hispanic, 15-year-old, "at risk" students and their parents to participate in the study. This amounted to 827 invitations. We stated the purpose of our project as an effort to discover how "at risk" students stay in school. Our letters were printed on University of Texas letterhead, specifically from the Center for Mexican American Studies. Our letters and those from the schools were in both English and Spanish.

We received 107 signed consent forms from these parents. We deleted seven families from our sample because they were not of Mexican origin or because they did not give us information allowing us to get in touch with them. This constitutes a response rate of 13%, a seemingly low but not unusual response rate for an "at risk" Hispanic population. More important, our group of volunteers was similar demographically to the larger group of 827, who were part of the same cohort identified by the district as part of the class of 1991. The specific comparisons are in Table 1.1.

Most of the differences are extremely small between our sample of volunteers and the larger, eligible pool of students labeled "at risk" within the same cohort. Our sample contained a slightly higher percentage of female students, but was similar in the other characteristics in the table. The characteristics included in the table are those most frequently cited in the literature on dropouts as relevant to the causes of dropping out.

In our study, we designated students as "low income" if they had received some form of meal subsidy (full or partial) from the schools, or if they had a sibling who received this subsidy. The school district used the income guidelines established by the U.S. Department of Agriculture to determine eligibility for lunch assistance. The guidelines are based on a combination of family size and income. During the time period of our study, about 42% of all students in the district were qualified to receive this type of subsidy.

Although our sample consists of many overage students, being overage for grade level was relatively common in this school district, particularly for Hispanics. On average, during the first year of our study, about 19% of all elementary school students, 4% of middle school students, and 18% of high

TABLE 1.1.   Comparison of Our Sample with the Larger Pool of Eligible Nonparticipants

	Our Sample (N=100) %	Eligible Pool (N=827) %
Female	53	47
Low income	53	51
Limited English	13	9
Overage	77	72
Special Ed.	10	13
Gifted	1	0
Graduated	31	39

school students had been retained at least one grade. The percentage of Hispanic students who were overage was greater than that of other students. For example, during the 1990–91 school year, the average percentage of ninth-grade Hispanics who were overage by one or more years was 63.3%; overall (i.e., for all students) that percentage was 49.7%.[20]

Almost all of the students in our sample were comfortable speaking in English; a relatively small percentage of our sample participated in Limited English Proficiency (LEP) programs during the time of our study. Yet, almost all students in our sample experienced a skills deficit in reading: they were in higher grades than their reading skills supported easily. The average grade equivalent in reading for the students in our sample was around sixth-grade level (6.4, to be precise) at the beginning of the study. At the same time, our students were scattered across five grades, ranging from seventh to eleventh grade.

The percentage of our sample receiving special educational services was close to the district average. Around 11% of all students in the district received special educational services, a level comparable to that of the other major urban school districts in Texas.

All of the students in our sample should have been members of the graduating class of 1991. At the end of June 1991, only 15% of the students in our sample had graduated. In contrast, 66% of all Hispanic students who were in the district's class of 1991 graduated in June 1991.[21] Thus, the students in our sample were much less likely than the district's typical Hispanic student to graduate. The best performing students in the class of 1991 were non-Hispanic Whites, of whom 82% graduated in June 1991. Because many of the students in our sample (21%) were in middle school when we began the study, due to grade retentions, we extended by one year the duration of the study. More students from our sample graduated in 1992, bringing up to 31% the percentage of students from our sample who graduated. This percentage is slightly lower than the 39% of our comparison sample of eligible nonparticipants who graduated in 1992.

Our interviews with students and their parents indicated that many of the students in our sample had already begun the process of dropping out of school when we began our study. We observed many cases in which the school kept a student on their rosters even though he or she had accumulated more than 50% absences. Some of our students never made it to high school classrooms. One of the strengths of this study is that we selected students to study who were 15 years old, regardless of their grade level. As we followed them over time, we were able to observe the process of dropping out or graduating.

Most (70%) of the parents we interviewed were the mothers of students in our sample. The remainder were divided between the fathers (17%) and other adults (13%), such as legal guardians or stepfathers. At the time of our initial survey, most parents were living with a spouse, although some divorces and remarriages occurred during the four years of our study (see Table 1.2).

The majority of the parents in our sample were born in the U.S., and most of the Mexican-born parents were living in the U.S. legally. On our initial questionnaire, 25% of the parents reported speaking only Spanish, 14% spoke mostly Spanish, 46% spoke mostly English, and 15% spoke only English. Parents were asked what language the 15-year-old spoke mostly at home. They reported that only 6% of the adolescents spoke only Spanish, 15% spoke mostly Spanish, 36% spoke mostly English, and 43% spoke only English. The families most likely to speak only Spanish were recent immigrants. The difference between the percentage of adolescents speaking only English compared to that of the parents suggests a shift to English dominance typical in second- and third-generation Mexican-origin students. In our interviews, we saw a wide range of abilities to use Spanish. Some parents were illiterate in Spanish. Others spoke a mixture of English and Spanish, code-switching in conversations with the bilingual interviewers. This pattern of blending of English and Spanish is also typical of second- and third-generation Mexican Americans.[22]

The average number of years of school completed by the parents in the study was 8.7. While this level of educational attainment may appear low, this is not unusual for Hispanics. Many of our Mexican immigrant parents had no education at all. In 1990, the U.S. Census found that about 16% of Mexican-origin adults (25 years or older) had less than five years of education, while nationally only about 1% of the U.S. population had this low an educational

TABLE 1.2.   Description of the Parents at Beginning of Study

Spanish speaking	29%
Mexican born	25%
Educational attainment (all parents)	8.7 years
Educational attainment (U.S. born only)	10.5 years
Single parent	25%

attainment. The U.S.-born parents had attended a greater number of years of school than the Mexican-born parents; still, only 39% of the U.S.-born parents in our study had graduated from high school. Nationally, about 44% of Mexican-origin adults had four or more years of high school; for the U.S. population as a whole, 78% had this level of education.[23]

Our Procedures and Measurements

Our data about individual students and their families came from four sources: (1) an initial survey of the sample of 100 families, using separate but similar questionnaires for parents and students; (2) in-depth, tape-recorded interviews with 26 of the 100 families, one set of interviews at the beginning and one at the end of the study; (3) annual follow-up telephone interviews with the 100 families; and (4) information from the school district about each of the 100 students participating in our study. Copies of our questionnaires and all interview questions may be found in the Appendixes.

After we received the signed consent forms from the volunteering families, we recruited Latino and/or bilingual university students from a variety of disciplinary backgrounds to work with us as research assistants. The research assistants worked in pairs to make appointments with the volunteering families to interview at least one parent and the specific "at risk" student. The research assistants traveled to the homes to collect the initial survey data. When the student and parent were available simultaneously, the research assistants suggested that they talk to the parent and child separately (they explained this in terms of efficiency). One research assistant would take the student to a separate room and interview him or her there, while the other interviewed the parent or parents, usually in the front room. When the student or parent was missing, they made another appointment and returned to the home to complete the initial interviews.

Our first source of information about our volunteering families came from their responses to our questionnaires. During our initial home visits, the research assistants read each item from the questionnaire and recorded the parent's or student's responses directly on the questionnaire. The parents' questionnaire contained 117 items and focused on a variety of topics, including the parent's understanding of the reasons their child was designated as "at risk," the size and composition of their family and household, their own educational attainment, and their expectations for the child's educational attainment.

The students' questionnaire contained 100 items, 77 of them similar in content to items from the parents' questionnaire, but worded to reflect the student's perspective. For example, one item on the students' questionnaire was: "I make good grades in school." The comparable item on the parents' questionnaire was: "My child makes good grades in school." We asked the parents and children comparable questions in order to assess the degree of similarity in their answers. The remaining items on the students' questionnaire inquired about how hard the students tried in a variety of classes.

Most of the items on the initial questionnaire provided a list of possible answers, which were read out loud to the respondent by the research assistant, who then recorded the respondent's answers. Other items required the respondent to give a number, for example to estimate how many hours the student spent per week on homework.

Our second source of information was the ethnographic work we did with a subset of our larger sample. We stratified this subsample by the educational attainment of the parents, because numerous studies indicate that the educational attainment of parents is highly correlated with that of their children.[24] Further, our specific categories of parental education reflected the actual educational attainment of the parents in our larger sample of 100. These categories were: elementary school or less (N=7), secondary school dropout (N=7), high school graduate (N=6), and training beyond high school graduation (N=6).

We began our ethnographic work a few months after our initial interviews with the 100 families. Harriett Romo and one research assistant returned to the 26 families of our ethnographic subsample and interviewed the student and the parent again. This time, the interviews consisted of a series of tape-recorded, open-ended questions. For both students and parents, the questions focused on what it meant to be "at risk," experiences in school, goals and aspirations, friends and siblings, and characteristics of parent-child communication and control. The interview questions for the students and parents were similar in content. For example, the students were asked, "How do you get your parents to do what you want them to do?" The comparable question asked of parents about the target child was: "How do you get your son (or daughter) to do what you want him (or her) to do?"

At the end of the four-year period of our study, we conducted another set of tape-recorded parent and student interviews with the families in the ethnographic subsample. These occurred during the summer or early fall of 1991. For those who had graduated, we asked them about their last year of high school and what had helped them earn their diploma. We also asked them about their coursework and their future plans. For those who had dropped out of school, we asked them what had caused them to drop out, what they had been doing, and what their future plans were. We asked the parents about the strategies they used to keep their adolescents in school and/or what experiences they had had with the school district relevant to their child's dropping out.

Our third source of information about the families came from telephone interviews. Twice, at yearly intervals, we telephoned the students and parents of our larger sample of 100 to assess school progress. Using an interview guide, we asked specific questions and recorded the responses. We followed up on unusual or unexpected answers. We traveled to the homes of families without telephones. We talked to the parents and students separately. During the fall of 1989 and the fall of 1990, we asked the students and their parents about significant events that had happened to them since our last contact. In 1989, we asked them about the student's schoolwork, if the student were still attending school, and if not, what the student was doing now, how they spent their summer, and about any changes in their peer groups. In 1990, we asked more extensive questions about what was helping the student stay in school or what caused the student to leave school, whom the parent or student relied on for help in school, and generally encouraged our respondents to tell us of any changes in their lives which had occurred since our last communication.

Our efforts at keeping in touch with our respondents were successful in that we were able to keep track of almost all of our original sample. Ultimately, we were able to determine who graduated and who did not, among the total sample. However, we were not able to make contact with all of the original respondents at all the times of our data collection. For example, we were not able to have our final interview with 4 of the parents and 6 of the students from the ethnographic subsample ($N=26$).

Throughout the course of data collection, we worked closely with our research assistants, organizing seminars for the assistants to discuss problems and solutions. We studied the data they were collecting and transformed it into information useful for the production of this book.

Our fourth source of information about the students—the school district—provided us with the following about each student in our larger sample: the number of years overage for grade level, the percentile and grade equivalents for their most recent standardized test performance in reading and mathematics, the reasons the student had been originally designated as "at risk" of dropping out, whether the student qualified for free or reduced-price lunch, attendance rates, course schedules for each student, total credits earned by the 1991–92 school year, and when the student dropped out or graduated.

These four sources of information served as the core of the data we had about the families. As mentioned above, we embellished our knowledge of their lives by fieldwork in their schools, neighborhoods, and recreational areas, as well as through interviews with relevant others, such as school administrators.

OVERVIEW

This book provides insights into how schools function to reproduce educational and social inequality in our country.[25] The research literature about inequality demonstrates clearly that the educational level of parents is linked to the occupational outcomes of their children.[26] This literature, however, has never explained adequately how the schools maintain these inequalities across generations. Some have argued that the low level of educational and occupational attainment of Hispanics in the U.S. is caused by characteristics of the Hispanic culture and Hispanic families. Many studies of Hispanic culture conclude that Hispanic culture does not value education and that the poor child-rearing practices of Hispanic families prevent students from achieving.[27]

In the process of interviewing the students and their parents, we learned that they valued education. The majority of the parents tried their best to help their children achieve in school. We also learned how the schools discouraged Hispanic students from staying in school and graduating.

Each of the chapters at the core of this book presents the cases of specific individuals as they attempted to graduate from high school. Table 1.3 summarizes the background characteristics of these adolescents and their families. Chapter 2 describes the cases of Robert and James, two victims of the school's *tracking* policy. Robert was able to graduate from high school, but the coursework his school channeled him into did not prepare him for college-level work. Robert flunked out of college in his first year. James dropped out of high school, bored to exhaustion with low-level courses that led him nowhere.

Chapter 3 focuses on the effects of *grade retention* on two students, Richard and Alice. Richard was retained a grade in middle school, but he was able to overcome this grade retention through a program that accelerated his pace, thereby allowing him to graduate on time. Alice was retained in first grade and was never given the opportunity to make up the grade. State laws changed between the year Richard graduated and the year Alice was scheduled to receive

TABLE 1.3. Description of the Cases Highlighted in This Book

Student (Parent)	Household Composition	Home Language	Education		Employment	
			Student	Parent	Student	Parent
Chapter 2—Tracking						
Robert (Roland)	2 siblings 2 parents	English	H.S. diploma	B.A.	None	Accounting clerk
James (Petra)	5 siblings 2 parents	Bilingual	Dropout	6 years	Grocery bagger	Stockroom clerk
Chapter 3—Grade retention						
Richard (Maria Elena)	3 siblings Parents divorced Moved in with girlfriend, became father	English	H.S. diploma	Associate's Degree	Electrician's helper	Childcare administrator
Alice (Jessie)	8 sisters Mother died Lived with father	English	No diploma, failed exit exam	7 years	Grocery checker	Utility inspector
Chapter 4—Gangs						
Ramona (Paula)	8 siblings Parents divorced 4 nieces/nephews	Bilingual	H.S. diploma	6 years	Clerical worker	Disabled

TABLE 1.3. Description of the Cases Highlighted in This Book (*Continued*)

Student (Parent)	Household Composition	Home Language	Education		Employment	
			Student	Parent	Student	Parent
Salvador (Suzanna)	3 siblings Stepfather	English	dropout	GED	Graphic artist	Catering administrator
Chapter 5—Teen Motherhood						
Norma (Alfredo)	2 siblings Parents divorced Lived with father, had two children	English	H.S. diploma	H.S. diploma	Welfare program	Policeman
Kathy (Caroline)	5 siblings 2 parents	English	Dropout	H.S. diploma	None	Nurse's aide
Lupe (Graciela)	8 siblings 2 parents Had one child & boyfriend moved in	Spanish	Dropout	7 years	None	Cook's assistant
Chapter 6—Immigrant Students						
Linda (George)	3 siblings 2 parents	Bilingual	H.S. diploma	GED	Grocery checker	Lab technician

TABLE 1.3. Description of the Cases Highlighted in This Book (*Continued*)

Student (Parent)	Household Composition	Home Language	Education		Employment	
			Student	Parent	Student	Parent
Enrique	12 siblings 2 parents Lived with brother, then married, became father	Spanish	Dropout	None	Restaurant cashier	Migrant farmworker
Chapter 7—GED						
Martin, Jr. (Martin, Sr.)	2 siblings 2 parents	English	GED	GED	None	Industrial plant manager
Felipe (Juan Felipe)	3 stepsiblings Lived with stepmother & father	English	GED	Law degree	Worked for Dad	Lawyer
Chapter 8—Bureaucratic Glitches						
Pedro (The Garcías)	7 siblings 2 parents 3 nieces/nephews	Spanish	Dropout	None	Cutlery salesman	Construction worker

her diploma. The new law required Alice to pass a standardized test before she could graduate. She tried to pass four times, and eventually gave up. Alice never received her diploma, despite having accumulated enough credits to graduate.

In Chapter 4 we describe the approach the schools have taken to *gang involvement*. One student, Ramona, had only a peripheral involvement in gang life and was able to "stay back" from her gang friends so that she could attend school and graduate. We describe how school policies, notably the "no pass/no play" law,[28] actually facilitated her involvement in gang life by preventing her from participating in extracurricular activities. In contrast, Salvador was deeply involved in gang life and remained loyal to his "brothers." He dropped out. This chapter explains how school failure combined with family problems drove students into gang involvement and how changes in school policy can make school attendance more rewarding than gang involvement.

We describe the relationship between *teen motherhood* and school policies in Chapter 5. Norma was able to graduate despite having had one child and being pregnant with her second when she marched across the stage. Norma attributed her early motherhood to her lack of education about contraception and sexuality. Kathy and Lupe became mothers after they had dropped out. For these teen moms, the schools had discouraged their school attendance, and neither saw a future career emanating from their high school diploma.

Chapter 6 describes the impact of the infusion of the children of undocumented *immigrants into schools*. Linda was a second-generation Mexican American who got into fights with girls in order to defend her honor. She graduated, despite having become so overwhelmed by peer rejection that she attempted suicide in her senior year. Enrique was the son of undocumented immigrants and also got into school fights brought about by tensions between himself and native-born Mexican Americans. He dropped out in order to get a job and help support his parents.

The seventh chapter considers the value of a *GED* for two of our students, Martin, Jr. and Felipe. Martin, Jr. dropped out midyear after completing only a fraction of the credits he needed to graduate. He was 18 and passed the GED test the first time he took it. Felipe dropped out after completing his sophomore year in order to get his GED and enroll in community college. He had been retained two grades in elementary school due to learning disabilities, and he decided that at age 18 he was too old to stay in high school.

The eighth chapter describes our efforts to return a dropout to school and the *bureaucratic glitches* we encountered in this lengthy process. Pedro was the son of illiterate Mexican immigrants. His parents worked long hours and were unable to do any of the paperwork involved in returning Pedro to school. They worked double shifts and night shifts and thus were unable to keep Pedro on a regular schedule. He dropped out but continued to harbor the dream of graduating from high school and college.

Chapter 9 brings together all the individual stories from the previous chapters and describes parental influences on high school graduation. We describe seven strategies that parents used that helped their "at risk" children stay in school and graduate. The final chapter integrates the policy recommendations made at the end of each chapter into one comprehensive set of seven recommended changes for the schools.

Their Perspectives

This book tells the stories of students and their families as they struggled along the path toward high school graduation. We have tried to present the perspectives of the students and their parents fairly, as they wished to be understood. We have included the actual statements from the transcribed interviews whenever possible to capture the character and language of our volunteers. Some of their stories brought tears to our eyes as we listened; sometimes they cried as they talked. We tried to capture the intensity of our interviews and the stress involved both in being an "at risk" youth trying to achieve a high school diploma and in being the parent of such a youth.

We discovered that dropping out or staying in school was a dynamic process in which some students stopped attending for a period of time, and then returned, and then stopped attending again, and so on. We observed how precariously close the majority of these "at risk" students were to dropping out at several points along their pathway to graduation.

We also learned how much the schools had overestimated the educational, financial, and emotional resources of the parents in this sample. During the time we observed them, most of the parents were doing the best they could for their children. And yet, in many cases, their "best" was so constrained by their own lack of education, mental and physical health, and financial resources that they could do little to help their adolescent children.

Finally, we learned that while there were many individual teachers, office staff, and administrators who helped individual students graduate on time, the school system as a whole impeded our students' progress toward graduation. Consequently, this book is not just about the youth and their families, but also about the strengths and weaknesses of the school system.

TWO

The Tracking of Hispanic Students

"You're

not

college

material."

This chapter tells the stories of Robert and James and explains how academic tracking in middle and high school contributes to the relatively high Hispanic dropout rates in high school and college. Nationally, Hispanics drop out of school at higher rates than African Americans or non-Hispanic Whites. Robert, the most academically successful student in our sample, not only graduated from high school, but entered a four-year college. We examine the difficulties he and his parents had in getting him into college preparatory courses in middle and high school. We demonstrate how his inadequate preparation in secondary school made it almost inevitable that Robert would drop out of college in his first year. James never made it to college. The school district retained James twice in seventh grade and tracked him into the lowest-level classes. Consequently, he found academic coursework uninteresting and slow. He dropped out of high school. We demonstrate how schools use norm-referenced tests to track students and how this tracking practice reduces the likelihood that Hispanic students will acquire the skills they need to graduate from high school, succeed in college, or obtain a good job.

ROBERT

More than anything else, Robert and his parents wanted Robert to go to college. His father, Roland, was the youngest of twelve children. Roland was the first in his family to graduate from high school and the only one to go to college. He was able to go to college because his military service in Vietnam made him eligible for financial support as a veteran. He credited his college degree to his own hard work while at college. Roland explained, "Well, it was kinda hard for me to go to college when I didn't have all the prerequisites for college. And it was a lot harder for me to study, I mean I had to really study. And I found out that it was not like high school. I mean, I really had to study. I mean I had to reread and read."

Because of the difficulty Roland had in doing college work, he knew that his son needed to take college-preparatory coursework while in middle and high school. But Robert's school stymied Roland's efforts to prepare his son for college. Roland explained the problem this way, "One thing I didn't like about the school was that Robert wanted to take Algebra and they wouldn't let him take Algebra because they said his seventh-grade scores showed that he did not have the ability. So I went down there and talked to 'em about it. He was taking just Fundamentals of Math. The teacher said he couldn't take Algebra because of his grade he made in seventh or sixth grade. He wanted to take Algebra and they told him because of his scores in the seventh grade, he did not have the aptitude for Algebra."

Roland continued, "So I asked the teacher, 'Well, what is his average right now?' He says, 'A+.' 'Well, what has he done?' 'Well, he's made all 100s on the tests.' 'How about the pop quizzes?' '100s.' 'And what is the average of the class?' 'Well, most of them are 70s and 80s.' And I said, 'Well, don't you think since he's making 100s and all that, he knows the information already and you should put him up?' 'Yeah, but his scores in the seventh grade show that he doesn't have the aptitude.' They finally let him get into Pre-Algebra and he had a 93 average in there. When he finally went in there, I could see that it was easy for him. He was making 100s. Robert said, 'We're just going over the same things I did last year and the year before that. Just making the problems a little bit harder, that's it. I already know it.' So that's the only problem I had, when the teacher said to him, *'Well, you're not college material.'*"

Despite this setback, Robert and his father thought that the courses Robert was taking in high school would prepare him for college. When we first interviewed him, Robert told us that he was surprised that he had been labeled as "at risk" of dropping out because he was definitely going to graduate from high school and go to college. Robert thought that the reason he had been labeled "at risk" was the F he had received in a photography class. This F plus the fact that he failed to pass the writing portion of the statewide achievement test twice caused his "at risk" designation.

During the time of our study, Robert lived with his parents and his younger brother in a neatly kept three-bedroom house in a Mexican American enclave that had survived the encroachment of businesses and apartments in the area. Many members of Robert's extended family lived in the same neighborhood—a grandmother lived next door, an aunt and uncle across the street, and other aunts and cousins in the area. An uncle often helped Robert with schoolwork. All of these relatives kept track of Robert, which helped explain how

Robert managed to stay out of gang activities, despite their prevalence in his neighborhood.

Robert grew up with an older sister who had dropped out of school in the ninth grade. She became involved with a gang of girls and ran away from home at the age of 16. After the gang leader went to jail for stabbing and killing a man, the gang disbanded. Robert felt that he had to make up for what his sister had done to his parents. He explained it this way, "They want me to go to college, and I do, too. My sister didn't do so good and they expect me to do it. They'd kill me if I didn't finish high school."

Robert's parents frequently used the example of his sister to bolster their arguments in favor of high school graduation. His sister visited the family about once a month, usually asking for money. She had been able to get a job, but it paid poorly and she frequently found herself short of the money she needed. She told Robert that she too wanted him to graduate from high school. "Don't be like me, get a career," she told Robert. To make the point, she bought him his senior ring when he was in the tenth grade.

Roland and his wife, Anita, learned from the bad experience they had with their daughter and became much more strict with their sons. They encouraged Robert to participate in sports, specifically soccer, so that he would have a strong connection to a wholesome group of friends.

Playing soccer was important to Robert throughout high school. If his grades dropped, the school threatened him with suspension from the soccer team. Whenever this happened, he pulled up his grades and stayed on the team. Several times during our interviews with Robert, he mentioned his soccer tournaments with pride and excitement. His father served as a booster of the soccer club and knew the soccer schedule as well as Robert did. Soccer season spanned almost the entire year. Often, when Robert wanted to go out late on Friday night, Roland would remind him that he had a soccer match or practice early Saturday morning.

Robert described his closest friends as his "neighborhood friends." His best friend lived across the street and belonged to a gang. This friend dropped out of high school because he "flunked" a grade twice and became discouraged. According to Roland, this best friend would "rather have the money in his pocket right now than an education later." Robert did not see his "school friends" outside of school. He knew that they did better in school than his neighborhood friends. Robert sometimes did not fit in with his neighborhood friends. He explained, "I'm like the only one that really makes decent grades and all of that stuff." Students who made the honor roll were considered "nerds" by his "neighborhood friends." The stigma associated with being a nerd was especially strong during his middle school years.[1]

Robert attended the same elementary, junior high, and high school his father had attended until he was transferred to a new high school in his sophomore year because of school district boundary changes. The new school, one of the largest high schools in the city, had an enrollment of almost 2,500 students. Robert told us he liked his old school better because "there were lots of Mexicans there and everyone was friendly." At the new school, Robert found it hard to fit in because he felt the "white kids didn't like the Mexicans." Nonetheless, he told us that "I like going. I like talking to everybody. Not so much doing all the work, but I like going."

None of Robert's parents or siblings spoke Spanish at home. They were emphatic when they told us that they spoke only English. Nonetheless, Roland knew that Robert would need a foreign language to get into college and he told his son to take Spanish. Robert began taking Spanish in the ninth grade, but he told us that he felt uncomfortable in the class. Robert explained, "And, Spanish, I don't like volunteering there. I don't volunteer there. She gets mad at me. They expect me to volunteer since I'm Mexican, but I don't do it. The teacher gets mad at me. There are only, like, two or three Mexicans in there. I told them, 'You know, if I knew Spanish, why would I be taking the class?' They always expect me to do things and I don't do it." Despite the encouragement of his teacher to take honors-level Spanish classes, he stopped taking Spanish classes after two years.

He became discouraged in math also. School records show that Robert failed Algebra and repeated it in summer school. He explained that he didn't "ace" summer school, but "it wasn't any problem." He also explained that he had failed the first time because his "social life was too fun."

His failure tracked him into Informal Geometry, a remedial class. When Robert finally enrolled in the regular Geometry class, he was reluctant to ask the teacher for help even though he was having a difficult time keeping up. As a senior, he felt uncomfortable admitting he did not understand. He elaborated, "In my Geometry class I was a senior and most of them were sophomores and maybe some freshmen and I just felt I didn't want to be embarrassed in front of them. There were other seniors in there. I just didn't want to say I didn't understand that or something like that. I didn't want to do it in class."

While Robert was in high school, both he and his parents felt he could have done better in school if he had tried harder. Robert rationalized his mediocre performance by attributing it to his lack of motivation: "I'll just do what I can and especially just enough to pass. I don't care about honor rolls. I don't really go all out. . . . My parents get mad when I get failing progress reports, 'cause there's no need for it. I know I can do it." His self-confidence was based partially on his successes in social studies classes. For example, after Robert graduated from high school, he told us that when he was in the ninth grade, he outperformed a classmate on a Geography final. This classmate later went on to become class valedictorian. He reminded her then, "I still beat you!"

Robert finally received some helpful attention from a high school counselor in his senior year because he worked in the counselor's office. He consulted with the counselor about applying to college. He took the SAT exam and made a total score of 830, which was a reasonable score given that he had not taken much math or science coursework, nor had he taken honors-level English.[2] He attended a citywide college fair and gathered information about several colleges in the state. He wanted to attend the major university in the area, but he did not have the SAT scores or the grades to be admitted. So, he applied to another university about 35 miles from his home, the same four-year state university that his father had attended. The counselor helped him complete the application and wrote a letter of recommendation for him. Still, Robert's SAT scores were beneath the usual admission standard, and admission was delayed. He did not get an acceptance notice until the day of his high school graduation.

The family's plan was for Robert to commute to college and live at home the first year so that he could concentrate on his studies. They thought that this was a better idea than letting him get a job during the school year to pay for the expense of living on campus. When we visited him in late August, he was wearing a cap with the college logo on it and told us that he had gone to freshman orientation. There he was pleased to discover that many of his classmates from his first high school were also going to be freshmen. His main disappointment was that the university did not have a soccer team; he had to settle for taking soccer classes.

We telephoned him one year later. He told us that he had dropped out of college. He told us that he just couldn't seem to do the work. His first semester he made mostly Ds. The second semester he made two Fs and withdrew from the rest of his classes to keep from failing them. He reported that a turning point came when a history professor returned a major paper and wrote on it, "I can't believe you actually passed college English." Robert had forgotten the date the assignment was due, and when he remembered it, he had only one weekend to write his paper. This failure was especially devastating to him because history had been one of his favorite subjects.

Robert never went to talk to any of his professors about his courses or his grades at college. He did not get to know any of the students in his classes. When we last talked to him, he was planning to enroll in the local community college to try to bring up his grade point average.

Analysis

Robert and his parents thought that he was getting the kind of middle and high school education that would prepare him for college. They were wrong. Robert rarely took honors-level courses, taking instead general-level English, social studies, business, and computer science courses. He was prevented from taking college-preparatory mathematics courses and had to repeat Algebra in summer school, once he was finally allowed to take it. His repeated failure of the statewide standardized writing composition test in high school should have alerted him and his teachers that he needed to improve his writing skills. However, nowhere in his transcript nor in Robert's memory was there an indication that this warning signal elicited remedial training. Quite the contrary, Robert's taking of general-level classes meant that he had fewer writing assignments than he would have if he had taken honors-level English courses.

While members of Robert's family unanimously believed that Robert must go to college to get a good job, his neighborhood friends had all given up on education and the prospect of having good jobs. Robert had an active social life dominated by his neighborhood friends. This conflict between family and peer values made it difficult for him to study and make good grades. He preferred to avoid taking challenging courses; after all, his teacher had actively discouraged him from doing so in mathematics. He blamed his poor grades on his not trying hard enough, his laziness, his lack of organizational skills. By avoiding challenging courses in high school, he was able to avoid the issue of whether he had the ability to do college-level work. If he had worked hard in honors-level courses and failed, he would have confirmed what his middle school teacher had told him—that he was not college material. If he had worked hard in honors-level courses and done well, then he would have been totally rejected by his neighborhood friends.

JAMES

When James was 15 years old and still in the seventh grade, he told us that he expected to graduate from high school. He thought that he had been designated as "at risk" of dropping out because of his bad grades, a situation which he blamed on his friends and his teachers. About his friends, he said that they would make fun of him if he tried to do well in school. To win their approval, he would skip classes; he would not do his homework, or if he did, he would not hand it in. About his teachers, he said that because they would not explain assignments, he would not do them. Consequently, he failed. He said that his teachers refused to answer his questions about assignments because they thought he had not been paying attention.

At age 15, James was given the opportunity to participate in a special middle school program aimed at accelerating his pace of course completion. He spent the next two years trying hard and making good grades, even making the honor roll a few times. Part of the credit for James' persistence can be given to his mother, who talked to him about the importance of getting a high school diploma in order to get a good job. Petra persuaded him to try harder in school by pointing out what happened to his five older siblings. She explained, "I have two children that dropped out and I have three that graduated. I have six. The ones who graduated are doing real well now. Two of them are married and have their own homes and they have good jobs and are doing fine. And the other one has a good job. And the two who dropped out, they are not bad kids, but they can't find jobs. I say, 'Look, James, do you want to be like your sisters, the ones who graduated? Look at the ones who dropped out. You wanna be like that? That's the way you're going to be.'"

One of his sisters graduated from high school and worked her way up to the status of manager at the local office of a federal agency. She told James that she would get him a job at her agency, if he got his high school diploma.

Even though James and his mother told us that he was taking college-preparatory coursework, James believed early on that he would not be able to go to college. Petra remembered James telling her, "We don't have the money for me to go to college. How am I going to make it if you don't have the money?"

Although Petra wanted James to get his high school diploma, her own lack of an education made it impossible for her to help James with his schoolwork. She had dropped out of school in the sixth grade. She explained, "Well, I just went to sixth. If it was up to me I would have kept going because I love school. And I was good in school, but in those days they didn't force you to go. If you didn't go, they didn't say anything. They don't talk to your parents or see why you're not going. And my parents, they used to, well my father, he used to go to work in the fields to other towns and he used to pull us out of school and take us to work. But if my father would have been like me, personally I would have probably accomplished something." When we first met her, Petra had been working in the stockroom of a department store for over a decade.

James' father also encouraged James to get his high school diploma. James' grandfather had removed James' father from school after the third grade to work in the fields. James' father would frequently use himself as an example of what happens to a man when he doesn't get an education, often telling James, "Look at me. I didn't went to school. . . . If my parents had of sent me to school I would be in a better job. Look at me." James' father had worked for many years at an iron rod manufacturer.

James' burst of energy lasted two years. School records indicate that he was taking middle school classes throughout his 15th and 16th years, and was only beginning to take high school–level classes when he was 17. James took the lowest-level English, mathematics, and science courses, so low, in fact, that some of them did not yield credits toward high school graduation. By the time James was 18, he had accumulated only 9 of the 21 credits he needed to graduate.

One of James' talents was drawing. Petra told us that he always "got an A in art classes since kindergarten," and that he often sat around drawing at home and at school. During James' first year in the high school, an art teacher displayed one of his drawings. She told his mother "to save it for a scholarship." James took art classes during his two-year achievement spurt, through his middle school program. However, the school counselor discouraged James from taking art by telling him that he thought James needed to take vocational coursework focused around a grocery store job.

When he had just turned 18, the school staff advised James to participate in vocational classes that involved receiving course credit for his work at a grocery store. James' work schedule was different from his mother's, and they saw very little of each other during this, his last, school year. Petra complained at that time, "He never talks about school. He comes in and does his homework and leaves for work. When I come home from work he is already gone to work, and when he comes home from work I am already asleep."

At the beginning of his last year of school, James began to feel frustrated about the slowness of his progress. In the vocational program, he could spend years accumulating enough credits for graduation. He had an active social life in addition to his part-time work. He was spending a lot of time with his girlfriend. He told us that he was feeling tired of school. In fact, he would feel so tired that he did not go. He was surprised to find out how easy it was for him not to go to school. By the end of the school year, he had piled up a 57% absence rate. Contrasting work with school, he told us, "Work keeps me there cause it's like for the money and like, if you don't go, they call you and tell you. You have a chance of getting fired. School is like, they don't call you. They don't care if you are not there. At work you are scared of getting fired and that's what keeps you going to work. School is like, so you miss a day, so what?"

Then, his girlfriend dropped out. To be with her, James stopped attending school, but then he began to feel uneasy about this. In March, he went back to school to see what he could do to get back on track. His teachers told him that he had missed so much school, that "you might as well not even come." This made him angry and he went to the counselor to help him get into another program, one aimed at accelerating students in high school. But this program was full, and the counselor told James that he would have to wait his turn for a slot.[3] This was especially painful to James, because a friend of his, a girl who was one year younger than he, was given a slot in this program ahead of him. He described himself as "astonished" that the counselor did not put him in the program immediately. He explained, "I'm already 18, I should have been graduated!" That summer, he told us that he planned to try to get into this program at another school in the fall, but our records indicate that he did not reenroll in any of the district's high schools.

Analysis

Essentially, James never recovered from his grade retentions. His dropping out can be linked clearly to his perception that his movement toward graduation was too slow. As his mother put it, being a "big kid with all those little kids" sapped his motivation to keep trying. Despite his own efforts to make up for lost middle school time, he entered high school at an advanced age. We could only agree with James that it was astonishing that his high school did not automatically place him in the accelerated high school program. If there had been a smooth transition from his middle school acceleration program to a high school acceleration program, it is likely that James would have stayed in school long enough to graduate. Just before his last year of school, he had two consecutive years of good grades and school attendance. It was clear that he had changed his attitude about school. But his high school stuck him in a regularly paced vocational program that allowed him to go to school part-time and work part-time. This was not what James needed; it is what his high school had available.

Harriett Romo spoke to James about one of his vocational courses.

> HR (reading from the course list): "And when you went into high school, what course was this? your last period. Intro Industrial something . . ."
>
> James: "Oh, I think it was some special kind of class where all they talk to you about is life and school and everything else. It was kinda to help you out in life."
>
> HR: "Was it helpful?"
>
> James: "Yeah, it was nice. The teacher would talk to you about the world and life, you know. Everything."
>
> HR: "And how many kids were in that class?"
>
> James: "Not that many. It would start off with about 10 and then you went down all the way through the year and it was like 3 left, I think."

HR: "What was happening to the people in it?"
James: "They all gave up on school."

The high school had written off students like James. The vocational program they placed him in became a gateway for dropping out.

THE PARENTS

Both Robert and James had the benefit of growing up with both of their biological parents. Yet Robert graduated from high school and James did not. Our findings suggest that having two parents is not a significant factor in determining whether the student graduated or dropped out.[4] Instead, these two sets of parents differed in their educational attainment and the degree to which they worked together to monitor the daily activities of their sons.

Robert's parents were some of the best-educated parents in our sample. His father had a college degree, and his mother had a high school diploma. In contrast, James' parents were some of the least-educated people in our sample. His mother had completed sixth grade, and his father, third grade. The educational attainment difference between the two sets of parents affected their knowledge of schooling, their ability to help their sons with their schoolwork, and their willingness to be an advocate for their sons.

Roland visited Robert's school, talked to teachers, and gave Robert advice about what courses to take. In contrast, James' mother told us when James was 15 that she had not talked to anyone at his school, including teachers and administrative staff, for the past four years. She explained, "I used to go when he was closer but when he went to middle school, I think I went one time only and I told the teacher there, 'It's too far for me to come over here. If they could put him closer. It's far over there and I don't drive,' and the teacher said, 'There is the bus, it can bring you, it stops at Govalle.' But you have to be there about 3:45 and I work until 5, and she said, 'Well, you can take off from work.'" Petra told us what was not apparent to this teacher, that if Petra had taken off from her job, she would definitely have lost her pay for the work time missed and perhaps put her job in jeopardy.

Not surprisingly, we found statistical support in our sample for the importance of parental education in determining a student's chance of graduating.[5] In general, students, like Robert, with better-educated parents were more likely to graduate from high school than students, like James, with less-educated parents. This statistical finding is not caused by less-educated parents caring less about education. Our interview results indicate that all of the parents wanted at least a high school education for their children. For example, James' mother, Petra, told us that she desperately wanted an education for her son and herself. Petra told us, "I would like to study again, even though I'm old. I would just like to study. I think that if I could study it would encourage James more and help him because there is another problem he had. Because I didn't have an education I couldn't help him with his homework. He had to call his sisters over to try to help him with his homework." She worried that her grandchildren would ask her questions that she could not answer and would be embarrassed about her.

Our finding of a statistical relationship between the educational level of parents and the educational attainment of their offspring is consistent with a substantial amount of research results indicating that American schools are institutional systems that function to perpetuate inequality.[6] American schools have followed practices that unwittingly result in the children of poorly educated parents getting less education, and in the children of better-educated parents getting more.[7] Not only are less-educated parents less able to train their children in such skills as vocabulary and mathematical problem solving, they don't understand the procedures and processes of American schooling and therefore are unable to help their children meet the challenges of secondary school.[8]

The second important difference between the two families was the extent to which the parents worked as a team to keep their son in school. Robert's parents had responded to the problems of their older daughter by making significant changes in the ways they brought up Robert. Roland and Anita had worked out a way of getting their son to do his homework. Before Anita went to work the night shift at the post office, she would make a deal with Robert that if he sat down at the kitchen table and began his homework, she would wash and iron his clothes. Robert was very concerned that he wore just the right clothes to school, and his parents would buy him only one or two of an item, if he would do his homework. Then, because he had only one of the "in" shirts, for example, he needed to have it washed and ironed every night. His mother would do this as he sat at the kitchen table and did his homework. Carefully and slowly, she ironed his clothes while her son worked on his homework. By the time that Anita had to go to work, Roland had arrived at home to supervise both Robert and his younger brother. In this way, his parents worked as a team to make certain that Robert got his homework done and stayed out of trouble.

In contrast, there is no evidence from our interviews that James' parents worked as a team to keep their son in school. James' father spent little time with his son; in fact, over the four years we visited the family, we rarely saw him. When James was 15, his mother felt she had some control over him. Petra had little hesitation in telling James what to do: "I just tell him." She repeated,

"I just tell him. I just talk to him. Sometimes he says, 'I don't know; I don't want to do it.' I say, 'You have to do it. If not, then don't ask me if you want to go here, you want to go there.'" Since Petra did not drive, it was her husband who had the control lever for James. In exchange for his cooperation, his father would drive James where he wanted to go.

However, James' parents lost control of him when he got his own car to go to the job that was part of his vocational program. Before his last year in high school, his mother gave him the down payment to buy the car, and James maintained it with the money he made at the grocery store. Suddenly, he didn't need his parents to take him places. During James' last year in school, none of his siblings lived at home and his mother had little opportunity to monitor his daily school attendance because of conflicting work schedules.

In contrast, Roland had authority within his family. When Robert was 15, we asked Roland what he did when his son disagreed with him about a family rule. He explained, "No, he doesn't disagree that much. He knows better." When we asked Robert what happened when he did something his parents didn't want him to do, he explained it to us clearly. "I usually get in trouble. But it all depends. If it's something I'm not supposed to do and I do it, then I get in trouble. But if it's something they want me to do, but I don't do it, then I really don't know." He added, "They talk to me. They really don't punish me. They don't hit me or anything. I know what's right and what's wrong." When we asked him how much say he had in family decision making, he said, "Well, I don't have a say or anything. As long as I'm under their roof, what they say, goes."

Nonetheless, Robert knew how to get his parents to do what he wanted them to do. "I do something they want me to do first. You know, make them happy, do something they want me to do, don't get them mad at me. I ask for something and they'll get it for me. If I bug them, they'll get it for me."

Thus, the parents of Robert and James differed in significant ways. Robert's parents were better educated, they worked as a team to make certain he did his homework and stayed out of trouble, and they had established a power-sharing relationship with their son. In contrast, James' parents were less educated, the mother shouldered almost all the childrearing responsibilities alone, and the parents gave up what control they had of their son when they helped him buy a car.

THE ADOLESCENTS

In the tenth grade when we began interviewing him for the study, Robert had scored a 12.2 grade equivalent score in reading and an 11.9 grade equivalent in math on the Iowa Test of Basic Skills. This placed him at the 69th percentile in reading and the 67th percentile in math, making him among the highest-scoring students in our larger sample of 100. Only two students in our sample performed better than he did on the standardized tests. These scores suggest that, with the appropriate high school preparation, Robert had the potential to go on to do college-level work.

And yet, he did not take honors-level coursework, the level of coursework which would have prepared him better for college-level work. Except in the case of Spanish, he was not encouraged to take honors-level courses, possibly because he showed little eagerness to work hard and had marginal (for honors-level courses) standardized test scores.

Part of Robert's difficulty in motivating himself to take more challenging courses was his inability to see the linkages between what he might be learning in honors classes and future occupations. Robert was motivated to work hard in his social studies classes, but he added, "I don't see it taking me anywhere. I feel like if I go into social studies, I'll have to leave this area, and I don't want to leave. I want to stay here. I don't believe there's any real positions for social studies, unless I might be a teacher and I don't, no offense, I don't really want to be a teacher. I love school, but not that much."

Robert never had a clear idea of what type of career he wanted. When we first interviewed him as a high school freshman, he indicated that he wanted to be "a computer something." Over time, he explored a few possibilities, including becoming an accountant, like his father. But when we last interviewed him, he had few clear goals, other than to get a job that paid well. We asked him to describe himself and he hesitated, "It's hard. I think I'm ambitious. Basically I'm honest, kind, loving."

In contrast, James always knew that he wanted to be an artist. He liked his art classes very much. Describing his art classes, James told us, "The teacher there, you know, I talked to her a lot and she would talk to me a lot. We got along real good and she'd tell me I'm doing a real good job and keep it up. She made me feel good about myself. And I drew. I never drew before that class. Real good. She liked it and she would put it up on walls and she would tell the whole school."

Even after he had dropped out, James told us that he hoped to be success-ful: "I still have it in mind that I really want to be successful. Work my way up with my best skills that I have. I have real good skills in art and . . . you know, trying to work my way up."

James defined success in art this way: "I really want to be noticed, you know, people looking up towards me, like, you know, telling me that I'm doing a good job or I can say, do something real big, like I'm real good at art. I can draw like a drawing and put it up in the gallery and be noticed or something like that. That way I can know that I'm being successful."

Thus, although James had academic difficulties, he still had ambition and wanted to work hard and become successful. When James entered the ninth grade, he scored in the 41st percentile in reading and the 23d percentile in mathematics, which put him at the 9.0 grade level in reading, but only the 7.8 grade level in mathematics. These scores indicate a low to average level of achievement, and yet, other students in our sample with such scores did manage to accumulate enough credits to graduate from high school. It seems likely that if James had been placed in an accelerated program that included art training, he would have persisted long enough to graduate from high school.

THE SCHOOLS

It is ironic that when Robert and James were 15 years old, they and their parents thought that they were taking college-preparatory courses. The truth is that both boys had been tracked by their schools to low-level courses when they were 12 years old.[9] Robert was assigned to the general track by his standardized test scores in mathematics, and James was consigned to the vocational track by his scores and his repeated course failures. Neither boy understood that his fate had been sealed early in his middle school years. Both assumed that they still had a chance to graduate from high school and go to college.

Despite Roland's protest to one teacher about his son's math placement and despite Robert's strong performance in the low-level mathematics classes, the school staff did not place Robert in the college track. If he had been allowed to take the higher-level math courses in middle school, he could have stayed in the college track in high school. Because he was tracked into the low-level mathematics courses in middle school, Robert could not take the full set of mathematics courses he needed in order to do well on his SATs and in college.[10] Robert graduated before he had a chance to take Calculus or Trigonometry. He was not even eligible to take Chemistry or Physics until his last year of high school because Algebra was a prerequisite for these courses. Further, once tracked into low-level mathematics courses, scheduling conflicts made it unlikely that Robert could have enrolled in honors-level English courses, even if he had been allowed to.

James' belief that he was taking college-preparatory coursework even after he had repeated the seventh grade twice was an indication of how out of touch he was with the educational system. His parents could not guide him because they had fewer scholastic skills and less knowledge of the educational system than he did. James had to rely on the advice of peers, teachers, and counselors who guided him into the lowest possible courses. James found his high school coursework to be easy. He did not drop out of high school because the school-work was too hard for him. On the contrary, he dropped out because he was frustrated that his high school failed to enroll him into an accelerated voca-tional program that would have helped him make up for the time he had lost in middle school.

It has been common practice in the school district studied to assign students to tracks on the basis of standardized test scores.[11] Since counselors each have a caseload of between 500 and 1000 students, they do not have the time to get to know all of their students. The work of counselors, therefore, revolves around scheduling classes for students based on their "numbers," that is, their standardized test scores and their grades. Based on these numbers, they track students into college-preparatory, regular, or vocational coursework.

Few students in our sample questioned what courses their counselors had assigned them to. Their acceptance resulted from neither the students nor their parents understanding the long-term consequences of their being tracked in the non-college-preparatory courses.[12] For example, Robert's father understood the consequences of his son's mathematics tracking, but he did not understand the consequences of his son's failure to take honors-level English courses. Robert should have been taking honors-level English and social stud-ies courses to prepare him for college. Indeed, our survey of the materials that the school district made available to students for their high school coursework planning revealed no relationship between taking honors courses and college attendance. Nonetheless, our conversations with students enrolled in these classes indicated that honors students understood fully that taking honors-level courses would help them gain admission into college and to perform bet-ter in college. But students not enrolled in these courses had no idea of what opportunities had been denied them.

Transcripts of numerous students in our sample showed that our students frequently took a full schedule of low-level courses—so low, in fact, that some of them yielded no credits toward graduation. The students' transcripts indi-cated that these courses were not regarded by the schools as building upon each other in a logical fashion. It was common to find students taking English IIIA and English IIIB simultaneously. It was also common to find students re-peating a failed course with a semester interval in between. For example, the students who failed Pre-Algebra in the fall had to wait until the following fall to repeat the course because it was not offered every semester. This meant that students fell even further behind in their progress toward taking the science and mathematics courses they would need to enter college or a high-technology training program.

Both James and Robert saw their school problems as caused by themselves. They took the blame because their teachers, counselors, and parents told them that they should have tried harder and persisted. These adults all failed to appreciate the insidious effects of tracking on these young men's motivation. Robert was capable of earning a college degree and James was capable of earning a high school diploma. Labeling these young men as "not college material" and tracking them into unchallenging coursework discouraged them from trying hard and persisting in school. Neither adolescent nor his parents realized the part the school's tracking had played in causing his school problems.

Robert and James both left high school with few skills that would enable them to get a job paying above minimum wage or one offering possibilities for advancement. The local community college became an alternative for Robert after he had flunked out of a four-year college. It might have been better for Robert to have entered the community college first, build up scholastic skills and a good grade point average there, and then transfer to a four-year college.[13] The route he took resulted in a poor first-year grade point average, which jeopardized a later transfer to another university. For his part, James regarded his job as a checker at a grocery store as "going nowhere." He wanted to be successful in art, but when we last talked to him, he had no plans to get more art training. James told us that he had a sense of being adrift, of having lost something important by leaving school, but he was unable to get himself back to school.

Tracking and Norm-Referenced Tests

Tracking can take many forms, but it always involves grouping students for instructional purposes on the basis of their "ability." In Texas, tracking begins in kindergarten with the identification of "Gifted and Talented" students. State law requires the identification of talented and gifted children in kindergarten and requires that children so identified receive educational enrichment.[14] In the Austin Independent School District, "Gifted and Talented" students are placed in the Aim High program, a program designed to enrich their learning. Teachers labeled students as "Gifted and Talented" because they scored high on standardized ability tests. By the end of the first two months of first grade, almost all first graders knew which students participated in the Aim High program. By the beginning of the third grade, all students who were not in the Aim High program understood that they were in the other program, which they called the "Aim Low" program.

What difference does this make? What difference does it make to a third grader that she is in the "Aim Low" program or to a middle school student that he is "not college material"? It makes a major difference. There is a substantial research literature demonstrating that the simple act of labeling people significantly affects their behavior.[15] Students who are labeled "Gifted and Talented" are much more likely to behave accordingly; students *not* so labeled are much more likely to behave in ungifted and untalented ways.

Furthermore, the effects of labeling extend for long periods of time because labeling changes the way teachers, counselors, and peers treat the students. Teachers and counselors behave differently around students labeled as "not college material." They expect less from them in terms of intellectual performance, and students generally meet their expectations.[16] Over time, this treatment and the labeling itself affects the way the students think of themselves. Students labeled as "college material" become more confident about their academic potential and therefore pay more attention and participate more in class. In contrast, students labeled as "not college material" become less confident about their academic potential and therefore pay less attention and participate less in class. Students who are confident of their potential are more motivated to try harder and to seek out academic challenges. Since going to college is the only option that most elementary and secondary teachers clearly associate with success,[17] the schools' exclusion of children from this category in early middle school inevitably results in the low motivation of non-college-track students.

Since labeling students causes harm to those labeled as "not gifted and talented" or "not college material," why do schools continue to do it? Labeling continues because various laws either directly require it, as in the case of gifted students, or indirectly promote it through the mandated use of norm-referenced tests and tracking.

Students are tracked into coursework in secondary schools based on their norm-referenced test scores, or NRTs. Federal laws, most notably Chapter 1—a federal program aimed at improving the educational outcomes of children from disadvantaged backgrounds—require that all schools receiving this type of federal assistance use NRTs.[18] Nationally, one of the most commonly used NRTs is the Iowa Test of Basic Skills, or ITBS. The ITBS purports to assess the extent to which students have mastered skills which the ITBS regards as essential to instruction. These include listening, word analysis, vocabulary, reading, language, work-study, and mathematics. These standardized tests are created by experts who invent multiple-choice items based on "subjective considerations." These considerations "have to do with the match between the skills objectives represented by the items and instructional objectives and analysis of the mental processes required of the pupil to select the correct response to each item and to reject the alternatives."[19]

Typically, these new items are first tried out on students in Iowa, and depending on how well the items work in generating a range of scores, a smaller number of items are selected for another test given to thousands of students in a variety of locations throughout the U.S., excluding Iowa. On the basis of the performance of these non-Iowa students, *norms* are created, which designate what percentile and grade level specific scores represent.

The ITBS *Manual* presents the purpose of the test as providing information which can be used in improving instruction for individual students. This is probably why the implementers of Chapter 1 in Texas thought the ITBS scores would be useful in helping disadvantaged children. However, the *Manual* also provides other information about the ITBS scores that indicates that they are not useful in assessing the extent to which students are improving. Specifically, the *Manual* presents the results of research indicating that there is a strong correlation (ranging from .70 to .80) between fourth graders' ITBS scores and their twelfth-grade ITBS scores.[20]

What does this correlation mean? The *Manual* sees this as establishing the "predictive validity" of the tests. *Predictive validity* is a psychometric term that reflects the merit of a test. Tests are considered better the more predictive validity they have. It is considered good if the scores of a group of people from one point in time are statistically related to their scores at a later point in time. While this high predictive validity demonstrates the stability of the ITBS scores, it also indicates that most students do not change their relative position over time. For example, a fourth-grade student who scores at the 40th percentile is highly likely to be at the 40th percentile when a senior in high school, despite the fact that the student has been attending school regularly and earning passing grades in all courses and will graduate from high school.

In attempting to explain this stability of scores, the *Manual* faulted the schools for not altering their instructional practices so that low-scoring students could improve.[21] However, the overwhelming evidence suggests that the percentile score of a given student does not change much over time, despite the efforts of teachers and students to improve. That is, it is highly unlikely that a student like Robert would be able to shift from the 47th to the 90th percentile in mathematics, even if he had studied 10 hours a day under the guidance of a high school math teacher.

Compounding the problem, high schools have used the scores to do what is suggested in the *Manual*: track students into "appropriate" coursework. These scores have been used for tracking because the ITBS *Manual* states that the skills assessed by the test "reflect the extent to which pupils can profit from later instruction."[22] ITBS scores are used to track students into coursework that holds the highest-scoring students to the highest academic standards, the middle-range-scoring students to mediocre academic standards, and the lowest-scoring students to the lowest academic standards. The result is that lower-scoring students are educated to a lower standard than are higher-scoring students. This instructional tracking based on percentile scores makes the stability of ITBS scores over time almost certain.

In addition to blaming schools, the *Manual* suggests that students maintained their relative percentile position over time because higher ability students are more "able to benefit from their schooling than are lower ability students."[23] Specifically, this means that even if average ability students work hard at school, paying attention and completing their schoolwork, they are likely to remain at roughly the same percentile because brighter students will have been learning much more with the same amount of effort. This suggests that creators of the ITBS recognize that the scores generated by the test have been more sensitive to differences in I.Q.—a common, but controversial measure of intelligence—than to an individual's gain in knowledge.

POLICY RECOMMENDATIONS

When we originally began this study, we believed that staying in school and graduating from high school was in the best interest of all students. We assumed that all high school graduates were trained to meet standards high enough so that they could obtain good jobs, jobs which paid above the minimum wage. We wanted to find ways that schools and parents could keep students in school long enough to graduate because we assumed that a high school diploma helped graduates get decent jobs. We have learned that many of our high school students dropped out because they correctly perceived that the education the schools were providing them was at such a low level that they would not be able to achieve their goal of a good life even after graduation.

After interviewing the students and their families for four years, we learned that many aspects of schooling in Austin are dysfunctional. In particular, we now recognize that it is simply not in the best interest for students to persist in the low-level tracks. The content of the courses and the level at which they are aimed prepare students for a lifetime of minimum-wage jobs.[24] Given this, we must join the growing number of Americans who demand that low-level classes cease.[25]

Some educators have argued that raising standards and eliminating low-level courses will cause more students to drop out. This argument cannot be supported with the data from the present study. All of our students were assigned to the lowest- or general-level tracks. The overwhelming majority of them (79%) told us that neither their mathematics nor their English courses were too difficult for them. In fact, the majority (73%) rated some of their classes as boring or dull. Virtually none of the students who dropped out told us that they dropped out because their coursework was too difficult. Instead, their coursework was at such a low level that it failed to motivate them to stay in school.

Certainly the high number of students who drop out of school now demonstrates that tracking is not an effective method of improving graduation rates. The low-level courses our students were tracked into did not significantly increase their skills. On the contrary, tracking into low-level courses only limited their opportunities to learn.

In her book *Crossing the Tracks*, Anne Wheelock[26] describes schools that have succeeded in untracking students. These schools have extended to all students the learning opportunities usually reserved for the "Gifted and Talented." She found that when "low track" students are exposed to grade-level curriculum, high expectations, and concrete support, they made significant gains in achievement and self-esteem.

When our current system of tracking began at the beginning of the 20th century, public schools needed to produce only two kinds of students: the small percentage who would be going to college, and the larger group who would be working on the assembly line or on the farm. Our assessment instruments were geared to sort students into two categories: those who were college bound, and everybody else. Assembly lines and farms did not require high-level skills then, but within this century, the technical innovations in most workplaces require that workers have higher skills. By the end of the 20th century, our economy and the jobs available in it have changed so that earning a middle-class income requires much higher reading, writing, and mathematics skills than before. It simply does not make sense for our schools to track students into unchallenging coursework that prepares them for jobs that pay at or near minimum wage.[27]

Thanks to the U.S. Department of Labor, we now have a description of the skills that will be needed in the workplace of the 21st century. The secretary of labor established a commission (the Secretary's Commission on Achieving

Necessary Skills, or SCANS Commission) to define the skills necessary for being employed in a high-performance workplace, those with jobs that generate good incomes for blue- and white-collar employees.[28] These skills include what they call "Foundation Skills": strong English language and mathematics skills, problem-solving skills, as well as personal qualities, such as sociability. In addition, the commission recommended the following five "Workplace Competencies":

1. Knowing how to allocate time, money, materials, space, and staff.

2. Knowing how to work in teams, teach others, negotiate, and work well with people from culturally diverse backgrounds.

3. Knowing how to use information, especially in relation to computer processing.

4. Understanding social, organizational, and technological systems so that they know how to monitor and correct the performance of themselves and others.

5. Knowing how to select and use tools, apply technology to specific tasks, and maintain equipment.

The SCANS Commission acknowledged that in order to train American students to the needed, high standards, U.S. schools will need to be "reinvented." Part of this reinvention will involve retraining teachers. Continuous training and retraining is an integral part of successful American industry and should be a part of American education. Teachers and administrative staff should be routinely trained by their school districts to meet the challenges of training all students for a job with a decent future.

One promising instructional technique that can train students in most of the skills needed for a high-performance workplace is called cooperative learning. Championed by Robert Slavin, this is an instructional method involving students working together to master material originally presented by teachers. Cooperative learning techniques can be applied to elementary and secondary school classrooms containing students of mixed abilities.[29]

There are many forms of cooperative learning, and these techniques have been studied and evaluated extensively. The results of these studies demonstrate that students of all abilities benefit from participation in mixed-ability learning teams. These benefits include measurable gains in academic skills as well as other benefits that are important to students who have not previously experienced much success in school. Specifically, cooperative learning makes it easier for low-achieving students to form relationships with high-achieving students. In this way, cooperative learning promotes positive academic peer norms. When cooperative learning is done effectively with young adolescents, it becomes "cool" to get schoolwork done, to ask questions about assignments, and to care about what one is learning.

If Robert's and James' teachers had used cooperative learning techniques, then these two youth might not have been as conflicted about the disparities in the academic norms between their neighborhood friends and their classmates. Robert's lack of motivation to work hard in high school can be attributed partially to his difficulty in bridging the gap between his more academically oriented classmates and his antiacademic neighborhood friends. Similarly, James had trouble passing seventh grade because he was frequently distracted by his antiacademic friends. Cooperative learning, done effectively, might have provided students such as Robert and James with the peer support they needed to work hard on schoolwork.

Using cooperative learning techniques requires significant amounts of teacher training and planning. Teachers need to learn how to group students into teams containing a mix of student abilities so that, on balance, the teams are about equal in ability. In order for cooperative learning to work, there must be team rewards, so that any team reaching the standard gets an award. One important component of cooperative learning is the avoidance of making just one student or one team the winner, thereby making all others automatically losers. Also, individual student accountability needs to be built into each cooperative learning task. The extent of skills improvement for each student must be part of the team's total score.

Experiencing cooperative learning throughout their K–12 education will make students more able to work as team members later in adult life. The high-performance workplaces of the 21st century will be organized around the team concept. This is why the SCANS Commission makes teamwork skills one of its priority skills for high school graduates to acquire. American students have not been trained in teamwork skills. Instead, American schools have traditionally trained students to be competitive against each other. This training makes students less able to work in teams once they enter the workplace.

A common complaint against organizing students into teams is the "free rider" problem. That is, some students don't do their share of the work and put a burden on other, harder-working students. There are several solutions to this problem.[30] For example, teachers can structure the nature of the task so that the contributions of each individual are indispensable and cannot be compensated for by others. Also, the "free-rider" problem can be solved by establishing from the outset penalties for individuals for nonparticipation. Overall, training students in teamwork requires much planning on the part of teachers, and therefore careful attention to the retraining of teachers in cooperative learning techniques will be needed.

Many school districts across the country have tried to eliminate tracking, but only a few have succeeded. Those who try to eliminate tracking often encounter opposition. Opposition has come from several sources among teachers. Untracking schools is contrary to what most of them have been taught. Teachers and counselors have all been trained to believe in norm-referenced tests. Test scores are presented as objective, scientific measures of what students are able to do. Moreover, teachers have been trained to believe that it is easier to teach students who have been grouped by ability. Most teachers have not been trained how to teach classrooms filled with students of mixed abilities and skills.

Many parents of "college material" students oppose changes to the status quo, particularly changes that involve mingling their children with those who are considered to be of lesser ability.[31] They oppose changes because the current educational system benefits their children and they have no interest in giving up these advantages. "College material" students frequently get the best teachers. School counselors spend most of their time helping such students gain access to college. Because their parents are likely to be well educated, in prestigious occupations, and well connected to school board members, their opposition to any proposed elimination of tracking in elementary or secondary schools prevents many schools from untracking.

The national debate about tracking rarely includes a discussion about the use of norm-referenced tests to track students. And yet this is at the heart of the tracking problem for minority youth. Because Mexican-origin students score lower than non-Hispanic Whites on most norm-referenced tests, they are overrepresented in the lower tracks and underrepresented in the higher tracks. Since only students in the highest tracks are educated to do college-level work, the overwhelming majority of Mexican-origin youth are not trained up to the standard required for success in college. Instead, their lower scores have channeled them into lower-level coursework that is known to promote apathy, feelings of exclusion, and disregard about completing classroom tasks and doing assigned work.[32] We should not be surprised that, given their disproportionate placement in lower tracks, Mexican-origin students are the most likely to drop out.

The results of our study also lead us to recommend that schools be more effective in communicating honestly to parents and students about the consequences of taking a specific sequence of courses. The district we studied simply did not make it clear to our students or their parents that they were *not* taking college-preparatory courses. We discovered that few of the students in our study understood that they were not being prepared to go to college. When they were 15 years old, 66% of the students indicated that most of the courses they were taking were preparing them for college. Similarly, 61% of their parents thought that their children were taking college-preparatory courses. And yet, of our sample of 100, only Robert enrolled in a four-year college, and he flunked out his first year.

Schools must also change the ways they work with parents. Hispanic families value education and promote their children's success in school as best they can. We found that the schools did not make parents partners in the process of enhancing each student's academic success. Instead, the schools either viewed the parents as the problem or they ignored the parents' desires.

Key to making students like James and Robert successful is the role of school counselors. Currently, school counselors are overburdened and have little time to counsel students individually or monitor their performance in coursework. Their job has been primarily that of course scheduler, in which they sort students into high, medium, and low tracks. Instead, they should be focusing their efforts on motivating all students to meet high skills standards so that they can obtain good jobs when they complete their educations.

Essential to untracking schools is the discontinuation of norm-referenced tests like those used in the school district we studied. Norm-referenced tests have been useful because they provided a basis for sorting students into tracks. But if schools are untracked, then there is no need for this type of standardized test. There will, however, be a need for other types of standardized tests, those which assess how far a student is from meeting absolute standards in basic subjects, such as English, mathematics, history, and science. These tests assess whether a student has mastered a specified amount of information and/or has acquired a skill. Known as criterion-referenced tests, they provide information about the specific areas of learning students need to master if they fail to meet the absolute standard. Unlike norm-referenced tests, which force some students to be losers, criterion-referenced tests make it possible for all students to succeed.[33]

We recommend that skills standards be made explicit to students and their parents. The use of criterion-referenced tests will help both students and parents understand what is expected of them in order to obtain a high school diploma and go on to a technical training program or college.

Since uneducated parents have almost no understanding of the American educational and training system, the schools cannot assume that these parents will provide the vocational guidance their students need. Instead, the schools must take more of the responsibility for advising students about future vocational options and the links between course-taking sequences and these options. The schools will need to link course content and course sequences to vocational outcomes. If this had happened, Robert would have understood what jobs were available for someone who went into social studies, the topic that fascinated him. James would have taken courses organized around his consistent career goal, art. In so doing, the schools would have been more effective in motivating the students to work hard in school and acquire the skills they needed to get a good job.

THREE

Caught in the Web of School Policies

"Why me?"

This chapter describes how the enforcement of high standards by teachers, schools, and states does not automatically lead to higher skill acquisition for all students. We tell the stories of Richard and Alice. Richard was held back a grade in middle school, but was able to make up for lost time by participating in a special program. He graduated on time. Alice was retained in first grade, and the schools never allowed her to make up the lost time. Although Alice accumulated enough credits for graduation, she did not receive her diploma because she was not able to pass the standardized test required for graduation, even after four tries. We argue that forcing students to repeat grades, or withholding their high school diplomas, does little to bring their skills up to the desired standards. Instead, grade retention, especially in elementary school, leads to long-term motivational problems that make dropping out of school much more likely. This chapter demonstrates that many of the current approaches taken in both elementary and secondary schools to raise the level of student performance fail to bring all students up to the new standards.

RICHARD

Richard flunked the seventh grade. This event was brought about largely by the turmoil of his early middle school years. He described his problems as stemming from his drug use, his "drinking problem," and his friends, a group of friends who he claimed got him involved in gang activities, including at least one drive-by shooting. While in middle school, he drank heavily and smoked marijuana with his friends. He had spent a few days in jail and was on probation when the school district transferred him from his regular middle school to a special school within the district. This alternative school enrolled a small number of students, all with similar legal and disciplinary problems. The staff included more teachers per student than regular schools and a full-time psychologist.

Fortunately, the special school had a program to accelerate students who had flunked a grade, so Richard could get back on track with his age mates within a year. He tried hard in his new school. When his schoolwork gave him trouble, Richard explained that he would "just ask the teacher for more help. Sometimes I'd stay after school and, you know, the teacher would just sit there, and he'd explain to me, and we'd just go through it. You know, go to school early in the morning and get there an hour earlier and go study with the teacher. That's how I did it."

In this way, he was able to skip eighth grade, enter ninth grade with his age mates, and stay on track. We interviewed him as he entered the eleventh grade, confident that he would graduate from high school. His confidence stemmed from the fact that he had only two more years to go. He also knew that if he wanted to get into the military, he would need a high school diploma. It was important to his mother that he graduate, but Richard also wanted his high school diploma. He acknowledged, "I'm not gonna do it just to satisfy her and everybody else, you know. I do it for myself."

In addition to going to school, he worked 30 hours a week, divided between two jobs, one as a dietary aide at a nursing home and the other as a game-room attendant at a pizza establishment. He did his work at the nursing home before school and his work at the restaurant after school and on weekends. His school coordinated this work schedule as part of his vocational program. Richard thought that one of the reasons he had been able to stay on track academically now that he was in high school was his busy schedule with school and work that left little time to get in trouble.

Richard had begun working at age 7. He had borrowed his grandfather's lawnmower (the grandfather provided the gas) and mowed lawns during summer vacation. He did this for several years and earned the money he spent on clothes and school supplies. His parents' divorce fostered in him a concern about money, and he thought his mother and three sisters needed his help financially. This ability to earn money also nurtured in him a fierce independence, which was further promoted by his mother's preoccupation with her own education during his elementary school years.

Maria Elena worked part-time and took college courses. She had begun having children at age 16. She told us, "I quit school to get married and got pregnant and had a child and went back to school and quit school and finally got my GED and had four kids before I went back to school. And we all went to school together. Like, I would get up early in the morning and drop some of the kids off at my dad's and mom's, one of them off at a place to catch the bus, and then I would take off and catch the bus, go to school in the afternoons, pick them up after school from my mom, go home, and go to night school. So we kinda went to school together. I mean, I should have spent a lot more time at home with the kids and maybe we wouldn't have run into some of the rough edges we ran into. But I don't begrudge what we did and how we did it, because my kids are very independent. They grew up without a dad. They had a dad and he was always real good about supporting them, but he was never around that much. He was a very responsible person, I can say that much. But due to his absence and my doing other things like going to school and so forth, they grew up very independent."

By the time we met her, Maria Elena had completed the two-year program at the local community college and had taken college courses at two nearby universities. She served about 20 hours a week on various volunteer activities, particularly an organization designed to help teen mothers. She lived in a small frame house in a low-income Mexican American neighborhood. Her second husband, a Mexican construction worker with a fifth-grade education, took little interest in her children. Mexican American art decorated her living room walls and included a prominent acrylic painting of Mexican farmworkers picking lettuce. She actively participated in community protests against discrimination and demonstrated her pride in her Mexican heritage in the curios on her bookshelves and tables. As a result of her activism, the mayor appointed her to the governing board of one of the city's agencies, and she served on major school district committees. Her college experience and community activity helped her gain the skills and knowledge she needed to help her children complete their high school education.

Maria Elena's assertiveness resulted in Richard's participation in many school programs thought to be effective in keeping "at risk" children in school. For example, a college student tutored him in government, and an IBM employee mentored him. Richard volunteered during the summer in a recreation program for young Mexican American youth. He participated in a peer-assisted learning program at his high school, helping elementary schoolchildren with their schoolwork and their personal problems. Later, after he had graduated, he said of the training he received to be a tutor: "That class helped me a lot." He felt comfortable talking with teachers who would give him encouragement, and several helped him during his school career. Referring to a specific English teacher, he said, "She's the one that influenced me the most about staying in school."

Further, Richard's mother felt strongly about being involved in the school and did not hesitate to seek help from school staff. Explaining her approach,

Maria Elena said, "I go directly to the school. I'll go to the principal. I'll go to the teachers. I'll go to the counselors. I'll go with whoever will listen to me. Because I know what I want for my son and if there's a problem, we need to work on it. . . . I usually go to the top, and I know a lot of people consider that really hateful, but that's my son they are dealing with. And even though he's not special to anybody, he is special to me. And I know what I want. I know what is best for him. I just have to guide him along that road. So that's why I go to the top. I go to the teachers."

After his junior year in high school, Richard fell in love with a young Mexican American woman, Susan, who was a teen mother living alone with her child in her own house. Richard had met Susan at the same day-care center where his mother worked when Susan brought her son there to be cared for while she finished high school. While they were dating, Susan became pregnant. Richard's mother and older sister conferenced with Susan and Richard about the implications of this pregnancy. Richard and his family did not support an abortion, but Susan had an abortion anyway. Richard felt hurt and angry. He had wanted the baby.

Around this time, the school year began and Richard returned to school for his senior year. He found his life situation changed. He explained it this way. After the abortion, Richard and Susan broke up. Then they got back together again. They tried to improve their relationship. Things were going well, Susan invited him to live with her in her house, and he moved in. He had more bills to pay now that he wasn't living with his mother, so he became more concerned about making money. He began to think that if he could enroll in the night program, he could work full-time at a day job. He found such a day job working at an ice company. Simultaneously, he began drinking heavily again, he failed geometry, and he had a disagreement with the principal of his alternative school; so, he stopped attending. Richard did not regard himself as a "dropout." Instead he saw this as a temporary shift away from the special school he had been attending toward a different program, which he called night school.

His decision to stop attending came at a bad time. Richard had to wait for a place in the night school program. Susan had graduated from high school by attending the same program, and she encouraged him to enroll as soon as possible. He filed the application for admission, got himself to the interview, and completed the tests necessary for acceptance in the night program.

Susan became pregnant again, but this time Richard persuaded her that he would support the baby. After a four-month wait, the school district offered him a place in the night program. He returned to school and quit the ice company job. Susan gave birth to Amber two months before Richard graduated from high school. He spent about 10 months in night school and earned a high school diploma, about one month later than he would have if he had stayed in the regular school program.

We interviewed Richard and his mother again shortly after his graduation. Richard still lived with Susan. He worked as an electrician's helper, wiring new homes. He described the pay as good, but the work hard. We asked him if getting a diploma had made a difference in his job prospects. He answered, "No, not really. It didn't. Actually, it didn't. A lot of people say when you graduate and you get a diploma it's going to help you find a better job and it's going to make a difference, but it doesn't. I don't see where they think that. You know, these days you have to go to college and go four or five years or something to make good money. And still that's probably not enough."

We asked him if he planned to go to college. Richard was uncertain: "Uh, maybe. I don't know. Well, I wanted to go into the air force. If I can't get into the air force, I'm going to try to get into the coast guard, and if both of them fail, I want to take some courses at ACC [Austin Community College] to be an EMT."

An EMT is an Emergency Medical Technician. Richard had met some EMTs at a hospital and had asked them how they got their jobs. They told him about the training, and they encouraged him to consider it. A shortage of EMTs in Texas and elsewhere created a good job market in that field. Although the EMT position paid the same as that of an electrician, he thought he would like the work better.

Analysis

Richard was fortunate in many ways. He received the opportunity to participate in all of the most successful programs for "at risk" youth in the school district, especially the program that allowed students to make up for lost time because of grade retention. This was critical, because it made him see high school graduation as within his grasp. Even when he stopped attending high school for four months, he knew how to reenter school and how to complete his education. He was confident in his ability to graduate. Richard was also determined to get his regular high school diploma instead of the GED. He believed "the GED is not worth anything. A diploma says more. A GED says you got your basic skills and basically that's all the diploma is. But I didn't want the GED. I didn't want it. A diploma says more."

When we first interviewed Richard's mother, she believed that he was "at risk" of dropping out of high school, and this realization motivated her to spend time at the school he attended, asking for help for her son. She also spent time with him at home, asking him daily, "How was school?" and having serious talks with him weekly about his schoolwork and his social life.

Richard's biological father paid his child support regularly, never missing a payment. His father had dropped out of high school, joined the army at age 17, went to Vietnam, and became a sergeant by age 18. He had earned his GED and continued to serve in the army reserves. The army had trained him to be a mechanic, and he used these skills to get a job in Austin when he left the service. He has worked for the same car dealership as a mechanic for almost 20 years, earning the promotion to assistant service manager.

Richard's father had a major impact on Richard's life for both the good and the bad. On the positive side, his father worked hard and behaved responsibly, and Richard identified strongly with him. Richard looked like the clean-cut, well-built military man he wanted to be. It was Richard's father who had encouraged him to graduate from high school so that he could join the military. Richard saw his father's strict discipline with the children he had with his second wife, and wished that he had grown up in his father's home. Throughout his childhood, Richard had expressed his wish that his father and mother would get back together again, a hope he continued to nurture even after he graduated from high school.

On the negative side, Richard's father had a long-standing drinking problem and inadvertently encouraged his son's abuse of alcohol. He gave Richard a car when he was 15 years old, despite the fact that the boy could not have a driver's license, due to his age and his status as a probationer. Richard had been caught driving this car with a concealed weapon and without a license, an offense which jeopardized his chances to get into the air force.

Thus, Richard had a mother who actively promoted his interests in school and a divorced father who stayed involved with him. Additionally, Richard was able to graduate before the standards for graduation increased. During Richard's high school years, students needed to pass a relatively easy standardized test before graduation, called the TEAMS (Texas Educational Assessment of Minimum Skills) test. Richard passed this standardized test, even though he had not done well on standardized tests throughout his education. In tenth grade, for example, he scored 7.5 and 7.6 grade equivalents in reading and math, respectively, indicating that his basic skills were below his grade level. In the eleventh grade, his reading score had improved to 9.6, but his math score had stayed relatively low, at 7.0 grade equivalent.

The next class of high school graduates, those graduating at the end of the 1991–92 school year, had to pass a more difficult test, called the Texas Assessment of Academic Skills (TAAS). The shift from the TEAMS to the TAAS test represented part of a larger state plan to increase the achievement standards required to obtain a high school diploma. The TAAS test was more challenging than the TEAMS test in several ways: not only were students expected to do multiple-choice items on such topics as English grammar and spelling, but also they had to write essays that were evaluated by trained experts, external to their school. Likewise, the mathematics section required students to demonstrate mastery of relatively complex mathematical concepts and operations, and to engage in fairly advanced problem solving. Age mates of Richard's, those who were, like him, one year behind in grade level, were required to pass the more difficult TAAS test before they were allowed to graduate.

ALICE

Alice was one of these students. Alice's academic difficulties began in the first grade when her mother became seriously ill with breast cancer. In the middle of this family crisis, Alice's teachers decided that she should repeat the first grade. Alice was devastated by her mother's death in 1981, when she was 8 years old and in the first grade for the second time. Nonetheless, with the help of her father and her seven older sisters, the life of Alice and her younger sister settled down.

Her father, Jesse, had only completed seventh grade when he stopped attending school to help support his parents. Despite his low level of education, Jesse rose to a job as an inspector in one of the city's utility departments. With this modest income, he and his wife brought up nine children, all daughters. After his wife died, he supervised his daughters as best he could. As each of his daughters graduated from high school, she moved out of the house. During the time we studied them, Jesse shared his two-bedroom house with Alice and her younger sister. They were joined briefly by an older sister, her husband, and children during the first year of our study. The well-kept house sat on the edge of the oldest Mexican American neighborhood in the city.

After first grade, Alice made satisfactory progress throughout her elementary school years with the help of special education services. She described herself as doing fairly well in middle school, but things began to fall apart when she entered high school. Some of Alice's sisters tried to prepare her for college. Three of them were attending college at that time. With their encouragement, when Alice entered ninth grade, she enrolled in a special, college-preparatory magnet program that happened to be at her high school. She flunked the ninth grade, so that she became two years behind grade level. Alice explained her early academic difficulties in high school this way: "I just wasn't doing really good in school at all, I mean, I guess high school wasn't for me or something. I don't know, but I would do good in my classes for a while but then I would start slacking off. Then I started, next thing you know, I would be passing like four of my classes and failing the rest. And so, it was like, it had been going on for the whole semester. I was there physically but mentally I wasn't there."

Indeed, Alice had an outstanding attendance record, never being absent more than 5% of the school days during the four years she and her family participated in our study. In fact, the year she flunked ninth grade, she had a perfect attendance record.

We asked her what caused her to have these mental lapses. She told us, "Ever since my mother passed away, you know, we've just, it's just been ups and downs. It's more of, 'You have to be perfect,' 'You have to be good.' My other sisters did good, 'Why can't you do better?' You know. 'Cause, you know, it's true that all my sisters, yeah, they done real good and everything. They're real good A students and everything. Now it came down to me and it's like, 'Well, you know. What's wrong with you?' 'We expect more than this, what happened?' And, to me, it's a lot of pressure because I've taken classes I didn't even want to take, but I've took 'em because a lot of my family's telling me, 'You need to take this and you need to take that.' And I was like, 'Well why?' you know. 'Why can't I just take it in college?' you know. I mean, what I'm going for, it's a big thing. But can't this stuff wait? But, they were like, 'No, you need this. You need that. You need Chemistry. You need Physics. You need Geometry. You need all that.' I was like trying to pass and I just never could and it was just piling up and that was troubling me a whole lot 'cause I was having too much in one class and then having to study something else. I just couldn't think right. It was just too fast. History was giving me a lot of trouble. History and my math was giving me a whole lot of trouble. A whole lot. I'm not strong in math, I'm not. I know that. Everything else was fine. But that Latin was killing me and math and history was killing me real bad."

To avoid the pressure, Alice skipped classes, electing to go to the library to study rather than face another class that demanded too much of her. When she skipped classes, she missed assignments and critical information needed to do her schoolwork. Consequently, her grades suffered. And when she neared failure, the school notified her father. A teacher or principal called him, or he received computerized notices from the school. Her father told her sisters, and they came home to lecture her.

It was during her second try at ninth grade that Alice entered our study. We asked her how she felt, knowing that she had been labeled as "at risk" of dropping out of school. She answered, "Well, I mean, when I found that out, I was like, *'Why me?'* . . . I feel, ah, when somebody thinks that, I mean, I feel very sad. . . . I don't really have too much belief in myself that I can really do it and

I am more depressed about it. And then it just draws in my mind. And when I go to school, I mean, I just keep thinking about it." At that time, she said she thought she might drop out.

Alice told us that she knew that she was "slow," but this did not prevent her from trying hard in school. What distressed her most were some of her classmates in ninth and tenth grade who did not try. She explained, "I dislike some of the students who are there, and you know, they just give up on their work. I mean, they're very intelligent. They just really blow it off. And I wish I had that much intelligence like theirs, you know. I mean, I'm over here, working real hard to get an A, and they don't worry about it because they already have an A."

Her desire to be on a college-preparatory track in high school was consistent with her occupational interests. Over the years, Alice told us that she wanted to be an attorney, a psychologist, an architect, a dancer, a clothes designer, a marine biologist, a soldier, and an engineer. All of these occupations require either college and graduate degrees or specialized training after high school. Her vocational interests became more realistic when one of her sisters recognized that Alice needed more of a vocational education and helped her get a summer job as a carry-out at a grocery store.

When Alice began what she hoped would be her last year of high school, her sister helped her to shift from the regular high school program into the same self-paced vocational program that Richard had participated in. She continued working at the grocery store, and when school started, she earned a promotion to the job of checker. Because the vocational program allowed her to make up one of the years she had been retained, she earned all her credits toward graduation during this year. Still, she had to pass the TAAS test in order to graduate.

It would not be easy for her to pass this standardized test. In her first year in ninth grade, she scored at the 12th and 9th percentiles in reading and mathematics, respectively, on the Iowa Test of Basic Skills. She improved the second year she spent in ninth grade, scoring at the 36th and 26th percentiles in reading and mathematics, respectively.

Throughout all this, Alice maintained a positive attitude about school. She explained, "I really do like school, because in some of the classes, I mean, I really understand the stuff and I really get into it and I wanna learn more about it." Although she had had some bad experiences with some teachers, she felt close to other teachers and felt they encouraged her a lot. "I get real close to them as being friends. They're more like friends, but they're just older and they're my teachers."

Alice failed almost all the sections of the TAAS test when she first took it in the eleventh grade. She was hardly alone. Only 28% of the Hispanic students in her grade at her high school passed all sections of the TAAS test.[1] With the help of computerized training offered in her vocational program during her senior year, she practiced the skills she needed to pass the TAAS test. The second time she took it, she passed about half of the sections.

By the end of her senior year, when most seniors were planning for the senior prom and graduation, Alice felt left out. She had completed all of her credits for graduation, but she could not obtain her diploma or participate in the graduation ceremonies because she had not passed the TAAS test. The Texas Education Agency estimated that about 8,000 students were in Alice's situation at that time.[2]

Alice had to wait for the July administration of the test to try again. Just prior to the July administration, the school district provided six weeks of one and one-half hours of daily training in the skills tested on the TAAS. Her father loaned her his car so that she could get to the distant site of this training program. He took the bus to work. Although Alice failed again, she came closer to passing than ever before.

The school year began again, but Alice did not return to school. She had been conscientiously attending classes in the school district for 13 years and had earned all her credits for graduation. She was 19 years old. When we left her, she was waiting for the October administration of the TAAS test in the hope that this, her fourth, time she might pass the test and get her high school diploma.

Analysis

Despite Alice's determination to overcome her two grade retentions and meet the TAAS standards, she did not obtain her diploma because of state educational policies requiring students to meet high standards without requiring schools to bring all students up to these standards.

We presume that Alice's sisters thought they were doing the best thing for her when they initially advised her to enter the college-preparatory program. They knew that she had scholastic trouble in elementary school. Perhaps they thought that the disruption caused by her mother's death had caused her early academic difficulties and that now she was capable of doing college-preparatory work. Apparently, they had no reason to believe that she would not be able to succeed in a highly competitive program. No high school counselor explained to Alice, Jesse, or the older sisters that Alice entered high school with very low basic skills and that it was unlikely that she would be able to keep up with the demands of the college-preparatory coursework.

It is likely that Alice was able to get into the competitive college-track program because no one at her high school had the job of making certain that the courses she took were appropriate for her. No one employee of the high school she entered knew her academic history and advised her about what courses to take, given the level of skills she had.

The sisters' efforts to put Alice in a college-preparatory track in high school also reflected the widely held view that high schools do not have good vocational programs. Alice's sisters may have felt that the risk of her failure in the college track was worth taking, because in the U.S., general or vocational tracks are perceived to be dumping grounds for losers and misfits. They wanted more for Alice.

Alice had little realistic preparation in either middle or early high school for a career. School officials encouraged her to have high aspirations. Her career goals required not only baccalaureate degrees, but graduate degrees as well. Only the intervention of one of her sisters, who got her a job at a grocery store, gave Alice a realistic view of the kinds of jobs she might be qualified for once she graduated from high school.

THE PARENTS

Both Alice and Richard spent a large part of their childhoods in single-parent homes, a situation that national statistics indicate is strongly associated with grade retention, regardless of whether it is a mother- or father-only household.[3] Nonetheless, Richard and Alice had families that gave them the desire to graduate from high school and supported their efforts to overcome their grade retentions. Both Jesse and Maria Elena were involved in their children's education and did all that they could to promote their children's educational progress.

Maria Elena was particularly philosophical in her approach to childrearing. Reflecting on her life, she said, "I had parents who told me what to do, and from my very early age I remember I've always wanted to be a mother. I always told them when I have kids I won't tell them what to do. If I know how they wanted to be, maybe help them along that line. 'Cause I'm not going to be here forever. My kids have learned to make decisions on their own from a young age out of necessity because we were a single-parent family."

Her desire to guide, but not to dictate to, her son did not prevent her from setting limits on Richard. "He knows his limits and I still don't hesitate to restrict him if he [over]steps his bounds." She expressed disapproval of Richard's gang friends. "I don't like his friends. But at this age the only thing I can do is tell him, 'I don't like your friends.' . . . And I tell him why I don't like his friends: 'I don't like your friend because he's a gang member,' or because 'I feel that maybe he puts a lot of pressure on you,' the drug situation, or whatever the reason might be. But he respects me. I mean, we have to meet halfway somewhere, and if I don't want them in my house, he just doesn't bring them."

When we asked Maria Elena how she got Richard to do what she wanted him to do, she talked about three strategies: asking, telling, and making deals. She found asking him the most effective strategy, and she used it most often. Although she did not want to be an authoritarian parent, she resorted to telling him what to do when nothing else seemed to work. Sometimes she made deals and kept them, especially when money was the issue.

Jesse combined both direct and indirect techniques for encouraging Alice to stay in school to graduate. He asked teachers to call him if Alice had problems. He had a two-way radio in his work truck and could receive calls even when he worked out in the field. He scrutinized her report cards and any other report he received from her school. He called family meetings, talked to her about her school failures, and admonished her to keep trying. He would tell her: "Don't go out there and just take the test. You're gonna have to do a lot of studying so that you'll be ready for the test."

He would give her advice: "Now you might be slow, but you can still reach high school, and finish high school, and go to college if you want to. . . . If the rest of the girls did it, you can do it too. . . . Don't think that 'cause you're slow, or you don't make good grades, you're gonna stay behind. No, don't go for that. You go for it. Like today, if you mess up on some test, all you gotta do is try to make it tomorrow, or the next time. Try to make it right next time, better than what you did today."

In addition to coaching Alice, Jesse would seek help from his older daughters because he felt he couldn't do enough for Alice. Jesse conceded, "A man was not meant to take care of girls by himself." Jesse had only a seventh-grade education, and he had nothing in his background or experience to draw upon to help Alice with her homework or advise her about careers and coursework.

When we asked Jesse how he made the rules in his house, he reflected for a while and said, "Yeah, like I got 'em from my dad. My dad used to say, 'Nobody besides me raises the voice around here,' which was right." Like his father, Jesse raised his voice when his daughters got out of line. Jesse declared that he made the rules in the house. When we asked him what happened when someone broke the rules, he declared, "I'm the only one that can break the rules."

Alice confirmed his assertion. When we asked her who made the rules in her house, she said, "My dad does. . . . I really don't get my way." Later she stepped back from this dramatic assessment, saying, "Yeah, once in a while, I mean, yeah, I get my way, if I really explain everything to him and tell him precisely what time, when, and stuff like that. . . . Yeah, I mean, I get my way once in a while."

Jesse had no tolerance for early dating. He reported that when Alice was 14 she asked him when she would be old enough to date. He felt awkward having to answer the question and tried to put her off, but she persisted. They agreed upon the age of 17 or 18. But by the time she was 16, she pressed him to let her go out on a date with a boy. Jesse refused, pushing it off to maybe 16½. At about that time, Jesse relented, but only if he talked to the boy beforehand and enforced a relatively early curfew. One of Alice's teachers told us that she carefully chose the boys she dated.

Both Maria Elena and Jesse valued education and did all they could as single parents to bring up their children properly. They supported their children's efforts at staying in school and becoming responsible adults.

THE ADOLESCENTS

By the time Richard and Alice were 18, they were mature and self-confident. They had jobs and some optimism about their futures, even though they acknowledged that they had problems.

Richard described himself in both positive and negative terms: "I guess I'm just a nice guy and hardworking and there are things about myself I don't like that I would like to change. I have a drinking problem and it's got, it's, right now it's not that bad, but I admit that I am alcoholic, but, um, that's one thing in life that I hope to take care of."

Richard had received some counseling for his drinking problems. He explained, "It started in junior high. I went to counseling but all the counselors have been White people and I don't like talking to White people about my problems. I'd rather talk to somebody of my own race."

He had turned to his girlfriend. "Little by little my girlfriend Susan she's helping me out. She's helped me out a whole lot since we first started going out, you know. I used to always drink a lot. And when we met, I still drank. She stayed here with me for a while and I would go to work. I would get out of work. I would go out drinking. I would leave her here, didn't care. I would go out and come home drunk and, you know. But basically she's helped me out a whole lot to slow down and stop. It's not that bad as it used to be."

His mother understood the importance of this relationship for Richard. She explained, "I don't know if it's his way of being or what it is. He gets what he wants most of the time. He always wanted to be a father. He always wanted to have one girl love him forever and ever."

Alice seemed upbeat when we asked her to describe herself at the beginning of her senior year. She described herself as "patient, understanding, willing. And I have a lot of ideas. I'm energetic around people. I'm a real outgoing person, pretty much when I'm around the customers. I'm a really hard worker and I am a very responsible, independent person and, you know, just real easy to work with."

When we asked her what she wanted most to achieve in life, she told us that she wanted to be able to provide for her children and to give them a better time in school than she had had. She wanted to get married, have a family, and a job.

Alice was unlucky in many important ways. Most notably, her mother had died during her childhood, and schoolwork was hard for her. On the other hand, her father and sisters paid close attention to her schooling and encouraged her persistence, her family had an adequate, if modest, income, and she was attractive. Alice had beautiful, long black hair, a pretty face, and the body of a dancer.

After Alice completed all her credits for graduation, she worked as a checker at the same grocery store where she had worked during high school. She seemed to perform adequately on her job without the diploma. Nonetheless, she wanted to receive her diploma because she did not want to be the first daughter in her family not to graduate from high school. She also had the desire to go to community college. She explained, "I don't want to be one of those people to be working at any little job. I want to make something out of myself. I want to go to school and just make something out of myself."

THE TEST

In the early 1980s, Texas legislators became concerned that high school graduates had low levels of skills. Employers complained that many graduates were functionally illiterate and lacked even the most fundamental math skills, such as the ability to make change. As a result, legislators passed laws that required students to pass a standardized test of basic skills before they could obtain their diploma. The standardized test was to make certain that all high school graduates had the skills thought to be essential for success in the world of work after high school.[4]

The plan was to increase the standards for graduation gradually so that students and teachers would have time to prepare students to pass all sections of the exit-level test in order to obtain their high school diploma. Students in the third, fifth, seventh, ninth, and eleventh grades took the test each year. The law mandated remediation by schools for students who failed any portion of these standardized tests at any grade level. In this way, all students were thought to have a chance to acquire all the skills necessary to graduate. Students who flunked the exit-level test were supposed to continue taking it until they passed it in order to obtain their diplomas.

The Texas Educational Assessment of Minimum Skills (TEAMS) became the first statewide standardized test used. It was a minimum-standards test. It did not have a writing section, and the mathematics problems were simple and mostly computational in nature. Critics of the public school system argued that the test was too easy and did not truly assess the kinds of skills a citizen would need to get a good job after graduation. The Texas Assessment of Academic Skills (TAAS) test replaced the TEAMS test. It was supposed to assess higher-order thinking skills and to determine if students had the skills believed to be needed in order to succeed in the world of work after high school.

Passing the TAAS test emerged as a challenge for students in Texas. The first year schools administered the TAAS test (1990–91), only half of the state's eleventh graders passed it. Students in the Austin Independent School District did slightly better with 53% passing all sections. Minority children fared worse, with only 40% of the Hispanic and 30% of African American students in the Austin school district passing this exit-level test.[5]

The challenge of passing the TAAS test became greater. In the 1991–92 school year, in order to graduate, students had to answer correctly 60% of the questions on the TAAS. Alice had to meet this standard. For students planning to graduate during the 1992–93 school year, the passing standards increased: students had to answer 70% of the questions correctly.

As part of the TAAS test, students write one essay, which is evaluated by trained graders external to the school. When these graders judge an essay to be inadequate, they give a brief explanation. Students and their teachers use this feedback to help the student and teacher overcome the writing skills deficit.

The TAAS reading comprehension subtests contained more complex, longer, and more interesting passages, compared to the TEAMS reading passages. Not only were students expected to understand the meaning of words, but they were supposed to be able to summarize reading passages and distinguish supporting from nonsupporting ideas and fact from nonfact. The test required them to draw inferences, to generalize, and to understand relationships and outcomes.

The mathematics section of the TAAS test also demanded many more skills than did the mathematics section of the TEAMS test. The mathematics section contained many word problems with extraneous information included to test the students' skills at solving problems. The items reflected real-world problems. In addition to demonstrating skills in mathematical concepts and operations, students had to solve problems using estimation, solution strategies, and mathematical representation and to evaluate the reasonableness of a solution.

Most of the test questions changed each time the TAAS test was administered, so that a student like Alice could not simply memorize the answers from one administration to the next. She needed to be able to demonstrate that she had the requisite thinking skills. Although intelligence undoubtedly influences a student's performance on the TAAS test, the skills required to be demonstrated by the test can be learned by people of normal intelligence. Guided practice in the types of skills required by the TAAS test improves performance. This was why Alice improved her level of performance each of the three times she took the test. Nonetheless, after three tries, she still failed to pass all the sections of the TAAS exam.

THE SCHOOLS

During the 1980s, Austin schools commonly used grade retention for remediation. A report[6] compiled by the district's office of research and evaluation indicated that in the 1990–1991 school year, approximately 22% of all students enrolled in the district were overage, indicating that they had been retained. In Austin, as in other cities throughout the nation, one of the main factors in predicting who will drop out of school is grade retention, with students who are overage by two years being highly likely to leave school before graduation. In Austin, as elsewhere, most of these retentions occurred in elementary school.

Grade retentions have commonly occurred in the early years of elementary school in Austin, when teachers judged some children to be unable to succeed at the next grade. Children frequently flunked kindergarten because their teachers deemed them too immature. They assigned them to a grade level variously labeled as prefirst or transitional. Teachers retained other students after first grade because the students could not read grade-level material or perform addition and subtraction correctly.

Administrators and teachers thought that simply repeating the grade would remediate the maturity or skills deficits of these children and that they would be able to meet the high standards better in the future because of an extra year in kindergarten or first grade. Several investigations of this belief have been done in Austin and elsewhere, and the evidence is clear that simply repeating a grade does not bring about the desired boost in the child's academic or behavioral performance.[7]

To see if this finding would be repeated with data from our sample, we conducted statistical analyses of the data provided to us by the school district and found that grade retention was strongly related to the students' sex and their standardized test scores.[8] Boys in our sample were much more likely to have been retained than were girls, a finding that is consistent with national trends. Our novel findings involved associations between having been retained in elementary school and doing poorly on standardized tests in high school. This suggests that the second try at a given grade does not bring these students up to the same skill levels as "at risk" students who were not retained. The skills deficits of retained students persisted despite their grade repetition and remained with them throughout high school.

We also correlated grade retention with other student and parent characteristics. Our results were interesting for the associations we did not find. For example, having been retained was not associated with the students' beliefs about the value of staying in school, or their perception that their English or mathematics classes were too hard for them, or the low-income status of their families, or their reports of speaking Spanish at home. These results argue against interpretations that blame grade retention on the antischool values of some students, or coursework that is too difficult, or poverty, or speaking Spanish, at least for this sample of "at risk" Mexican-origin youth.[9]

If it is the responsibility of the schools to educate all students to the level of skills necessary to pass the TAAS test, then Alice's story demonstrates that our schools are not fulfilling their responsibility. Alice's experiences in school shed light on the nature of the problem and the solution.

"At risk" students like Alice should have received the best teaching available in the district. She needed enrichment from talented teachers able to motivate her to learn up to the standards necessary for passing the exit-level test. But Alice frequently found herself in classrooms taught by the least competent teachers. For example, while explaining to us why she had to take two English classes simultaneously one semester, Alice said that she had failed one of the courses the first time, "because the teacher that we had, she wasn't very good. The whole class that she had at that time, she failed the whole class. By the end of the year she had failed all her classes. They fired her. So I had to take it again. All the other teachers knew that she was no good. They finally changed that and got a better teacher and that's when we had to take it over again."

The students had to bear the burden of this teacher who flunked everyone instead of teaching all students to perform up to her standards. The school district had to pay double the cost of providing this course for Alice and for all the other students whom the incompetent teacher flunked.

Our knowledge of the poor quality of teaching Alice received was based not only on her reports but also on our own observations. We witnessed firsthand one of Alice's vocational education teachers as he belittled his students while teaching them little. With the permission of the program coordinator, Harriett Romo spent a typical school day with Alice during her senior year.[10] This school day consisted of two hours of work in the self-paced academic program and one hour in a vocational class. Then Alice would eat lunch and go to work. The school required her to take the vocational class because she worked part-time and went to school part-time.

When we entered the vocational classroom, the teacher sat slumped casually behind a large mechanical drawing desk. Four students sat in the desks in front, while one student sat apart, in the rear of the classroom, by himself. The teacher handed out some student career magazines, and the students read some of the articles. The teacher thumbed through one of the magazines and called the students' attention to an article about not getting accepted by your first-choice college and how to deal with the disappointment. He pointed out to the students the several colleges they could go to in the area and emphasized that one of them did not have very high standards and asked the students which one that was. The students did not answer, but after prodding, one student responded with the name of the local community college. The teacher emphasized that the students did not have to have high test scores or good grades to get in there (obviously implying that the students in this classroom were all eligible to be admitted there).

The teacher found another article in the magazine and pointed out a self-inventory that asked readers to rank what they considered most important in a job—including wealth, independence, creativity, etc.—and asked the students what they wanted most in a job. One muttered "independence," but the teacher did not hear him. Alice turned to Harriett Romo and whispered "benefits," an item that was not on the inventory. Harriett agreed and suggested that Alice volunteer that answer. She shook her head, "no."

The teacher asked the class what they wanted to be, but no one responded. He continued to prod, and finally one girl said she wanted to be something that started with the letter "s" and had five more letters. She seemed embarrassed to tell the group. The teacher started trying to guess. He asked for more clues. He laughed and said, "Why am I doing this? Why don't you tell me what you want to be?" She laughed and said the student sitting next to her knew. He laughed too. Finally she told him that she wanted to be a singer. The teacher asked what kind of singer, and she retorted, "A Mexican singer." The teacher responded, "Well, you are Mexican. All you have to do is sing and you will be a Mexican singer." She laughed and the class laughed.

Harriett asked Alice if she had ever discussed her desire to be a manager of a supermarket in this class. She replied that the teacher would joke about it and tease her in front of the class and that, therefore, she did not want to bring it up. The class continued in this manner, with students very reluctant to participate and the teacher finding articles in the magazine and making comments about them.

The teacher told Alice that she could go back to her self-paced class if she preferred. She did and as we walked down the hall, Alice explained that none of the students liked that class. She said that the students always disagreed with the teacher and that he always put them down. In contrast, the teacher in the self-paced program always worked with them in a positive and supportive manner.

Alice talked more about the social life at the school, explaining that the school separated the alternative programs from the rest of the school. She had very few opportunities to see friends in the regular high school. She reported that teachers and other students belittled the students in the alternative programs, calling them dumb or saying that they did not work as hard as the other students. The school had not notified the graduating seniors in her program about the prom or the graduation activities and they had almost missed them. Alice talked to the senior advisor about this and got the senior newsletter sent to students in the alternative programs. The stigma of being in the special programs bothered her, although she liked the program, the program coordinator, and the other students very much.

Alice could be motivated to work hard, to answer questions, and to solve problems. When Harriett asked her how she felt about school, she responded, "School? For one thing, I like school. I really do like school, because, I mean, in some of the classes, I mean, I really understand the stuff and I really get into it. And I want to learn more about it. This one class I really enjoy, because it talks about different things that's been in my life, too, I mean like my past and with my family. Like where did I come from, like if I am Latin American or Spanish or Indian. I think it's kind of exciting to find out what tribe you're from or if you're from Spain, you know, when those people that came, the first, you know." Unfortunately, many of her teachers were not skilled enough to engage Alice in the learning process.

During the last year of Alice's schooling, she spent only three hours a day in academic preparation. During these hours, the teachers expected her to be teaching herself, through self-paced practice, the skills she would need to pass the TAAS test. Alice's training for the math sections of the TAAS test consisted of practicing test items on a computer and occasional tutoring from the teacher when she did not understand the computer tasks. The computer program had been designed by the program coordinator, based on instructions from the Texas Education Agency, but had not been evaluated in terms of its ability to improve students' performance on the TAAS test. Harriett Romo watched her go through her practice one day, and saw that Alice did not read the main part of the question carefully. She would glance at the question, go quickly to the answers, choose one, which was wrong, then skim over the remedial instruction, go back to the question (not reading it), choose another answer, and continue in this manner until she hit the right answer. Harriett had been trying to read the question and choose the correct answer along with Alice and did not have time to finish reading the question before Alice would change the screen to choose an answer.

Harriett Romo asked her why she rushed through the practice items. Alice explained that she had learned to rush through tests in her regular classrooms so she could finish. She had simply continued to use the same approach when trying to practice for the TAAS test. No one had instructed her how to take this test or how to get the most benefit from the computer program. In the self-paced alternative program, she was expected to teach herself. Although she made measurable progress each time she took the test, it is likely that her performance would have been improved if she had five to six hours of classroom instruction daily with teachers who knew how to teach Alice and how to direct the instruction to the level of skills she needed to pass the TAAS test.

POLICY RECOMMENDATIONS

Flunking students was commonplace during the 1970s and 1980s in American schools. Among people 20 years old and younger, nearly one in five has flunked at least one grade before reaching high school in the U.S.[11] Now the evidence is clear that being held back one grade strongly increases the likelihood that a student will drop out of school. Being held back two grades makes dropping out almost a certainty.[12] Most of the children who were held back were harmed by this experience. Schoolchildren rank grade retention as one of the worst things that can happen to a child, just below death of a parent and going blind.[13] While retained students may continue to attend school and perform reasonably well in elementary school, the negative effects of grade retention become more obvious during adolescence, when retained students become aware of their differences compared to their classmates and drop out of school.

Texas schools have been especially prone to use grade retention, with over 35% of the state's ninth graders being at least one year overage for grade in 1990.[14] Figure 3.1 displays the percentage of ninth graders in the 1989–1990 school year by ethnicity and whether they were overage for grade by two or more years, an index generally used to measure grade retention. Hispanic students have been much more likely than other students to be two or more years overage for grade. This has also been true at the national level, with Hispanic and other minority students being much more likely to be overage for grade level.[15]

The responsibility for getting an education at the elementary and secondary level has been thought to rest primarily with the students and their families. Educators have resisted tying student outcomes to evaluations of teacher and school effectiveness. Thus, when a student fails a course or an entire grade, the student bears the stigma of failure, not the teacher or the school or the school district.

Instead, school districts (and the taxpayers who support them) are left to pay the additional cost of offering the course or the entire year of schooling again. The financial costs of simply adding the extra year for students is significant. It is estimated that grade retention has added an additional 8% to the costs of operating American public schools.[16] But this cost is only a small part of the overall costs that society must bear when students lose hope and drop out of school.

Many educational leaders are demanding that schools assume more responsibility for educating all students up to standards that will allow them to be qualified for decent jobs upon graduation. Furthermore, these educators expect schools to bring all students up to these standards in a reasonable amount of time. While students and families need to assume a large part of the

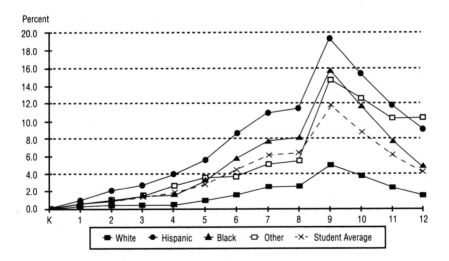

FIGURE 3.1.   Percentage of 1989–1990 students two or more years overage for grade by grade and ethnicity. *Source:* Texas Education Agency (1991). Older is better, right? Not really. *Research Briefs,* Issue 91.1.

responsibility for meeting high academic standards, these leaders argue that students and families should not be expected to bear all of this responsibility.

The Texas commissioner of education, Lionel "Skip" Meno, went so far as to suggest that the results of the TAAS test should be used to evaluate the quality of schools, teachers, and school districts, but not students. He argued that when students flunk the TAAS test at any level, the burden for remediation should be placed on the district's administrators, the school's administrators, the teachers, and the students. For this reason, Meno argued that passing the TAAS test should not be a requirement for an individual to obtain a high school diploma. Instead, scores on the TAAS test should be one method of evaluating school and district-level administrators and teachers.[17]

Part of the reason why students like Alice have trouble passing the TAAS test is that they are in the general or vocational track. Teachers and administrators have low academic expectations for students in the non-college-track programs and fail to train them up to the level of skills they will need to get a good job in the future. While clearly Alice could not meet the demands of an honors-level, college-preparatory track, she was capable of learning much more than what she was offered during her last year of high school. American public schools in general, and Texas schools in particular, expect too little of non-college-track students, and this jeopardizes their opportunities to acquire the skills they need to obtain good jobs upon graduation.

Another part of the problem lies in the preparation that students receive in elementary school. Most elementary school teachers simply do not know how to teach a classroom full of students who range widely in reading and mathematics abilities. It has become acceptable among teachers to assume that not all students can learn, or at least perform at the desired level, and so they seek scientific-sounding justifications, like IQ scores or learning disabilities, for why they cannot obtain the desired performance from all children.[18]

In the United States, teachers emphasize innate learning abilities and disabilities from the time children enter preschool. In Japan, elementary school teachers fiercely maintain the belief that all children are equal in their ability to meet the elementary school standards. They deny the relevance of any innate abilities in terms of determining who can meet the teachers' high expectations. Learning disabilities are unknown. Instead, Japanese primary teachers emphasize the importance of hard work and persistence. In their view, with enough effort on the part of students and teachers, all students can acquire all the skills they need. Students who work the hardest to meet the standards are seen as the best students. Researcher Harold Stevenson proposes that such a belief system helps to explain why Japanese elementary students outscore American students in both reading and mathematics.[19]

According to carefully conducted research, the gap between U.S. and Japanese students cannot be explained in terms of the superior intellectual abilities of Japanese schoolchildren. Instead, scholars such as Stevenson argue that this difference can be explained in terms of the quality of the teaching that goes on in Japanese elementary schools and the substantially greater time Japanese students spend learning in school. Not only do Japanese students spend 60 more days a year in school than do Texas students, for example, but also they spend many more hours each day on learning mathematics and reading than do Texas schoolchildren.

All students should be taught to have the skills they need to obtain good jobs upon graduation from high school. No students should be allowed to fail to achieve this standard. In order to do this, schools will need to assume more of the responsibility for educating all students and make fundamental changes in the way they go about educating students.

Grade retention must be eliminated. Schools need to create new ways of bringing low-achieving students up to the standards set by the standardized tests. Another part of assuring that students meet higher achievement standards will require convincing teachers that all students can meet these standards. Finally, we must hold teachers and their administrators accountable for making certain that all students do meet the standards.

This accountability will require that teachers keep track of individual students as they progress (or fail to) from one level of skill to another, from one course to another, from elementary to secondary school. This will involve re-organizing schools so that teachers in separate grade levels and content areas keep track of the progress of the same students over a period of several years. Students need to have teachers who are aware of their academic histories so that the students get the kind of attention they need to make continuous progress toward earning their high school diploma.

Another part of this change will require schools to use time more effectively. Given the high number of retained students already in our schools, these students will need to be given the opportunity for making up lost time by accelerating the pace of their learning. This will require that the schools move away from the current yearlong or courselong method of crediting students to a system of education which promotes a student's rate of progress based on skill acquisition, not the simple passage of time. In this way, students with skills deficits will be given extra tutoring after school, on Saturdays, and throughout the summer so that their skills will meet or exceed what they will need after high school graduation to get a good job or go to college. The costs of this approach should not be much greater, and may indeed be much less, than the costs of giving retained students the second try at an entire year of schooling.

Teachers and schools need to be trained in how to motivate all students to work hard. In elementary schools at least, the highest awards should be given to students who work the hardest. This will mean that equivalent spelling awards will go not only to the best spellers, for example, but also to the students who have tried the hardest to spell. Such an award system will motivate the most able students to keep trying to attain high standards of excellence, while at the same time, giving less able students the incentive to attain their highest possible level of achievement.

Part of this retraining will involve convincing teachers that the true measure of their professional success is the academic success of their least able students. At present, prestige among teachers is pegged to the outstanding performance of a few star students. Peer prestige among both teachers and students needs to be directed toward the attainment of high academic skills for all students in the class.

Finally, at the secondary level, the academic performance of non-college-track students needs to be raised. These students need to be offered challenging courses taught by exciting and committed teachers. Vocational programs like the one Alice participated in need to be replaced by ones that encourage students to live up to their potential.

FOUR

"My

own

gang."

Gang Involvement and Educational Attainment

This chapter describes the important interrelationships between youth gangs, school failure, family supervision, and the educational progress of "at risk" Mexican-origin youth. Participation in gangs has been relatively common among "at risk" youth, but such participation has not led inevitably to dropping out of school. This chapter examines the gang involvement of two students, Ramona and Salvador. For students like Ramona, gangs offered a way of gaining peer popularity and status. Because her family was able to discourage her gang involvement, Ramona "backed off," became a model student, and graduated. For others, like Salvador, gangs became a source of dependable, supporting relationships, which were not available from their families. Salvador's involvement in "bad" gangs deepened, ultimately hindering his educational progress.

RAMONA

Ramona was thin, delicate, and quite pretty. She had made satisfactory progress in school up until she entered high school. Then she found that many of her teachers relied exclusively on lecturing as a teaching method. She told us, "The problem is that I hate it when the teachers stand up there and just lecture. They just talk and talk. It gets me bored and makes me want to fall asleep. Sometimes I end up falling asleep."

Often, she did not understand the words the teachers used, nor did she understand the homework assigned at the end of the class. When she asked for help, her teachers told her that she should already know that material or that they did not have the time to help her. Ramona became discouraged, but she passed the ninth grade and entered the tenth.

Every day, as she walked to high school, she passed a halfway house for male juvenile offenders. Most of its residents had been arrested at least 10 times, typically for auto theft, assault, or, drug-related offenses. The residents would call out to Ramona and her older sister Alba, who was one year ahead of Ramona and attended the same high school. Enrolled in the same high school, these young men would follow the sisters into the building and hang around Ramona's and Alba's lockers, waiting for them between classes and after school. When she began tenth grade, Ramona became romantically involved with one of these boys. Ramona explained, "I was doing pretty good in ninth grade. Then I hanged around with this guy from the halfway house, and I just stopped doing my work, and stopped going to class and everything. I started being late in the mornings, so I didn't do too good in tenth grade because of my friend."

Although the halfway house staff supervised the residents closely during nonschool hours, they relied on the school to keep track of the students during school hours. Ramona's boyfriend encouraged her to skip school[1] with him, and they would spend many hours each school day hanging around a laundromat near the high school with other truant students.

One semester she had a math teacher who penalized tardy students by placing them in the "last desk," a position that required them to do a lot of problems on the board. The teacher intended this strategy to encourage punctuality. However, Ramona used breaks between classes as opportunities to talk to her boyfriend from the halfway house, so she frequently found herself standing in the hallway when the bell rang. Although math was one of her stronger subjects, she began skipping the class rather than having to sit in the "last desk."

That year she made four failing grades and the principal scheduled her to go to summer school, but she did not have enough money to pay the tuition. The school gave her a form to fill out for assistance, but Ramona explained, "They gave me a form to go to summer school, but I lost it, so I didn't give it back in. And I couldn't get another sheet. So, I got left out." Ramona began falling behind.

Instead of encouraging her to attend summer school, Alba helped Ramona get a job at the same restaurant where she worked. Half of their wages went to their mother to pay the family bills. In addition to working, Ramona spent the summer practicing her flute and memorizing music for the upcoming school year when she would march in the band.

When we interviewed Ramona, one of us went with her to her bedroom while the other one interviewed her mother in the front room. Two single beds took up most of the space in the bedroom she shared with Alba. The walls were decorated with posters of rock music stars, and a few well-worn stuffed animals adorned the neatly made beds. At that time, Ramona told us that she would sometimes hang around with gang members because they "liked to do fun things," but that she herself was not really a gang member.

Ramona's family had lived in the same small frame house for 18 years. The house was in northeast Austin, in a low-income, predominantly African American neighborhood. High rates of unemployment plagued the residents of this area, and in midmorning it was common to see young men working on cars, walking to the store, or sitting and talking in small groups in the yards. Like the other houses on her block, Ramona's house was in poor condition—it needed paint, the kitchen cabinets had no doors, and the screens were torn. There were several cars parked on the lawn. Ramona's family income was among the lowest in the city, and at the time of our interviews the family could not afford a telephone.

Usually, 10 people lived in this house—Ramona, four of her eight siblings, four nieces and nephews, and Ramona's mother, Paula, who had dropped out of school in the sixth grade to help support her parents. Paula waited until she was 22 to marry and begin raising a family. Ramona's father left the family in the late 1970s and only recently began sending some child support because the Texas attorney general had forced him to. After her divorce, Paula worked as a hotel maid for several years until her poor health prevented her from continuing. She was both obese and diabetic. Even though Paula collected every form of family assistance the state of Texas could provide, she still needed the money that Alba's and Ramona's restaurant jobs provided.

Each of Ramona's oldest three sisters had dropped out of school when they became pregnant at the age of 13.[2] The reason that Ramona lived with three of her nieces and nephews was that Paula had taken them in because she believed that their mother, one of Ramona's older sisters, was not a responsible parent. Each child had had a different father, and their mother took little interest in them. The fourth one, a boy, had been abandoned by another one of her older sisters, and Paula had adopted him. He had been living with Ramona, like a younger brother, for the past six years.

We discovered by reading the local newspaper that a major drug raid had occurred in Ramona's neighborhood just after one of our visits to this family. The raid resulted in five arrests at four suspected "crack houses" within a three-block area near Ramona's house—one house was on her street, two were on the street immediately east, and one was located directly behind her house.

Early in her high school years, Ramona played the flute in the high school marching band. She identified her "good" friends as students who were also in the band. They were "good" because they helped her with her homework and answered the questions she could not get answered by teachers. But she continued working during tenth grade, and her work schedule forced her to miss practices and trips, and then her grades became so low that she was prevented by state law from participating in extracurricular activities. At this point, Ramona told us that she almost dropped out of school because it seemed to her that there was no way she could succeed.

She became more involved with her "bad" friends, the girls who went with gang members. She admired gang members and described herself as a "wanna-be," someone who is not in the gangs but who hangs around with gang members and wants to be with them. Her girlfriends, including herself and her sister Alba, looked up to the gangs. They had parties and did fun things that she liked doing. But then "they got too wild." She witnessed or heard accounts of acts of serious violence, like "shooting people just for the fun of it." Gang members were "getting locked up." She and Alba decided to "stay back."

Their mother had repeatedly expressed dislike for their gang friends. Alba and Ramona talked about their gang friends for a long time and finally decided that they did not want to be that "bad." They concluded that "ganging up on people in fights was not fair and if you want to show people that you got something, you got to do it yourself." They did not need their gang friends. Ramona concluded that her family, especially Alba, was *my own gang."*[3]

About the time that Ramona first began disengaging from gang activity, the school staff advised her that she would be held back in the eleventh grade. The thought of flunking a grade devastated Ramona. She sought help from Alba, who had managed to graduate from high school with the help of a special program that allowed students to accelerate the process of earning credits toward graduation. Alba had participated in this program, and even though she had missed more days of school than Ramona, she earned her diploma—becoming the first of Paula's children to graduate from high school.

Alba recommended the program to Ramona, but there was one problem: more students wanted to get into that program than there was space available. Ramona had to compete with other students for a place in this program. Because Alba had been able to get into it, Ramona thought that she could qualify, if only she played the game right. Ramona knew that you had to "talk to the right people" and "be persistent, keep bugging them [school staff]," "talking to them and letting them know that you are really serious about finishing" to get into the special program. Ramona began acting like a model student, particularly around teachers whose courses she had failed. As she repeated their courses, she began to "act like the good students": paying attention in class, doing the assignments, and not talking back to teachers. The teachers noticed the change, and one told her she was "a bright student and if she really wanted to do it, she could do it."

With the assistance of these teachers, Ramona enrolled in this self-paced, alternative program. When she could not keep up with the schoolwork because of her work schedule, again the teachers helped her get into a program of part-time school and part-time work. Ramona explained that it didn't matter at her work whether she had a high school diploma or not: "At the fast-food job they don't care if you graduated or not—you come to work or they get someone else to do the work."

Her transformation from a "bad" to a model student was facilitated by the sending of her halfway-house boyfriend to jail for drug possession. When her boyfriend returned from jail, he wanted to resume their relationship. Ramona was vulnerable. She had no other boyfriend, and her sister Alba had moved into her own apartment after graduation. The boyfriend immediately returned to using crack. Ramona tried to help him, sometimes staying out of school to keep him from doing drugs. She went with him to a drug counselor who took a great deal of interest in her and recommended that she visit a local free clinic for birth control, which she did. With each visit to the drug counselor, Ramona began to be more influenced by her. Ramona told us that the drug counselor helped her understand her need to help others and helped her put it into perspective. Ramona recalled her asking, "I know you want to help your boyfriend, but shouldn't you really be helping yourself?" Ramona decided that her boyfriend was not trying to help himself and told him, "You gotta do something, you know, 'cause I can't always do it for you." He began getting help from his sister and went to live with family members in Colorado.

Although Ramona had told us when she was 16 that she wanted to be an elementary school teacher, her vocational interests shifted as she approached high school graduation. Her interest in secretarial work emerged in the eleventh grade when a vice-principal helped Ramona get into a "communications class"—a class that Ramona described as a "typing class."

Ramona persisted in her schoolwork and eventually graduated on time. During her last year, when tempted to give up, she would reflect upon the outcomes of her "bad" friends, most of whom had become heavily involved in gangs and had dropped out of school. Ultimately, those girls "got even more 'bad'" than she was—involved in fights and drugs, living with their boyfriends, getting pregnant—and Ramona didn't like what they were doing.

She also received a lot of encouragement to graduate from her mother and her sisters, especially those who had dropped out. She told us, "I don't like being in the gangs. . . . My older sister tells me, 'Don't drop out. If you graduate, we'll give you a party, we'll give you a car, we'll give you anything you want.' I just don't go to bed with guys. I just take it slow and everything, so I don't worry about getting pregnant. I worry more about my sisters. I don't know if they're gonna make it or not."

Through the drug counselor, she got into a job-training program. Ramona left her restaurant job and began attending a secretarial school three nights a week. Ramona told us that the class taught her "how to work in an office building, how to build up typing skills, and other skills." The job-training program enabled her to get a job, after her high school graduation, working 15–18 hours a week as a file clerk at an auto company service department.

Ramona believed that office work represented a step up for her. She compared the clerk position to her fast-food job: "You don't sweat as much, there is air conditioning, they don't bullshit you as much, the work is not greasy and dirty." Her "number one goal" was to move up into a "state job." She believed that state jobs "pay more, pay when you are sick, and you get vacations."

When we left Ramona, her plans centered around getting a state job. She insisted that she was different from her sisters in that she did not drop out, she did not have children she could not support, and she was not working in a restaurant. She described herself as "someone that ain't going to let anyone tell me, put me down, you know. Someone who is willing to do something, you know, someone who really cares for other people than myself."

Ramona tried to get Alba into the same job-training program that had helped her, but Alba now had a four-month-old child to support and was reluctant to leave her fast-food job. Ramona had not given up on Alba, but at our last interview, Alba had missed the deadline for applying to this program and would have to wait for the next class.

Ramona contrasted work against school, saying "school, it wasn't really nothing for me. You know, it was like you go to school, you learn, you forget about it. You know, you go back to school, you learn again, and during the summer you forget about everything you learned. It's a waste of time." Describing her friends, she added, "It's like they go to school for the fun of it. They don't go to school to learn, really. They go to school to have fun, meet friends, talk around to their friends. That's what school is to me, to other people I see. It's weird, man. . . . But work, it's like you have to, it's mandatory. You want to get paid, you gotta be there. If you don't wanna work, you might as well leave."

Thinking back on high school, she explained that English classes were particularly difficult—especially the grammar. The teachers acted as if she should already know the material from the earlier grades and "they don't want to teach it because they don't have enough time." Having to answer questions from texts that she could not understand became a major obstacle that almost caused her to drop out. She explained that she was "not really into reading and did not understand all the words." Ramona described her many teachers who refused to accept that she had not been taught the basic skills to do the work they assigned. She could not stay after school for tutoring because she had to work. The year she had to repeat classes, Ramona enrolled in the English course she had failed and the next English course at the same time. That is when she started "backing off." She said she felt at times that she could never do all the work and that that is why she skipped and almost didn't pass.

Her Informal Geometry class was difficult because of all the "word problems." Even though she graduated from high school, she worried about her lack of writing skills. She said, "I can write if I can write in words I understand." Ramona did not consider attending college because she believed that college work would be too hard for her.

Analysis

Ramona's case brings into focus the two meanings of the word *gang*. First, there are the groups of youth who spend most of their time hanging around together, partying, and occasionally, engaging in violence. Like 60% of the students we studied, Ramona had friends who were involved in gangs. She liked to attend some of their parties—they were, after all, near where she lived, and she had few alternative forms of recreation.

As long as Ramona played in the school band, she was part of a group that facilitated her school attendance. But her family's financial needs and state law ("no pass/no play") conspired to sever her relationship to this group of "good" friends. Ironically, legislators passed this state law in order to improve the school performance of football players, not to drive girls like Ramona into more involvement in gangs. When her access to her "good" friends ended, gang involvement provided her with an alternative means of satisfying her needs to belong to a peer group.

There was a second way that Ramona used the word *gang*—when she referred to her family. Her continuous conversations with her sister Alba and her other older sisters helped her to distance herself from the other type of gang, the "bad" people. Furthermore, her three oldest sisters discouraged Ramona's gang involvement directly, through their admonitions, and indirectly, through their own poor outcomes. Her mother continuously pointed out the weaknesses of these "bad" friends and the mistakes of her sisters. While Paula was unable to prevent Ramona from interacting with gang members (many of whom were either fellow students or neighbors), Paula's negative commentary about them gave Ramona reason to "back off."

The "bad" gang pulled Ramona away from her schoolwork, while her family pulled Ramona away from these friends and encouraged school completion. For most of the students we studied, these two forces competed for the student's affiliations, and their academic outcomes were largely determined by which force prevailed. In Ramona's case, her family prevailed and Ramona disengaged from her peer gang enough to continue in school until completion. In other cases, as we will see below, the gang prevailed and the students dropped out of high school.

SALVADOR

Siblings played an important role in helping Ramona disengage from gangs and stay in school. Other students, like Salvador, found that the examples of more successful siblings actually pushed them toward further involvement in gangs. Salvador was the "black sheep" of his sibling group. His mother, Suzanna, dropped out of school when she became pregnant with Salvador, and as an unmarried teenager, she had considered giving Salvador to an older couple she knew. Suzanna chose not to give him up and, instead, let Salvador visit this couple each summer for at least a couple of weeks. Soon after Salvador was born, Suzanna married a man who worked with computers at an insurance company. This man, Bill, legally adopted Salvador, although he never took an active part in his upbringing. With Bill, Suzanna had two children, a son a year younger than Salvador and later a daughter.

These two children were academically inclined. Comparing Salvador to his younger brother, Johnny, Suzanna said, "Johnny did all As except for one B. . . . Salvador had low grades but they said that he did pass all his classes with very good grades, but he got low grades because of his tardiness. Johnny has real good discipline. He's a real disciplined child, and maybe 'cause he took karate when he was younger, . . . he was into sports where Salvador didn't like sports. And Johnny would come home, look at his cartoons, do his homework, look at another cartoon, do more homework, and finish his homework before I get home at six. Whereas Salvador can go home and sit and sit and sit, and he'd do nothing—not even watch TV!"

Suzanna had earned a GED and was working as a catering administrator during most of the three years we studied her son. She attributed Salvador's academic problems to his enrollment in bilingual classes in elementary school, during a time when he had not lived with his mother but with an aunt who only spoke Spanish. For years, Salvador pretended that he did not know any English, and the teachers expected very little of him. It was only after Salvador returned to living with his mother that the teachers learned that Salvador could speak English. This experience resulted not only in Salvador's low reading skills but also in teaching him that he could avoid working hard in school by deceiving teachers.

Salvador was in middle school when Suzanna divorced Bill. Salvador took the divorce very hard and found comfort in the company of peers.[4] He became involved with the same gang that had attracted Ramona. At first, his mother did not recognize his peers as gang members. She thought that it "was cute that they called each other 'Bro'"; she believed that they called each other brothers because they did not have fathers. She saw Salvador's friends as well-behaved neighborhood boys. Describing them then, Suzanna said, "They are real polite. They clean up after themselves. I've never seen them dirty. They always look neat, and they eat in my house. They put the plates up. I mean, these are polite little guys. These guys aren't bad kids. They just need someone to be with because all their parents are divorced or separated or they don't have parents at all. They live with their grandparents. They just want somebody to hang around with, somebody they can call family, and they call each other 'brothers.'"

Salvador lived with his mother, his younger brother and sister, and his mother's new husband in a small three-bedroom, brick tract house in a Southeast Austin neighborhood. The neighborhood was predominantly Mexican origin and working class. A boarded-up house across the street was for sale. Very few adults remained at home during the day in this neighborhood, but after work hours, large vans, pickup trucks, and recent-model family cars lined the curbs. Iron bars protected the windows of Salvador's house. A recessed front entry, off a small concrete porch, and an iron door at the front walkway prevented a visitor from seeing who opened the front door. Several times when we tried to schedule an interview, someone opened the door a crack to tell us Salvador was not at home. Salvador fought with rival gang members who lived on the same street, and his house had been a target of drive-by shootings.

By the time we first interviewed Salvador and his mother, the school district had enrolled Salvador in one of its special schools for troubled adolescents, because he had been caught stealing a car. The personnel at this school figured out that the only thing Salvador liked about school was art. He and his gang "brothers" spray-painted graffiti, and the school attempted to channel this interest into a positive skill by teaching them how to do airbrush art on canvases. To encourage Salvador's attendance throughout the school day, they arranged his schedule so that art was his last class of the day. At first, he appeared to be making progress in this special school, completing eighth and ninth grade in two years.

His brother Johnny, who enrolled in honors courses in a regular high school, complained about the easy life that Salvador had: "How come he gets to get all the dummy classes and passes, and I have to be an A student?" Johnny and his sister made fun of Salvador, telling him that he was "street smart but not school smart." His younger sister recited the Ten Commandments in his face.[5] Their teasing hurt Salvador, who retorted that he would rather be "street smart than school smart," and he called them "nerds." He would leave home on Fridays and not return until Sunday. Even though Johnny and Salvador went to different high schools, Salvador had a reputation as a gang member, and the principal of Johnny's high school kept an eye on Johnny "because he was Salvador's brother." This angered Johnny and his mother.

During summer vacation, when Salvador turned 16 years old, he participated in a county-sponsored youth program that provided art materials and considerable encouragement to produce a painting to enter a contest. He worked furiously on this project, eventually producing a large canvas picturing a rose with a tear drop on it, with the phrase, "Happy Mother's Day." He won first place. His prize included a free lunch for his family at a local restaurant. When his family arrived with Salvador, they discovered that Salvador had invited all of his gang friends too. They cheered Salvador when the contest's sponsors recognized him for his achievement.

Another part of his prize involved free art lessons at a local community college. But Salvador never took the classes, explaining, "I just don't have the time. I want to go out with my friends."

Salvador returned to the special school, but by this time he had begun leading groups of male students out of that school during the day. The principal expelled Salvador and dumped him back into his regular school. Once there, his gang involvement deepened, leading to a critical event. One night, he and a few of his gang friends decided to shoot guns in a park. They claimed to be practicing with targets. Responding to a call, the police came and as they approached the boys, one officer thought he saw one of them point a gun at him. The police officer shot this boy, who was standing next to Salvador. The boy died.

Salvador returned to school, but his life was never the same. Sometimes he started crying in the high school hallways, and would run out of the building. Once an assistant principal chased after him, trying to help. Salvador knew he needed help, so he went to Bill, his mother's ex-husband. Not knowing what else to do, Bill got him drunk. After his divorce from Salvador's mother, Bill drank even more heavily. He gave Salvador the kind of "help" he gave himself. Salvador took up alcohol as a means of dampening the pain. But the pain remained, and the alcohol only made Salvador's school attendance more difficult. Salvador decided to give up. He officially dropped out of school in January 1991.

As a result of Salvador's having witnessed the policeman kill his friend, a lawyer representing one of the boys involved got Salvador and his client jobs at a government agency. Salvador explained, "The only reason I got this job was because of my friend's lawyer. I'd rather have my friend back than a job." Nonetheless, Salvador took advantage of this job opportunity. He began as a file clerk at a warehouse. Then he was moved to the main building downtown and he filed there. After three months, he advanced to the graphics department, where he could use his art talent.

When we left him, Salvador was making $1,000 a month. His relationship with his sister had changed. She had stopped reciting the Ten Commandments to him, and he paid her to clean his room. Despite a major layoff at the agency, which included two of his friends, Salvador managed to keep his job. An administrator at the agency had intervened with the school district on his behalf, trying to get Salvador back into school so that he could graduate. Salvador told us, "The people I'm working with are nice. They talk to me and say 'Hi! How are you doing?'"—something he told us his teachers had never done.

Having a good job transformed Salvador into a more mature, respectable-looking young man. His abuse of alcohol lessened, according to his mother: "Five days in a row he is sober. He used to not be able to go two days. He used to get drunk, just drunk."

Despite these changes, Salvador still saw himself primarily as a gang member. He had not thought about what he would be doing next year. He explained, "I figure it day by day, I guess." Harriett Romo asked him what he would like to see happen in the future:

> Salvador: "I don't know. I guess clear my friend's name. They put him down pretty bad."
> HR: "How do you think you can do that?"
> Salvador: "Put him [the policeman] in jail. Do something to him instead of him going free."

Salvador became misty-eyed when he told about what had happened to his friend. He made it clear to us that despite everything, he was loyal to his gang: "Once you're in it, you're in it. You're in it forever."

Although he applied to the alternative program, the one that had helped Ramona and Alba to graduate, Salvador did not get into it because of his history as a gang member. He could not bring himself to reenter a regular high school program because he knew that if he did, his younger brother Johnny would graduate from high school ahead of him.

Analysis

When we statistically tested the relationship between having gang-involved friends at age 15 and whether the student dropped out or graduated by age 19, we could find no association. Some gang members dropped out, while others graduated from high school. Our results are consistent with the results of other studies of Hispanic gangs.[6] The reason for this finding is clear when we consider the stories of Ramona and Salvador. Some teenagers, like Ramona, get involved solely in the social aspects of the gangs. Ramona was able to socialize with gang members and keep up her schoolwork. As her sister Alba later explained, "She just wanted to be popular." Studies of "at risk" youth indicate that students who experience little success in school turn to peer groups and delinquent behaviors as a route of gaining status and success.[7] Gang membership is one important way for "at risk" youth to establish a positive sense of identity.

Other teenagers, such as Salvador, get involved in gangs early in adolescence in response to family dysfunction and stress. His mother neglected him during his early years, and not long after he was finally accepted into her new family, she divorced his newly adopted father. This trauma, combined with his early history, led him to become deeply involved in gang life while in middle school. Gang behaviors—such as skipping classes, arriving late, not doing homework, and fighting on school grounds—interfered with his school progress. This did not concern him, since from an early age he had been encouraged to believe that school was something of a joke. Although it is clear that Salvador had the mental abilities to complete high school coursework, his deep involvement in gangs during his adolescence made it almost inevitable that he would not be able to meet the requirements for high school graduation.

THE PARENTS

Consistent with the results of other researchers,[8] our statistical analyses indicated that living in a single-parent family at age 15 was *not* associated with whether the student was involved in gangs at that time. These other studies found that the quality of family relationships was important in determining delinquency.

For example, Paula and Suzanna were different in the degree of control they had over Ramona and Salvador, respectively. Ramona's mother had learned from the mistakes she had made with her three oldest children and tried a new approach on Alba and Ramona. Paula had been too trusting of her three oldest girls, believing that if she took them to the school, the school would do the rest. She drove the three girls to middle school every day, on the way to her hotel job, and watched them enter the building. She returned at the end of the school day and picked them up from the school building. She assumed that they had attended classes. Later she discovered from letters sent by the school that they had been skipping. She became more restrictive; they responded by getting pregnant, dropping out of school, and moving out of her house.

With Alba and Ramona, Paula changed her tactics. She realized that the school would not take responsibility for motivating her daughters to attend school. She had to make them want to graduate from high school. So, she made certain they left the house on time every morning, but she did not follow them to school. At home, she continuously preached to Ramona and Alba about the value of an education, pointing to the failures of their older sisters, and arousing their loyalty to the family as a reason for graduating from high school. She also pointed out the flaws of their gang friends and, for Ramona, the weaknesses of her drug-addicted boyfriend. Then, Paula asked her oldest three daughters to tell Ramona and Alba that they should finish high school. This they did, relentlessly. They gave repeated, sincere testimonials about how much they wished they had finished high school. Paula never stopped sending the message, refocusing on the younger children once Ramona and Alba graduated from high school and moved out. Paula had learned how to make her children want to graduate from high school. When we asked Paula how she got Ramona to do what she wanted her to do, Paula said matter-of-factly, "I tell her what to do." She also used the full force of her family to reinforce her message to graduate from high school.

Suzanna approached her son's problems differently. She had given birth to Salvador as an unmarried teen mother and gave him up to her sister to rear. That Salvador spent several years in bilingual classrooms with teachers who did not know he spoke English suggests that his mother and aunt paid little attention to his schooling. It was only after Salvador became an adolescent that he entered Suzanna's new family. By that time, Suzanna had married and had two other children with her husband. Then, Suzanna realized that Salvador had been intentionally misleading the teachers into thinking he could speak only Spanish. Nonetheless, Suzanna blamed Salvador's academic difficulties largely on the school and the teachers, especially those in elementary school. She saw herself as a good mother because she loved her children. In retrospect, she realized she should have brought him up differently, disciplining him more and giving him educational gifts instead of toys. With the support of a marriage, she had brought up her last two children with more discipline and more of an educational orientation.

Even when Salvador moved into his mother's new family, she remained largely out of touch with his problems. She did not worry about Salvador's involvement with his gang friends because they seemed harmless to her at first. After Salvador stole a car at the age of 15, Suzanna realized the seriousness of his gang involvement. When she had to pay $500 to repair the stolen car, Suzanna took Salvador to the bank to withdraw the money. At that time, she tried to give him a moral lesson by making certain that he realized the severity of what he had done. Afterward, when he transferred to a school for troubled students, she made spontaneous visits to the school around lunchtime to make sure he was there. If she found him there, she rewarded him by taking him to lunch.

Salvador did not feel a part of Suzanna's new family. Although Suzanna tried to draw Salvador into the family life by bringing him out of his room into the front room to watch TV with the other children, Salvador interacted little with his family, preferring his gang friends. At home with the family, he preferred sitting in his room alone with the door shut.

When we asked Suzanna how she got Salvador to do what she wanted, she said, "We compromise a lot." When it came to household chores, Salvador would do what he was supposed to, but on his own schedule. For example, he would wash the dinner dishes around midnight, after everyone had gone to bed. If Suzanna found out that he skipped school, she grounded him for the weekend. Sometimes, nothing she did seemed to get through and she yelled at him. Salvador tried to calm her down saying, "Hey! It's not worth it. Just get out of here. Just go for a walk. . . ." Suzanna added, "They've told me they're raising me."

Salvador's attempts at controlling his mother became clearer to Suzanna when she first divorced Bill. Salvador grilled her when she came home late, and he sternly disciplined his sister for minor transgressions. It occurred to her then that Salvador was trying to be "the man of the house." While she asserted her authority with Salvador at that time, she still felt uncomfortable with the responsibility for controlling her children alone.

And what about the biological fathers of these children? Ramona's father simply left his family, not paying any child support for over a decade, until the state's attorney general forced him to do so. Ramona was usually animated when we talked to her, but when the topic of her father came up, her face darkened. She was almost in tears when she said that she did not want to have anything to do with him, even though she knew he lived in the same town she did. He had remarried twice since leaving Paula and their eight children.

At least Ramona had a mother who had supported her, emotionally and financially, throughout her childhood. Salvador did not. He grew up knowing that his mother almost gave him up for adoption because she was not married to his biological father. Suzanna had told Salvador many times that he caused her to drop out of school. Suzanna portrayed Salvador's father as totally uneducated and living in a rural shack. When Suzanna became frustrated with Salvador, she brought up his biological father and told Salvador that he should not want to be like him. Salvador would retort that there was nothing he could do about his failures because he had inherited his father's low abilities. In contrast, his gang friends recognized him as a leader and supported him when he needed them.

Both Ramona and Salvador suffered from the realization that their biological fathers had no interest in them.

THE ADOLESCENTS

When we first met Ramona, she had a negative attitude toward school. She found school difficult, largely because of her weak reading and writing skills. Although she had never been retained a grade, her standardized test scores indicated that her reading skills were about three grade levels below the level of courses she was taking. This reading deficit almost caused her to drop out of school because she found much of her schoolwork to be too difficult. She failed the state required exit-level exam in writing. Her math skills were basically on par with her grade level, but here again, if the teacher used word problems and expected the students to write about mathematics, then Ramona had difficulties. It hurt her to fail, but she did. To cope with her pain, she would skip classes or talk back to teachers. However, during the three years we studied her, her skill scores improved substantially, from 9.9 to 13.4 grade equivalents in math, and from 7.4 to 9.4 grade equivalents in reading.

Ramona wanted to be the first in her family to graduate from high school, and in order to do this, she consciously transformed herself into a model student, making herself appear to school staff as worthy of the special program. She reached out to teachers, school administrators, and drug counselors for help. As importantly, she made the most out of the help they gave her. She graduated from high school and she continued working "little by little" toward her goal of getting a state job.

In contrast, when we first met Salvador, he had just been through a difficult year, part of it in a correctional facility for auto theft and part in a school for troubled students. Because he had been absent or tardy so often, he had been held back two grades in school. During the time of our study, his skills, as measured by standardized tests, changed little. In 1988, his grade equivalents in reading and mathematics were 8.6 and 8.5, respectively; one year later, they were 9.1 and 8.5.

By the time Salvador was 18, his life had no direction, even though he liked his state job. His mother and the personnel director of the state agency where he worked pressed Salvador to go back to school to get a GED or a diploma. In response to their pressure, Salvador attended a few sessions of a course at a middle school to prepare for the GED exam. He stopped attending, saying, "I tried once. It didn't work out." He had no particular complaint about the course or the teacher, although he indicated he did not like the "English grammar."

Many people tried to help Salvador: the faculty and counselors at the special school, the staff involved in the summer art contests, various mentors, various teachers, administrators, and counselors at the regular school he attended. The attorney representing the killed gang member had gotten him his job, which paid more than Ramona's job did even after her high school graduation. After graduation, her part-time job at an automotive parts department expanded to a full-time job, but she earned minimum hourly wage rates, the same as before her graduation. Salvador recognized that his good job was the result of what others had done for him. He told us he planned to stay at the job at the state agency "as long as they'll keep me there."

THE GANG

While many studies of gangs have portrayed them as part of the assimilation process for the children of immigrants,[9] the gang that attracted Ramona and captured Salvador contained Mexican Americans and Mexican immigrants. According to Officers Mark Gil and Robert Martinez of the Austin Police Department Gang Liaison Unit,[10] The Brothers began in the East Austin Mexican American community as a neighborhood gang but expanded beyond this neighborhood with satellite groups in several other neighborhoods, including the Northeast Austin neighborhood of Ramona and the Southeast Austin neighborhood of Salvador. These satellite groups were part of the approximately 92 gang groups in the Austin area in 1992. The Brothers often included two or three generations of parents, children, and grandchildren in their membership. Consequently, their ages ranged widely, from about 12 to 37.

According to Gil and Martinez, there was no overarching authority uniting these subgroups of The Brothers; in fact, they functioned so autonomously that it is likely that Salvador and Ramona did not know each other. Within each satellite group there was no formal chain of command; they were loosely organized like friendship networks. Although most of the active members of The Brothers were males, females also took more active roles in such activities as shootings and thefts.

Entry into The Brothers was linked to friendships formed in school and family relationships. For many families, gang life has become a routine part of the growing-up process. It was not unusual for sons, fathers, uncles, brothers, and cousins to belong to the same group. Officers Gil and Martinez described the recruitment process this way: gang members continuously recruited from the large numbers of Austin youth who experienced failure at school and who were not closely supervised by their parents. Typically, older gang members invited such youth to parties where there were girls (like Ramona), drugs, and music. These parties often involved binge drinking. The older gang members flattered the vulnerable egos of young adolescents by paying attention to them and sharing stories of gang exploits, like drive-by shootings and fights with rival gangs.

Once youth were attracted to gang life, these "wanna-bes" had to prove themselves by such rituals as "walking the line," which involved being beaten up by a number of gang members. In addition, gangs required the new recruits to steal, starting with thefts of six-packs of beer and culminating with major crimes, such as car thefts or drive-by shootings.

THE SCHOOLS

Several individual teachers, school counselors, and administrators tried to help both Ramona and Salvador, often beyond the call of duty. These individuals together with special programs made a difference for Ramona. And they might have made a difference for Salvador if his personal and family problems had been less severe.

Nonetheless, as organizational settings, the schools did not function optimally to help students like Ramona and Salvador acquire the skills they needed to become successful adults. Instead, the schools tracked these two students into low-level courses and programs that grouped them with active gang members and offered few social activities that could compete with gang attentions. Youth like Ramona and Salvador were turned off by school long before they became involved in gangs. Our statistical results indicated that youth involved with gangs found schoolwork to be unimportant.[11]

The following assessment by one of our gang-involved students who dropped out of school was typical: "I wasn't interested in English, math, stuff like that. . . . I just went ahead and gave up doing all that English and math stuff. I just went ahead and dropped on down to the lower classes because they were easier and I didn't have to learn new things. . . . Ever since I went to the first grade I didn't like school. I just had my mind set then to quit, try to quit in the seventh or eighth grade."

It is a safe assumption that students like Ramona and Salvador would have been much more motivated to go to school if they were genuinely interested in what they were learning. Neither Ramona nor Salvador could think of a time in a classroom when the teaching excited them. In part this was due to the assumption of many teachers and administrators that students performing at average or below average levels should not be expected to meet the academic standards of the college-bound students. Average students with attendance problems were frequently tracked into uninspiring coursework. Given all this, it was not surprising that our statistical analyses indicated that students who had gang-involved friends skipped classes much more than did others. Curiously, such students were as likely as others to arrive on campus each day, but once there, they often left school for more interesting activities elsewhere.

We found that the schools Ramona and Salvador attended were porous buildings, with little or nothing holding students inside. School data show that Salvador missed over 40% of the state-required school days during the last semester he was enrolled, and Ramona missed 26% of her school days during the same semester. School officials regard class attendance as the responsibility of students, and they regard students as the responsibility of the parents. Therefore, school officials responded to evidence of skipping by attempting to get the parents to solve the problem for them. The schools called or wrote to parents in an effort to get the parents to prevent student absences. While parents tried to motivate their children to attend school, they could not force them to attend classes where the students were bored, humiliated, or defeated.

In the school district we studied, there was no districtwide policy about gangs; each high school handled "the gang problem" differently. While some schools ignored the problem, other schools dealt with incidents of fighting, weapon possession, truancy, and absences, due to juvenile detention or assault, on a case-by-case basis. A few other high schools approached the problem affirmatively, incorporating gang life into school activities. In one high school with a large concentration of The Brothers, a vice-principal encouraged a charismatic "Bro" to run for student body vice-president; he did, and won. At the same school, the administration sponsored retreats for gang members to talk out problems. Yet another school brought in a dispute-resolution specialist, who worked with gang members to help them learn nonviolent ways to resolve conflicts between rival gangs.

One vice-principal at a high school with a high proportion of The Brothers largely blamed the parents for the affinity of many students for gang life. He believed that the parents did not pay enough attention to their children and that many parents facilitated the gang involvement of their adolescents by not discouraging it. He explained that while the Mexican-origin parents provided a supportive family structure for their children, many lacked the skills needed to control adolescents. Many were actually afraid of their children and incapable of taking action to stop their son's or daughter's involvement in gang life. The vice-principal's advice to these parents was, "Lock the kids out, if the kid keeps breaking the rules, take away support. Kick them out of the house." This advice reflected the method routinely used by Austin high schools to respond to gang behavior in school—expulsion.

Yet, according to our research, expulsion from school or home does little to stop gang behavior. It merely pushes the adolescent toward deeper involvement in gang life. Many of the parents we interviewed, those who had sons or daughters involved in gangs, said that it was not uncommon for the adolescent friends of their children to live with them for indefinite periods. Many parents accepted this as a way of maintaining some contact with (and therefore, some control over) their gang-involved sons and daughters. Expulsion from home and/or school was a contributing factor in youths' dropping out of school and becoming more deeply involved in the criminal aspects of gang life.

In addition to expulsion, the school district created and maintained schools for "troubled" youth, where they sent students with a variety of behavior problems. The rationale for these schools was that the special staff could provide more individualized attention and thereby improve the student's school behavior. These schools mixed youth whom the police called "policy breakers" (that is, they had broken the school rules) with students who had committed serious and often violent crimes. This is what happened to Salvador. After spending time in juvenile detention for stealing a car, he was sent to one of these alternative schools, where he was able to acquire new criminal skills by interacting with other students. He began to incite more naive students to get deeper into trouble.

Salvador's experience in the alternative program was not unusual. The most recent evaluation of these alternative schools, conducted by the district's own evaluation staff, reported that students who attended these special schools were much more likely to drop out of school than were groups of comparable students.[12] Clearly, the district's policy of throwing such students out of regular high school and concentrating them in these alternative schools did not improve these students' chances of getting a high school diploma and quite possibly increased their level of gang activity.

POLICY RECOMMENDATIONS

Our policy recommendations are aimed at reducing the negative impact that gangs have on educational progress, not on eliminating gangs, per se, because the point of this book is to explore ways of fostering higher graduation rates among Hispanic youth. Gangs play an important part in the socialization of youth and are established in many Hispanic families and communities. Our focus is on rechanneling the affiliative needs of youth toward activities more compatible with educational attainment.

Like other researchers, we found that gang involvement was often instigated by academic failure.[13] Students who are defeated in school turn to gangs as a source of self-esteem and peer popularity. If families and schools are ineffective in turning the adolescents away from gangs, their involvement will deepen, leading to behaviors, such as fighting in school, that make expulsion from school likely. Expulsion has been the primary action that schools and families have taken when overwhelmed by the aggressive behavior of youth. The desire to "throw gang members out" of school or families is understandable, but it does not solve the joint problems of discouraging the criminal aspects of gang life and encouraging school performance. The evidence indicates that this "throwing away of the problem" merely encourages the youths to engage in criminal actions as well as to drop out of school. It is clear that both families and schools need to develop more effective strategies to motivate all students to stay on the academic path toward high school completion.

The need to expand opportunities for parents to learn how to bring up academically successful adolescents is great within the Mexican-origin population. Mothers like Paula and Suzanna had no formal training in parenting skills. Paula learned from the school failures of her first three children, and had the savvy to change her behavior when trying to motivate her fourth and fifth children to complete their high school education. Both Paula and Suzanna were poorly educated and had few opportunities to learn the skills they needed to parent effectively. In particular, Suzanna was a teen mother and made many mistakes with Salvador, including not paying enough attention to him, not disciplining him, and not responding negatively when she first realized he was involved in a gang. She tried to make up for these mistakes during Salvador's early adolescence, and she had consulted with school administrators and succeeded in keeping Salvador in a job, in her home, and out of jail, even if she had not succeeded in getting him to complete his education. Nonetheless, Salvador's case is a good example of how parental neglect before and during middle childhood causes almost irremediable problems in adolescence.

The need for more successful strategies for dealing with adolescents is demonstrated by the difficulties experienced by these and other parents we interviewed. Parents expressed much skepticism and disillusionment with the efforts previously offered by the schools. Because gang activity and school failure are such common experiences in their neighborhoods, parents often do not perceive them as problems that they can solve. Police officers Gil and Martinez complained that many parents were unaware of the extent of gang involvement of their sons and daughters. Moreover, health problems, irregular work hours, and economic and family crises make it difficult for these parents to obtain help in solving gang problems. Parents like Paula and Suzanna might have recognized that they were making mistakes earlier if they had had community resources to support their parenting.

Most parents learn to parent effectively from their own parents and by comparing their parenting strategies with those of other parents. If parents see that their children are deficient in some way, then they become motivated to do something about it. It is likely, however, that when Paula compared her children to others in her neighborhood or family, she did not see them as remarkably different. Indeed, there are thousands of students like Ramona and Salvador who are having difficulty in school and are enticed by peers into gang life. If anything, Ramona had more ability and motivation than most of the youth growing up in her neighborhood. For her part, Suzanna had been overwhelmed with her own problems during her youth and early marriage, and had not paid attention to Salvador's development during his early years.

The extended family network of aunts, grandparents, and in-laws that traditionally taught young mothers parenting skills was not in place to help Paula and Suzanna. Their friends, neighbors, and significant others were dealing with similar problems with their own children and had few solutions. An alternative could be parent support centers in Hispanic communities that reach out to new parents at the birth of each child and follow that child until he or she graduates from high school. To be effective these centers would have to be staffed by community members and provide information about normal child and adolescent development as well as advice on how to solve problems.

Joyce Epstein notes that at middle and high school levels families and schools traditionally work separately to solve students' social, academic, and personal problems, such as truancy, failure, grade retention, and discipline issues.[14] Secondary schools have made few efforts to reach out to parents and involve them in meaningful activities. The parents of adolescents, like Suzanna and Paula, who need information and help in formulating coping strategies to help their adolescents deal with gangs, sex, drug abuse, and school failure are presently receiving the least attention and support from the schools.

There are examples of restructured schools that are providing a supportive learning community for adolescents. A notable success is the Koln-Holweide Comprehensive School in Cologne, Germany.[15] This school enrolls 2,000 students, in grades 5–10, and nests each student into a table group of five or six mixed-ability students who work together all day, for an entire school year. Sitting around a table, each group is taught by a team of teachers who follow the same cohort of 85–90 students during the six years they are enrolled in the school. The students and teachers are part of a school community that supports the learning of all students while at the same time sanctioning students who stray too far from community norms. Students have little motivation to skip school because the nature of the cooperative learning that goes on in the class makes learning personally rewarding for each student. Furthermore, they develop strong personal relations with members of their table group and their teachers, and they know they would be missed if they skipped. Because all members of a table group help each other learn, students are never embarrassed about not knowing the material. When a student has a question, he or she is supposed to ask members of the table group first and then the teacher. Thus, bright and/or prepared students gain status socially because they can be resources for their peers while slower and/or less prepared students gain status because they are able to acquire all the skills necessary to complete their schoolwork without being publicly labeled or ridiculed. Such table groups make school a more attractive place to be. Students are excited about being there, and they feel part of a group of students and adults who care about each other.

Students who attend Koln-Holweide have no motivation to skip school. A peer culture is created that supports learning and school attendance. Only about 1% of the students drop out, compared to the German average of 14%, and 60% score well enough on exit exams to be admitted to college, compared to a national average of 27%. These results cannot be explained in terms of the advantaged backgrounds of the students. The student body is heterogeneous demographically, with 30% being immigrants and about 25% having unemployed parents.

Although no schools like Koln-Holweide exist in the U.S., several states have established academies—that is, schools within regular high schools that keep groups of students together with the same, small number of faculty for the last three years of high school. In California, there are more than 50 such academies, which are based on local business-school partnerships.[16] Such academies have the following features: block scheduling of 100–120 students, a small core of teachers who work together to plan and implement the program, coordinated coursework that consists of rigorous academic courses organized around an occupational theme, and the use of a rich array of motivators, including parental support, paid work experience, and a mentor program.

California academies have been functioning for 10 years, and several evaluations of them have been conducted. Students who participate in academies have been found to have better attendance, earn more credits, fail fewer courses, and have higher grade point averages than comparable students in regular high school. Moreover, the dropout rate for academy students is half that of comparable students.[17] As importantly, the students who emerge from such academies have strong workplace skills and are much more likely to obtain a good job in local industry and/or pursue further training in the occupational area they have been trained in. The major problem with academies is that they serve a relatively small proportion of the students who need them. Students like Ramona would have been admitted into such an academy, but it is unlikely that Salvador would have been selected, given his record as a troublemaker.

FIVE

"I

wanted

him."

Teen
Motherhood

This chapter discusses the interrelationships between teen motherhood, family relationships, and school attendance. We tell the stories of three teen mothers—Norma, Kathy, and Lupe. Norma was able to graduate from high school despite her motherhood because her father sacrificed so that she would have the time to go to school and study. For Norma, teen motherhood was unintended, the consequence of sexual activity without contraception. Kathy and Lupe became mothers after they had already dropped out of school. Kathy was not motivated to attend classes, and she became pregnant in the hope of finding a way to get away from her troubled family. Lupe was unable to understand her English-speaking teachers, and she suffered when they gave her bad grades. For Lupe, teen motherhood was a way of attaining the praise and respect of others. This chapter describes the type of interventions needed to stem the number of teen pregnancies among youth "at risk" of dropping out of high school. Essentially, such interventions need to give teens strong motivation to avoid pregnancy by giving them real prospects for obtaining good jobs with their high school diploma.

NORMA

Norma became pregnant for the first time when she was 16 years old and repeating the ninth grade. She received "no credit" for most of her ninth-grade courses the first time she took them because she had skipped so many classes. This pregnancy was the culmination of her tumultuous entry into high school. During her first two years, school officials suspended her from high school for fighting with girls. She spent a brief period in an alternative school for troubled students. She attributed her problems to the fact that she had "discovered boys" and that it was easy to skip classes without her father finding out.

At the very beginning of ninth grade, Norma appeared to be making a good adjustment to high school life. She became wholeheartedly engaged in the social life of the school. She told us, "I was in band, the marching band. I went to summer band before I started my freshman year and that was fun, I liked that. I was elected homecoming princess for my freshman class." But then she found that the rewards of skipping with her friends were greater than the daily consequences of missing classes. She told us that, beginning the second half of the school year, "I started not going to school and then I didn't like band anymore because we weren't marching. I got out of band and I went into track but by that time I was skipping and wasn't doing my schoolwork so I wasn't able to run track for the school. They didn't pay that close attention so I wouldn't go to school. If my friends or a guy I was talking to at that time wanted to leave, we would just go off. I wasn't doing my schoolwork. I think I got about 3 credits, no I got 4 credits my freshman year." And then, during her sophomore year, she became pregnant with her son.

During her first two years of high school, Norma spent a lot of time with her boyfriend outside of school. They had met when they were 12 years old and remained close friends and confidants, even though Ruben had dropped out of school after completing the eighth grade. Norma described to us how she felt sorry for him because of his family: "They were just so depressed with their lives they just didn't want to lift themselves up, that's the way I saw it. So he didn't have a real happy home life. The thing about me and Ruben was for the first time he met someone who saw him as a person and that is how I saw him. I didn't see him as a boy. We were friends for a while and then we got closer in time and I saw him as a person because he confided a lot of his life to me and he told me a lot and I told him a lot. I tried to help him because it was so sad. I felt so bad because I knew what he could have; I knew how his parents *could* treat him because of how my dad treated us. I felt spoiled. We weren't just boyfriend and girlfriend who saw each other and kissed and hugged and all kinds of stuff you know. We were people. We could sit with each other and not have to kiss and hug, and talk. And that was nice and I think he liked it."

Norma would take Ruben to her home when her father was not there. Alfredo was a policeman, and he worked three nights a week. He had brought up Norma and her two brothers alone after his wife left him and the children when Norma was four years old. Norma's biological mother simply moved out and into her own place in the same town. She worked as a secretary and visited the children on birthdays and holidays, but she remained at an emotional distance from them.

Alfredo remarried about the same time Norma entered high school. The new wife and her child moved into Norma's house, a neatly kept three-bedroom brick home on the east side of town. The house was one of several built as affordable housing in the area. The living room had a large upholstered sofa and matching chair and a large TV. The living room opened onto a dining area furnished with a modern dining table spread with a lace tablecloth. A vase of silk flowers adorned the center of the table. A large matching china cabinet took up most of the wall behind the table.

Norma never accepted her stepmother. Alfredo believed that Norma engaged in many of her delinquent behaviors at that time in order to drive his new wife out of the house. Norma's stepmother disapproved of the permissive way that Alfredo dealt with Norma's transgressions.

When Norma suspected she was pregnant, she went to the high school nurse for a pregnancy test. She told us, "I was happy when I found out I was pregnant. It's not that I wanted to get pregnant or I planned to get pregnant. If I could go back, I would have waited. I would have done something. I didn't use protection at all. I would have waited, but I didn't. I mean it just happened and I wasn't going to have an abortion or give him away because to me his father—I was with him for like three years at that point. We grew up together. He wasn't just my boyfriend—he was my friend. I don't believe in abortion. *I wanted him.* I was happy when I was pregnant because I wanted him.

"You know, my dad never knew what I was doing, how I felt about my boyfriend. That was a hard thing for me to explain to my dad. I was the only girl and it was always being banged into my head, 'You'll always be a little girl.' And that didn't help. I think that is the worst thing anyone could tell a little girl—'You'll always be a little girl'—because maybe she will but she's still growing and she needs to talk about the other side of her."

Alfredo tried to persuade Norma to get an abortion, but she refused. "I didn't want to. I really did not because I felt it was wrong," she explained.

During that summer, she went to summer school to make up some of her lost credits, and her mother took her on a long weekend to the beach. In August, the school district changed the high school boundaries in order to maintain "ethnic balance." Norma was assigned to a new high school, one which had previously served a predominantly White student population.

She arrived at her new school in the later stages of her pregnancy. She enrolled in honors courses and took her schoolwork seriously. Norma knew she was different—there were few minority students in her new school, and pregnant students were a rarity. "They would just kinda look and stare because I was really different." Her isolation helped her focus more on her studies. "I had a 3.5 average and I think that's good but the reason why I had that average was that not many people talked to me. I didn't eat lunch with anyone. I would go to the library and do my work and I was making good grades there. I had nothing else to do but work, so I did."

Despite her academic achievements, one of the vice-principals tried to persuade her to go to the district's school for pregnant students. Norma refused. She told the vice-principal, "I have a right to this kind of education just as much as everyone else. Just because I am pregnant does not mean that I can't come to school here." She had learned at the alternative school that the school for pregnant students did not offer high-level academic courses. Norma wanted to take honors courses, and she did well in them.

The vice-principal threatened her. He reminded her that she could only be absent seven days before she would begin losing credits, something she could not afford to do. The vice-principal called Alfredo and persuaded him that going to this special school was right for Norma, but she persisted. She told the vice-principal, "Look at my grades. I'm making good grades. There's no reason why you can't excuse my absences. I am pregnant. The only time my doctor's appointments are is during the day, not after school." The vice-principal gave up.

With the help of several sympathetic teachers, Norma continued her high-level academic work even though her son was born on December 4, near the end of the fall school term. She named him Ruben, after his father. She returned to school after the holidays.

The arrival of the baby created many problems for the family. Alfredo had eight dependents at that time, and money was short. Nonetheless, he paid for baby-sitting the infant while Norma was in school. The father of Norma's baby was unable to provide any support for the child because he was unemployed. After the baby's birth, he harassed Norma and her family because they denied him access to the baby. Alfredo got a peace bond against him to keep him away from Norma. Then Alfredo's mother came to live with them because she was frail and almost blind. Thus, in addition to caring for a baby, Norma and her younger brother were expected to take care of their grandmother when they were not in school.

To relieve the financial burden from her father for the expenses of her baby, Norma investigated what welfare was available to her and found out that she was eligible for WIC. This program provided some support for her new baby, but it was not enough. So, by the beginning of the summer, she took a part-time job at a grocery store. Despite the increased demands on her time, she continued in school, enrolling in night school and summer school to make up the credits she had missed during her first two years of high school.

During summer school she found a new boyfriend. He also attended summer school, making up lost credits so that he could graduate on time. They became intimate and their relationship continued into the first semester of their senior year, even though they attended different schools. Norma became pregnant again.

Alfredo took the news very hard, fearing that she would never graduate. He explained, "When she became pregnant the second time, that really, it was even worse than the first time for me. Because I said, 'How is she going to do it now?' you know, and I could only see that I was going to be a father again. I was going to be the one that was going to have to provide. I had provided for Ruben (the baby), all of his day-care, all of his Pampers, all his milk. She had gotten some help from [Texas Department of] Human Resources to get some food stamps and things of that nature, but it just wasn't enough. You know, especially the day-care, I was having to pay that and that took away from the rest of the family. . . . You could only see problems ahead, it wasn't the end of the rainbow, it was the end of the world. So the second baby made it even harder for me and I really got upset with Norma and for a long time I could never accept her being pregnant again. It put a big stress on my family. Me and my wife had trouble. We had already gone through one baby and here we're going through another one and it seemed like we were never going to get out of raising children. And that was the hard thing to try to cope with. I'm getting divorced because my wife could not handle the second baby. But it took its toll on everybody. My youngest son, we were all helping Norma. That put a big stress on us. We were having to give up our time and try to help Norma with the babies. And my mother was here and she also had trouble coping with the situation. I mean she loved her granddaughter and she loved the babies, but we could tell that it affected everybody."

Norma persisted in school, making up lost credits and working part-time in the grocery store. During her last semester, she transferred to her boyfriend's high school to be with him. They graduated together. When she walked across the stage to receive her diploma, she was eight-months pregnant with her second child. She described the experience this way: "I knew the way people were looking at me and I knew they were stereotyping me, but I was proud because I was thinking, 'God, I am pregnant. I'm eight-months pregnant but I still got it and I still did it on time.' And it's real good, it's a real good feeling to get that diploma. . . . You can tell someone and tell someone but they never know until they receive the diploma. It makes a lot of difference. It gives you a lot of new hope for more."

One month later, Norma received a telephone call from Ruben, the father of her first child, the day before she went into labor with her second. He was calling from prison. He had been convicted of stabbing a 15-year-old boy to death. Norma said that Ruben told her that he was proud of her graduating on time. She said, "I talked to him and he congratulated me and he told me 'I knew you'd do it.' That made me feel good."

When asked to reflect upon why she was able to graduate on time despite all of her academic and personal problems, she credited her family for a large part of her success. "I think I had the most family support anyone could ever have. And that helped, that helped a lot. . . . From the beginning, my dad and my grandma, they raised me and my brothers, they always emphasized school to us, not like, you better do it, but they made it sound good. They made it something that we wanted to do. And so, to me, it would have been too abnormal for me to leave school and it was normal for me to stay. It wasn't hard."

About six months after graduation, Norma began a jobs program designed to make teen mothers employable. In her case, this meant that in addition to "every kind of welfare there is," she told us that she received day-care for her children while she went to community college. She was training to become a physical therapy assistant in a two-year program. She hoped that ultimately she would be able to get four years of training and become a physical therapist.

Norma was still seeing the father of her second child, although she did not want to marry him. She explained, "I guess some people think I'm a hypocrite on that part because I don't even think about marriage. I'm not saying I don't want to get married. It's just not a subject that is on my mind right now because I know where me and my boyfriend stand and I don't think getting married will do anything for us right now. If anything, getting married will take away all the chances I have right now."

After one year in this program, an apartment for Norma and her children became available in subsidized housing. She was about to move into her own place when we last interviewed her. She explained, "Me and my two kids were in one room, the smallest room in the house. My dad, he needs his life. He's 42 and he's getting a divorce and he's helped me along. He needs to be able to enjoy life and not worry about who is crying or this Pamper's dirty. He went through that alone for the past twenty years. He's not done yet because he still has my little brother."

Analysis

Norma was able to obtain her high school diploma because she had the determination and the academic skills she needed and her family supported her, both emotionally and financially. She had not expected to get pregnant, although she was involved in a sexual relationship with her boyfriend. Other teenage girls may get reliable information about sex from their mothers, but Norma's mother did not live with her. Her father had not talked to her about sex because he still considered her a child, not a sexually active young woman. The coursework in her school health and science classes never addressed the issues of contraception, the pleasures associated with sexual intercourse, or the consequences of becoming a teen mother.[1]

One might wonder why Norma was not able to learn from her first pregnancy and avoid the second. Essentially, the answer to this question is that Norma had little motivation to avoid a second pregnancy at the time of the second conception. Her first pregnancy had been a positive experience for her. She felt good being pregnant, and it changed her life, for the better. She was able to settle down and get serious about her life. She took more advanced courses and obtained good grades.

She explained her feelings at that time, "I wasn't embarrassed because I knew who I was. I knew what I did and to me it wasn't bad. It wasn't bad because I didn't feel bad about it. I felt good. I felt good. . . . It wasn't hard, I wasn't embarrassed. I wasn't ashamed. I used to like to talk about it, when people would ask me what it was like and 'can I feel your stomach?' and stuff like that."

Not only did she feel good about the changes that motherhood made in her life, she was rewarded for her second pregnancy by the departure of her father's second wife. Norma had never developed a good relationship with her stepmother. She told us, "Me and her, we were distant from each other. We hardly talked. . . . She made it clear that I was taking advantage of my dad and that wasn't true. She would never talk. It was like I didn't exist. And I was like, OK, you don't exist either."

The first pregnancy had caused her father and stepmother to argue. The second pregnancy was more than her new stepmother could bear. She moved out of the house. Later, she divorced Norma's father. Since Norma regarded her stepmother as an intruder in her family, Norma was probably happy that she had been able to drive her out of the house.

After Norma had her first child, she transferred to a school with a child care center for teen mothers. She developed a network of friends who were also teen mothers. She told us, "There were a lot of girls there that are mothers. They don't have just one child, they have two, like me. . . . It wasn't nothing abnormal for them." Thus, she had peer support and encouragement to have a second child. Now she had a close group of friends with common interests and bonds that she didn't have before her children were born.

Her father, and to some extent her brothers, helped Norma take care of her first baby so that she was shielded from the costs and primary responsibility of taking care of a newborn. Alfredo paid for baby-sitters and for the baby's needs. The state also provided assistance in the form of Medicaid, food stamps, and AFDC.

Why should she have wanted to avoid a second pregnancy when the first brought with it so many rewards?

The reality of parenthood did not become clear to Norma until her newborn child became old enough to take up a lot of her time and energy. But by that time, she was pregnant again.

We asked her what she planned to do for her daughter when the child became an adolescent. Norma answered, "I want to get involved with her school and her teachers. Make sure she stays in there and likes it and enjoys it and then after she starts getting into boys, I'll be honest with her because I was 16 when I got pregnant, a young age. I was having a sexual life so she might too. I'll probably talk to her about that and give her what she needs and tell her, 'You don't have to tell me, just use it if you have to.' The protection. Then I wouldn't want her to hide her boyfriends. My boyfriend was not allowed to come near this house, but that didn't stop me."

KATHY

Kathy returned to high school for the fall term, but found repeating the ninth grade for the third time both embarrassing and boring. She became pregnant at age 17, about four months after she had officially dropped out of high school. Although she had become pregnant in January, she delayed telling her father, Paco, until Easter because she knew that he would not take it well.

And he didn't. Kathy's mother told us that Paco became enraged and called Kathy "worthless." As Kathy's mother explained it, the revelation of the pregnancy only reminded Paco of all the frustrations and disappointments in his life. Kathy's parents had worked hard so that their five children would be able to concentrate on their studies and not have to give up school for work. Paco had been forced to quit school after the sixth grade to work to support his parents and siblings. He didn't want this to happen to his children. Instead, he wanted his children to earn high school diplomas and get good jobs and then marry and start families.

But Kathy's three older siblings had all dropped out of school. The oldest sister had begun childbearing when a teenager and now had three children, a husband, and a job. The second oldest, a sister, had a baby and no husband or job. The one closest in age to Kathy was an older brother, and he had not found a job since dropping out. He spent most of his time at home watching television. Her younger sister was 13 and still attended middle school, although it was uncertain how long this would last, given that she was sneaking out of the house at night to hang out with friends at a convenience store parking lot in the neighborhood. Paco was angry that despite his sacrifices, his children failed to obtain the education he had hoped for them.

What really magnified Paco's anger about Kathy's pregnancy was that the father of her baby was Black. To Paco, this was the ultimate humiliation. He told his wife that his friends would ridicule him about having a Black grandchild.

He threw Kathy out of the house.

Kathy had been dating Jamal, the father of the baby, for over a year at the time of the baby's conception. Kathy's mother, Caroline, had been promoting the idea of Kathy getting married, and Kathy was in love with Jamal. According to Caroline, Jamal lived with his unemployed mother and had only met his biological father for the first time when Jamal was 17. Although he had dropped out of school and had no job at the time, Caroline saw Jamal as a good prospect for Kathy. She described Jamal as looking for "office work, like proofreading." The main work that Kathy seemed interested in was homemaking. The only thing that she told us she liked in high school was the cake decorating she had learned in one of her courses.

Although we do not know her thoughts and feelings at the time, we do know that Kathy intended to get pregnant because she stopped taking her birth-control pills just before the conception in January. Perhaps she thought Jamal would marry her and they could live together with their baby, not too far away from her family.

With little adult supervision, Kathy had ample opportunity to bring about this pregnancy. Around this time, Caroline and Paco worked long hours and spent little time at home. Caroline worked daily from 3 P.M. to 9 A.M. as a sitter for an elderly person, and Paco worked for the city's sanitation department from 2 A.M. to 10 A.M. They expected Kathy to take care of the housework and to supervise her younger sister. Kathy had been playing the substitute mother role in the household since her two older sisters moved out. Little was expected of her older brother.

Kathy's family lived in one of the poorest sections of Southeast Austin. Caroline wished the family could move to a better house, but she told us that they could not afford anything better. Because the landlord refused to install screen doors and because the family could not afford air-conditioning, the front and back doors stayed wide open most of the year. There were few adornments or pictures on the walls, although school pictures of the children hung in the living room above the television.

After Kathy learned of her pregnancy, she considered having an abortion, but Caroline talked her out of it, reminding Kathy of the misfortunes of a friend of Kathy's who had had three abortions. Caroline talked to Jamal about his responsibilities to the child. Jamal told Caroline he was not ready to get married, but that he would do what he could to support the baby after it came. Kathy became angry with Jamal and said she didn't want to have anything to do with him. By the sixth month of her pregnancy, she had not been in contact with Jamal for a long time.

After her father threw her out, Kathy went to live with her married sister, who lived nearby. Her sister paid Kathy to baby-sit her three children when the sister was at work. Kathy visited her mother when her father left the house.

When we last interviewed Kathy, she was making one of these visits. She told us that the most important things for her to achieve in life were "graduating and having a healthy baby." She received prenatal care and WIC and looked, to us, to be healthy. But she was far from happy, describing herself as "just a confused young girl about to have a baby." Her immediate problem was to find a place to live after the baby arrived in three months. Her sister's place was crowded already, and she knew she couldn't stay there.

Caroline considered divorcing her husband and finding a place where Kathy, the new baby, and Kathy's younger sister could all live together. The children had discussed the divorce, and only the son had decided to stay with his father. It was hard, though, for Kathy's mother to leave her husband. Caroline was very religious, and she and Paco took their commitment to each other seriously. When Harriett Romo interviewed Kathy last, they sat in Kathy's parents' bedroom, and the only adornment on the wall was an altar where several votive candles burned next to a picture of the family. By refusing to allow Kathy to come home, Paco was forcing Caroline to choose between him and her grandchild. Caroline accepted her daughter's baby as her grandchild, no matter what "color, race or breed."

Completing her high school diploma would be a difficult goal for Kathy to achieve. Caroline and Kathy seemed to think that all Kathy needed to do was to return to school for about one year and Kathy would be able to graduate. Caroline told us that Kathy lacked just 5 credits for graduation. Kathy told us that she had talked to someone at the district's school for teen mothers and thought she might be able to enroll there, in the fall, when she turned 18.

From school records, we knew that Kathy had accumulated only 2 of the 21 credits she needed to earn a high school diploma. Thus, in order to graduate, Kathy would need to attend classes for about three more years.

There was a high degree of discrepancy between Kathy's understanding of her academic situation and the school's interpretation of her standing throughout the time we studied the family. The mother could not arrange meetings with counselors and school administrators in order to get information about Kathy's academic situation directly. Therefore, Caroline was dependent on Kathy to give her the correct information. Kathy either did not understand her school status or was intentionally misleading her mother.

When we first interviewed them, Kathy was 15. Caroline told us that Kathy should have been given some credits for attending an alternative school, but these credits never appeared on Kathy's record. Caroline told us that she could not get an explanation from the alternative school or Kathy's subsequent regular high school about why these credits did not appear on Kathy's grade card.

One year later, Caroline told us that the school had not made good on another deal that Kathy had made with an administrator. Kathy had told her mother that by going to 14 night classes, she could erase all of her absences. Kathy told us she had attended all 14 night sessions, but she still received no academic credits for any of her classes. Caroline had tried to resolve this discrepancy with the administrator who had made the deal with Kathy, but since he was not on staff during the summer, he was not available to explain it to her when she tried to contact him just after the school year ended. Kathy had to repeat the ninth grade for the third time as a consequence of this failed deal.

Analysis

Kathy did not drop out of high school because she was pregnant. She had not been attending school regularly for years before she became pregnant. From the school's perspective, Kathy had an "attendance problem." Going to school every day and attending all her classes throughout the day was something Kathy did not do, at least from the time she entered this school district, when she was placed in the eighth grade.

From the outset, Kathy and her family found themselves at odds with the expectations of the school district. When she first tried to enter a middle school in the district, at age 14, Kathy was prevented from attending because she did not have her immunizations. Kathy and her siblings stayed home from school for one week while Caroline looked for a clinic that would give the shots and bill her later.

Then, when Kathy began attending school, she felt alone and unhappy. She had lived most of her life in a small city in South Texas, and she felt out of place in her new school. She would skip classes; then, when she found out she could get away with it, she would skip entire days of school. Because of her poor attendance record in eighth grade, the district sent her to an alternative school for the first semester of what Kathy thought was ninth grade. Whatever the school district tried to do for her at this alternative school simply did not work. When she was transferred to a regular high school, halfway through the school year, she stayed home. She said that she feared that some girls were going to attack her. She told us that female students had been verbally abusive to her, and she took them seriously. She also saw her brother skipping school, and she did what he did. Her mother would let her stay home for weeks with a sore throat. Absences piled up, accumulating to 50% during her first attempt at ninth grade. She was not given credit for the time she did attend school and was required to repeat the entire year.

Her second try at ninth grade was a small improvement over her first in that she was absent 26% of that school year. Still, given the attendance laws of Texas, she was unable to earn credits for classes when she missed that much. When she was assigned to classes she didn't like, or to classes with teachers she didn't like, she would simply skip the class. She would frequently sit through two lunch periods, talking to her friends.

Her mother moved to withdraw her officially from school when she stopped attending after her third try at ninth grade. As Caroline saw it, Kathy was better off "checking herself out of school" before she accumulated more of a bad school record. When Kathy was ready to go to school, she "could check herself back in." It was clear to Caroline, if not Kathy, that Kathy could not maintain the student role long enough to graduate from high school.

Kathy may have thought that getting pregnant would result in her marriage to Jamal and a place of her own. She wanted to succeed at being a wife, mother, and homemaker. This did not work out for Kathy, and she and her mother were left trying to figure out what to do and where to live when the baby arrived.

LUPE

Lupe used the strategy of becoming a mother to raise her status in her family, and for her, it worked. She became pregnant when she was 17 years old and still a ninth grader in high school. Lupe's family had moved from one area of the city to another, and she was expected to attend a new high school. But only one of her new teachers spoke Spanish, and she had difficulty understanding all the others. These English-speaking teachers could not understand Lupe when she asked for help. So, she started flunking courses. This discouraged her and she stopped attending school. Somehow she got the sister of one of her friends to sign papers and make official excuses to cover her truancy. However, eventually Lupe's mother, Graciela, was required to go to court to explain why her daughter did not attend school. At court, someone explained to her in Spanish what was going on, and Graciela told the judge that she had no idea that her daughter was not going to school. She and her daughter rode the same city bus in the morning, and Lupe got off near her high school, while Graciela went on to her work.

Graciela had assumed that Lupe was going to school. After the court appearance, Lupe and her mother talked about Lupe's school situation, and Lupe convinced her mother that she no longer wanted to go to school. At that point Graciela officially withdrew Lupe from school to avoid further court appearances and resultant fines. The Texas Education Code had been amended to fine parents if a child was voluntarily out of school for 10 or more days. The fines ranged from $5 to $25 for the first offense, from $10 to $50 for the second offense, and not less than $25 and up to $100 for subsequent offenses.[2] Each day the student remained out of school constituted a separate offense. Graciela was concerned that if she forced Lupe to return to school, Lupe would skip school again, and Graciela would have to pay big fines in court.

By that time, Lupe was two-months pregnant, but Graciela did not know it. In fact, Graciela did not discover that Lupe was pregnant until just six weeks before the birth when Graciela finally noticed Lupe's swollen stomach. The father of the baby was a friend of Lupe's whom she had known since she arrived in the U.S. from Mexico. Lupe and Pablo had been in the same bilingual program since fourth grade. Pablo had also dropped out of high school.

After the pregnancy was discovered, Pablo moved into Lupe's family apartment and started working to contribute financially to Lupe's family. When Pablo moved in, the family included Lupe, her parents, and her eight younger siblings. As the eldest, Lupe had the job of supervising her younger siblings. She had carried this major responsibility for several years. When she was 16 years old, she told us that when her siblings became sick, she had to stay out of school to care for them. She also told us that taking care of her eight younger siblings made it difficult, if not impossible, for her to do her homework every night.

Lupe's family lived in an apartment complex inhabited by other Mexican immigrants. Many of the neighboring families came from the same rural village where Lupe's parents had grown up. The children moved freely from apartment to apartment, and the only English words one could hear were those voiced by children occasionally practicing what they had learned in school or from watching television. Although Lupe's parents had lived in the U.S. for almost eight years, they could speak no English. They did not have legal papers to work in the U.S.; nonetheless, both were employed and worked long hours.

Even though Lupe began her American schooling when she was 10 years old, she had little command of the English language by the time she was 18 years old. At our last interview, just after she had become a mother, she spoke to us solely in Spanish. Even though she had been enrolled in bilingual programs throughout her elementary, middle, and high school years, she did not feel comfortable with English. She explained her reason for dropping out of high school thus: "Como le decía, tenía ganas de ir—pero no, no podía. Los grados—bajitos. O sea que no iba a pasar y me volví ahí para mi casa. Y me daban ganas de regresar y regresar otra vez, pero me pasaba lo mismo. Y yo le decía a mi maestro que yo necesitaba un maestro bilingüe porque no le entendía. Y tal vez, o sea, él no podía hacer nada." (Like I told you, I wanted to go [to school], but no, I couldn't. The grades, very low. Or probably I wasn't going to pass and I came back home. And I wanted to return and I returned again, but the same thing happened to me. And I told my teacher that I needed a bilingual teacher because I didn't understand him. And maybe, or who knows, he couldn't do anything.)

Lupe failed many courses. Not surprisingly, she had accumulated zero credits toward graduation by the time she officially dropped out of school.

Analysis

Lupe is a good example of the many immigrant youth who are caught between two worlds—the world of rural Mexico and the world of the urban U.S.A. Like her parents, she never learned much English because she did not perceive a strong need to learn it. She lived in a Mexican enclave within the U.S. Her parents worked for Spanish-speaking employers and with fellow Spanish-speaking workers. Tragically, Lupe never received much of an education in Spanish either, and so her skills at reading, writing, and speaking Spanish were low. Thus, Lupe's options for employment were limited to menial jobs. Her American education did not empower her to get a decent job in either Mexico or the U.S. At our last interview, she told us of her occasional trips back home to Mexico and her ability to get past the border guards by speaking English. Apparently, her American education had provided her with little else than the skills necessary to get past border guards more easily.

Lupe did not drop out of school because she became pregnant. She stopped attending school and then became pregnant. Lupe no longer wanted to go to school because she could not understand most of her teachers and they gave her failing grades. It was relatively easy for her to stop attending school because most of her peers, including Pablo, had also dropped out. We asked Graciela how she gauged Lupe's success at school. Graciela told us that she assumed that if she heard nothing from the school, everything must be all right.

But since the family had no telephone and Lupe was the only person who could translate the contents of the letters from the school, Graciela was essentially ignorant of Lupe's academic status.

Lupe had worked as the surrogate mother of her younger siblings for many years. It was easy for her to take the step from older sister to new mother. When Pablo moved in, he and Lupe got their own bed, and they attained adult status within the family. Even though they were not married, they had formed a union in the eyes of Lupe's parents. Such unions are common in rural Mexico; furthermore, it is common for a teen pregnancy to form the basis of such unions. Lupe and her family were not concerned that Lupe had received no prenatal care or that her baby was not born in a hospital. Prenatal care and hospital births are not common in rural Mexico.

THE PARENTS

Norma's father, Alfredo, provided support both financially and emotionally and made many personal sacrifices so that Norma could graduate from high school on time. Alfredo defined himself primarily in terms of his children: "I am a parent that cares about his children. I want the best for them, and by the best I don't mean that they have to be the president of the United States or anything like that—I think so long as they do something that is healthy and honest and is something they enjoy."

Then he reflected further on himself, "I have a lot of patience. I think that's my biggest virtue. I will help anybody as long as they can help themselves. I am a very giving man. I think I give more than I receive. . . . If I was to put it into two or three words, I'm patient, I'm loving, I'm sympathetic."

Alfredo had little control over Norma. At the beginning of our study, he told us that he had not taken seriously Norma's designation as "at risk" of dropping out, although he had talked to her about her academic situation. He described her as both "headstrong" and "stubborn." He positioned himself to solve her problems, since he was unable to prevent them.

Nonetheless, from both Alfredo's comments and those of Norma, we can see that Alfredo instilled a desire for education in his daughter. He monitored Norma's status with her school and supported her through summer and night schools to make up her "skipped" coursework. He had taught her that a high school diploma was worth personal sacrifice. Both of Norma's parents had graduated from high school, and they wanted at least a high school education for their children.

In contrast to the clear message about education that Alfredo conveyed to his children, Caroline was the embodiment of contradictions. While she told us repeatedly that she wanted Kathy to graduate from high school, she spoke of her own high school diploma from a Catholic school as "not worth a shit," in terms of its value in getting her a good job. She found herself competing with college students who were willing to do low-level jobs to support their education.

Although Caroline appeared to visitors to be the matriarch of the family, very much in control of the household, she acknowledged that she could not force her children to go to school if they did not want to. She complained, "These children do not want to go to school. What can I do to keep them in school?"

She explained her approach to discipline this way: "I used to be real strict with them when they were younger. If they did not do what they were told to do, they would not get to go out to play, they would not get to go out to the movies or whatever. I would put a stop to that until it would finally sink in. When I say something, I mean it. I found out that spanking them was not con-ducive because it only hurts for a while and that's it. I found out that punishing them, taking things that they liked most away from them was more conducive than, you know, spanking them."

Both Caroline and Kathy agreed that Paco was especially hostile toward Kathy. When we asked Caroline what Paco did to help Kathy stay in school, she replied, "Nothing, except reinforce the fact that she needs to have her ed-ucation." When we probed further, asking what he did to encourage her, Car-oline said, "He threatens her. If she doesn't go to school, he is going to send her away. It really hurts her."

Paco had little status in the family. Caroline described him as an alcoholic. His oldest daughter treated him as though he did not exist. We witnessed this during one of our visits, when she commenced talking to us in English while we were in the middle of a conversation with Paco in Spanish. He was the only person in the family who could not speak English. According to Caroline, the family's disrespect for Paco finally got to him. Just before Kathy became preg-nant, Caroline described their home as like "a war zone" because Paco wanted the kids to do whatever he told them to do. She said that he felt that his children did not show him enough respect. He tried to take charge of them by ordering them around, becoming verbally abusive to them when they ignored him.

In contrast, Lupe's father had an established role within the family as a breadwinner and disciplinarian, even though he had attended only three years of school in Mexico. The parent we talked to most often was Graciela, Lupe's mother, who worked six days a week in a Mexican restaurant. She repeatedly told us of her desire for her children to get a high school diploma. Graciela had completed only seven years of schooling in Mexico and believed that her·

lack of education had diminished her chances for a good life. She told us that she encouraged her children to go to school by telling them that the family was poor because she and her husband had little education. She said, "Les digo, 'si no estudian van a, van a andar como nosotros.'" (I tell them, 'If you don't study, you're going to be like us.') Repeating a phrase common among Mexican immigrants, she told us that she tried to encourage her children to get a high school diploma "porque uno de pobre no tiene otra cosa más que, que dejarles" (because a poor person doesn't have anything else to leave them).

Because Graciela worked long hours at a restaurant, she had a pressing, daily need for baby-sitting. This need took priority over Lupe's need for an education. Watching over younger siblings earned Lupe an important place in her family. When school attendance became painful for Lupe, she dropped out of school to become a full-time mother to her siblings and her own new baby.

When Lupe was 16, we asked Graciela who made the rules in the house. Graciela at first did not understand the question, so we repeated it and gave an example. She said flatly, "Oh, pues, no tenemos reglas" (Oh, well, we don't have rules), explaining, "Sí, no, pos aquí, ellos me obedecen en todo, a mí y a su papá. Ellos saben que tienen, todo lo que les decimos nosotros lo tienen que hacer." (Yes, no, well here, they obey me about everything, me and their father. They know that they have to, everything that we tell them, they have to do.) When we probed further about what would happen if Lupe did not do what Graciela told her, she said, "No, ella me obedece. Por eso no tengo problema, porque ella, ella, si yo le digo, 'yo quiero que hagas esto,' ella lo hace. Conmigo así es, nunca me dice que no." (No, she obeys. That's why I don't have a problem because if I tell her, 'I want you to do this,' she does it. With me, that's how she is. She never tells me no.)

This type of parental control method is known as authoritarian.[3] Neither Lupe nor her mother understood the value of general rules of behavior that parents establish for all children to follow, such as rules about household chores or homework. Graciela had only one rule: Obey parents. Lupe was not given the opportunity to negotiate with her parents. Therefore, when she could no longer bear to attend school, she simply misled her mother into thinking that she was attending. When she discovered she was pregnant, she hid it.

THE ADOLESCENTS

Norma, the teen mother who graduated from high school, was one of the most academically skilled students in our sample, scoring a 10.4 grade equivalent in reading and a 13.4 grade equivalent in math when she entered high school and

12.0 and 14.1 grade equivalents in reading and math, respectively, when she repeated the ninth grade. Thus, Norma had twelfth-grade and beyond reading and math skills when she was still trying to accumulate enough credits to be a high school sophomore.

Just before she became pregnant, Norma told us she wanted to go into business or advertising for a career. She expected to attend college. Four years later, her specific career goals had changed, but she was attending community college and hoped to complete four years of higher education to qualify as a physical therapist.

Norma's pregnancies during high school cost her the chance to be a cheerleader and to have an active social life. On the other hand, her determination to complete her education drove her to work long hours as a student, an employee, and a mother.

As she prepared to move out of her father's house into her own place with her children, she had a sense of her own strengths and weaknesses. She explained, "I believe in myself. I believe I can do what everyone else can do. I am very sensitive in ways. . . . But because of what I believe, I don't give up."

In contrast, Kathy gave up easily. When she didn't feel comfortable in school, she simply avoided it. At the beginning of her third year in ninth grade, her mother drove her to school, and Kathy would stand a few minutes in the lobby and then walk home.

Because Kathy so rarely attended classes, she missed most of the days of standardized testing and we have only one set of scores for her. She took the test during her second attempt at ninth grade and scored at the 8.0 grade equivalent in reading and the 7.3 grade equivalent in mathematics. This score meant that she was below grade level in her basic skills, but not as far below as some of her peers who managed to pass ninth grade and eventually graduate from high school.

Kathy maintained the same career goals throughout the three years we studied her. She wanted to be a cosmetologist; specifically, she wanted to cut hair. She also aspired to be a model. While she was very pretty, she was no taller than 5′2″ and she had little appreciation of the odds against her earning money in legitimate modeling. Her ambition to become a model was encouraged by a scam which snared her when she was 16. Kathy told us proudly that she had been selected out of 3,000 applicants to be a finalist in a cover-girl contest that summer. She sat for her photographs, but then was asked to pay $75 for the prints. She did not have the money, but this confirmed in her the belief that she had a real chance to be a model. During this same summer, she got a job at a national retail store in the accessory department. Her stay there was brief. Kathy told us she quit the job because the manager did not give her enough hours; Caroline explained Kathy's short stay as due to her lack of acceptable clothing. "They told her not to come back until she had a better wardrobe. Her school clothes were not good enough," she said.

Concern about work clothes never became an issue for Lupe because she never left home to do her job of caring for her younger siblings. Otherwise, her life revolved around local dances and her friends. She felt comfortable going to school with her Mexican immigrant friends. When we asked her about the main obstacles to continuing school, she mentioned the threats and insults of English-speaking Mexican American girls. Lupe had been disciplined in middle school for fighting with such girls on school property.

When Lupe was 15 and still in middle school, she saw herself as about average academically and her mother described her grades as in the A–B range. Lupe could have this belief about herself because she compared herself solely to her peers in the bilingual program, many of whom had come from the same rural village in Mexico. Graciela could have this belief about Lupe because she was dependent upon her daughter for information about Lupe's academic status. Lupe did not have a realistic understanding of how low her skills were until she was mainstreamed into regular classes in high school.

Although Lupe had attended American schools for eight years, her reading grade equivalent scores never went beyond 4.9. Her math skills were slightly better, improving from 6.2 when she was in eighth grade (and 16 years old) to 7.2 when she was in the ninth grade (one year later). There is little evidence that her scholastic skills improved beyond this, because she started skipping school a few months after her ninth-grade scores were assessed. Then she stopped attending altogether.

When we first met Lupe, she told us that she wanted to be a secretary or doctor. She mentioned that she might want to go to college. When we asked her to fantasize about what she would like most in life, she said she wanted to have a lot of money so that she could take her parents back to Mexico to live.

During our last interview with Lupe, soon after she became 18, she answered our question, who is Lupe? She responded by emphasizing her new status as mother: "Bueno, ella es una persona que, uh, quiso estudiar pero no pudo. También no escuchaba a mi mamá; muchas veces que ella me decía cosas y no hacía caso. Pero ahora, ya tengo mi bebé y sé que es lo que cuenta. Creo que ya ella ha cambiado; ya pienso diferente. Ahora pienso al igual que mi mamá. Pienso, las cosas que ella me decía—ahora las comprendo, que ella tenía razón." (Well, she is a person that, uh, wanted to study but couldn't. Also I didn't listen to my mother; many times she told me things and I didn't pay attention. But now, now I have my baby and I know what is important. I believe that now she has changed; now I think differently. Now I think the same as my mother. I think the things that she told me—now I understand them, that she was right.)

We asked her to tell us what things her mother had told her. She said, "Que ahora, que ahora, ahora voy a saber lo que es ser mamá, lo que a uno le preocupa, los hijos. Y yo pienso que ahora ya yo soy diferente que ahora voy a pensar mejor." (That now, that now, now I'm going to know what it is to be a mother, what it is that one worries about, the children. And I think that now, already I'm different that now I'm going to think better.)

It is important to note that both Norma and Kathy received government-subsidized prenatal care and other types of social welfare to help them support their pregnancies and babies. Lupe did not. Her lack of prenatal care was probably the result of a combination of factors, including her desire to hide her pregnancy from her parents and the ineligibity of illegal aliens for government-supported health benefits. If she had attempted to obtain medical care during her pregnancy, she would have put the chances of her family ever receiving U.S. citizenship in jeopardy. In order to qualify for citizenship, she and her family would have to demonstrate that they were self-supporting and not dependent on government support.[4]

THE SCHOOLS

We found only a weak association between becoming a teen mother and dropping out of high school in our sample of youth.[5] Many girls who dropped out were neither pregnant nor mothers at the time they left school. Indeed, Kathy and Lupe did not drop out of school because they became mothers. Our results are consistent with those of other studies of Hispanic youth, indicating that dropping out often precedes pregnancy.[6] Another reason why we did not find a strong link between becoming a teen mother and dropping out was the existence of programs within some high schools that helped mothers stay in school. As we saw in the case of Norma, some teen mothers were able to graduate. However, Norma's case also typifies a common problem that teen mothers have: staying in college-preparatory coursework. School administrators assumed that any teen who became a mother must have low academic aspirations; therefore, the schools did not provide challenging coursework for such students. This made it likely that teen mothers, even if they did graduate and attempted to attend college, would have less success in higher education than other students.

Teens like Lupe and Kathy were making little academic progress, and although they voiced their desire to get a high school diploma even after they had dropped out of school, it was highly unlikely that they would ever reenter high school or any other educational institution. In order to make progress toward graduation, they had to attend school regularly, but their schools failed to motivate them to do so. The schools' lack of holding power for Lupe and Kathy suggests that the schools had not made them feel involved in the academic life of the school.

Indeed, public schools in the U.S. have promoted the achievement of boys much more than the achievement of girls. When children enter school, girls have the advantage in academic skills, but by the time they graduate from high school, boys have the advantage in science and mathematics and are on a par in verbal skills.[7] Schools need to become more gender neutral in promoting achievement, at all levels. Schools also need to provide social environments where both male and female students can feel accepted and appreciated.

Some argue that parents should be responsible for the sex education of their children. While it is desirable for parents to do the job of educating their children about sexuality, our experience with Norma, Kathy, and Lupe indicates that many parents do not prepare their children adequately to avoid teen motherhood. Norma's father was reluctant to talk to her about the subject. Kathy's mother knew her daughter was sexually active and using contraception, but she was unable or unwilling to stop her daughter's intentional pregnancy. Graciela was unaware that her daughter was not only sexually active, but about to become a mother. If parents are unable to educate their children about sex and sexuality, then schools and communities must assume responsibility for doing so.

Finally, it is fair to conclude that the sex education provided by the schools did not meet the needs of Norma, Kathy, or Lupe. Sex education in the school district varied widely, with most schools opting to provide very little and only a few schools opting to provide a more comprehensive program. In secondary schools, the school district nested sex education within its science curriculum, primarily in the form of reproductive biology. But this academic approach left a lot unsaid. As Norma described it, "They don't even talk about a male and a female coming together. All they talk about is what happens when a sperm and an egg meet," she said.

Simply knowing what happens when the sperm meets the egg did not prevent Norma or the other girls from becoming mothers. Sex education needs to be more comprehensive and must integrate information about reproduction with the developmental needs of teens. Research indicates that effective programs to prevent teen pregnancy must address the needs of both males and females and give teens:

- incentives to participate,
- a supportive peer group that promotes the idea of avoiding pregnancy,
- positive relationships with adult and peer mentors,
- information about risky behaviors,
- skills to cope with peer influences,
- accurate and explicit information about sex so that they can make decisions about sexual activity that are based on medical science.[8]

Such programs can be offered by schools, but if political opposition makes this impossible, then schools can support such programs within the community.

TEEN MOTHERHOOD

The American Problem

The teen pregnancy rate in the U.S. is much higher than the rate in the other industrialized nations.[9] This is not because our teens engage in more sexual activity. Their rate of sexual activity is comparable to that of teens from other industrialized nations. Our high rates of teen pregnancy are brought about by the infrequent and ineffective use of contraceptives by our sexually active teenagers.

This infrequent and ineffective use of contraceptives is caused by three important factors. First, our programs to prevent teen pregnancy are ineffective. Several studies have demonstrated that the typical American approach to sex education has no effect on the sexual behavior of our teens.[10] The ineffectiveness of our sex education programs is hardly surprising given our national ambivalence about sexuality. American teens are continuously bombarded by messages promoting sexual activity, but teens have also been led to believe that being "prepared" for sex with contraceptives reflects poorly on their character. Furthermore, many young teenagers are ignorant about reproductive facts, and believe that they are, for example, too young to get pregnant, or have sex too infrequently to get pregnant.[11] Thus, although by 15 years of age, 25% of all American females have engaged in sexual intercourse, very few of these teens have used contraceptives effectively.[12]

Second, American teenage females have relatively more difficulty gaining continuous access to contraceptives than do teens in other industrialized countries.[13] This difficulty is caused largely by a health care delivery system that puts health care, including contraceptives, more within the domain of private health practitioners than within the domain of public health clinics. Consequently, most teens are dependent on their parents to obtain contraceptives, because the parents must make the doctor's appointments and pay the bill in order to get contraceptives. Furthermore, teens who cannot afford private practitioners have grave difficulty gaining continuous access to contraceptives. Given the ambivalence that young teens and their parents have about sexual activity, many sexually active teens simply do not get the contraceptives they need.

In Texas, even though it is legal for female adolescents to obtain contraceptives without parental consent, it is difficult for adolescents, especially young ones, to gain continuous access to contraceptives. There are few free clinics serving their needs. Moreover, sexually active Latina teens may find it difficult to reconcile their cultural traditions with the American message to practice sex safely. On the one hand, traditional Mexican culture values motherhood and large families much more highly than does contemporary American culture. Teens like Lupe are attracted to teen motherhood as a means of achieving success. On the other hand, young Latinas are supposed to be ignorant about sexual matters before marriage. Therefore, they fear that their reputations would be ruined if they are seen in a family planning clinic.[14]

Third, young Americans having serious academic difficulties have little motivation to avoid parenthood and, therefore, little motivation to avoid sexual activity or to use contraception.[15] They realize that simply having a high school diploma won't guarantee them a good income and a happy family life. In contrast, students who are doing well in school are motivated to avoid parenthood because they believe that premature parenting will interfere with their attainment of their educational goals. They expect that achieving these goals will lead them directly into good jobs, careers, and marriages.

Students who are failing in school know that they have little to lose and something to gain if they become teen parents. Even if teens know reproductive facts and have access to contraceptives, they may become parents in order to obtain the rewards they perceive to be associated with becoming a parent. These rewards include raising one's status in the family, forming unions or marriages, being valued as a parent, and receiving gifts and attention for the baby.[16]

The division in motivation to postpone childbearing between the college and the noncollege bound is a reflection of the current wage differential in the U.S. between those with only high school diplomas versus those with college degrees. Immediately after World War II, those who had a high school diploma were able to earn considerably more money than those who did not. But since the early 1970s, the major income divide has been between those with a college education and those with high school or less education.[17] At the same time, employers have been reluctant to hire teens with just a high school diploma, preferring to wait until such individuals mature into their 20s to give them entry-level jobs with a future.[18] Consequently, for most of the teens in our sample, earning a high school diploma would not give them an immediate competitive edge in the job market. Thus, students who had a hard time earning enough credits to advance to the tenth grade did not perceive themselves as losing much by becoming teen parents. Even if their parenthood made it less likely they would earn a high school diploma, this diploma would make little immediate difference in their life circumstances.

The Austin and Texas Problem

Teen parenthood was relatively common in the environment in which our families lived. In 1991, Texas led the nation in births to girls 14 and younger, had the second highest rates of births to 15–17 year olds, and ranked second in the nation in the number of births to girls age 19 and under.[19] Vital statistics for the state suggest that Hispanic female adolescents contribute disproportionately to the incidence of teen motherhood in the state, as Table 5.1 indicates.

Teen motherhood has been relatively common in Texas, particularly among Hispanics. During the years of our study, the difference between His-

TABLE 5.1.   Percentage of Live Births to Teen Mothers by Age Group and Ethnicity in Texas, 1988–1991

Year	Age Group	Ethnicity		
		Anglo	Hispanic	Black
1988	Less than 15	17	42	41
	15–19	37	42	21
1989	Less than 15	17	48	35
	15–19	36	42	22
1990	Less than 15	17	48	35
	15–19	35	43	22
1991	Less than 15	18	50	32
	15–19	33	46	21

NOTE: Anglo refers to White babies without Spanish surnames. Hispanic refers to White babies with Spanish surnames. Black refers to African American babies regardless of their surnames. These data are from the Texas Department of Health and include all births within the state.

panic youths and others was greatest for births to mothers less than 15 years of age. This finding is similar to what has been found nationally with Hispanics.[20]

The few published studies on this topic suggest that there is a strong emphasis on remaining a virgin until marriage among Mexican-origin youth.[21] Of the three young mothers described in this chapter, only Lupe showed signs of holding this value. Lupe hid her pregnancy from her parents, and when it was discovered, it formed the basis of a union between Lupe and Pablo. However, neither Norma nor Kathy expressed concern about remaining a virgin until marriage. Norma expressed no shame about her sexual behavior nor about remaining unmarried after two children. Kathy's mother knew enough about Kathy's sex life to know that she had been taking birth control pills and then stopped taking them. Caroline knew of Kathy's sexual relationship with Jamal and appeared to approve of it at that time.

Teen motherhood is relatively common in the Austin area. The Travis County statistics for teen births are similar to those for the state. Overall, the county reported a birthrate in 1990 for females aged 10–19 of 35.7 per 1000, which ranked Travis County about midway among the Texas counties in birthrates to teen mothers. By ethnicity, Hispanic teens had the highest teen birthrate, 67.5; Blacks, the second highest, 56.9; and Anglos, the lowest, 15.8. The sheer commonness of pregnant and parenting teens has made teen parenthood more socially acceptable among minority youth in Austin.[22]

Teen motherhood was relatively common in our sample of "at risk" Mexican-origin youth. By the time that our female students had become 18 years old, 34% (14 out of 41) were mothers, some with more than one child. Most of these (8 out of 14, or 57%) had become mothers before they were 16.

And yet, when these teens were 15 years old, 90% (37 out of 41) of them told us that they did not expect to start a family in the next three years. Those who did expect to start a family at that time were pregnant or had already become a parent. Neither Norma, Kathy, nor Lupe indicated when they were 15 that they expected to start a family before they were 18. And yet, by 18, all three were mothers.

Norma, Kathy, and Lupe were typical of the females in our sample who became teen mothers. Our statistical results indicated that female students who became mothers were much more likely to have had disciplinary problems at school—particularly, fighting with other girls.[23] Teens who became mothers reported having many friends and/or siblings who had dropped out of school.[24] They also indicated to us when they were 15 that they felt that their teachers expected them to drop out.[25]

Norma differed from Kathy and Lupe in that she wanted to go to high school and had strong academic skills. Combined with substantial family support, these skills and her own motivation to get an education facilitated her completion of high school and success in community college. Lupe and Kathy had much less motivation to go to high school and were much weaker academically. At the time of our first interview, most of the girls in our sample who later became teen mothers did not expect to go to college.[26]

Academic responsibilities could not compete with peer influences in the lives of Norma, Kathy, and Lupe when they entered high school. The parents sent their daughters to school, only to have them skip school to hang out with their friends. Skipping school gave teens opportunities for sexual exploration. Norma told us that sexual intercourse was commonplace: "Everybody does it." Norma, Kathy, and Lupe rationalized their sexual behavior because they perceived themselves as having a significant relationship with the fathers of their babies when the babies were conceived. This rationalization is common among teen mothers, according to the results of a national survey.[27]

POLICY RECOMMENDATIONS

When national policymakers first designed programs to discourage teen parenthood in the U.S., they assumed that all schools needed to do was to educate teens about reproductive facts and that teens would use this information to postpone childbearing. However, sex education at the local level met with much opposition, and many students did not receive the type of sex education they needed. Policymakers then identified lack of access to contraceptives as a major cause of teen motherhood. The idea was that teens would postpone parenthood if they had easier access to contraceptives. But this also met with opposition at the local level, especially when associated with schools.

More extensive study of the problem of teen pregnancies made it clear that education and access are not enough to reduce the rate of teen parenthood.[28] Any effort to discourage teen pregnancies must involving motivating teens to want to avoid teen parenthood. Indeed, some teenagers become mothers and fathers intentionally. Nationally, it is estimated that about 20% of pregnant teens intended to get pregnant.[29]

The public schools could play a major part in stemming the number of teen pregnancies by giving all teens good reasons to avoid parenthood. The most fundamental way they can do this is by making all students believe that they can succeed in school and that school success will lead to a better life. At present, many school practices create failure and make it impossible for all students to succeed. In truth, the majority of Hispanic students in public secondary schools in Texas have been designated as "at risk" of dropping out of school. The high rates of course cutting, truancy, teen motherhood and dropping out we found in our sample of "at risk" students indicate that schools have failed to make all students believe that staying in school will improve their lives.

Families, schools, and communities must work together to foster the belief in adolescents that a teen pregnancy will place obstacles in the pathway toward a better life. The students in our study had little to lose by becoming parents because in our city, high school dropouts competed with high school graduates for the same, low-paying jobs. Any effort to prevent teen motherhood should focus on linking good jobs and other attractive outcomes to high school graduation. These efforts could include challenging vocational training programs that prepare adolescents, particularly young women, for careers with upward mobility. They could also promote going to community colleges or universities for all students. The schools and communities should be more active in creating scholarships for a wider range of students to pursue postsecondary educational opportunities.

SIX

"Well, she's Mexican. She's going to drop out." Immigrant and Second-Generation Students

This chapter introduces Linda and Enrique and the topic of Mexican immigration to the U.S. In the early 1980s, a U.S. Supreme Court ruling forced school districts in Texas to admit the children of "illegal" immigrants into their classrooms. Linda was a second-generation Mexican American and a versatile athlete who played on the varsity volleyball, basketball, and softball teams. Because she was sensitive to being mistaken for a Mexican immigrant, she became involved in many school fights. She even attempted suicide in response to peer rejection and violence. Although Linda recovered and graduated from high school, she ended up confused about her future direction. Enrique was a bright student and a Mexican citizen whose large and extended family immigrated to the U.S. in 1980 without immigration documents and who later qualified as a legal resident under the amnesty provisions of the 1986 Immigration Reform and Control Act (IRCA). Enrique's family pressured him to drop out of school so that he could work full-time to support his parents. He dropped out, helped his parents, and then went to work in a restaurant. We describe the ways schools have failed to meet the needs of immigrant and second generation children. We argue that some of the violence in the schools we studied was brought about by the tensions created over immigration and that the schools could play an important role in reducing this violence.

LINDA

Linda was a versatile athlete. By the time she was in the tenth grade, she played on varsity teams almost all year long, participating in volleyball in the fall, basketball in the winter, and softball in the spring and summer. Her parents spoke proudly of her sports ability and attended her games as often as they could.

Her father, George, grew up in the Austin area, but like many of his siblings, he dropped out of school—in his case, in fifth grade. As a young boy, George helped his family financially by picking cotton. Later, he earned a GED and got a job cleaning an animal laboratory, a job he had held for 27 years when we last talked to him. This job paid reasonably well, providing him and his family full benefits, including health and retirement. He and his wife talked about moving to Mexico after he retired because his retirement income would go further there and his wife would be nearer her family. His wife, and Linda's mother, Estella, had been born and educated in Mexico, completing 6 years of school and learning the tailoring trade there. She had worked as a seamstress for over ten years at a fashionable men's shop in Austin.

Linda lived with her three siblings and parents in a comfortably furnished, three-bedroom brick house located in a South Austin residential neighborhood. The house was located on the corner of a busy street, but a large lawn helped to mute the traffic noise. The living room was decorated with a painted mural of wildflowers on one wall and was furnished with a large television set, a comfortable sofa, and several chairs. There was a den to the rear of the house and a dining area with a round maple table and chairs. Typically, we began our visits in the living room, and after a short time, went to the kitchen to do the interviews.

During our first visit in the kitchen, George told us that he had assumed Linda had been designated as "at risk" of dropping out of school because she was Hispanic. He drew this conclusion based on two lines of evidence: (1) he knew that Hispanic kids were more likely to drop out than others, and (2) he had experienced prejudice as a student. He felt that he had been discriminated against in school because he spoke only Spanish as a child. He told us, "I could hardly speak English at all when I started going there in 1938, no, 1940. I was six years old and they turned me down because I couldn't speak English and the teacher couldn't speak Spanish. So I think two years later I went back and I was eight years old. They took me in and I still couldn't speak English. I remember me and another friend just staring at the teacher. I didn't know what she was saying or anything. And you know, it still goes on."

George had strong memories of discrimination and still felt uncomfortable about dealing with the schools. He expected discrimination from the Anglo teachers and principals, and he told us that some of the coaches were prejudiced against Mexicans because they let the Anglo students play more during games. As a result, he had been reluctant to go to Linda's school. He explained, "You feel like you're not gonna understand anything they say and you won't be able to, uh, if you have some questions, you won't be able to bring it out because [stuttering], you know, feeling inferior or something. You know what I mean?"

Linda was keenly aware of the prejudice within the schools against Mexicans. When she was 15, she denied to us that she was truly at risk of dropping out of school. When we asked her what she would do if the school district thought that she was likely to drop out, she responded, "That'd make me want more to try harder, to bring up my grades. Because I don't want people to think, '*Well, she's Mexican, she's gonna drop out,*' I don't want people thinking *that* of me. You know, I'm going to try hard."

Linda was embarrassed by her parents and discouraged them from going to her high school. In fact, Linda chose to go to a high school more distant from her home because her father had expressed a preference for a closer one. He told her that he would be able to watch more of her practice sessions if Linda went to the school closer to home. Linda explained, "I do not want my dad watching me, you know. He'd embarrass me." She felt even more strongly about her mother because Estella spoke little English. Linda's reluctance to include her parents in school activities plus their feelings of inadequacy caused George and Estella to confine their school visits to attending their daughter's games.

Although Linda spent much of her time in sports activities, during our interviews she talked more about the fights she and her friends had in school than about her wins and losses at sports. For example, she described her first fight in high school: "I have a lot of fights. It used to be like five girls and almost all of us had had a fight. [She laughs] I had a fight at the beginning of the school year. And it was just so dumb. I thought it was real dumb. [She laughs] A girl said I called her a name, and I did 'cause I was so, that girl had always, she just always, she just always look at me really ugly, you know. 'Cause, see, when I called her a name it was a Friday, and it was after school. I was ready to leave because I had my volleyball uniform on 'cause we had a game that day. So, you know, I called her a name . . . So the next thing you know, that Monday, you know, her and her friend, her friend had already hated me. We hated each other from the very beginning because of this guy. It was 'cause of a guy, but I mean, that wasn't the reason why we fought."

Linda continued, "So, one morning, they told me, they said, 'Can I talk to you?' and I said, 'Fine, about what?' I was scared because I never got into a fight in my whole life. She goes, 'You know about what.' And I said, 'Ok, fine.' So we went, and it was outside in the commons, it's this open area, you know, and they have vending machines there and everything and tables and everything . . . I guess they got up and then the girl that I called names, she goes,

'Why'd you call me a name?' this and that, we just started really arguing. I don't remember how it happened. It was weird, 'cause I'd never had a fight and the girl pushed me, so then we started fighting. I don't think we got on the ground, but they stopped us. There was a lot of people and next thing you know there was so many people in the commons, it was just full. OK? . . . And I had my jacket on, so I was uncomfortable and I took it off and I was mad because her friend had come, while I was fighting that girl, her friend JoAnn, she had come and pulled my hair. So, I ended up fighting her after that 'cause I took off my jacket and I went up to her 'cause I was mad, you know, I mean, they were both trying to fight me and then, I don't know, we stopped. They stopped us." For Linda, defending her honor was of utmost importance, and fighting was a way to do that.

Many of Linda's friends also played on the sports teams. They wanted her to go out with them, to concerts and nightclubs. But Linda's parents refused to let her stay out past midnight. Many of her Mexican American peers stayed out much later, and it bothered Linda that her parents were so strict. She and her parents argued frequently about permission to go to certain concerts or stay out late. When she was 15, she told us, "Like if there's times that I've wanted to do something real bad, and they don't let me, I said, 'God, you know, it makes me so mad!' I'll cry for the longest time, you know. I'll go to my room and all I do is tell myself, 'Oh, you know, it's just another day. I'm sure there'll be parties later on.' That's what I tell myself, if I didn't I'd probably end up like killing myself or something."

The parents' experiences with their oldest child, a son who had dropped out of high school and still lived at home, sleeping all day and staying up all night, fueled their concern. In response to his bad outcomes, they became more strict with their remaining children, three daughters. It was easy for them to become more strict with their daughters because they also believed that it was not proper for girls to be out on the streets alone. Linda was the middle daughter. All the girls had to endure their father's close surveillance. For example, when Harriett Romo first visited the family, Linda and her parents explained a critical event.

George: "She [Linda] gets mad because I won't let her drive. She doesn't realize she doesn't have a license and the cops can stop you for anything and if she doesn't have a driver's license . . . they'll either cancel my insurance or it'll go up sky high. I can't afford to pay more insurance already. So I can't make her realize this, you know, and . . ."

Estella: "They think we are old-fashioned."

George: "Did I tell you about the time I let her drive the pickup to school?"

Linda: "Tell them. I don't care."

George: "She said, 'Daddy, let me drive that truck over there,' you know, and it was during the . . ."

Linda: "Spring break."

George: "Spring break. So there wasn't much traffic going on. So I let her drive it by herself, you know. For some reason, I don't know why, I went over there. I don't know why. I did not go looking for her. I went over there for something or I happened to pass by there and I didn't see the pickup around there. And I asked somebody. They were practicing. . . . And I said, 'Where's Linda?' They said, 'She hasn't shown up.' I'll be damned."

Estella: "You know, la primera vez. . . ." (The first time.)

George: "¡Una vez! (One time!) But she doesn't drive it anymore. She will not drive anymore. If she gets a ticket, that's it until you're 18 and get your driver's license then."

Estella: "I think it was amigos porque se juntó con esa amiga más grande que ella y le ha dicho, 'Vente. Let's go to this place.'" (I think it was friends because she was with an older girlfriend and she told her, "Come on, let's go to this place.")

Linda: "I went to the park."

George: "Your parents are more important than your friends."

Estella: "You were supposed to be in practice."

George made a practice of checking the odometer whenever Linda or her older sister used the car. He challenged their stories if the odometer indicated they had driven someplace farther or closer than where they said they had gone.

George was very protective of Linda and her sisters, taking them to and from school and work every day and escorting them to movies or parties. Linda chafed at the close supervision by her parents. She explained, "It's embarrassing, you know, when I have a friend come over to stay over, and you know I have to tell them, 'Oh, we've got to come home by twelve.' . . . If you go there at nine, things are barely starting. People are barely starting to get there by eleven. God, and then everybody's there, and you're having fun. That's when I have to come home!"

However, even when Linda was 16 she acknowledged that some limits were good. "Yeah, I can see my friends, the ones that got pregnant or whatever, they stayed out *real* late. Or the ones that got into fights or got stabbed or whatever,

I mean because their parents didn't care." Despite this insight, Linda remained intensely attached to her friends and resented the strict control of her parents.

The highlight of her senior year was that her volleyball team made it to the state playoffs. But soon after that, she got into a fight with her best friend. Apparently, Linda did something with that girl's boyfriend—Linda wouldn't tell us what. The two girls abruptly ended their three-year-long friendship. The ex-girlfriend turned the other girls against her.

Distraught, Linda took an overdose of sleeping pills. Her condition was discovered before the pills could have their lethal effect. Her parents rushed Linda to the hospital, where she stayed several days. Her parents took the doctor's advice of obtaining counseling for her. The mother recalled, "Estuvo pesado. Sólo después de eso, ella no quería, no quería volver a la escuela. Y dije, 'Mi hija, tienes que volver, tienes que volver porque lo que pasó, hace cuenta que no pasó. No vale la pena.'" (It was very serious. Only after that, she did not want, did not want to return to school. I told her, 'Honey, you have to return, you have to return, because what happened, you have to pretend it didn't happen. It is not worth it.')

Linda did return to school, but she began to distance herself from many of her former friends. These girls noticed the change in her behavior, and they interpreted it as a rejection. Her former best friend spread ill feelings about her. A group of girls began following Linda from class to class during finals week of the fall semester. They tried to provoke her into fighting. She refused to fight them. One of Linda's friends told her that one of the girls had a knife. Tensions reached the breaking point when a girl leaving a classroom with Linda said out loud, "They're just stupid," and all the girls jumped on her. A teacher broke up the fight and sent them all to the office. The assistant principal said he was going to expel all of them, but he allowed them to finish their final exams and enforced the expulsions after the break between semesters.

Frightened by what their daughter told them was going on in the school, George and Estella together went to talk to the assistant principal. They explained the situation to him and said they believed that Linda was not responsible for the fighting. They reported to us that the assistant principal seemed sympathetic and promised to investigate the allegation about the knife. He reduced Linda's punishment to an in-school suspension. For once, Linda was pleased that her parents had gone to the school and stood up for her.

To stay away from the girls she had fought, Linda quit sports, telling her coaches and friends that she needed to get a job and did not have the time anymore to be on the team. Her last semester of high school was busy; she worked at a grocery store as a cashier and completed her courses successfully enough to graduate on time.

Linda's parents gave her a big party, including a mariachi band, to celebrate her graduation. Linda told us that she felt good about graduating: "I felt like I had accomplished something." She continued working at the same grocery store job. Because the owners could not give her full-time work, she continued to work 16 hours per week at minimum wage with no benefits. She told us that she had already learned all she could possibly learn on that job, such as "the types of vegetables and names of things in the store." She tried to remain optimistic, explaining, "I know sooner or later, I am going to like working."

When we last saw her, she was wearing a bright orange sundress and big loop earrings. She told us that the reality of being a graduate had not quite sunk in yet. She did have some regrets about her high school experience, especially that she had not taken the math and science courses that would prepare her for college. Instead, she had followed her girlfriend's advice to take the easier courses so that she would not jeopardize her eligibility for sports. "I made a mistake because that was almost a year thrown away by those two classes when I could have taken Geometry and Algebra II my junior year, and Calculus or Trig my senior year."

We asked her why she hadn't consulted one of the counselors about what courses to take. She said, "They were always too busy. I never went and asked them anything, and I don't think they would have told me. I never really went to them. I regret it 'cause my last year I worked at the counselor's office as an office aide and it was wonderful. They are just like any other person, but I always thought they were too busy."

Linda told us that she planned to take classes at the local community college in the fall, although as of mid-June, she had not taken the ACT or even requested an application for admission to the community college or a course catalog. She received information from a Catholic university in Austin, but the envelope remained unopened, sitting in her room. She thought that the university was too expensive. She was still in contact with her old coaches, one of whom tried to talk her into joining an exhibition softball team so that she could travel around the state and perhaps get recruited by a college to play sports. The coach thought she had a good chance of getting a sports scholarship at a small college in East Texas, but Linda did not want to get involved with the team again. Some of the girls she had fought with would be on the traveling team, and she preferred to stay home and away from conflict.

When we were about to leave, we asked her if there was anything she wanted to know from us. Linda paused and said, "Is it really hard in the real world? A lot of people, ones that just graduated, they are just so scared to get into the real world."

Analysis

Linda was like the 34% of the students in our sample who had at least one Mexican-born parent. Although Linda herself was born in the U.S., the fact that her mother was Mexican and spoke little English made Linda feel different from her friends who were Mexican American. She feared that the other students would see her as a Mexican and not an American.

Linda was desperate to be accepted by her peers. To protect her image, she fought other girls over matters that were silly, even by her own admission. But she had to protect her honor and her reputation. Acceptance by her peers was almost more important to her than her own life.

Her parents ruined her efforts to be like all the other girls by keeping her under close surveillance and rarely granting her the privileges routinely granted by other parents. She spent almost all of her high school years arguing with her parents about their "old-fashioned" ways. Nonetheless, they held firm in their demands, continuously explaining why they made the decisions they did. In the end, she acknowledged the value of their support and their high standards, even if she thought they were unreasonable at times.

In our analyses of our sample, we found that the children of Mexican-born parents were as likely to graduate from high school as the children of U.S.-born parents.[1] Key to Linda's ability to graduate was not the nationality of her parents, but their financial security and the control they maintained of her social life. Indeed, Linda gave her parents much of the credit for her being able to graduate from high school. Her parents' resources were critical in helping Linda survive her high school years and graduate. Her father's job provided the family with sufficient income to own a home and with sufficient time to drive the daughters to and from school every day. The father's job also provided benefits including mental health coverage, so that Linda could get professional counseling when she needed it.

Linda also told us that the bad experiences of some of her classmates who had dropped out helped her maintain her motivation to stay in school. She spent some of her time reflecting on "the people that didn't make it and what they were going through," and this drove her not to be a dropout.

ENRIQUE

Enrique's immigrant parents lacked such resources. Having no formal education at all, they were illiterate in Spanish and spoke no English. They came to the United States in 1983, when Enrique was 10. Their eight oldest sons had worked in the U.S. for many years and had saved up enough money to bring them and the five younger children to Austin from a rural area in central Mexico. No one in the family had legal immigration documents at the time of entry into the U.S.[2]

Several of the older brothers had established large families of their own in Austin. They located a two-bedroom apartment near their own rental houses for their parents and younger siblings, paid the deposit and rent for them, and helped them get settled.

Because Enrique had never attended school in Mexico, he was placed in a second-grade classroom in Austin, putting him with children about two years younger than himself. He spoke no English. The school provided intensive English as a Second Language (ESL) instruction, grouping Enrique with other immigrant children for several class periods each day. Enrique continued in ESL classes until sixth grade. He recalled, "By then I had some basic idea of what I was saying but it wasn't perfected. I still had problems trying to get the words together, but after a while I had a better understanding of what I was saying."

In response to a court-ordered desegregation plan, the Austin school district bussed Enrique and some of his schoolmates across town to attend a predominantly Anglo school. Enrique recalled experiencing prejudice at that school. He told us, "Basically, all Hispanics were together and all the Whites were together. They would call us wetbacks. That would hurt me. I would get into a fight. I did not like to be called a wetback. That is not an appropriate word to use on a person."

By the time he got to junior high, Enrique was making the honor roll. In seventh grade, his teachers selected him into the National Honor Society, and in eighth grade they chose him to receive the Hispanic Achievement Award, a recognition given to only a few students in the school district. He was the only one to receive the award from his junior high school.

At different times during this period, immigration officers apprehended and deported Enrique's father and two of his older brothers. The family pooled their money to come up with the $500 to $600 per person to get the deported family members back to Austin.

Enrique's high school teachers decided that he should move to the upper tracks in some courses, but not English. In fact, his failure of the reading-comprehension portion of the state-mandated, standardized test got him designated as "at risk" of dropping out. He explained it this way: "As soon as I got through with my final exams, all the teachers told me I had done very well on them. They decided to move me up into higher courses and I agreed with some of them. Not the Geometry. I passed the Algebra class. The teacher thought I was good enough to go into Geometry. I didn't think so, but she said, 'Yeah, you'll do all right.' And that's what she did."

He also took one vocational course in ninth grade. He described it to us: "I took Introduction to American Energy and Power, like a mechanics course, but the teacher there didn't seem to really care 'cause I don't think we ever lifted a pencil there to do work. We had workshop in his office and in the back. We would read books as part of it, and then we would go back and look at all the equipment and machinery. And we did take tests every once in a while, but they were real simple tests. I didn't like it in the beginning. I don't think it helped me a lot. Classes that interest me, I get good grades in. If it wasn't interesting, my grades would go down. And every other class, I did very well except Geometry and I was not ready for that."

Meanwhile, Enrique's parents struggled financially and decided to join one of the older brothers in Florida on the migrant stream harvesting citrus crops. Enrique wanted to continue to go to school in Austin, and so he moved in with another one of his older brothers. In fact, Enrique was living with Antonio, Antonio's wife, and their two children when Harriett Romo first interviewed him. They shared a two-bedroom apartment. Antonio had no education, but his wife had completed nine years of schooling in Mexico. Since the apartment was in another neighborhood, Enrique had to attend a high school different from the one his old middle school friends attended. Soon after entering this new school, some students got Enrique into a fight and he was suspended from school for a day. This suspension angered Enrique because although he did not start the fight, he got the same penalty as the students who did.

Nonetheless, he continued his schoolwork successfully. When Enrique was about to finish ninth grade at age 16, his father was hurt in an accident in Florida, and the parents began having serious financial troubles. His older brothers put pressure on Enrique to go to Florida to help them out. He explained, "Basically, my brother said that instead of being in school I should be working and helping out my parents." Typically, the family solved such problems by sending the oldest single male in the family to help the parents. This would have been Enrique's next older brother. But this brother was in his junior year in high school and was working half-days and going to school half-days, and the older brothers thought that he was already contributing financially to the family. So they pressured Enrique to go to Florida where he could work and go to school. At the same time, tension had developed between him and his sister-in-law. She felt that he was imposing on them and not helping out financially.

Enrique had no one to turn to for support. He went to the school counselor and talked about his problem. He reported to us: "I kinda explained the situation to her, what was going on and what I was gonna do, and I told her that I would probably drop out within the next year or so, not because I wanted to, but because my brother, he wanted me to start working. . . . She told me to stay in and not to listen to them 'cause school was one of the most important things in life that you have to accomplish. One of your main goals to accomplish. I tried to listen to her, but the pressure was just too high for me."

Enrique remained in high school in Austin long enough to take his final exams and get credit for the ninth grade. Then he left for Florida to join his parents. In Florida, he enrolled himself in high school and worked in the fields. The town was a small rural community of about 5,000 residents. While there, he was approved for legal residence in the U.S. under the amnesty provision of the 1986 Immigration Reform and Control Act. After several months, an older brother came to check on the family's situation and found the conditions they were living in deplorable. He brought them all back to Austin.

While in Florida, Enrique met a 15-year-old female student whose family also worked in the fields, and they began seeing one another regularly. When Enrique's parents decided to return to Austin, Enrique gave his girlfriend the choice of coming with him or not seeing him again. He told us that she decided to leave her family because her father was abusing her. And so Enrique returned to Austin with a girlfriend.

Enrique wanted to start his own family so that his brothers would not expect him to drop everything to help his parents again. He married his girlfriend and she got pregnant and they moved into their own apartment in Austin. Enrique got a job in a Mexican restaurant, and his wife worked in a fast-food restaurant. After the baby arrived prematurely, his wife stayed home to care for her.

Harriett Romo learned of Enrique's return to Austin from one of his older brothers. He told us where Enrique was working. Harriett went there to have lunch. He appeared to be a model employee, bussing tables, washing dishes, serving food and drinks, and working the cash register. When he got a break, he sat at Harriett's table and told her about his experiences with his parents in Florida. He said that he considered himself a very successful person: "I did what I had to do. It turned out good for me. Even if I would have had my diploma, it probably wouldn't have helped me up there [in Florida]. I would probably be working the fields for $28 per day working from eight to five. My brother got his diploma, and he is working in construction now. He's not making very much either. We probably make the same amount, and he's killing himself up there. Hurting his back doing all this heavy lifting. I'm not." Enrique had enough influence with the manager to get his younger sister a job at the same restaurant. He believed things were turning out "OK so far" for him and his family. He boasted, "I have a nice car, my own apartment, a checkbook, and money in the bank."

Although he compared his job favorably to that of his older brother, who had finished high school, Enrique envied his brother's diploma. Then, one day, he saw his opportunity to return to school. He said, "I was watching TV and they had an orientation meeting for evening school and I called the school and they said to drop by and take the test and if I passed it they would admit me. So I did it as fast as I could."

He told us, "I decided to go back because I wanted to achieve a goal that I did not achieve and that I meant to achieve but just did not have the opportunity to. My brother, he can brag a lot, but he kinda posted that diploma on the wall and said, 'Baby sure feels good.' And I started laughing every time. And I kinda thought in my head, 'I'm gonna get mine.' Even if I have to pay for it, I'll get it."

Even though he had been out of school for two years, Enrique was able to pick up where he had left off in the Austin schools. He told us that he had done well on the placement tests and that he hoped to transfer some of his credits from the Florida high school and get his diploma about one month after his 20th birthday.

Although Enrique was eager to complete his high school education, he was not complimentary about the program at the evening school. It was self-paced with each classroom under the direction of one teacher. He didn't like it "because it's not like, not all the teachers know [the subjects]. Some are teachers at other high schools, teachers from around. If I'm taking a math course and ask my teacher, she won't be able to help me 'cause she won't know 'cause that's not her subject. So I would probably have to go and look for another teacher and ask him. And as you go on, the problems get harder and I would probably have to stay there all night trying to find out how to do the problems."

But before Enrique could graduate, he discovered that his teenage wife had been seeing another man. She was bored with Enrique's long work hours and late nights at school. Enrique took their child and moved in with one of his older brothers. He told us that he was planning to contact legal aid about a divorce. He still planned to get his diploma.

Analysis

The poverty and lack of schooling of Enrique's parents and older brothers were major determinants of his dropping out of school. For Enrique's family, his attaining the age of 16 meant that Enrique was regarded as able to earn money, and this ability was valued more than his academic abilities.

We found that students like Enrique who came from low-income families were much more likely to drop out than were students from families with better incomes.[3] This finding within our small sample is consistent with research results of all students in the Austin school district as well as research results based on national samples.[4] Based on our experience with Enrique, we think that many of these low-income dropouts left school as soon as they were old enough to get a job and generate income for their families. Given the high degree of emotional and financial support adolescents need to succeed in high school, it is not surprising that a bright teen like Enrique dropped out. His family simply could not support him; instead they needed his support.

THE PARENTS

Although the parents of the two teens had some similarities, the differences between them were major. Linda's parents placed the education of their children near the top of their life priorities. They could afford to do this because they had an adequate income to support the basic needs of their family. They also had some education, enough to appreciate what an education can do for a person. Linda's parents wanted their daughter to graduate from high school and were willing to expend a great deal of their energy every day to make sure this happened.

Part of this energy was devoted to supervising Linda and her sisters. Linda's father had no difficulty with our question about how he and his wife got Linda to do what they wanted her to do. "We just tell her to do it," he said. "When she has something that she wants to do, we tell her to do this first, clean the house, and then you can go." This answer was reflected in the response that Linda gave us independently about how she got her parents to do what she wanted. She explained, "Well, first of all, before I even ask, I have to clean up. If I don't, that's the first thing he's gonna tell me. He's gonna say, 'Look at the housework. Look at this, you haven't done your bed.'" Thus, although her parents were strict, Linda and her parents had worked out a method of giving her permission to do some things with her friends.

In contrast, Enrique's parents and older brothers could articulate the connection between education and good jobs, but their financial needs took priority over the support that Enrique needed to continue his schooling. Not only could his parents not support Enrique through his high school years, they had few resources to guide him in his education. When he was 16, Enrique described family decision making regarding him this way: "We talk it over and they say, 'Sure, if that's what you wanna do.' Like with school, they say, 'Are you sure you wanna stay in school?' I say, 'Yeah, I wanna stay in school.' 'OK, fine, you're gonna stay with me, as long as you want to. Whenever you wanna leave is up to you."

During the same school year, Enrique described his parents as not caring about whether he graduated from high school. They had no understanding of the significance of Enrique's academic successes. When Enrique returned from Florida, he discovered that he no longer had his award certificates. "I saved them in a folder when I left," he explained. "When I came back home, I think my mom got rid of them. Kinda regret it for not putting them in a safer place. I wish I had them."

When he was 19, we asked him if he ever thought about going to college. He answered, "Not really. I never thought I could go to college because of my folks. I don't think they would let me, or have the money to send me to college for at least a year or two. I don't think they would have done that for me."

Antonio, his brother, revealed a great deal about the family's philosophy of schooling to us, when he explained why some students drop out of school. He said, "Unos papaces no tienen el dinero para darles a sus hijos el colegio que se necesita. Y otra es, que los alumnos no quieren estudiar, que se les hace muy difícil la escuela. Ha habido que varias personas han tenido que dejar de estudiar, porque tienen que ayudarles a los padres a trabajar, porque no les ajusta el dinero que tienen ellos, para darles. So, que ellos ya están grandes piensan mejor ayudar en la casa. Se dedican a trabajar y dejan el estudio, por cierta razón, que tienen que ayudar a sus padres a trabajar." (Some parents don't have the money to give to their children the schooling they need. And some students don't want to study; for them school is very difficult. There have been several persons who have had to stop studying because they have to help their parents work, because it just isn't enough, the money that they have, to give it to them. So, because they are now older, they think it is better to help at home. They dedicate themselves to work and leave studying, rightly so, because they have to help their parents work.)

THE ADOLESCENTS

Linda and Enrique were very different students. Linda rarely tried hard to excel in her coursework and impressed her peers as more of an athlete than a scholar. When it came to grades, she just wanted to do well enough to remain eligible for sports. When 16, she explained it to us this way: "Sports is almost everything to me, you know. I'll do anything to play sports, 'cause, you know, I love sports. I think sports have kept me in school a lot, you know, 'cause I'm always, I mean, I try so hard to pass, you know, have passing grades." The school monitored the grades of sports team members and issued weekly "Progress Reports" on students who were doing poorly in their coursework. Coaches got copies of these Progress Reports and would send team members with Progress Reports to study halls in order to improve their academic performance.

Linda was confident that she could get good grades if she wanted to. She explained this to us: "Sometimes I feel I can do so good, you know, just if I do it. I think I'm lazy that's all it is. Because sometimes, like in Physical Science, all there is to do is read and answer the questions, right? But I get so lazy that I don't want to read it, but then there's times like, when I was scared of failing last semester. I got real scared. I said, 'God, you know, I can't fail. I barely got the credits that I need.' So I really started to do my work, and you know, I saw myself and I said, 'Why can't I do this every six weeks?' It's just, I don't try hard. I guess that's why."

One of the reasons that she did not maintain her motivation to do her schoolwork was to spite her parents. When she was 16, Linda complained, "They'll tell me, 'Get off the phone. You should do your work.' They make me so mad because sometimes I don't have homework or sometimes I'm doing my homework on the phone. They'll tell me, 'Get off. Get off. Get off,' you know. I get off but it makes me so mad, it just makes me want to not do it. So I just sit there and I say, 'I'm not going to do it.'"

Despite her uninspired academic performance, she scored in the 46th percentile in English and the 73d percentile in math on the ITBS when she was in the ninth grade. A low score on the reading portion of the ITBS the previous year caused Linda to be labeled as "at risk" of dropping out. She explained: "I really didn't care. Like the math, it was real easy for me and I did them. But reading, I cannot stand doing. I said, 'I'm not going to read it. I'm just going to guess, you know.' And so, that's what I did, and I guess my grades kinda went down on that."

When Linda was 15, she told us she had no idea what kind of job she wanted to have when she grew up. Later, she talked to us about joining the air force and then going to college or simply going directly to college and then becoming a coach. But these career objectives brought with them many personal conflicts for her. Her parents disapproved of the air force idea. They told her they did not want her to live that far away from home. She thought the only way she could go to a four-year college was with a sports scholarship, but after she dropped out of sports in her senior year, she assumed that attending a four-year college was impossible for her. She also rationalized her choice to give up becoming a coach because, she told us, her coaches had always talked about how poorly they were paid and she wanted to earn more money than they did.

Thus, after graduation, she had no career goals. She told us that her goals were "to be happy, to have a family and be happy with my friends, and not have problems with my family." She described herself as "a person who always tries to look at the bright side of things and a person who is always there to help other people, if I could in any way help them."

In contrast to Linda, Enrique tried hard in school and took pride in his academic achievements. Nonetheless, he scored lower on the standardized tests than did Linda, especially in English. When he was in the ninth grade, he scored in the 26th percentile in English and the 66th percentile in mathematics. Linda's English score (46th percentile) was probably higher than Enrique's because she spoke mostly English at home, as did her father and siblings.[5] In contrast, Enrique used English only at school and did not use it to communicate with any of his family members. Since his family did not speak it, and he did not see his English-speaking friends outside of school, his English skills could not be reinforced and extended in his everyday conversations.

The two students also differed markedly in their relationships with peers. Unlike Linda, Enrique did not strive for peer acceptance. He indicated to us several times that he did not have many friends in school. His brothers also described him as very serious-minded and not social. He did not participate in extracurricular activities and socialized with only a few youth who played basketball near his brother's apartment. His lack of drive for peer acceptance probably stemmed from the fact that his social needs were met by his large family. As the 10th child in a 13-child family, he had his 12 siblings, eight siblings-in-law, and countless cousins, nieces, and nephews as a social network.

Linda's desire for peer acceptance reflected her greater assimilation into the American culture. Linda wanted to be known as a Mexican American, not a Mexican. In contrast, Enrique was comfortable being thought of as a Mexican, although he didn't want people calling him a "wetback."

As he entered high school, Enrique intended to graduate from high school, get a sports scholarship, and go to college and major in something "like engineering, dealing with design or something like that." He stressed several times that he wanted to "be somebody." When we asked him what it meant to be somebody, he said, "You know, like a doctor or lawyer, someone people will respect."

When we last interviewed him, at age 19, Enrique's goals had become more realistic. His major goals at that time were: (1) to graduate from high school, (2) to go to college for two years so that he could become a restaurant manager, and (3) to own five cars. Why five cars? He laughed, "In case they break down."

We asked him if any of the courses he had taken in high school helped him now. He answered, "Not that I know. I would probably say my math skills. My ability to count cash and think and remember and not to short out—all *that* I learned in elementary school. My classes like Algebra and stuff like that and dealing with fractions—I don't use any of that stuff now."

He saw himself as a "nice and hard-working person who loves to spend his money, who someday would like to retire and be a wealthy man so he wouldn't have to worry about working for the rest of his life."

MEXICAN IMMIGRATION TO THE U.S.

Most Mexican-origin people living in the U.S. are either the children of immigrants or are themselves immigrants from Mexico.[6] Since the 1960s, a high percentage of immigrants to the U.S., especially "undocumented" immigrants, have come from Mexico.[7] Hundreds of thousands of Mexicans have come to the U.S. in search of economic opportunities not available to them in Mexico. Mexican immigrants distinguished themselves by their sheer number and concentration in the southwestern states of California and Texas. Recent Mexican immigrants also have less education compared to the American average as well as to other immigrant groups.[8] This distinction became even more pronounced after 1975, when many low-skilled and uneducated Mexicans came north to the U.S. to escape severe economic conditions in Mexico.[9] Linda's mother was typical of the pre-1975 immigrant from Mexico. She completed sixth grade and learned a trade in Mexico before coming to the U.S. Enrique's parents were more typical of post-1975 immigrants from Mexico. When they arrived, they did not have even a first-grade education, and their limited skills could only provide their children with a standard of living at the poverty level.

In general, sociologists have found that many European immigrant groups to the U.S. have become more assimilated into the American mainstream with each generation.[10] Commonly used indicators of this assimilation are the proportion who complete high school, complete college, and become naturalized. Recent research has indicated an alarming trend among the Mexican-origin population within the U.S. There is mounting evidence that the Mexican-origin population has not followed the general assimilation trend, although this conclusion remains controversial at present.[11] Instead, the third generation of Mexican-origin immigrants is not surpassing the educational attainment of the second generation. Furthermore, Mexican-origin immigrants have a lower rate of becoming naturalized citizens of the U.S. than do other recent immigrant groups.[12]

Many have speculated about why recent immigrants from Mexico have not assimilated to the same degree as have other immigrants. Some have argued that this lack of assimilation is caused by discrimination.[13] Others point out that the American economy has restructured so that there are proportionately fewer low-skilled jobs that pay well now than in the past.[14] Because of this lack of economic opportunity, few Mexican-origin families have been able to assimilate. We believe that both of these explanations have some merit, but still, we argue that part of the problem is that American schools have failed to educate Mexican-origin students so that they can assimilate into the rest of U.S. society. American schools are not prepared to deal with families like Enrique's, families with virtually no comprehension of American education, families that do not qualify for welfare because they are here illegally, and families that have traditionally relied on their adolescent children to contribute to the family's income. Because the schools do not have programs that allow students as young as 16 to earn money while staying in school, students like Enrique drop out before completing high school.[15]

THE SCHOOLS

The surge of immigration from Mexico to the U.S. during the 1970s and 1980s has had a special impact on Texas schools. A critical issue in Texas education has been whether the student is a legal immigrant or an illegal one. Just before Enrique entered school in Austin, another school district in Texas refused to admit the children of illegal immigrants. In the case of *Plyler* v. *Doe*, a Texas school district argued that local tax dollars should not be used to pay for the education of children who were not legally in the U.S. By a 5–4 vote, the U.S. Supreme Court decided in 1982 that American public school districts had the obligation to educate the children of illegal aliens.[16] Public schools in Texas admitted these students. Still, there remained a great deal of animosity toward children of immigrants.

Both Linda and Enrique perceived the schools they attended as hostile to Mexicans. Enrique was called a "wetback," and Linda wanted to avoid being confused for a Mexican at any cost. The friction between native and immigrant Mexican-origin students caused Linda and Enrique to become involved in fights in school. The fights in Linda's and Enrique's high schools were frequently between Mexican and Mexican American students.

According to statistics kept by the school district for Linda's school in her senior year, Hispanic and African American students were much more likely to be involved in fighting in school than were Anglo students. While 38% of all students in her school were Hispanic, they accounted for 50% of the students involved in fighting with other students. Ten percent of the high school's students were African American, and they accounted for 37% of the students involved in fights. In contrast, 52% of all high school students were Anglos, and they accounted for only 13% of the students involved in fighting.[17] School administrators were quick to point out that these figures did not represent an absolutely perfect count of the frequency of violence in the schools, but rather reflected the number of times the administrators chose to make a disciplinary report. Administrators were motivated to make an abusive-conduct report in order to amass a record for a specific student that might eventually justify the suspension or expulsion of that student. Several of the parents in our study complained that Mexican-origin students were more likely to be "written up" than were Anglo students.

The district's statistics about the incidence of fighting in Linda's school during her senior year also demonstrate that only minority students were involved in incidences of girls fighting. Of all the fights involving Hispanics, about 20% involved girls. The same percentage held for African American students. On the other hand, of all the fights involving Anglos, none involved girls.[18]

According to school district administrators, the district had no systemwide program to prevent violence during the time that Linda was in school. Instead, it was the responsibility of an assistant principal at each school to deal with each disciplinary incident after it happened, on an individual student basis. Unless this assistant principal could clearly identify a perpetrator and a victim, then the usual procedure was for all the students involved in a fight to receive the same penalty, ranging from detention (the required presence of a student in a given classroom before or after school), to in-school suspension (the required presence of a student for three or fewer days in a classroom that substitutes for a regular class), to suspension from school (the required absence of the student from school for no more than six days), to expulsion from school (the required absence of the student from school for a period which can extend to the end of the current school year).[19]

Instead of dealing directly with the tension between immigrant and native students, the Austin schools responded to the influx of immigrants primarily by labeling the immigrant students as limited in English proficiency (LEP), grouping them together, and providing them with minimal English language training. In the Austin schools, about 90% of the students whose native language was not English spoke Spanish.[20]

During our fieldwork for this project, Harriett Romo sat in on an English as a Second Language classroom at the junior high school level. The teacher was Mexican American. The class dialogue focused around the problem of a young woman planning her wedding and deciding where to purchase her wedding dress. The students repeated phrases related to the wedding plans.

The 10 students represented a wide range of English skills. The class included 3 limited-English-speaking Chinese siblings whose parents taught at a nearby university, 5 Mexican American students who spoke English but needed assistance with reading and writing, and 2 Mexican students who spoke little or no English. The Chinese students sat near the front of the class and dominated the teacher-student interaction, asking questions and raising their hands for help on the written exercise. The two Mexican students sat at the back corner of the classroom and did not participate. Both were physically larger than the other students, suggesting that they were much older. One had his head on the desk for most of the class period.[21]

The problem with such ESL classes is that they emphasize oral language and do not address the students' academic needs, such as learning the social studies or science content provided solely to them in English.[22] In the case of the children of Mexican immigrants, such knowledge cannot be supplied by their parents because Mexican immigrant parents are, on the average, very poorly educated.

During the time of our study, elementary school–aged students typically were trained in basic concepts in their native language, while learning English on the side. Many of these ESL programs were assigned to staff who were not specifically trained in language acquisition or the special needs of immigrant students. The programs operated on the premise that a LEP student had a deficit rather than the potential to be bilingual.[23] Enrique attended such a program until sixth grade. Once he entered middle school, he was mainstreamed into regular courses and was no longer classified as limited English proficient. Non-English-speaking students who entered the Austin schools as adolescents received their ESL training solely in the core subjects of reading, writing, and basic math.

Overall, standards for graduation for students are higher than they have ever been, requiring relatively high levels of English reading comprehension and writing skills. Children who enter school speaking primarily Spanish are expected to meet the same English standards required of native-born children. And yet, Mexican students are not given longer school days or school years or well-trained language teachers to compensate for their limited English background. They are expected to learn much more in school with the same quantity of education (in terms of hours per day, days per year) as native students. Thus, students who enter American schools in late elementary school or later and who have parents who are poorly educated and speak no English are likely to drop out. They recognize that they will not have the opportunity to acquire the skills they will need to meet the high school graduation standards.

The school district's Office of Research and Evaluation conducted annual evaluations of the performance of the district's LEP programs. They discovered that students in secondary schools who received training for their limited English proficiency during the late 1980s and early 1990s were much more likely to drop out of school compared to district averages. Specifically, the year that Linda became a senior, 16.5% of high school students who received LEP services dropped out, compared to a districtwide annual dropout rate of 9.8%.[24] Students who cannot pass the standardized English tests or function in a regular classroom often give up on school because they realize that they will not be able to achieve the high school diploma.

The school district designated both Linda and Enrique as "at risk" of dropping out because of low scores on standardized reading tests. For Linda, an American-born daughter of a Mexican mother and American father, her extremely low scores were most probably caused by her decision to fill in her answer sheet randomly. For Enrique, a Mexican-born son of Mexican parents, his low score was probably caused by his lack of opportunity to practice reading and writing English outside of school.

We found that lack of English skills was not a problem limited to only foreign-born children or the children of foreign-born parents. Many native-born students had weak English skills as well. While less than 2% of the Austin school students were categorized as immigrant or refugee during the time of our study, 7% of all Austin students received special services for limited English speakers. This finding is consistent with the results of a national survey of adult literacy conducted in 1992 by the Educational Testing Service under contract with the National Center for Education Statistics. Of the 10 racial or ethnic groups considered in the analysis, Hispanics of Mexican origin had the lowest average performance on literacy tests, with over half of the respondents scoring at the lowest level.[25] Many native-born students have parents whose English skills are so poor that the parents cannot understand the messages sent out by the schools about their children. Furthermore, they cannot help their children acquire the literacy skills they need to graduate.

POLICY RECOMMENDATIONS

Historically, American schools have had the job of assimilating the children of immigrants into the American mainstream. In general, the waves of immigrants who came to the U.S. in the 1970s and 1980s created needs that most schools were not ready or willing to meet. Many of their needs go beyond providing ESL instruction.[26] Specifically, one of the important needs of immigrants and their children is to be accepted into a school community. And yet, the high frequency of violence among Mexican immigrant and Mexican American students suggests that the newcomers have not been accepted. Many Texas teachers and school staff, ambivalent about the presence of high concentrations of "undocumented" immigrants from Mexico in their schools, have not promoted respect for and acceptance of the children of immigrants.

As part of our initial survey of the families in our sample, we asked the parents of the students whether their children were afraid to go to school. Only 16% of the parents said yes. But three years later, all of these children had dropped out of school. Fear of going to school was a major factor in dropping out for the students. While this fear drove some students to drop out, it also had other negative effects on students like Linda. For her, the violence turned inward. She was driven to take her own life because she felt rejected and unaccepted as an American girl. Although she was saved by her parents from her attempted suicide, she gave up her plans to go to college on a sports scholarship because she feared the violence from her teammates.

At present, most schools do not see themselves as having the job of training students in social harmony. Instead, they see themselves as institutions that train students in narrowly defined academic skills. School officials, teachers, and many parents simply want violent students to be removed from the school. But the expulsion approach does not deal with the underlying causes of the violence. Consequently, violence will continue to unnerve both students and teachers. Prevention of violent acts in school would contribute significantly toward making schools places where all students can learn and teachers can teach.

We argue that students, faculty, and administrators need to learn how to get along in a mutually respectful and satisfying manner. This training and its everyday practice can be packaged as part of the process of learning how to be a good citizen of one's school, community, state, nation, and world. This is needed for all students, not just those who have trouble with the English language. This training could include not only formal training in the mediation of conflict, but also informal training in recognizing and coping with misunderstandings, insults, racial and ethnic conflicts, and hurt feelings. At present, no comprehensive school program exists that integrates all the necessary elements, including conflict-meditation and anger-reduction training, and the universal participation of students in school decision making. Schools could play a major role in reducing the amount of youth violence in the U.S., if such training were considered an important part of each school's mission.

This new form of citizenship training could also serve the function of educating students and their parents in positive ways of communicating with various immigrant and ethnic groups in order to promote respect for cultural and racial differences. A recent commission on the education of immigrant children argued that administrators and teachers need to lead students and their parents toward acceptance of the immigrant children. According to the commission's report, school personnel could take steps to stem the violence against immigrants by "providing visible administrative leadership which models respect for different languages and cultures, setting a firm expectation that harassment of students who are different will not be tolerated, integrating all groups of students for purposes of instruction and extracurricular activities, providing students with assistance in coping with socially threatening situations, and developing quality multicultural education programs."[27]

In addition, school personnel need to understand that the parents of immigrant children typically rely on the school to make educational decisions for the student. These parents are reluctant to enter the school to meet with teachers and administrators. Some parents are hesitant to come to "back-to-school" nights or participate in student-teacher meetings for a variety of reasons, including that many cannot read the announcements, that school meetings remind them of their own negative school experiences, and that they are discouraged by their children from going to school.[28] While school leaders should reach out to such parents in nonthreatening and culturally sensitive ways, they need to understand that they will have to take the initiative in solving the school-related problems of students. They cannot expect immigrant parents to solve these problems for them.[29] The abilities of many parents, foreign- or native-born, are simply not up to the task of solving the school-related problems of their children. Furthermore, schools need to assume primary responsibility for linking students to training beyond high school since many parents of immigrant students have no idea how students enroll in college or other training programs after high school.

In Linda's case, her parents took no part in helping her make decisions about high school course taking, college enrollment, or any other form of training. They had no understanding of how one gained admission to a college or how students paid for their education. Linda became angry with her parents when they attempted to talk to school personnel. She was embarrassed by them and discouraged them from participating in her high school life. It was only after her attempted suicide and the fight involving a knife that Linda's parents felt compelled to walk into the office of the assistant principal to speak up for their daughter.

In Enrique's case, his parents had transferred the responsibility for his education to Enrique and his older brother once Enrique became a teen. Enrique's parents were much too burdened with their own problems to supervise him or monitor his schoolwork. When Enrique's parents needed financial assistance, the family believed that Enrique had the obligation to help them out. Enrique went to the school counselor for help. But all she did was preach to him about the value of education. She should have tried to find Enrique a job so that he could have sent his parents money while remaining in school. Enrique's case is a prime example of how American public schools have failed to understand the reality of the lives of immigrant families and have not responded in helpful ways to meeting the needs of the children from such families. Schools with high concentrations of such immigrant children are sometimes overwhelmed by their special needs.

During our field research, we became painfully aware of the gap between the expectations of the schools and the real limits of some parents. For example, one immigrant mother told us of receiving a letter from the school about her son. But since the letter was solely in English and she understood no English, she had no idea what it was about. Her son was not very helpful in explaining it to her, misleading her into thinking that it was not important. When an older sister visited, the mother showed the letter to her and discovered that her son had been suspended from school for possessing a knife. The letter informed the mother of a hearing date; by the time the letter was correctly translated to the mother, that date had passed and the suspension was irrevocable. Soon thereafter, this student dropped out of school.

While it is not possible to have a translator for every possible language in every school, it is reasonable to require the presence of at least one Spanish-speaking staff member in schools with high concentrations of Spanish-speaking parents. Not only could such persons be responsible for informing Spanish-speaking parents of the expectations of American schools, but also they could help educate the school personnel and student body about the culture of the immigrant children. While a few of the schools we studied had a staff person to work with Spanish-speaking parents, many schools with high concentrations of LEP students did not.

Finally, we recommend that children of immigrants be given many opportunities to learn English. School districts should provide English instruction tailored to the needs of students whose parents are not literate in English. This means that English instruction should include not only speech and listening, but also reading comprehension and writing as well as instruction in content areas. This expanded English instruction should be offered on a 12-month a year basis, on Saturday mornings, and before and after school.

The costs for the expanded instruction time and the Spanish-speaking staff member, where needed, should be borne by the federal government and be based on the number of foreign-born parents sending children to the school. It is essential that the cost of such personnel be paid for by the federal government, because immigrants are not evenly distributed across the states nor are they evenly distributed across all school districts within states. Immigrant children, especially those with special needs, tend to be concentrated in states and school districts with budgets that are already inadequate to meet the need of the native school population. We can hardly be surprised by the negative reaction of states and school districts to immigrant children. Those states and school districts with disproportionate numbers of immigrant students should not have to draw on already overstretched budgets to serve the many needs of immigrant children. It would be in the best interest of all Americans to promote the assimilation of immigrant children, and it is only reasonable that the federal government pay at least some of the extra costs of educating limited-English-speaking students.[30]

SEVEN

"I didn't Going

want to be for the

20 when GED

I graduated."

This chapter examines the value of the GED for "at risk" students. We consider the cases of Martin, Jr. and Felipe, who chose to stop attending high school and to earn their GED instead. Martin, Jr. had serious motivational problems and could not stay awake during his high school classes. Since he was making little progress in accumulating credits for graduation, he stopped attending. Felipe had serious learning disabilities, but worked hard in school and had accumulated enough credits to be a high school junior. He was two years behind because his elementary school teachers had dealt with his learning disabilities by retaining him twice. Both students intended to use their GED as a way of entering community college. We argue that the GED ought to be replaced by an educational system that prevents student failure and provides services for students in school. If we had an educational system that prevented student failure in school and provided the services students needed to succeed, the GED would be unnecessary, except for adults.

MARTIN, JR.

Martin was tall and thin with long black hair drawn back in a ponytail. He wore an earring in one ear and dressed like the hard rock musician he wanted to be. He smiled easily as he came forward to greet Harriett Romo when she arrived in his home in North Austin. His family lived in a middle-class neighborhood of stone tract houses. Harriett usually talked to Martin, Jr. and his father while sitting on the modern circular sofa in the den. This room had a new beige carpet, a large stone fireplace, and one wall covered with family photographs, including the graduation pictures of Martin's two older sisters.

Martin explained why he had dropped out of high school in the middle of the school year, about six months before he turned 18: "I just started slacking off real bad. I was skipping a lot of classes, dropping on a lot of my work. Basically, in my mind, I didn't see any reason why I should keep going. So, I just stopped going." Indeed, he had accumulated only 8 of the 21 credits needed to graduate from high school.

He described school as "a basic waste of time." He was falling asleep in class and not getting any of the work done. He blamed himself: "I have nothing against the teachers. They were doing their jobs. It was just me not wanting to do the work or pay attention, basically, my problems."

His parents were disappointed, but not surprised. His father, Martin, Sr. had told us three years earlier that he half expected his son to drop out of high school. Martin, Jr.'s problem then was lack of motivation. Throughout the three years we followed him and his family, nothing seemed to inspire him to do his schoolwork. Martin, Jr. continued in school for two and a half years, and his parents continued to hope that something would turn him around. But nothing did.

Martin, Sr. was distressed not only because Martin, Jr. was his namesake and only son, but also because he wanted all of his children to get good educations so that they would never have to live in poverty. Martin, Sr. had been poor, and had worked his way up to be a floor manager at a manufacturing plant owned by an international electronics company. His wife had also grown up in poverty, and together they continuously gave Martin, Jr. the same message about school: "Stay in school. Don't become a bum."

Several of Martin, Jr.'s friends left school at about the same time, and together they decided to take the GED test and enroll in the local community college. Martin, Jr. knew of people who had obtained the GED before going to community college; indeed, his father had taken this route. On his own, Martin, Jr. signed up for the test, took it, and passed, receiving his certificate in the mail. His family gave him a party to celebrate getting his GED.

When Harriett last talked to him, Martin, Jr. had postponed enrolling in the community college so that he could work during the summer to make money. But he was having trouble finding a job. He told us that he wasn't picky about what job he got, just as long as he could make money for his car and for tuition. Still, no offers. He was depressed, telling us, "I have this idea in my head I'm cursed. If I had a stack of all the applications that I've put in, it would be so high and no calls, nothing. It gets annoying after a while."

Martin, Jr. had been employed before. He worked around 18 hours a week at a sandwich shop when we first interviewed him at age 15. He left that job, he said, because the manager made him feel unappreciated. He then worked for a discount drugstore, but was never able to get more than nine hours of work a week. He told us that he quit because it didn't pay him enough to cover the cost of transportation.

He knew that he didn't really need a job. He lived at home, his parents paid his living expenses, and they had offered to pay his tuition to college. He understood this, saying, "They just want me in school, period."

According to Martin, Sr., his son's school problems first appeared in fifth grade and then grew worse in middle school. Martin, Jr.'s transition from child to adolescent did not go well. Martin, Sr. thought that several events were key. When his two older sisters were in high school, Martin, Sr.'s mother repeatedly reminded them that their father had been a straight-A student and challenged them to live up to his example. As a child, Martin, Jr. would watch his grandmother saying this to his sisters and concluded that he also had to live up to his father's record or be a failure. Martin, Sr. told us, "So my son hears all this and I think he felt caught. He never could measure up and I think that's what devastated him."

Martin, Jr. also had some insight about the reasons for his lack of motivation. When he was 16, he told us of a middle school English teacher who had told him that he was "worthless" and that he would never amount to anything. Martin, Jr. explained his reaction to this teacher thus: "It makes me mad, it makes me feel like they think that I'm worthless or something. 'Why are you even here?' you know. It just upsets me a lot. I always figured that reverse psychology never worked on me. . . . They're thinking that I'm just going to prove them wrong. But every time they tell me stuff like that it just breaks me down more than it motivates me."

Two years later, Martin Jr. told us the same story, in response to a question about any problems he might have had in middle or high school.

> Martin, Jr.: "I had some problems that occurred. Had an English teacher who kept telling me I wasn't going to amount to anything. That was a big discouragement. When you are young and you have an adult telling you something like that, that really bugs you because you actually start to believe it."
>
> HR: "Why was she telling you that?"
>
> Martin, Jr.: "It was a guy. I really don't know. It's been a while so it's really hard to remember but it just sticks out in my head all the time."

Martin, Jr. had trouble sleeping. He spent many hours alone in his room, which was at one end of the house, away from all the other bedrooms. The isolation of his bedroom was a metaphor for the isolation he felt from his family. When he was 16, he explained his family situation this way: "The way it's been ever since I've been small: my sisters had each other, my sisters had my mother, my dad had my mother, and my mother had my father. Me, being the smallest and being the only boy, I had nobody. So, the only other people I could turn to were my friends."

He would talk on the telephone to his friends while in his room alone. Although Martin, Jr. liked to portray himself as having many different types of friends in school, his father described his friends as former "drug addicts and alcoholics. They've all been rehabilitating. He feels that he's responsible for his friends, not to drink, not to take drugs, and that type of stuff, so he takes a lot on himself. . . . I think that his friends affect his grades because he worries too much about them rather than doing the things that he needs to do to be successful with his homework."

Martin, Jr. was already turned off by school when we first interviewed him. He told us, "There's nothing about school that I really like. I can handle oral things. I can have a discussion in class and sit there all day and listen, but when it comes to writing things down and looking through a book, I think it's the thing that upsets me a lot. If I have somebody there who can relay the answers to me if I get them wrong instead of saying, 'Well go through chapters one through six and find the answer.'"

He elaborated, "I'm not good with people telling me what I have to do. Constructive criticism, that's not bad, but when I start getting ordered around, I don't get rebellious, I get upset within myself."

After Martin, Jr. left school, his father began treating him differently, more like an adult, and when Harriett last talked to him, Martin, Sr. thought he had seen glimpses of improved behavior. Martin, Sr. remarked, "When he was in school, he wasn't as outgoing as he is now. He seems to be going out with his friends more, which we try to encourage, because he used to stick in his room and stay there all day. We told him he had to do his homework and he would be there all night, trying to do the little bit of homework he had to do so he would stay there all night. Procrastinating and not doing it. Do a little bit, then go off. So, he goes out more and he's with his friends. I give him more freedom now."

Furthermore, when we asked Martin, Sr. about his plans for his son, he responded, "I quit having plans for him. It lies on his shoulders now. I'm here to help him whatever he decides to do. It's up to him now to decide what he wants. I've already given him everything I can think of that I would like him to do or pursue. It's up to him to decide what he wants to do."

Elaborating further, Martin, Sr. said, "And my wife tells me to push him, but I say, he's got to do a little on his own, make his own mind up. I was always pushing real hard and now I try to back off a little bit so as not to be as forceful as I can be. Try to let him make his own decisions. Give him space to do that. You gotta give him a little time. You have to look at the positives. He's still here, he's not out on drugs and stuff, so you have to look at the positives."

Analysis

Martin, Jr. knew that having a GED was no substitute for a high school diploma. He was having trouble finding a job after getting his GED. Still, getting the GED gave him a way of reassuring his parents after he had already stopped attending school.

Understanding Martin, Jr.'s lack of motivation is difficult. His father had some insight about his son's fear of measuring up. Other aspects of the problem, his father did not understand. It revolved around Martin's parents' emphasis on ability. We saw this when Martin, Sr. tried to explain his son's problem.

Martin, Sr.: "I never doubted that he's got the mental ability to do the work. I think if he really wanted to, he could have aced any of those classes he was taking. If he really wanted to. . . . Anything he does, he does real well at. That's why it was always so discouraging when he would quit. He had successes."

HR: "And he didn't have to work to get them?"

Martin, Sr.: "No, it was so easy for him. He played little league, soccer. He was always the number one player. It was always so easy for him. He was a natural. And I said, 'Man, if you could build on those things, imagine the success you would have.' I said, 'Those other kids work so hard to get to where they are, and you come out here and mess around and you get picked number one. Think about that, those things you are able to do.' That's what's so amazing. Things would come so easy for him."

This emphasis on having "the right stuff," and the deemphasis on working hard, was clearly part of Martin, Jr.'s problem. Working hard threatened his sense of identity, which was firmly rooted in the abilities of his father. If Martin, Jr. tried hard and failed, then everyone would know that he was not a "chip off the old block." But if Martin, Jr. didn't try and he failed, then he and his family could continue to believe that he had the ability to succeed, the ability to be like his father. By not trying, he could be seen as simply lacking motivation.

While "acting unmotivated" helped Martin, Jr. cope with his school problems, this behavior infuriated his mother. Martin, Sr. described her response to her son: "My wife jumps all over Martin. To put it bluntly, she's direct and she doesn't tolerate much. So I try to put the rings on her and say, 'Look, I'm trying to work with him. Trying to be understanding. Trying to be more supportive.' But she can only take so much and she'll jump all over him and let him have it. And so, he gets all mad. And I say, 'Look, your mother is only trying to help you, too. She may be doing it a different way, but she's trying.' You have to understand. She won't stand for it too long. She's like, 'Do it right now. Do it right away. And go for it.' She's always been a leader. Goes after it and gets it done. Within the family, she's the one that goes out and gets things done, and she expects Martin to do the same."

As soon as Martin, Jr. recognized that he would have to work hard to accomplish something, he lost interest in it. For example, we showed Martin, Jr. his course list for one semester, and asked him about a soccer course he had taken. Martin, Jr. told us, "Took soccer because I had played a lot when I was a kid and when I went out there and played during school, I realized I was done with that sport." When asked "Why is that?" Martin, Jr. replied, "I don't know. The coordination was gone. I couldn't play the way I did when I was younger."

Rather than risk the possibility of not being the best player, as he was when he was a child, he gave up playing the sport altogether.

FELIPE

Felipe looked like a professional when he received us from behind his large desk in the suite of rooms occupied by his father's law office. He was working for his father, maintaining his father's computer network, which he had helped his father select and use. Felipe was tall and had curly black hair. He wore a dress shirt and slacks. When we last talked to him, he had just withdrawn from high school after completing two years. He was 18, but he only had 12 of the 21 credits needed to graduate from high school. He explained his withdrawal: "I was just too old for it. You're supposed to outgrow high school and *I didn't want to be 20 when I graduated.*"

Indeed, if he had not been retained two grades in elementary school, he would have been in the process of graduating from high school, not withdrawing from it, the time we last interviewed him. Nonetheless, he had a well-articulated plan to go to college. He reeled off the dates for the GED and college-placement tests he would need to take in order to enroll in the local community college. He explained to us what courses he would have to take in community college and how he would accumulate enough credits to enroll in the University of Texas and major in computer science.

He understood the skills he needed to get this bachelor's degree: "reading, mathematics, determination, enjoying your work, basically."

Felipe's educational problems became evident in Brownsville, Texas, a town on the Mexican border, where his mother moved after her divorce from his father, Juan Felipe. Felipe was the youngest of Juan Felipe's three children with his first wife, and when she took Felipe from Austin to Brownsville, the schools there did not know what grade level to put him in. At first, they put him ahead a year, and then, they decided to retain him in the third grade. Felipe's mother and teacher both recommended that he be retained, and although Juan Felipe had some doubts, he felt that he could not do anything about their decision. Juan Felipe's misgivings about Felipe's educational progress grew, and he eventually obtained custody of Felipe, moving him back to Austin and placing him in the sixth grade in a private school.

There Felipe began his career as a teacher's pet, helping teachers with their use of computers and other machines. Much to Juan Felipe's amazement, at the end of the school year, the teachers at the private school recommended that Felipe spend another year in sixth grade. The decision shocked Juan Felipe because he had received no prior indication that Felipe was having academic difficulties. Instead, the teachers at the private school had told Juan Felipe how helpful Felipe was to them. Juan Felipe suspected that this small school simply needed more students, and so he withdrew Felipe and put him back in public school to repeat the sixth grade.

From there Felipe went to a public junior high school which contained a magnet program in the sciences. Felipe was in this junior high program when we first interviewed him and his father. Juan Felipe acknowledged then that his son was at risk of dropping out of school: "Besides the fact that he's failed two grades, he now has consistently poor grades. His work is real sloppy. He has a tendency to turn in things late. Or, like recently, he worked on some big assignment and he got it up to a whole page, which to him is a lot, and then he lost it."

Juan Felipe went on to elaborate, "When he writes down a telephone number, the 4s look like 7s and the 7s look like 2s, and so I always tell him, 'Do it again in a way that somebody can read.' We tell him, it's almost an insult for a teacher when you turn that in because it looks like something that a third grader is doing."

Felipe and his father lived in a large house in the heart of the old Austin barrio with his stepmother and his three stepsiblings. The oldest of his stepsiblings was about nine years younger than he was, and Felipe was often called upon to babysit. Both Felipe and Juan Felipe said that his stepmother wanted Felipe to perform better in school and often became exasperated by his inability to focus on his schoolwork. Felipe frequently got distracted from his schoolwork. "He's always wanted to do mechanical, electrical stuff. If he had his way, he'd just be breaking apart radios and fixing them. . . . He'll bring home motors . . . and there's parts all over the place and he's not doing his academic work," explained Juan Felipe.

Felipe knew that his father and stepmother wanted him to try harder at his schoolwork. He told us when he was 16, "I think I try very hard, but my parents don't think I'm really trying that hard." He gave us examples of the things he worked hard on in school: "That virus in the computer, I had to figure out a way of getting it out of the system. Different things, like there's a program that somebody wanted me to copy that no one else could copy and I figured out how to do that. I finally got it copied—very simple, but that was basically the stuff that stays on my mind."

The science magnet program was good for Felipe because he liked working on the science projects. Felipe was popular with his teachers, especially the electronics lab instructors, and he stayed late at school, helping them. But his father faulted the school for not trying to get him to work harder. He explained, "This school has the policy of no homework on the weekends and I think it's something wrong with the school system. It seems to me that [the weekend] may be the time when some students can put in an hour or two on Saturday or an hour or two on Sunday."

Further, when Felipe left to live with his mother during the summer, his father thought that Felipe should be enrolled in summer school. But his mother did not seem concerned about Felipe's academic progress, and she allowed him to watch eight hours of television every day, according to Juan Felipe. He made several suggestions to his ex-wife for summer schools and summer jobs for Felipe, but Felipe usually spent the summer watching television, socializing with friends at the mall, and traveling with his mother's family.

Despite Felipe's poor grades in junior high, he signed up for honors-level courses when he entered high school. This probably appealed to Felipe because most of his friends at the magnet program planned to take honors-level classes in high school. Once in high school, however, Felipe did very poorly in the honors courses.

Juan Felipe explained his rationale for encouraging his son to take this college-preparatory coursework: "I see the idea is to learn something and seems like that, even though he was bombing out in every honors course, he was learning more than he would in the other courses. Here you have honors learning more, but bombing out greater. In the lower track, he would be learning less and probably just go to sleep. Boredom. And then I could see him saying, 'I don't want to continue school because I am bored.'"

When Harriett last talked to Juan Felipe, he expressed a great deal of pride in his son and positive expectations for his son's future. He said, "He's got a real good view of life. I think he's achieved about all the important things. He's got a real good disposition towards work and he enjoys work and he's social."

Analysis

Felipe's difficulty writing, his inability to complete his schoolwork, his reversed numbers and poor spelling indicate that he had learning disabilities. But rather than treat his learning difficulties directly, his schools retained him twice so that by the time he entered junior high school, he was two years behind the other students. Consequently, when Felipe was 18 and psychologically ready to leave high school, because of these grade retentions he was unable to graduate. Juan Felipe encouraged his son to complete his two years in high school, withdraw, take the GED, go on to community college, and then a four-year college. Juan Felipe himself had taken this route, eventually graduating from law school and passing the bar exam.

Juan Felipe assumed some of the responsibility for his son's grade retentions. This father told us that he made a mistake when he yielded to his ex-wife's recommendation for retention in third grade, and he felt betrayed by a private school when his son was retained the second time in sixth grade. It is likely that Felipe's many moves from parent to parent and from school to school made it difficult for his parents and teachers to identify and treat his learning disabilities.

Furthermore, Juan Felipe assumed some of the responsibility for his son's learning disabilities. He saw many similarities between his son's learning difficulties and his own. Juan Felipe confessed, "I still can't spell. And if you give me a phone number, you have to give it to me in three digits at a time."

Nonetheless, his father urged his son to try harder to make his written work clearer for the teachers, so that the teachers would know that he understood what he was doing. Juan Felipe told us that Felipe would retort, "You don't know how to spell either." And Juan Felipe said he would reply, "Yes, but at least I'm working on it."

Despite the existence of these very real problems, Juan Felipe maintained a positive attitude about his son's overall abilities, and his son internalized this positive attitude.

THE PARENTS

Both fathers identified strongly with their sons and wanted their sons to share in their own occupational success. These fathers were the most occupationally successful in our sample, and they put in many hours at work. Martin, Sr. worked about 50 hours a week, and Juan Felipe about 70. And yet, Martin, Sr.'s example discouraged his son's academic performance, while Juan Felipe's example gave his son reason to hope that he would be able to overcome his academic problems.

Martin, Sr. and his wife were baffled by their son's lack of interest in schoolwork. Martin, Sr. had moved up from poverty to the middle class by completing two years of college and working hard in electronics manufacturing. Taking care of his family and promoting education were important to him. "From an early age, I decided I was going to try to do something with education, work, or whatever, and I have always been family oriented so my family probably is the biggest part of my life, not just my own family, but my whole family. I have also wanted to be an example for my kids, for them to achieve what they can, as far as they can."

But Martin, Sr.'s success became more an impediment to Martin, Jr.'s achievement than an inspiration. Not only did it create a fear in Martin, Jr. that he could never measure up to his father, but also it created in the son an intense sensitivity to authority. Martin, Sr. learned that when he came home from work, he could not simply order people around the way he did at work. Referring to his son, Martin, Sr. explained, "If I want him to do things, I'll tell him that I want things done. He'll jump on me and ask how come I don't ask him. . . . I have to keep changing myself, you know, because I'm used to giving directions rather than asking."

Martin, Jr.'s mother was a "can do, no nonsense" kind of person who worked as a secretary at a labor union, despite the fact that she had completed only eight years of education. Martin, Sr. used lack of education as an excuse to explain her emotional tirades. Echoing his father's explanation of his mother's behavior, Martin, Jr. said, "My mother, you know, dropping out of school when she was in the eighth grade, you know, doesn't really look at things the way we do. My father says, well, your mother thinks with her heart, not with her head. She says things, and it's not like she's dumb or anything, because she knows exactly what we're talking about, but she talks from her feelings."

Juan Felipe also portrayed Felipe's stepmother as lacking in understanding of Felipe's circumstances. Juan Felipe acknowledged that his wife tried to be a good parent to Felipe, helping him with his homework and visiting his school; but he believed that because she had no experience with teenagers, she was often disappointed by his immaturity. Juan Felipe described her perspective this way: "I don't think that his stepmother puts herself in the mind of a teenager and appreciates that a teenager is not responsible to the extent that she is. She thinks, this is not how I would do it. You know, he'll wash the car for me, and he'll leave one door just totally a mess. He'll make the sandwiches in the morning and go off to school without them. He'll put things in the refrigerator that should be thrown out."

Despite Felipe's lapses in his schoolwork and his chores, Juan Felipe encouraged his son to think positively about his abilities and his future. Juan Felipe expected his son to go to college and do well in some sort of technical occupation.

Juan Felipe explained why he discouraged Felipe from continuing in school in a vocational program. He said, "I have a big problem with this vocational thing. I see a lot of people that could have gone on and enjoyed school, but were just pushed into this vocational thing. There are some of these kids who are frustrated they aren't going to the regular college. Too many people don't have that self-esteem."

THE ADOLESCENTS

At age 18, Martin, Jr. and Felipe had much in common. They were young Mexican American men whose financially secure parents actively supported their persistence in school. The two young men followed in their fathers' footsteps in taking the GED route to community college. And yet, their academic histories were very different. Elementary school was easy for Martin, Jr. His problems didn't become obvious until he entered middle school. In contrast, elementary school was very difficult for Felipe. He had more success in junior high school.

Given the downward spiral of Martin, Jr.'s educational performance, we found it difficult to be optimistic about his future. Martin, Jr. was designated as "at risk" of dropping out in secondary school because of his poor standardized test scores in reading and his accumulation of Fs. When he was 16, he scored in the 27th percentile in reading and the 30th percentile in mathematics. At that time, we asked him how he got his parents to do what he wanted them to do. He told us, "Tell them what they want to hear pretty much. Let them know I have the problem and let them know that I want the problem to be solved and I want things to be right. But then, I forget about it for a while."

Martin had developed a means of coping with his parents, one of telling them what they wanted to hear, so that they would get off his back. Thus, when Martin, Jr. was 18 and told us of his plans to go to community college, we were a little skeptical that he would ever attend classes, turn in assignments, and accumulate enough credits toward graduation from community college.

He himself seemed confused, commenting, "I talked about graduating from high school, but I said I wasn't going to go to college. I ended up not graduating from high school and I want to go to college. So, it's very confusing . . ."

He went on to describe himself as a "very confused person. Knows what he wants but doesn't know what he wants. He's lost in his dreams."

And what were those dreams? Music and sports. Martin had told us, consistently since he was 15, that he wanted to be a musician. He thought he had talent. He told us then, "I think as far as raw talent goes, I think so, you know, with the right, with the proper training, and with the proper teaching I think I can be even better. Enough to get to where I want to go, if I have the chance."

However, when we asked him about the likelihood that he would get the chance, he said, " The odds that I'll get the chance would be 100 to 1, I'd say."

By the time he was 17, Martin played the drums in a group with two other guys. Although together they had played a few parties, Martin, Jr. told us that they really needed another person before they had any chance of getting hired as a band.

Tennis was his second choice. He had played occasionally on his high school tennis team, but because of his poor grades, he was not always allowed to play. During our last interview, Martin said that he still dreamed of a future in tennis.

> HR: "What type of career or job do you see in tennis?"
> Martin: "Well, there are basically no jobs or careers in tennis unless you are a basic tennis player. Planned on playing tennis for school, and once I started I was going to work on my basics at community college and then transfer and then play for whatever school I decided to transfer to."
> HR: "You're pretty good at tennis?"
> Martin: "Hate to judge myself. I usually leave that up to other people."
> HR: "What do other people say?"
> Martin: "Most people say I have potential. The last guy I played with, I asked if he thought that I had the potential to play collegiate level and he said definitely. I'm not sure about myself."

Although Martin, Jr. was confused about his goals and unable to take steps to achieve them, Felipe had clear plans to enroll in community college and focus on a career in electronics. Felipe's experiences in elementary school—he had been retained two grade levels—had put him "at risk" of dropping out. But once in middle school, Felipe seemed to function better, scoring at the 85th percentile in reading and the 44th percentile in mathematics when he was 16 years old.

Felipe impressed us with his grasp of all the details about college course titles, credits needed, and so on. He told us that he had learned all this from reading the community college catalog and from talking to counselors and to people he knew who went to community college as well as the university he wanted to attend. His long-term goal was to graduate from the University of Texas "with maybe a bachelor's in computer science or a master's in computer science." If he did, this would be the culmination of a goal he had since he was 15, when he told us he wanted to be a laser technician or computer specialist.

This sense of organization and purpose pervaded Felipe's adolescence. Throughout our study of Felipe's family, he told us about the chores he did for his household. When he was 16 and attending junior high, he had a system. "In the mornings, I'm the only one awake. Everybody else is asleep because they don't wake up until seven o'clock. I like to take out the trash in the mornings when it's trash day. Or wash breakfast dishes—my breakfast dishes and stuff like that. But it depends on if there are dishes left over from dinner—I'll wash. Or, I'll put up the dishes."

These chores were tasks his stepmother wanted him to do, and in turn Felipe knew how to get his parents to do what he wanted them to do. He would "do a little bit more homework than normal." And sometimes, he'd "try to talk them into it."

Juan Felipe carefully nurtured in his son a sense of self-worth, but he was not reluctant to discipline Felipe. Perhaps because Felipe felt good about himself, he accepted the discipline he received. When we asked him what his parents did when he disobeyed, he told us, "I usually get a lecture. They won't let me go. Like the science club went on a field trip and I didn't get to go because I didn't mop the floor." He went on, "I really don't care about those punishments. They're just because I deserved them."

When we asked him whether he preferred working for his dad or going to school, he said, "I enjoy working here more than at school because here I get to make my own schedule; whereas in school, you finish one thing, for example, classes, you finish your work early and have thirty minutes or so left. You do nothing, except wait for another class. At least here, I can finish and start something else immediately."

When he was 18, we asked Felipe to describe himself. He hesitated and then said, "I'm smart. I keep on doing work. It is easy for me to adjust to just about any situation. Sort of blend in." Felipe had accomplished one of the main tasks of adolescence: gaining a positive identity.

THE GED

The U.S. Army originally used the GED in 1942 as a means of certifying the skills of military personnel who did not have high school diplomas. Beginning in 1953, civilians were also allowed to obtain high school equivalency certificates by examination, and in 1963 the certificate was given its current name, the General Equivalency Diploma. The army considered the GED the equivalent of the high school diploma until 1991, when it formally rejected the notion of equivalency. The army found that GED holders flunked basic training at twice the rate of those with high school diplomas, and therefore, they could no longer consider the GED as equivalent to the high school diploma.[1] Nonetheless, the U.S. Census continues to count GED holders as having attained a high school diploma.[2] And school districts across the nation remove from the dropout list students who earn a GED.

For both Martin, Jr. and Felipe, the GED became a socially acceptable way of dropping out of school. It was risky, however. If they failed to carry through with their plans to go to college, then their chances of getting jobs as good as their fathers' were low. Research has demonstrated that adults whose terminal degree is a GED have wages similar to those of high school dropouts, not high school graduates.[3] Only those GED exam takers who score at the top are likely to have incomes at age 25 and 28 as good as those of high school graduates.[4]

In light of this evidence, it is hard to argue that adolescents should be encouraged to exit school with the GED rather than the high school diploma. Why then were these students encouraged by their parents to take the GED? Both fathers and sons would have preferred graduation from high school.

Martin, Jr. had few options. He had no interest in school and had simply stopped attending in the middle of the year. Martin, Jr.'s family hoped success at the GED would motivate Martin to get more education, by enrolling in the community college.

Juan Felipe knew that Felipe had a good attitude toward school, but he worried that his son might feel too old to be in high school. Students like Felipe, who were two years behind, had a 90% chance of dropping out.[5] To avoid his son's becoming a dropout, Juan Felipe encouraged Felipe to create an alternative educational plan. Felipe attended classes regularly and took and passed all of his final exams. He completed all of this coursework, earning enough credits to be a junior, and then officially dropped out, so that he could sign up for the GED tests and enroll in community college. Juan Felipe thought that Felipe would be happier as a college student, at an age when his agemates were entering college.

THE SCHOOLS

American schools do not meet the needs of many students, and a growing number of students, nationwide, are completing their educations with exam certification and receiving the General Equivalency Diploma. For example, in 1968, only 2% of high school–credentialed persons had the GED; in 1987, that number grew to 11%; in 1993, almost 14% of high school–credentialed persons had the GED.[6] Most states restrict the GED to students who are at least 18 and officially withdrawn from school. School officials worry that if the GED were available to younger students, more students would terminate their schooling prematurely. Their concern is justified.

For example, in the fall of 1991, the school district conducted a survey of high school students in order to find out what they thought caused students to drop out of school.[7] From a list of 13 possible causes, students were asked to check all that applied. Table 7.1 presents the results.

Lack of interest in school is by far the most common reason cited by the peers of Felipe and Martin, Jr. for dropping out of school. "Lack of interest in school" was the phrase Martin, Jr. would repeat to us whenever we asked him why he was having academic difficulties. Serious personal problems came in second, and this cause also applied to Martin, Jr.

When Martin, Jr. was 16, he told us that his parents had tried to get him some psychological help. But Martin resisted, saying, "We talked about it and they said maybe this is the best thing to do and I said I guess maybe it is. Maybe we ought to find out because if I don't know what's going on, well somebody has to help me out. So, we were going to try, but then all of a sudden I changed my mind. I just said, well I'm not going to go and just unload on somebody I don't know. If I'm going take my problems to somebody, it's going to be somebody I know and somebody I trust."

Precisely. Martin, Jr. would have taken his problems to somebody he knew and trusted—such as an adult he saw every day in school. The kind of person Martin would talk to had to be respected and liked by all students. This type of school staff member would have to be effective at persuading students with serious problems to get professional mental health services. This type of staff member would be able to link the work of mental health professionals to the students' classroom experiences. This type of staff member would organize peer support groups for students with similar problems and create extracurric-

TABLE 7.1.   Percentage of Students Agreeing with Specific Reason for
Dropping Out
"If you know students who are seriously considering dropping out of school
or who have already dropped out, why do you think they are dropping out?"

Specific Reason	Percent
Lack of interest in school	53
Serious personal problems	39
Serious family problems	34
Poor grades	29
Alcohol and/or drug problems	29
Discipline problems	23
Gang and/or criminal involvement	23
Not enough support at school	19
Financial problems	18
I do not know anyone dropping out of school well enough to answer question	14
I do not know anyone dropping out	13
Not enough academic help at school	13
Low intelligence	11

NOTE: These data were collected during the fall of 1991 from 2,073 high school students in the Austin Independent School District.

ular activities that promoted the personal and social development of students.
What Martin, Jr. needed in his school was a staff member who did this work,
but no one at his school had such a job.

Indeed, the high school counselors had caseloads of 500–1,000 students
and spent most of their time scheduling courses. They were not required to
organize and recruit students into activities that promoted personal and social
development. Instead, counselors, when not busy scheduling courses, spent
their time helping students in the college-preparatory tracks apply to colleges.

Both Martin, Sr. and Martin, Jr. told us that their high school counselor
was not effective in helping them. Martin, Sr. expressed it best when Harriett
Romo asked him about the resources available to help them help his son in his
school. Martin, Sr. had just explained that Martin, Jr. "did not like the school
environment, it didn't agree with him. . . ."

> HR: "Other than the school, was there any place you could go for
> help with school problems?"
> Martin, Sr.: "Oh, yeah. Talked with friends and discuss about their
> children and our children, of course. Talked to Martin about going to

counseling and stuff to see if that would help. He would always frown on it, didn't really want to go. Talked about doing it but he never would agree."

HR: "So there aren't really a lot of resources?"

Martin, Sr.: "Not that I can think of, no. To go out and help you right away. You go and talk to the counselors and it's really a hurried thing. They got something else to do."

The same survey, mentioned above, asked high school students for solutions to the dropout problem. There were 12 options and the students could choose all that they thought would encourage students to achieve or stay in school. The results are in Table 7.2.

Again, these results make sense in the light of Martin, Jr.'s experience. In response to our prompting, Martin, Jr. described his coursework this way: "Everything was basically straightforward. Sit down, read the book, answer questions. Nothing that would really catch your attention or keep you from falling asleep."

Similarly, the schools would have served Felipe's interests better if they had a more coherent way of dealing with his learning disabilities than simply retaining him twice in elementary school. Felipe did not receive any services for his learning disabilities when he was in elementary school. The schools' knowledge of his problems may have been lost in his many transitions from city to city, school to school, and parent to parent. We know that during junior high school, Felipe received special education services that his father described as helping him with his study skills.

But Felipe did not seek special education services when he went to high school, and Juan Felipe told us that he had simply forgotten to request them for Felipe. His honors-level biology teacher did some research on Felipe and discovered that he was qualified for special education. Felipe began receiving special instruction in ninth grade. But in the tenth grade, Felipe declined these services because they conflicted with the honors courses he preferred to take.

Felipe's schools had not succeeded in helping him or his father understand or accept Felipe's learning disabilities. The special educators had not made clear to them that learning disabilities are permanent and that Felipe would always need help with academic work. They had not convinced Felipe or his father that their services would make a significant difference in Felipe's school success. They should have. According to the district's analysis, students like Felipe had a lower annual dropout rate than the district average. The annual dropout rate for high school students like Felipe, those receiving fewer than

TABLE 7.2.   Percentage of Students Agreeing with Specific Causes of
Achieving/Staying in School
    "Students at my school would be more motivated to achieve/stay in school if:"

Specific Causes	Percent
Class content was more relevant to "real life"	46
Schools had more flexible hours so that students could work at their own pace	43
More rewards and recognition were available for academic work	37
Classes trained students for real jobs	36
Counselors had more time to talk to students about personal problems	31
Each student had a caring faculty advisor	25
There were more school support groups for students to discuss personal problems	24
Parents were more involved	23
Personal support services such as health services and child care were offered on campus	20
Classes were graded pass/fail	13
No changes are needed; students are motivated to achieve and stay in school	8
Students had to learn more in each class	8

NOTE: These data were collected during the fall of 1991 from 2,084 high school students in the Austin Independent School District.

three hours of special education services a day, was 8.7%, while the annual dropout rate districtwide for high school students was 9.8%.[8]

If accurate assessments both of their needs and of applicable special services had been available to Martin, Jr. and Felipe from early elementary school onward, they might have been able to graduate from high school with their age mates. Felipe definitely needed special education services, and it is possible that Martin, Jr., too, needed this type of assistance in school. If they had received prompt and effective treatment for their school problems, they would not have needed to resort to the GED.

POLICY RECOMMENDATIONS

We argue that our educational resources should be redirected away from ineffective programs, such as the GED, and toward dropout prevention. Indeed,

Cameron and Heckman[9] attribute the rise of the GED to the existence of federally funded programs aimed at eliminating poverty and unemployment. Dropouts have been likely to come from low-income households, and the poverty programs promoting the GED were supposed to help dropouts from disadvantaged backgrounds get some form of educational certificate that would help them get out of poverty. Over time, these programs expanded to serve all youth, regardless of the income status of their families.

We recommend that the federal support for the GED be phased out and that these funds be redirected toward dropout prevention. At the secondary school level, the funds redirected from GED training and test administration could be used to prevent students from losing interest in school. For example, these funds could be used to create career academies that provide the individual attention and relevance to "real life" that many "at risk" students need in order to stay in school.

At the primary school level, the federal funds currently devoted to the education of children from disadvantaged backgrounds (known as Chapter 1) could be used to pay for the educational services needed so that all children are kept on track academically. The Chapter 1 program has been widely regarded as having failed at meeting its objective: improving the educational outcomes for children of poverty. Chapter 1 funds could be used to assist school districts in the reorganization of their elementary schools so that all students continue to make academic progress and attain the skills they will need to succeed in middle and high school. Keeping all students on track academically is one of the most powerful strategies that the U.S. government has to help children escape a lifetime of poverty.

Funds for the special education and counseling services that many students need in order to stay in school may be more difficult to find. Most school districts do not have sufficient funds to pay for the number of additional school staff needed to help all students keep up with their schoolwork. Local taxpayers have been reluctant to pay for these services, assuming that such services ought to be paid for by medical insurance and provided at sites outside the school. But schools are the ideal environment for providing many services to children and adolescents, not only because the students routinely attend school and are familiar with school personnel, but also because success in school depends on the delivery of these services.

Students like Martin, Jr. and Felipe had medical coverage, but their medical insurance did not help them. For Martin, Jr., his medical insurance covered only counseling outside of school—the type that he rejected because he didn't want to discuss his problems with strangers. Likewise, for Felipe, his medical coverage excluded the treatment of his learning disabilities, even though his disability was probably caused by a variation in his neurological development.[10]

We can only hope that revisions in the ways Americans pay for their health care will allow for some health services to be provided as a routine part of schooling for all students. Certainly, mental health services, as well as treatment for learning disabilities *in school* should be part of any overhaul of the American health care delivery system. The educational success of children is determined strongly by the existence of strong linkages between mental health and special education services and children's experiences within their classrooms. Furthermore, some educational and health services need to be provided more often than what most school systems currently provide. If Martin, Jr. had difficulty reading, then summer school classes and a Saturday morning program aimed at reading could have benefited him. Felipe's father was right that Felipe, because of his learning disabilities, would have benefited from weekend and summertime training, but the school systems were not organized to meet his needs. Not only were special education services limited to the nine-month school calendar, but also they did not follow him when he went to another city to spend his summer with his noncustodial parent.

Ultimately, schools need to reorganize so that meeting the needs of all students becomes their primary goal. At present, schools exist to provide an educational service, regardless of whether that service is effective in bringing all students up to the required level for high school graduation. We may always need some form of the GED, especially for adults. Nonetheless, our resources should not be spent on encouraging its prevalence, but on changing schools so that they keep all students moving forward on the pathway toward earning a high school diploma.

"*I guess*	# Bureaucratic
no one	# Glitches
wants me."	

This chapter tells the story of Pedro García and our efforts to return him to school. His story illustrates how the bureaucratic nature of our schools can create obstacles for students who wish to make educational progress. We describe the communication problems between schools and parents when schools refuse to accept the fact that many parents are not literate or able to understand English or the American educational system. We explain how theories of management, notably "scientific management," are at the core of American education and how these theories create administrative nightmares for students and parents. We make suggestions for new ways of managing schools that eliminate the layers of administrators and rules now common in urban school districts.

BACKGROUND

Harriett Romo first met the García family in 1982 when she was working on the research for her doctoral dissertation about undocumented immigrant families in Austin. The García family came from a small rural village in central Mexico and migrated to Texas in order to get jobs. Neither parent spoke English, and they were totally illiterate in Spanish. They did not know how to sign their names. In order to keep track of services for her family, the mother kept a notebook in which she taped the business cards of doctors, social workers, and other officials. She learned to recognize the logos from the cards, and in this way she was able to locate telephone numbers when she needed them.

When the family first moved to Austin, the mother attended several meetings at the elementary school her children attended. Harriett accompanied her to one of these meetings during which the parents were asked to play a Bingo game as a get-acquainted activity. The game required parents to go up to other parents and have them sign their Bingo cards. Every time Mrs. García was approached, she had to explain she could not write her name. By the time she left the meeting, she was shaking and tears welled in her eyes.

When the family came to Texas, they had six children. At that time, Mrs. García told Harriett that she believed that she already had more children than the family could take care of adequately. When Mrs. García went into labor with her seventh child, Harriett helped the midwife deliver the baby at the García home. When Mrs. García got pregnant with the eighth child, she wanted a hospital delivery that would include a sterilization. But when she went to the hospital for the delivery, she discovered that she could not get a sterilization because she had not applied for the sterilization in advance. Getting sterilized required an application process and a waiting period. Eventually, through Harriett's efforts, money was donated to Planned Parenthood so that Mrs. García could have a sterilization at a clinic.

The oldest child, Sofia, began school in the United States at age 13, right after the family arrived. She was placed in the sixth grade knowing little English and having attended little school in Mexico. She dropped out two years later after giving birth to her first child. By then, she had acquired a fairly good command of oral English and adequate English literacy skills to be able to handle bills and correspondence, telephone calls, doctors' visits, and other demands that confronted her parents.

The Garcías' next two children were also daughters. The second born was able to earn a high school diploma before her first baby arrived. However, the school district did not allow her to walk across the stage because she was pregnant. She received her diploma in the mail.

The third daughter did not succeed in avoiding motherhood before earning her high school diploma, and she dropped out after the birth of her first child. Although she tried to return to school, she was not able to juggle the roles of mother, student, and part-time worker, and she dropped out again. When we began our study of "at risk" youth in 1988, Harriett invited this daughter to participate because she was still in school at that time and the same age as all our other volunteer students. However, this daughter was making good grades, and the Garcías preferred that we consider their next child, Pedro, who was flunking out of school. Thus, although Pedro was only 14 when we began the study, we included him in our sample because he was otherwise qualified, being both "at risk" and Hispanic.

PEDRO

Pedro was four years old when he arrived in the U.S. and six when he began learning English in the first grade. Nonetheless, he was identified as "Gifted and Talented" and given special instruction in elementary school. His academic performance continued at a high level until the seventh grade when his involvement with his peer group led him to miss a lot of school. Even though he would get perfect scores on many of his junior high school exams, he received no credit for much of his junior high school coursework because of his unexcused absences. On the last day of seventh grade, he had a fight with another student in school, and when he returned to the eighth grade after the summer break, he discovered he had been assigned to a special school for students with severe behavioral problems. He attended this school for one semester, after which the principal recommended that he return to his home campus. However, Pedro wanted to go to a different school to be with his friends, and rather than work out this disagreement with the school district, Pedro simply spent the second semester of eighth grade at home, watching TV or working with one of his sisters as a janitor in the evenings.

On August 8, 1991, Harriett went to Pedro's house to interview him as part of our project. The family lived in a working-class residential area of Austin in a three-bedroom brick house. The walls and fences in the neighborhood were covered with gang graffiti. Several old appliances that Mr. García was trying to repair sat in the yard. Potted plants decorated the front porch. The regular school year began on August 26, and Harriett wondered if Pedro was planning to return.

When she arrived Pedro was in his room, and he had to be coaxed out by his sisters. Pedro was 16 at that time.

> HR: "Your sister said you were going to try to go back to school."
> Pedro: "Like, I mean, last year I didn't really go to school and the year before that I only went for like half a year and that's not going to do me any good because I've already seen what I can do without an education and it's nothing. It's not enough money."

Pedro had tried to get a better job but discovered that the major employers did not hire people as young as 16 for good jobs. He needed to be 18 and have a high school diploma in order to get any job with a future.

Pedro had a major problem in terms of the school bureaucracy. Because he had not accumulated enough credits in junior high school to qualify as a ninth grader, the district wanted him to return to junior high school. Pedro did not want to do that because his younger brother would be in the same grade at that school. Pedro wanted to go to high school with his friends and finish in two years. He thought that by combining summer school with hard work in a special program during the school year, he could finish high school in two years.

He had considered the GED and community-college route, but the types of jobs at the end of this educational pathway did not appeal to him. He wanted to be a lawyer or a doctor. He wanted to go to college, and he thought he needed a high school diploma. He wanted to get started in school and work right away.

Pedro told Harriett, "I mean right now, where I could start working right now and that I could make it a career or like, I could get trained for something. Like I could work there and the things I learned there I could use for something. I don't want to wait. I want to, right now."

Harriett and Pedro discussed his situation and agreed that at his age the best thing for him to do was to go back to school, and in the course of his studies job opportunities might arise. But the first step was getting him back in school. Pedro didn't know how to do this. It was still early in the afternoon on August 8, so Harriett decided to help Pedro get back in school. The following is her account of this quest.

RETURNING PEDRO TO SCHOOL

From Pedro's house on August 8, I looked up the telephone number and called the high school that, according to Pedro, he should attend. This was a Thursday, and school administrative staff were supposed to be on the school sites beginning August 1 to prepare for the beginning of school. The principal answered the telephone, and I explained Pedro's situation. She responded that the high school would need a letter from the junior high school showing the classes Pedro had passed; a copy of his last report card would do. I hung up and asked Pedro about the report card. We looked for it, but since Pedro had been out of school so long, he could find no recent report card at home.

I called the high school back, and the receptionist answered the telephone this time. I explained the situation again, including the fact that we had no recent report card. She suggested that I call the junior high school or call the student records office at the district level.

I decided to try the junior high school first. The person answering the telephone at the junior high school explained that the counselors would not return to school for another week and that they were the ones who would have to help me. The high school principal had given me the telephone number for the district-level office of secondary education, so I decided to try there. At this number, they referred me to the pupil services division. By this time, it was 4:00 P.M., and I got recorded telephone messages telling me that the district offices were only open from 7:30 A.M. to 4:00 P.M. One of the messages referred me to another number where I could leave a message. I left my name, telephone number, and a brief message about my desire to enroll a student who had been out of school for over a year and had no school documents.

By Monday, August 12, I had not received any response to my recorded message, so I began calling the school district office once again. I called the student records office, and the person answering listened to my description of the situation but informed me that the pupil records are confidential and that if I was not the parent of the student, they could not provide any information. I explained that I was a friend of the family, that the parents were illiterate and did not speak English. She transferred me to "Elizabeth." I repeated Pedro's story, and Elizabeth explained that they did not have any grades recorded at the district office, and I would have to get that information from the school. I explained that personnel at the school level had told me that I had to get this information from the district level because the school counselors had not returned to work yet. She offered to provide a letter showing what courses Pedro had taken. I provided my name and address, and she assured me that she would mail the information promptly. I called Pedro and told him that as soon as the letter arrived, I would take him to the high school to see what could be done.

On Tuesday afternoon, August 13, another district-level staff called my home responding to the recorded message I had left the week before. I felt that I had been successful, so I thanked the caller and explained that Elizabeth had taken my name and address and had promised to send me the information needed to enroll Pedro.

On August 14, worried that I had not received the letter showing the courses Pedro had taken, I called Elizabeth's office again. This time she told me that it was the school's responsibility to provide the record of the report card. I explained again that I had already contacted the school and that the counselors were not available. I reminded her that she had promised to send me a letter showing what courses he had taken. She left the phone to check her records. She returned and reported that she had mailed a letter on June 11, 1991. I was puzzled, since I had not called her until August 12. After checking parents' names and birth dates, she determined that she had confused Pedro with another child with the same last name. She seemed completely confused about which student we were talking about, but she emphasized that her office had no access to students' grades and that I would have to get that information at the school level. She said she had no record of my previous request for the letter, and explained that the "machine [a computer] was not doing things" for her and she could not help me. I never received a letter, and it was never clear what happened to my request for such a letter and her agreement to provide it.

I decided to call the alternative school that Pedro had mentioned and try to enroll him in the special programs the district provides for dropouts. No one thus far had known what kind of program Pedro qualified for, since he was 16 years old but had not completed the courses required for graduation from the junior high program. I called the alternative school listed in the telephone book, and the principal answered. I explained Pedro's situation. The principal responded that the alternative school only took students who had sufficient credits to be at the high school level. She told me I would have to call the district-level office and have them make an individual decision about the correct placement for Pedro. She explained that the new policy was to deal with overaged, middle school students on a case-by-case basis. I hung up, and then realized that I had not gotten a specific name or telephone number to call.

I had not had much luck at the district level with Elizabeth, so I decided to try the junior high school again, since that was the last school where Pedro was officially enrolled. I reasoned that more than a week had passed, so the counselors might be available on the school site now. The principal answered the phone at the junior high school and transferred me to the registrar's office. I told Pedro's story to the registrar and explained that I would like to get him back in school. She replied, "I don't know exactly what is needed . . . you probably need a report card or something." She put me on hold while she checked her computer. She was able to pull up Pedro's records after I gave her his birth date and the names of his parents. She did not bring up the issue that I was not his parent. She explained that he had enrolled at the junior high school in the fall of 1990, although he entered school a month late, on October 3. The records showed that he came for only a few days and was dropped from classes because of absences. He did not receive any grades, and as a result, he did not have a recent report card. She said she thought he was too old to attend classes at the junior high school, and transferred me to the attendance secretary to see if she had any official records for him.

The attendance secretary remembered Pedro. She explained that he did not pass the eighth grade and would need to be placed in a special program. According to her records, he received "straight 50s" (all failing grades) through the fourth six-week period because of absences. There were no grades at all for the last two grading periods. He was officially recorded as dropping out in January of 1991—two full school years after he started missing classes and failing. The secretary reported that she did not know "what they had him in—regular classes or not." She recalled that she had thought for a while that he would stay in. He had talked to her and told her that he felt too old to attend the classes at the junior high school. The secretary emphasized that she was "only the secretary and was not supposed to get involved," but she suggested that I call the high school principal and talk to her. She explained that since Pedro had not passed any of his eighth grade classes, he was not officially a high school student, but that her daughter attended this high school, and she felt the principal would try to help.

The name she gave me turned out to be the same name I had initially looked up in the telephone book and the same person I had spoken to when I began the effort to reenroll Pedro. It was now two weeks later, and thus far I had talked to nine different staff/offices trying to enroll Pedro—the high school principal, the secondary education office, the district registrar's office, the district-level pupil services office where I was referred to the extension office, "Elizabeth's office," the junior high school principal, the junior high school counselor, and the junior high school attendance secretary who had referred me back to the high school principal. We had made no progress.

Realizing that a telephone strategy wasn't working, I decided to take Pedro with me and go in person to the school. On Wednesday, August 21, I arrived at his house at 10 A.M. No one else was at home, and he was still asleep. He answered the door and got dressed quickly when I told him that we were going to the high school to try to enroll him. We drove to the high school, which was quite a distance from his home and not on a direct bus line. It would have been difficult for him to get to the school without a car.

We went to the main office. The principal was in a meeting with teachers, but a special education teacher assisting in the office talked with us. She asked if Pedro had ever been in any special education programs, and he responded that he had not. She suggested that we try the alternative school. I explained that I had called there and the principal told me they were only accepting students who were at high school level (ninth grade), and Pedro had not completed eighth grade. She suggested that we go down the hall and talk with the high school counselor.

We went to the counselor's office, but no one was there. We tried the office next door, and the secretary there began telephoning around to other offices to locate the counselor. The special education teacher came and told us that the counselor was in the hall putting up a bulletin board and we could talk to him there. The counselor, a small, balding Hispanic man in his late forties or early fifties, stopped his work and listened as I explained that Pedro had been out of school and we were trying to reenroll him. He immediately turned to Pedro and asked him why he was not in school. When Pedro replied that he was too old for eighth grade, the counselor gave him a brief lecture about how he had gone back to school at age 22, how he currently had several students who were that old and still in school, trying to graduate. He explained that he was the senior counselor and busy with scholarships and did not have time to try to help Pedro, who he said was not his responsibility. He elaborated on his responsibilities, emphasizing that he worked with the students who spoke no English at all and the graduating seniors. We would have to see the ninth-grade counselor, who was not there that day, or the registrar. He suggested that we go to the registrar's office. He was rushed and spoke in an annoyed tone. It was evident that he did not want to be bothered with Pedro's problem.

The registrar was in her office and asked us to sit down and wait a few minutes. She was Hispanic also, but needed Pedro to spell out his first and last name for her. She did not know what to do with Pedro either, since he had no eighth-grade credits but was now high school age. She offered to call the district office to see what could be done. The first number she called turned out to be a wrong number and connected her with the elementary school office. The person she spoke with recommended a junior high school counselor, and she called his office. No one answered. She decided to try again to reach the secondary education office and this time reached an associate superintendent. That person recommended that we try the alternative school. I explained that I had called the alternative school and the principal there had told us they were only taking students with high school credits. The registrar and the superintendent discussed Pedro's situation briefly, then she turned to us and explained that the superintendent told her the alternative school was testing for admission that same day at 2:00 P.M. and I should take Pedro there. If he could complete the test, he could enroll at the alternative school, earn enough credits to complete the eighth grade, and then transfer to his regular high school.

It was 11:00 A.M. and the testing was in three hours. We were about 25 minutes away from the testing location. I decided to take Pedro to get a hamburger, take him with me to run some errands, and then drop him off for the tests at 2:00. I wondered why no one that we had talked to previously had mentioned the tests. The registrar made several other calls to make sure Pedro's name was on the list to take the tests. As we waited, Pedro and I talked. He squirmed at each call that ended without resolving the issue. He commented at one point, "*I guess no one wants me.*" Finally, the test was arranged, and Pedro and I left, thanking the registrar for her assistance.

As we drove across town, Pedro talked about current events. He told me that his sisters brought home used newspapers for him every day from the fast-food restaurant where they worked. He read these newspapers and kept up with the television news. He talked about national leaders by name and expressed opinions about world events. He explained his concerns about the earth's ozone layer. As we ordered our hamburgers, Pedro noted in detail the differences in the menu between the restaurant where we ate and the fast-food restaurant where his sisters worked. After lunch, I drove Pedro to the alternative school for the tests.

As we arrived at the school at 1:45 P.M., several cars were lined up to get into the parking lot. The majority taking the tests were African American, but there were several Latinos and a small number of Anglo students as well. Many of them were accompanied by their mothers. Pedro looked around as we entered the building and commented, "This school is old." Trucks were delivering furniture, and several repair people worked on projects in various parts of the building. Boxes were piled in the dark hallways.

We entered the main office where two lines of students and parents, three deep, waited to be helped. A heavy-set African American woman directed people around. She informed me that Pedro could take the tests, but that "you still have to apply." She would hold the test results until she had a completed application on file for Pedro. She explained that the schools, not individuals, were supposed to send students to be tested for the alternative program. When I explained that Pedro had been out of school for a year and a half, she told us that the tests had been advertised in the newspaper and on TV. Neither Pedro nor I had seen these advertisements.

The woman directed everyone downstairs to the cafeteria for the tests. At this point, we still had no idea what type of tests Pedro was taking, but he did not seem nervous. I asked him how he did on tests, and he told me he had passed the test required for graduation with a high score and felt confident that he could read well. He expressed a little concern because he had been out of school for so long and worried that he might have forgotten some things. After we read the form that said a student had to have a sixth-grade reading and math ability to get into the program, Pedro felt confident that the tests would be no problem.

The test forms were all in English, as were the application forms and requests for family information. Pedro's parents would not have been able to fill out any of this paperwork, even if it had been in Spanish, since they were illiterate. The school director informed me that Pedro's parents and the school counselor had to sign the application forms before he would be considered, even though the forms were designed for students being referred directly from the school. I explained that Pedro had not been enrolled in school for over a year and that he had not been referred by the school, but she insisted we had to have the counselor referral anyway.

I left Pedro to take the tests. When I returned to the school after an hour and 45 minutes, Pedro had been waiting only a short time. He reported that the tests were like achievement tests, and he thought he had done well. He told me that he had talked to a math teacher whom he had known from the school for students with behavior problems. Pedro liked this African American teacher and seemed pleased that he was there. He expressed positive feelings about attending the school.

Although it was now 4 P.M., we decided to try to get the counselor referral signature to complete part of Pedro's application. His junior high school was on the other side of town near Pedro's house, about 25 minutes away. We arrived at the school at 4:30 and were relieved to see several cars still parked in the parking lot behind the school. We tried the front door, but it was locked. Pedro and I decided to drive around the back. The rear door was locked also, but we waited until someone came to the door. A woman came to the door and explained that the school was not open. I persisted, explaining that Pedro had attended the school previously, that we were trying to enroll him in the alternative school, and that the alternative program required a counselor's signature before he could enroll. She took the form and said she would try to find someone who would help us. Pedro and I waited outside the locked door. She returned shortly and reported that the principal was there and he would see Pedro. We went into his office. He remembered Pedro and agreed to sign the form for him. Pedro and I were both pleased. Pedro had never reported any negative feelings about the junior high school staff and repeatedly said they had given him "lots of chances."

The principal wrote on the form that Pedro had enrolled in an alternative learning program at the junior high school and signed the referral. Pedro looked over his shoulder and protested that he was never in the alternative program at the junior high school, that he had wanted those classes, but the principal never gave them to him. The principal ignored his complaints and gave him a brief lecture about taking advantage of this opportunity. We thanked him and headed to Pedro's house to have his parents sign the form. All the way home, Pedro protested that he had never been in the alternative learning program at the junior high and wondered why the principal said he was.

We arrived at Pedro's house, but his parents were not home. I knew from previous work with this family that the parents were illiterate. I also knew that immigrant children often took the responsibility of signing official forms for their parents, so I suggested that Pedro could sign for his parents. He did not feel comfortable doing that. As we pondered what to do, his older sister, Sofia, drove into the driveway. Pedro said she could sign the forms, and called her over to my car. Sofia took the forms and began teasing Pedro, "How long ya gonna stay this time? Huh? How long?" The younger brother and sisters laughed and joined in the teasing. Sofia signed the forms and Pedro thanked me. I assured him that I would return the forms to the alternative school.

On Friday morning, August 23, I took the forms over to the alternative school. The principal was not on the campus. The secretary told me she was not officially allowed to tell me if Pedro had passed the test until the principal had looked at the list and put her mark on it. I explained that he lived a long way away and I would like to let him know as soon as possible if he would be attending school on Monday. She decided she could go look and tell me if he had passed the tests, but it would not be official until late afternoon after the principal approved the list. She would call Pedro at that time. She looked up his scores and told me that he had passed. She asked which session he would like to attend. I had checked all three—8:00–11:00 A.M., 12:30–4:00 P.M., and the evening session—thinking that flexibility might give him more of an opportunity for admission. She decided to talk with him when they called about the scores to find out which session he preferred.

I inquired about transportation to the school on Monday when classes started. I knew this would be a problem because no one in Pedro's family could drive him to the school. The secretary told me that there were no school buses scheduled to pick up students in Pedro's neighborhood. She did say that I could call the district transportation office and try to arrange for a bus. A bus would not be available the first few days of school, but it could be made available after that. She looked through her files and could not find the phone number for the transportation office. She said I could look it up in the phone book.

I looked up the telephone number for the school district's main office and asked for the Office of Transportation. The director himself spoke to me about Pedro's situation. He told me that it was the school's responsibility to arrange for Pedro's transportation and that there was a school bus stop several blocks from Pedro's home. He also explained that there were no buses for half-day students, like Pedro, but that Pedro could take the public buses and use tokens provided by his school. In this way, Pedro would not have to pay for his own transportation.

I was amazed that the woman who worked in the school office had told me none of this. She had talked to me as if it were my responsibility to arrange bus transportation. I wondered how Pedro's parents could have coped with the bureaucratic maze of the school system. After all our efforts to get the application materials turned in before school began, Pedro would not be notified of his test results until late Friday and there would be no transportation to get him there the next Monday. No one had the correct number to call to arrange the bus, and it could not be arranged on Friday anyway because Pedro was not officially enrolled until the principal approved the list.

The school year started and I did not have an opportunity to find out if Pedro had gone to school until Thursday of that week. At 9:30 A.M. I called the alternative school to see if Pedro had enrolled. The secretary answering the phone turned to someone in the background, "Does the name Pedro ring a bell? When did he start? I don't have anything on him." She reported that he was accepted and had been called, but that he had not filled out the emergency forms that were necessary for enrollment.

Emergency forms? No one had mentioned the emergency forms during my visits to the school. When I asked for the registration forms on the morning I turned in his application forms, I was told that they could not give me the enrollment forms until after he had passed the tests and was officially accepted. The secretary explained, "There is no need to give the registration forms if he hasn't passed the test." I had discovered that the process of getting a student into an alternative classroom was complex. First, a student had to find out about the school and the admission tests. Next, the student had to apply, which included getting a counselor's recommendation and filling out application forms. Then, if the student passed the test and was approved by the principal, he or she had to fill out enrollment forms. Finally, the school had additional forms, required by law, such as the emergency-information forms, which had to be signed by parents in order for the enrollment to be complete. These stages of enrollment made it more complicated for Pedro to return to school.

I called Pedro's house and Sofia answered. When I asked for Pedro, she replied that he was in school. She explained that he had taken the city bus over to the school. Sofia knew about the emergency cards because she had filled them out and signed them for Pedro. I called the school again, but no one had seen Pedro, and no one had any record of him picking up the emergency forms. I told the receptionist about my conversation with his sister. She suggested that I leave my name and telephone number and said she would call me back.

At 10:30 A.M. the attendance clerk at the alternative school called my office and informed me that Pedro had shown up with the emergency cards. The office had sent him off to classes. I felt a tremendous sense of pride in Pedro for persisting and getting back to school. I felt that now that he was back in school, all would go well.

I heard nothing from Pedro or the alternative school for several weeks. Then on October 16, I received a message from the counselor at the alternative school requesting that I return his call. I called the next morning at 9 A.M. The phone rang and rang, but no one answered. I tried later the same day, and again no one answered. I tried several other times, on different days and still got no answer. I thought perhaps the message had been taken incorrectly and the number was wrong. I decided to go by the school to see what the message was about.

When I arrived, the school was cheery and attractive. I walked into the counselors' offices, and eight students sat or stood around in the small foyer waiting, but there was no one at the desk. I went next door to the main office where two secretaries worked behind a counter. A mother with two small children, one asleep on her shoulder, sat waiting on a bench. I asked if I could speak to one of the counselors. The secretary looked up and directed me back to the first room I had entered. I returned to that room to wait.

After a short while, a tall, thin African American man entered the waiting room. One of the secretaries had told him I was waiting to see him. He showed me into his office, a small cubicle with a desk, two chairs, and a couple of file cabinets. I apologized for taking so long to respond to his call. He told me that he had met Pedro at the school for students with discipline problems, and I realized that this was the teacher Pedro had liked and felt comfortable talking to. He showed me a list of names with Pedro's name highlighted and explained that Pedro had missed 40 days since school began. He explained that the pattern was that Pedro would show up and then miss several days, then show up again and miss. When I asked if transportation had been arranged for Pedro, the counselor could find no evidence that it had. Pedro's mother did not drive, and his father's license had been revoked because he had been caught driving while intoxicated too many times. Apparently, Pedro got to the school on the city bus, which cost him $2 every day, a significant expense for his family. I had not talked to Pedro since I enrolled him, and apparently he had not found out from the school about the bus tokens.

The counselor told me that the principal was ready to throw Pedro out of the school. The counselor was trying to give Pedro one last chance. He had talked to Pedro that very morning in the cafeteria and had promised to help him find a job if he attended school consistently for two weeks.

We began talking about Pedro. The counselor said that he knew Pedro was bright and that he had been assigned to the school for behavior problems because Pedro had been a member of a large and prominent gang. The counselor said that the fights Pedro had been involved in were gang related.

Pedro had not completed any course since enrolling in this alternative school. The counselor did not have any of Pedro's academic records because those were maintained by the teachers. Pedro had asked that they give him work to do at home, but the counselor explained that the program was not set up to do that because they wanted to be sure the students did their own work.

The counselor checked the enrollment file and reported that Pedro had scored at the eleventh grade level on the math test and twelfth grade level on reading on the admissions tests and that, therefore, he should not have trouble with the academic work. Since I had been a public school teacher, I asked if I could visit Pedro in his classroom and see how he was doing so that I could tutor him or help him at home. The counselor thought that would be a good idea and went to get his schedule from the main office. He came back shortly and said the principal would like to see me.

The principal, a formidable African American woman, asked if I were the parent or legal guardian of Pedro. I showed her my university ID card, indicating that I was a college professor, and I explained that I would like to volunteer at the school so that I could help Pedro. I also explained that I had known the family for a long time and had helped them in other difficult situations. She told me in no unclear terms that I could not have any information about Pedro's academic record or visit his classroom unless I were his legal guardian or parent. I would have to make an appointment with the teacher and bring the parents with me in order to have a conference about Pedro. I explained that his parents did not speak English and asked if his teachers spoke Spanish. The principal told me that the teacher did not speak Spanish, but that they had a bilingual counselor and I could set up the meeting for the parents with her. She insisted that the parents would have to take a day off from work and come to the school before I could be given any information about Pedro. After my prodding, she agreed that the parents could give me authority in writing to find out about Pedro, but she would not talk to them over the phone because she would not be able to discern whom she was talking to. When I explained that the parents did not read or write or speak English, she insisted that they would just have to come to the school. She gave me the bilingual counselor's telephone number and name and advised me to set up a conference about Pedro's work.

I found my face burning as she talked to me. I respected the legal constraints of student confidentiality and did not ask to see Pedro's grades or student files, but the principal's behavior made me angry. She showed little willingness to help Pedro or his parents. Overall, she made me feel very unwelcome and implied that I was acting improperly. Her major concern was to follow district policy and protect student privacy, not help students stay in school. She did, however, give me permission to visit a classroom—one not containing Pedro—so that I could see what the school's program was like.

I went home and called Pedro's house. I woke up his father who had been working all night. Mr. García worked illegally at a produce company loading and unloading fruit from 4 A.M. to 10 A.M. When I explained about needing their permission to try to help Pedro at school, he said he did not think Pedro was doing well because he stayed up late watching TV and was too tired to get up in the morning. Mr. García said that he could not come to the school because he worked all night, and after he slept a little, had to take care of his young children after school and his grandchildren in the evening while their mothers worked.

I offered to take Mrs. García home, if she could come to the school with Pedro on the city bus. But Mr. García explained that his wife had been working double shifts, even on her days off, because they needed extra money and that he did not think she could take time off to go to the school. Mr. García was concerned about Pedro but said that all he could do was talk to him. He could not make Pedro do anything that he did not want to do.

In short, neither he nor his wife was able to come to the school.

THE FAMILY

The Garcías had made significant progress since arriving in Austin. They first lived in a low-income, two-bedroom apartment, but they were forced out when the apartment owner transformed the units into a Section 8 low-income housing unit. The large García family did not conform to the federal guidelines regulating number of people per bedroom. Then the family moved into a small, high-rent, two-bedroom house in a predominantly Black neighborhood. This house was later condemned because of poor construction and inadequate plumbing. Next the family moved to a larger rental house shared with another family. Finally, they managed to get a loan to purchase a small, three-bedroom brick house. The loan agreement for the house included a balloon clause, and the parents and older children worked hard to make the house payments and to save money for the delayed mortgage payment. The people who lived in their neighborhood were primarily of Mexican origin, and there were several Mexican American gangs active in this area.

In order to pay their mortgage and to support their family, both parents worked as many jobs as they could find. Mr. García had operated heavy equipment on highway construction jobs when the family first immigrated to Austin, but with the Texas recession of the late 1980s and the newly enforced sanctions against employers for hiring undocumented workers, he had a difficult time finding consistent work during the time of our study.

Shortly after the family purchased their house, Mr. García spent almost a year in jail for drunk driving. This occurred while Pedro was in junior high school. Pedro was angry that his father had been taken away from him and the family. This was the period when Pedro became involved with gang members and started missing a lot of school.

After his father was released from jail, the police caught Pedro and a group of friends spraying graffiti on a wall. The police brought Pedro home and fined the parents $25 because he was not in school. From that time on, according to both Pedro and his parents, Pedro had little contact with his gang friends and either did janitorial work or stayed home at night.

Mrs. García and her Mexican-born children received their legal U.S. residency permits by applying under the 1986 Immigration Reform and Control Act amnesty program. She used the children's school records as documentation that the family had resided in the U.S. for the required time period. Her work site refused to provide official documentation.

Since Pedro's father had several drunk-driving arrests on his record, he was not eligible for legal resident status. During the early 1980s, Mr. García was picked up at one work site by immigration officers and deported. He was able to return to Austin within a week, by paying a smuggler. In 1991, however, Mr. García was fighting deportation again. This time, he was assisted by an attorney who had asked Harriett Romo to write a deposition describing the family history and the father's role in the family.

Throughout the course of our study, both parents expressed their belief that their children needed an education to get good jobs. They appreciated that their older daughters had gone to school and had learned things that benefited the entire family. Mr. García lamented that he had had no opportunity to go to school in Mexico and could not understand why Pedro had not taken advantage of the schooling opportunities in the U.S. Mr. García explained, "Mi esposa y yo, no tuvimos escuela, pues, por eso les decíamos a ellos ahora, verdad, que ellos tienen la oportunidad que le echen ganas, ¿verdad? Porque ya que nosotros no, no pudimos. Y por eso es que nos vamos dando una idea de como las muchachas, ya saben más o menos como va . . . como nosotros no, no sabemos. Por ejemplo, las respuestas o como se habla en la escuela, ¿verdad? Ellas nos ayudan. Por ejemplo, más Eva, porque ella es, es más activa, ¿no? Y eso nos, nos está sirviendo mucho para, para poder." (My wife and I didn't, didn't have school, uh, because of this we tell them [the children] they have the opportunity if they have the desire, true? Because now we couldn't, we couldn't [go to school]. And because of that we keep giving them the idea, that the daughters, now they know more or less; like we don't, we don't know. For example, the answers or how they speak in the school, right? The girls help us. For example, more Eva [one of his older daughters], because she is more active, right? And this serves us well, to get ahead.)

When asked what plans he had for Pedro, Mr. García told us, "A mí me gustaría pues en primer lugar que termine su escuela. Que fuera al colegio. Pues, sería una solución, sería lo que a él le gustaría, ¿verdad? Yo lo que trato de hacer es por su futuro no por mí. Porque ya para mí no, es decir no vale ya nada, ¿verdad? si yo estudiara." (I would like first of all for Pedro to finish school. And then go to college. This would be a solution, if it were what he wanted, right? What I want is for him, for his future, not for me. Because for me, it isn't worth it, right? if I were to study.)

Mr. García apologized for not being able to express himself well. He summed up our interview by saying, "Ellos van para adelante, y yo los dejo, ¿verdad? Y yo iría, ya voy para abajo, ¿verdad? Y espero un día, ¿verdad?, que cambie esta vida tanto como para ellos que para mí . . . pues, trabajando muy poco y por eso, pues . . . claro ya van para grandes, empiezan ellas a hablar con nostros sobre ya del futuro. Ya no es lo mismo, ¿verdad? que nostros." (They [his children] are going forward, and I let them go, right? And I am going, now I'm going down, true? And I hope one day, right? I hope this life changes for them and for me, because I am working very little, and because of this, well . . . clearly, they are growing up, they are beginning to talk with us about the future. Now it is not the same, right? the same as for us.)

THE SCHOOL

Recall that the principal at Pedro's alternative school had given Harriett Romo permission to visit a classroom as long as it did not contain Pedro. Harriett returned to the school two days after her initial contact with the principal and, with her permission, sat in a classroom for about one hour to observe. At the beginning of the period, the Mexican American teacher had 17 students. Students were given their own plastic containers of materials to study and were expected to complete the assignments on their own. When students needed help, they raised their hands and the teacher went to them and quietly answered their questions. Otherwise, the teacher sat at her desk and worked on her own stack of paperwork. She was responsible for 44 students. The only voices heard in the room were those of the teacher and the student as they talked about that student's individual problem.

There were no lectures, no group discussions, no demonstrations, no hands-on experiences for the students. Each student worked on something different, and they were not allowed to take any of these materials home. The students in this class worked on a variety of subjects, including Algebra I, Pre-Algebra, Geometry, World History, World Geography, English II, English IV, Health, Literature, U.S. History, and Economics. The teacher was positive and supportive. She seemed to be doing the best she could in a difficult classroom setting.

When a student passed the test for a course, four teachers had to sign off on the completion. The main teacher signing had to be certified in the subject being passed. The classroom teacher told us that some students had passed the course but were checked as "No Credit" because of absences.

Both the teacher and the counselor told Harriett that many students became discouraged because their progress was so slow. It was hard to stay motivated to learn when the students were isolated from one another, had little group work, and were expected to teach themselves almost everything. We were not surprised that the annual dropout rate for students in the seventh or eighth grade level at this school was almost 50%.[1]

GLITCHES

Pedro's experiences were not unusual. In our sample, 28% of the students reported having at least one problem with the administrative rules of the schools. Each of these administrative glitches were similar in severity to the one that Pedro experienced. The only difference was that we tried to resolve this problem with Pedro and in the process came to understand how hard these problems are to solve. In addition to excessive absences (Pedro's problem), these glitches often revolved around penalties for lost books, or incorrectly recorded grades, credits, or absences. Many parents told us that they tried to communicate with the school to resolve these problems, but the schools failed to respond to them in meaningful ways.

We conducted a few statistical analyses to determine if there was a connection between these administrative glitches and dropping out. When we correlated the incidence of glitches (recall that 28% of the students or their parents reported at least one of them) with the student's graduation status, we found no statistically significant relationship.[2] This finding suggested that there was no direct relationship between administrative glitches and dropping out. In general, parents who have the time, transportation, literacy skills, and emotional stamina to overcome administrative hassles can help their children get an education.

However, we found that the more children parents had, the greater the likelihood that their children would encounter problems with the school bureaucracy.[3] When parents had larger numbers of children, their ability to keep up with the administrative demands of the school system was overwhelmed. These parents did not have the time to spend closely monitoring each of their children's educational progress, and they often did not have the ability to untangle the administrative snarls that adolescents can create.

SCHOOL ADMINISTRATION

It is safe to say that American public schools operate under more laws, rules, policies, and court mandates than do the schools in any of the other nations of the industrialized world.[4] And yet, not only do our high schools graduate students with lower academic skills than do the other industrialized nations, but also our schools graduate a smaller proportion of our students. Is it possible that all of our laws, rules, policies, and court mandates not only retard student achievement but also promote dropping out?

We argue that they do. In earlier chapters, we demonstrated that such school policies as grade retention and tracking have limited the opportunities of American students to acquire the level of skills demonstrated by the students in other industrialized countries. In this chapter, we have focused on the role of administrative procedures in creating dropouts and keeping them out of school. We demonstrated how the bureaucratic maze that students and parents must navigate in order to return a student to school discourages students from trying.

One of the reasons the United States has the highest number of laws, etc., controlling the process of schooling is that American public education is still based on "scientific management."[5] One of the key concepts of scientific management is that production should be controlled from the top. Experts, such as scientists or engineers, determine how production should be done, and it is the expert's job to tell line-workers what to do.

Another key concept of scientific management is the breaking down of each part of the production process into its essential elements.[6] The lowest-level worker is supposed to go through the motions required by the detailed descriptions of the essential elements. The breaking down of the job into its tiniest elements is considered desirable because scientific managers believe that maximal efficiency results when line-workers pay attention only to their own small part of the overall production process.

According to scientific management, if everyone does their small part in production, then the completed product will result. Managers alone are responsible for larger pieces of the whole product, and in fact most managers are assigned responsibility for only part of the whole product. In this way, in order to account for the products of the entire organization, every manager has a manager and one supermanager at the top is responsible for everything.

When scientific management was applied to the public schools at the beginning of this century, students became the products and teachers became the line-workers. Teachers were placed at the bottom of the organizational hierarchy, transforming the teaching profession into a blue-collar occupation.[7] No other industrialized nation did this.[8] American teachers are managed by layers upon layers of administrators, ranging from the school, to the district, to the state level. At the top of each school is the principal, at the top of each district is the superintendent, at the top of each state education board or commission is an executive—called in Texas, the commissioner of education.

Scientific management became fashionable in the early part of the 20th century when the U.S. emerged as a major world leader largely because Americans generated mass quantities of products on assembly lines. The idea of applying this form of management to schools became popular because universal public education, including both primary and secondary schools, became available in the U.S. at the same time that the nation was impressing the world with the scale of its industrial mass production. Scientific management seemed an appropriate system to guide the education of the masses.[9] Its application has resulted in such common educational practices as grade levels, timed class periods devoted to separate subjects, and the screening out of students who fail to meet standards.

School boards are supposed to oversee the activities of each school district and make certain that they serve the interests of the community. In the organization of schools in the United States, principals, superintendents, and commissioners are appointed, but the members of school boards are elected. Although it may seem that the infusion of democratically elected public servants at this level of the organization serves the public interest, in fact, few members of a community actually participate in the process of electing school board members. In Austin, for example, since 1984, no more than 13% of the registered voters have voted in school board elections. The average percentage of eligible voters participating in these elections has been 7.8%. This low voter turnout makes it easy for ambitious people to use the school board as a launching pad for their political careers or for special interests, such as tax revolt.[10]

At each school, the principal is the one who ensures that the laws, rules, policies, and court mandates are enforced. Secondarily, the principal must supervise the teachers to make sure that they are going through the motions of doing the essential elements of education. Rarely is the education of students seen by principals as their responsibility. They assign this task to their underlings, the teachers.

As in industrial management, educational administrators gauge their success in terms of personal promotions to higher levels within the administrative hierarchy. Principals want to become promoted to area supervisor or superintendent status. Superintendents want to move up to other superintendent positions in larger and more prestigious districts. Fueling this upward movement is the tendency for school boards to vent their displeasure about school failures by firing superintendents. Thus, the chief executives of major school districts retain their jobs for only three to five years.[11]

The school district we studied is a typical example of administrative insta-
bility. During the course of our four-year study, the district had a succession of
four superintendents. Just after we were given permission to start the study,
the Austin Independent School District's superintendent took a job as commissioner of education in another state. Meanwhile, a high-level administrator
within the district assumed his responsibility, temporarily. An external search
for a permanent superintendent ended with the selection of a candidate who
did not enjoy the unanimous support of the school board. During his term as
superintendent, several board members succeeded in limiting his authority, at
one point preparing an alternative district budget. He spent much of his time
reacting to the demands of the school board and looking for a new job. When
he found one, as a superintendent in another state, he was replaced temporarily by another high-level district administrator.

During all of this administrative shuffle, almost everyone lost sight of the
main goal of the school district: *the education of children and youth.* Especially
neglected were the needs of students who had dropped out before becoming
tenth graders. No one was trying to streamline the reentry process for students
who stopped attending school during the eighth or ninth grades. This neglect
occurred despite the finding of the researchers within the school district that
most dropping out occurred during the ninth grade. The Office of Research
and Evaluation had created a four-page publication pointing out this fact and
had distributed it to the school board, the district's personnel, and concerned
citizens, including us.[12] Still, nothing happened to solve this problem.

POLICY RECOMMENDATIONS

We recommend that schools make it hard for students to drop out and easy for
them to return to school. At present, the reverse is true. Pedro was able to stay
home from school without the slightest interference from the school district.
Returning him to school took a considerable amount of time away from work
and other family members, and required access to transportation, English
speaking ability and literacy skills, familiarity with the various schools, patience and persistence. Once back, he was placed in an alternative school that
took scientific management to such an extreme that it was essentially a parody
of the theory. Specifically, the way the alternative school packaged instruction,
requiring it to be done individually and not at home, was an extreme application of the principles of scientific management. Rather than stimulate returned students and excite them about learning, this school forced them to
work entirely on their own, worksheet by worksheet, with the occasional assistance of a teacher. Being in the alternative school was not a rewarding experi-

ence; in fact, it seemed designed to punish students. Yet, by returning voluntarily to this school, the students were demonstrating their motivation to make up for past poor performance. The alternative school became a test of their desire to go back to school, and about half of the eighth grade students each year gave up.

Since poor attendance has been widely regarded by teachers and administrators as a precursor to dropping out, we argue that solving the problem of poor attendance should be a first step toward solving the problem of dropping out. The scientific management approach does not deal well with the problem of poor attendance. It treats the raw materials entering the production process as inert, like the raw materials at a car assembly plant. But adolescents are not passive recipients of whatever treatment they receive from teachers, staff, and other students. When they are repeatedly made to feel uncomfortable in classrooms, they can and do leave them for more appealing experiences outside the school building.

We recommend that schools make the act of nonattendance a bad experience and the act of class attendance a good experience. Sadly, the school personnel at the middle and high schools we studied took actions that made the reverse true. Students repeatedly told us that skipping classes was easy to do. They were surprised that they were able to walk out of the school without difficulty. In contrast, the requirement of presenting a permission slip for class reentry after skipping was a humiliating experience. It made the return to the classroom unpleasant. Making reentry to school a humiliating experience seemed to reflect the school philosophy of linking negative consequences to behaviors school staff wanted to change. Rather than discouraging skipping, however, this practice had just the opposite effect. Students decided that nonattendance was preferable to the negative reactions they ecountered from teachers and principals when they returned to school.

During one meeting of concerned community leaders, Toni Falbo listened as the principal of one high school explained how he attempted to discourage skipping. Teachers were supposed to keep accurate attendance records, and when students were found to be absent without permission from a class, they were required to present a permission slip to their teachers the next time they attended the class. The slips indicated that the student had been absent without permission. The principal reported that these students would often become surly and aggressive toward their teachers after presenting these slips.

When Toni told the principal that he was approaching the problem backward, that he was supposed to punish students *as* they were skipping and reward students as they were *returning* to class, the principal became confused. Several businessmen in the room took up Toni's point, trying to explain it to this principal. It was clear to the businessmen that workers are rewarded for showing up (i.e., they are paid) and punished for not showing up or for leaving work without permission (i.e., they are fired). But the principal never seemed to get the point, and the ineffective policy remained in place.

We argued that when students come to school they should be greeted warmly and encouraged to participate fully in schoolwork. If students received positive reactions for returning to school, they would have less desire to skip school. The negative attention should come when the students exit the building without permission, not later when they have decided to return. The principal needed to create and implement a system in which the act of skipping was monitored and punished, and would-be skippers were discouraged at all school exits. Simultaneously, the system would involve training teachers how to make their students feel accepted and rewarded for their attendance. Teachers have paid too little attention to student motivation.[13] The assumption has been that students are like raw materials, pulled by the assembly line to their next station.

American schools should abandon scientific management as an underlying organizational theory in favor of the management theories currently used by high-performance workplaces in American industry, such as Total Quality Management.[14] It is ironic that American schools have continued to use scientific management when many of the most successful American industries have abandoned it in favor of greater responsibility for line-workers and fewer layers of bureaucracy.

Following the model of the old assembly line, students in secondary schools are required to go through the motions of completing the essential elements of each course. More emphasis has been placed on sitting in the classroom and completing assignments than on acquiring specific skills. It is possible that Pedro could have mastered all the skills he needed for high school graduation in two full years, as he claimed when he was 16. But he was prevented from doing so, because the state and district bureaucracy required that students spend a specific amount of time in a seat in a classroom, doing the worksheets and tests. We believe that the "time in seat" method of measuring student progress should be abandoned in favor of a method that measures student skills.

Although we fully appreciate the value of "showing up," attendance can and should be separable from the mastery of scholastic skills. For most students, mastering skills will require the daily participation in academic work, such as reading textbooks, listening to class discussions, and taking tests. Mastering skills also requires that students are motivated to pay attention and apply themselves. But the "time in seat" approach has overemphasized the need for the student to go through the motions of learning and underemphasized the need for students and teachers to take responsibility for the student's mastery of specific skills. Graduation from high school should be based on the student's demonstration of skills and knowledge, regardless of how much time he or she spends in the classroom.

Also consonant with our recommendation to rid schools of scientific management is our strong recommendation that schools and school districts be totally restructured so that more authority and responsibility be given to teachers. Teachers are the ones whose work most directly influences the main goal of the school district: the education of students. In fact, every job at the school should be focused on enhancing the skills and knowledge of students. If a job does not directly add to student learning, it should be abolished. Janitors, school bus drivers, secretaries, and lunchroom personnel at school sites add directly to the learning environment of students, but many district-level personnel are far removed from what happens at the schools. At present, a top-heavy administrative structure and a myriad of school rules place the needs of school personnel ahead of the needs of students trying to get an education. The layers of principals and district-level administrators between teachers and the school board, currently common in American education, would no longer be needed if more of the decision-making authority were given to teachers and parents.

School districts should invest in both the staff and the technology needed to streamline the reentry process for dropouts. Ideally, there should be personnel at each school who continuously staff workstations during regular working hours, Monday through Friday, 12 months a year, to deal with returned students and/or any other administrative glitch involving the school district. Their workstations would be equipped with computers connected to a network that links all the necessary information about all the students enrolled in the school district. Information about all programs for making up credits and absences and obtaining special services should be available at these workstations. The telephones at these workstations should be staffed for 12 hours a day during critical times, such as the beginning and ending of the school year, and they should be equipped with answering machines so that parents or other adults can leave requests for help on a 24-hour-a-day basis. (See Chapter 10, pp. 246–247, for discussion of how these workstations are part of a comprehensive set of recommendations to make school success more accessible to Latino students.)

It would be the responsibility of these staff members to resolve successfully the administrative problems of the students. In order to do this, these staff members would have to have the authority to make decisions about the enrollment of students into specific schools, including making arrangements for transportation, free or reduced-priced lunches, and immunizations, and the resolution of disputes about absences, grades, and credits.

It would also be the responsibility of these staff members to communicate with the students and their parents in ways that are meaningful to them. This would also mean that part of their work would have to be done in languages other than English and during times other than regular work hours. In the school district we studied, the predominant alternative language that students and their parents spoke was Spanish, yet most schools did not have a Spanish-speaking translator available on campus to help parents communicate with school personnel. Teachers would be responsible for keeping records of student progress on the computer network so that when parents phone in to inquire about student progress, any staff member answering the phone can easily and quickly inform the parent.

Importantly, the job of school counselor needs to be radically redefined. We gained an insight into the weakness of the current counselor job when we learned from Mrs. García how one counselor had treated her. When Pedro was in the school for students with behavior problems, Mrs. García had taken off a day of work to talk with the counselor at that school. Her eyes filled with tears as she recounted this experience: "Yo llamé para allá, pero una de las consejeras de él me contestó muy, ¿cómo le dijera?, que groseramente, realmente. Yo ya no quise después hablar con ella ya, por lo que me dijo. Porque, que yo tenía la culpa que cuando haberle pegado cuando estaba chiquito; que lo haber agarrado a nalgadas o huarachazos a, cuando estaba chiquito, . . . si yo lo hubiera educado de otra manera cuando estaba chiquito, que no hubiera andado haciendo lo que andaba haciendo. Yo no, no creo yo que esto era, ha sido una mal para que ella me hubiera contestado a mí. Yo estaba pidiendo ayuda, y yo quería que él regresara a la escuela y acabara su escuela. Y ella . . . y eso fue lo que me contestó ella. 'Pues, ustedes tienen la culpa para no, no educarlos . . .' Yo después ya no quise yo llamar, por lo que me contestó ella. Y, pues, uno habla y pide ayuda y con lo que le sale, ¿verdad? Yo no, no hablé ya después, mejor . . ." (I called there but one of his counselors responded to me, how can I say it, very ugly, really. Then I didn't want to talk to her because of what she said to me. Because, she said I was at fault, that I should have hit him when he was small, that I should have smacked him or swatted him on his bottom when he was little, . . . if I had taught him in another way when he was small, that he wouldn't be doing what he is doing. I don't, I don't think that was it, she was wrong to have answered me that way. I was asking for help and I want him to return to school and complete his school, and she, and this was what she answered me, 'Well, you are to blame for not teaching them.' And well, one calls and asks for help and this is what comes out, right? I no, I won't talk to her again, that's best.)

Thus, Mrs. García's decision not to go to the last school Pedro attended to discuss Pedro's problems with school staff was very understandable. Why would anyone want to go to a school only to have a school counselor tell them that they are to blame for their child's problem? Pedro's mother had been totally alienated from school meetings by one incompetent counselor. Rather than spend her energy earning the trust of Mrs. García, this school counselor instead lectured her about what the counselor perceived to be the mother's shortcomings. While the counselor may have thought lecturing Mrs. García would make the parents take more responsibility for their son's behaviors, Mrs. García believed that the counselor was blaming her for being a poor mother. The aim of such blaming can only be to shift the responsibility for the child's problems away from the school and the counselor. Even if poor parenting during Pedro's early childhood was part of his problem, how could blaming his mother encourage her to take constructive action to help the adolescent-aged Pedro advance in his education?

As it turned out, Pedro did not stick it out in the alternative school. He got a job instead. Later, when he was 18, Pedro contacted Harriett Romo to tell her that he was now a cutlery salesman. She sent him to Toni Falbo, who, after listening to his salespitch, made a purchase. Afterward, she asked Pedro about his progress at attaining his high school diploma. He indicated that he still did not have a diploma, but that he wanted to get one through the local community college. She asked him if he had begun the process of applying for admission there, and he indicated that he had not. After encouraging Pedro to begin the application process soon, Toni asked Pedro about his plans for the future. Pedro announced that he wanted to go into public service. Toni advised him that in order to become a public servant in the U.S., he would need to become a U.S. citizen and at least a high school graduate. Pedro agreed and assured her that he still planned to go to college.

NINE

"Don't be like me — stay in school."

Cultural Boundaries, Family Resources, and Parental Actions

When we began our research, we intended to discover the strategies that Hispanic parents used to bring about the high school graduation of their "at risk" children. We planned to disseminate these strategies so that other parents could benefit from what we learned.

After four years of studying the families of "at risk" youth, we realized that in order for these strategies to have meaning, we have to place them within their own cultural and socioeconomic contexts. Our previous chapters have described the contexts and actions of individual families. This chapter combines what we have learned from all these families to create an overview of the cultural boundaries, family resources, and parental actions relevant to high school graduation. After portraying the cultural and socioeconomic contexts of these actions, we will describe the actions that parents took to help their children graduate from high school.

CULTURAL BOUNDARIES

Some have argued that the school problems of Hispanic students stem largely from a mismatch between the culture of the home versus the culture of the school.[1] Our experience convinces us that this simple mismatch model does not capture the complexities of the cultural differences we found in the families or the schools we studied. We found no single culture of the home, nor was there a single culture of the school. Furthermore, our statistical analyses indicate that characteristics of the home culture did not predict whether the student graduated. For example, such factors as the immigration status of the students or their parents or their frequency of speaking English at home had no statistically significant link to whether the student graduated from high school.[2]

The students we studied had to navigate the boundaries of three kinds of culture in order to graduate from high school. These three boundaries defined the cultures of the homes, the adult culture of the school system, and the student culture of each school.

Home Cultures

Because all of the students we studied were of Mexican origin, one might assume that they represented one culture. The cases we have highlighted in this book demonstrate that this assumption is not valid. We found no single Mexican-origin culture, but many home cultures, varying widely along important cultural dimensions. Some of the families in our sample were recent arrivals from Mexico; others were Mexican Americans, firmly entrenched in the American way of life. In some of the home cultures, only Spanish was spoken; in other homes, both Spanish and English were spoken; in others, only English was spoken.

Despite the variation in these important cultural dimensions, virtually all the parents and students we studied saw the high school diploma as a means to a better life. All of the parents wanted their children to get a high school diploma. In this sense, all the home cultures of the students we studied valued education.

The Adult Culture of the School System

The adult culture of the school system was more homogeneous than the home cultures of the students. This adult culture reflected the non-Hispanic White American tradition. In every way, the district's students were expected to meet academic and behavioral standards that emanated from the White American culture of the school. Most of the teachers, librarians, counselors, and administrators were White, and all were college educated. Even if some of the teachers, for example, were of Hispanic origin, they were often far removed from the cultures of working-class or low-income Mexican-origin families. Because of the educational levels required to be a teacher, librarian, counselor, or school administrator, it was almost inevitable that these school staff were oriented toward meeting middle-class needs by expressing middle-class values.

Not surprisingly, many of our students associated "doing well in school" with "being a White." For example, Alice, who accumulated enough credits to graduate, but could not pass the exit test, told us, "If you're in more of a White school, you see, well, you have to make it. You have to be able to pass, because then if you can't pass, you're just gonna think less of yourself. And Whites, too, are gonna think less of you. You can't just do it. You just can't be with them because they are more intelligent and you're not. . . . Because, I don't know, I just feel that I would have to do it. I would have to make myself do schoolwork in a White school. 'Cause I wanna be something. I wanna look at everybody and say, 'I did it. I've made it. I'm with everybody else now.'"

Some of the students we studied believed that they were not treated as well as White students were by school personnel. One student who dropped out described his experience: "If you're Mexican, they put you lower. If you're White, they put you higher, right? Most of my classes I have White people, right? It's like the teacher just looks at me and talks to me, but that's it. But when she talks with other people, she sits down and does it right with them. The teacher will just go over it with me. If I get it, I get it. If not, I don't. That's why I have to get it. If you're Mexican, they treat you sort of . . . if you're White, they treat you right and everything."

Most of the students we studied simply accepted that the White American culture was the culture of the school. They did not see their problems with school as caused by the conflict between their heritage and the culture of the school. Instead, when they entered high school, they attempted to find ways to be "with everybody else" and adjust to the culture of the school.

While the students were simply trying to fit in, some of the parents recognized that the schools were biased in favor of the White American culture. For example, Maria Elena told us, "You have kids from different areas of the city, different cultures, and I think the schools need more cultural activities. They need to have more activities to let the kids be aware that they should be proud of their backgrounds. This is not a White world . . . it's not a White world! . . . We change tremendously, we made it more than halfway and then the Mexicanos have been forced to go another 15%. . . . Society needs to change. We are oppressed but we don't need to sit back. And a good way to fight it is being the type of parent that I've been. The other way is the school system, it is so blind."

The Student Cultures of the Schools

The student cultures of the schools we studied reflected the ethnic, racial, and social class characteristics of each student body. Student cultures are very powerful in influencing student behavior. For some, the student culture is more powerful than the student's home culture or the adult school culture.

Many of the students we studied, particularly those from low-income families, had difficulty adjusting to the overwhelmingly middle-class and White American adult culture of the school. Part of the problem was that they could not find a proschool peer group to belong to. White American students from middle-class families had many such cliques to choose from. These predominantly White cliques were differentiated largely by the social and economic status of their families. For example, the "kickers" wore cowboy boots, dressed in jeans and western shirts, liked country music, and drove pickup trucks. The "preps" were described as wearing "a Polo and expensive shirts, shoes, and shorts and stuff like that. And expensive jewelry." Preps usually came from the wealthy White neighborhoods, while kickers usually came from the working-class White neighborhoods.

For Whites, there was also an array of antimainstream cliques to affiliate with. The "heads" or "potheads" were students who smoked marijuana or cigarettes in the school parking lots or nearby areas. "Skaters" rode skateboards and had their "hair long, covering their face." "Punk rockers," "new wavers," or "progressives" were identifiable by their black clothes and taste in particular musical styles.

There were two student groups within each school that received special recognition. The first was the "jocks," or those students on the varsity sports teams. The ethnic composition of the various school teams depended largely on the ethnic composition of the school. For the most part, the students on the teams came from a range of economic and ethnic/racial backgrounds. This made the jocks unlike other cliques at the school. One reason why the jocks were more mixed than other groups is that adults, notably coaches, had a firm hand in determining who was on the team.

The second special group consisted of "nerds." Nerds were students who performed well academically. They helped their teachers, handed in all their homework, and studied hard for exams. Anyone, regardless of ethnic, economic, or racial background, could be a nerd. But, most students used the term "nerd" to ridicule any peer who was doing too well in school.

None of the students we studied considered themselves to be in this latter group; in fact, nerds were the opposite of what most of our students wanted to be. Robert, who graduated from high school, but flunked out of college, told us that his "neighborhood friends" thought that anyone who did well in school was a nerd. He had to hide his school achievement from his "neighborhood friends" to avoid ridicule and rejection. Salvador, who was heavily involved in a gang and dropped out, called his half-siblings "nerds" whenever they made fun of his poor academic performance. James, who also dropped out, did not hand in his homework because he did not want to be perceived by his friends as a nerd. They called him "school boy."

The students told us that there was little mixing between White groups and Mexican American or African American groups. Felipe described the cliques at his school this way: "Basically there's Whites and then there's Mexican Americans and there's Blacks. They hang around the different parts of the school in groups. They mostly stay together. Every now and then one will mingle with the other. . . . There's like three different groups out of all the kids, and the Blacks are usually the largest, and then the kickers and then the preps. Or it depends on who's comin' to school that year. But this year it was the preps, the kickers, and the Blacks were like the biggest ones. The Hispanics were like the fourth, fifth ones. There's not many Hispanics who go to that school. That's basically it."

The students we interviewed made social class distinctions among Mexican-origin students. Most of the Mexican American youths did not identify with the "Mexicans" at their schools. Robert described the groups at his high school: "Well, there's a lot of snobs. Kickers and Blacks, Mexicans and gangs are there. Cowboys, a bunch of nerds, and you got your progressive people, progressive groups, new wavers. You know what a new waver is? They listen to new wave music, they dress in black. I'm not too much to that extent. At my old high school gangs were big, but at this new school, it's not really. . . . It's really Mexicans that think they're all big."

Martin, Jr., who was from a middle-class Mexican American family, rejected the "Mexican" students at his school and identified with the students who liked the music he did. He explained, "You have your 'heads,' people who listen to the music I do. You have your preps, pretty much the rich people, I guess you could say. You have your jocks. You have your, I don't know what you could say, your gangster-type people, you know, Mexicans, mostly, you know."

School staff at one high school claimed that one cause of common disruptions at the school was the conflicts between Mexican American and immigrant Mexican students. One of the immigrant students we interviewed described the "pandillas" as groups that ganged up on other students, particularly the recent immigrants.

Often the students did not perceive themselves as affiliating solely along ethnic and social class lines until conflict erupted with other groups. As Richard described it: "And, like, me and my cousin and some other fellas, we really just hang together. We just walk around together or go out to eat lunch. There's not really groups. It's just whoever. There's just people who hang out. You know, just friends. But mostly everyone talks to each other and nobody's snotty or nothin' like that. It's pretty cool. . . . There's a lot of Black guys there, and they think they're all big and bad. You know, like, last year they outnumbered the Mexicanos, so they thought that they were bad, you know. And like one day, we got in a fight with them."

Some students told us they stopped attending school because they feared being drawn into these fights. Parents told us that some students got into so many fights that the school administrators "pushed" these students out of school permanently. Administrators were interested in eliminating violence on their campuses and believed that the way to do this was to expel the troublemakers. They were concerned about the negative publicity associated with fights on campus. The general public expected administrators to take action to protect the majority of students who were not involved in fights. Some of the parents we interviewed felt that the administrators were too quick to expel Latino students instead of trying to resolve the conflicts between students.

The fact that only 31% of our sample were able to graduate suggests that, ultimately, most of the students we studied were not able to gain acceptance into a school-involved peer group. When these students felt rejected by the adults or peers within a school, they rejected the school. They dropped out.

FAMILY RESOURCES

Our statistical analyses indicated that two types of socioeconomic factors had a direct connection to whether the students graduated. Students with better-educated mothers or students with breadwinners who made more money were much more likely to graduate than were students whose parents had less education or income.[3]

Our experience with the families in our sample helped us understand why parental education and income were so important in determining children's educational outcomes. We became aware of the extent to which the schools had overestimated the resources of most of the parents in our sample. Many school personnel had assumed that all parents could read and write and that they had the means to involve themselves in the school. We knew that many of the parents we studied had little formal education and little knowledge about the fundamentals of the educational system. Although they worked long hours at various jobs, they still could not afford a telephone or a second car. Some could not understand or speak English at all. Many who could understand oral English had difficulty reading the cryptic and impersonal messages sent to them by the schools. Because of these limitations, many of the parents were unable to do the kinds of things that the schools expected them to do in order to keep their "at risk" children in school.

When parents are educated, they can get jobs that pay decently and provide health benefits. Better-educated people usually do not need to work two or three jobs a week in order to pay the bills. Furthermore, because they have health benefits, they and their children can get preventive health care and treatment when they are sick. This means that because chronic health problems are treated, their children miss less school time due to illness.

Appreciating the lack of the parents' education is critical to understanding the educational problems of Mexican-origin students in general. As we have mentioned in previous chapters, Mexican-origin adults as a group have the lowest levels of education of any Hispanic group in the U.S.[4] In our sample, 56% of the parents had completed fewer than 12 years of school. Indeed, 26% of our parents had completed fewer than 6 years of school. Six of our students had parents with no formal education at all.

Our analyses indicated that the standardized achievement-test scores of the children were strongly associated with the educational levels of their mothers and fathers.[5] This is not surprising because there is a substantial literature indicating that children score higher on standardized tests if their parents are better educated.[6] The uneducated Mexican-origin parents in our sample typically did not speak English at all, and they spoke a form of Spanish that is non-standard. Some were totally illiterate. Many of our parents told us that they could not help their children with their homework because they did not understand it. However, the uneducated Mexican-origin parents socialized their children carefully to acquire the skills they thought were essential for survival. These skills, such as helping the family and being a good employee, were often in conflict with the attainment of those skills needed for success inside the classroom.[7]

There are many consequences of having no more than an elementary school education in the contemporary Texas economy. Because of the abundance of people willing to do low-skill work, there is a lot of competition for these jobs. Therefore, if one or both of the parents in our sample had such jobs, they were reluctant to do anything that might jeopardize keeping their jobs. The least-educated parents in our sample tended to work whatever long hours their employers desired to make sure that they stayed in their employers' good graces. They knew they could not take time off from work to deal with their children's school problems without jeopardizing their employment.

Consequently, uneducated parents had less opportunity to monitor their children. And because poorly paid, low-level jobs are often done in the evenings and night, the parents had less opportunity to supervise their children's departure for school or their arrival home. Moreover, they were unable to control the time when their children went to bed or got up in the morning. Compounding this problem was the tendency for uneducated parents to have more children than educated parents had.[8] They had to divide what little time they had among a greater number of children. As a result, poorly educated parents had little time or energy to help their children when they had school problems.

Thus, many of our parents, especially the least-educated ones, were unable to be an advocate for their children when their children needed help in overcoming administrative obstacles within the school. Administrative problems, such as missed credits and too many absences, blocked the students' progress. These parents did not know when their advocacy was needed, they did not know how to be an advocate, and they were discouraged from doing so by their children. Many parents told us that their children begged them not to go to the schools because the students were ashamed of them.

Many of the students in our sample left school because their family needed the income their labor could generate. We were told of their need to work when we first interviewed them, when the students were 15 years old. Being able to help their family was a strong value among the students in our sample.[9] Yet, the school district did not allow students as young as 15 to integrate a work schedule with an academic schedule. Furthermore, even though they were 15 years old when we first interviewed them, 21% of our students were still in middle school because of grade retentions. The half-day work programs in the school district were available only to students in the later years of high school. Therefore, many students gave up going to school so that they could work full-time. And they were rewarded for their sacrifice by being treated like adults by their parents and siblings.

RECOGNIZING THE PROBLEM

The parents we studied took many actions they thought were essential for the well-being of their children. In this section, we focus on the actions that parents took in response to the school's designation of their child as "at risk" of dropping out. Before we could identify these actions, however, we had to discover the extent to which the parents understood that their child had been designated as "at risk." Did they recognize that their children had academic problems significant enough to warrant an "at risk" designation?

In theory, all the parents in our sample should have known that their children were "at risk" of dropping out of school. The Texas Legislature mandated that each school district notify parents in the event their children were "at risk" of dropping out of school, so that parents could take action to prevent their dropping out.[10] However, the Austin school district was reluctant to use the words *"at risk" of dropping out* because their research indicated that most of the students who qualified for "at risk" status would eventually graduate.[11] Therefore, the district sent the following letter to all of the parents in our sample in the fall of 1988, the first year that parental notification was mandated by the Texas law and the year our study began.

Dear Parent,

The legislature has established new standards that require all Texas schools to inform parents that their students may require additional academic support in order to meet grade promotion or graduation standards. Beginning the 1988–89 school year, parents are to receive a letter that explains the criteria used to identify their student's needs.

Students in grades 7–12 who are below the age of 21 years and who meet one or more of the following criteria, shall be identified:

- have not been promoted one or more times in grades 1 through 6 and continue to be unable to master the course requirements in grades 7 through 12;
- are two or more years below grade level in reading or mathematics;
- have failed at least two courses in one or more semesters and are not expected to graduate within four years of the time they entered the ninth grade; or
- have failed one or more of the reading, writing, or mathematics sections of the most recent TEAMS test beginning with the seventh grade.

Since the above listed criteria are very broad, a student may have been identified in error and may not be in need of receiving additional support. The attached printout states the reason(s) for your student's identification. Please contact your student's counselor at [phone number] to discuss any questions you may have concerning this letter.

We are looking forward to your student experiencing an outstanding academic year. Our staff is here to support your student's needs.

Sincerely,
Principal

It is easy to understand how most parents could have read this letter and missed the point that the school district had designated their child as "at risk" of dropping out. Indeed, we have evidence that most of the parents did not interpret the contents of this letter to mean that their child was "at risk" of dropping out. When we first interviewed the parents, soon after these letters had been sent out, only 36% of them told us that they thought their child was "at risk" of dropping out of school. Furthermore, only 23% could remember why their child had been designated as "at risk." Consequently, it was easy for parents to believe that their child was not really "at risk."[12] Thus, despite the law's intent, the majority of parents in our sample still did not understand that their children had a better-than-average chance of dropping out.

Recognizing the Problem and Dropping Out

Indeed, the importance of recognizing the risk is highlighted by comparing the recognition of the student's "at risk" status with the student's graduation status four years later.[13] In Table 9.1, we created a diagram describing four types of parents. The parents were divided into those who recognized the problem (Recognized Risk) versus those who did not (Did Not Recognize Risk), and then we divided them again into those whose children graduated (Graduate) versus those whose children did not (Dropout).

The distribution of parents into the four categories is also presented in this table. The parents we identified as *Alerted* responded to the school notification of their child's status with action aimed at solving the problem. The parents who *Denied* that their child was "at risk" believed that the school was mistaken and continued to support their child in school. The *Unable* parents recognized that their child had problems in school but felt unable to do anything about solving the problems. The parents in the *Out of Touch* category did not understand their child's academic situation.

The parents in the Alerted category told us that they recognized the risk when we first interviewed them, and four years later their children had graduated. Maria Elena, the mother of Richard in Chapter 3 (Grade Retention), was an Alerted parent. She gave the following portrayal of her son's "at risk" status: "He's been labeled at risk, but I'm sure he won't drop out. I don't consider him at risk, but yes, he fits the label. The drug use, the acting out, the grades.

TABLE 9.1. Four Categories of Parents: Recognizing the Risk by Graduation Status

Year four: Graduation Status	Year One: Recognized "At Risk?"	
	Recognized Risk	Did Not Recognize Risk
Graduate	Alerted (7%)	Denied (33%)
Dropout	Unable (30%)	Out of Touch (30%)

When he took his testing, he scored in the twenties under every subject. And that has a lot to do with why he is labeled 'at risk.'"

Alerted parents responded to the school district's notification in the way the Texas Legislature had intended. They accepted what the school told them, and they took action to solve the child's school problems.

Our interview data told us about the kinds of actions that Alerted parents took. They investigated alternative solutions to their child's problem; they went to schools, health clinics, and other centers of neighborhood services and met with the personnel; they insisted that their child get whatever he or she needed to succeed; they closely monitored their child's social and school activities; and they set limits on activities that they thought conflicted with schoolwork. Only 7% of the parents fit into this category.

The parents in the Denied category refused to accept the "at risk" label for their child, and perhaps in a sense, they were right, because by Year Four, their children had graduated. George, the father of Linda from Chapter 6 (Immigrants), was this type of parent. He gave the following assessment: "I don't think she is [at risk]. I don't feel like she's 'at risk' yet, anyway. Right now, I would say I don't think she is because she is involved in sports. As long as she wants to play this kind of volleyball and basketball, she knows she's got to keep her grades up. So I think as long as she's interested in playing some sport that she won't be much of a risk."

Many Denied parents were correct in thinking that their child would graduate, despite occasional academic mishaps. To avoid total school failure, Denied parents took actions, such as paying for their student's summer school courses to make up for the student's Fs. About 33% of the parents fit into this category.

Parents in the Unable category told us at Year One that their children were "at risk," and by Year Four their children had dropped out of school. Suzanna, the mother of Salvador from Chapter 4 (Gangs), was an Unable parent. From the outset, she believed that her son was "at risk" of dropping out of school: "I thought that he was determined not to make anything out of himself. He was just going to stay at home and just let me take care of him all his life."

Despite their recognition of the problem, Unable parents did not perceive themselves as being able to do anything about it. Some looked to others to solve this problem for them. Other parents in this category had grown discouraged when their earlier efforts to solve the problem had failed. About 30% of the parents were in this category.

Parents in the Out of Touch category did not believe that their children were "at risk." They were optimistic at the beginning, but by Year Four their children had dropped out. For example, when we asked Graciela, the mother of Lupe in Chapter 5 (Teen Motherhood), whether she thought that Lupe was "at risk" of dropping out, she said: "Pos, no, no. Yo creo que no. Ella le gusta la escuela, le gusta mucho." (No, I don't think so. She likes school, she likes it a lot.)

Graciela elaborated: "Pos, hablé con ella, y ella, me dijo que no, que ella sí quería seguir estudiando y me dijo que iba a tratar de ser mejor. Porque yo, pos no la regaño, porque ya está grande, me da cosa que si la regaño, pos a lo mejor, ¿verdad? Y éste, y ella, no parece que ya está haciendo caso. Y ella dice que ella, ahora ya quiere seguir estudiando, ya quiere seguir." (Well, no. I spoke with her and she told me no, that she wished to continue studying, and she told me that she was going to try to be better. Because I, well, I didn't scold her because now she is grown up, and it bothers me if I reprimand her, right? And this one doesn't think it is a big thing. And she said that she, now she wants to keep studying, now she wants to continue.)

How could Out of Touch parents be so wrong? We examined the information from our interviews with these parents to find the answer. We found that they relied primarily on what their children told them about their school status. Often these parents told us that their children liked school, were able to do well in school, and/or had a better attitude about school than did their older siblings, most of whom had dropped out. These parents told us that because they did not perceive their child as being "at risk," they took no action to try to prevent them from dropping out. About 30% of the parents were in the Out of Touch category.

The Emotional Involvement of Parents

We also found that Out of Touch parents were the least emotionally involved with their children. When we telephoned the parents periodically to check on the student's progress, Out of Touch parents were likely to give few details about the child's experiences. They gave us vague answers to our questions about their child's school or work activities. They expressed little emotion themselves and had little to say about their child's feelings.

In contrast, Alerted parents were the most in touch with the emotional state of their children. During our telephone interviews, these parents would discuss specific events and express intense feelings about them. These parents told us of their child's anger when unjust things happened. And they told us of their child's joy when good things happened. The parents would explain at length their own disappointment about their child's failures and their relief when their child succeeded. They knew what was happening in their child's life and how their child was reacting to these events.[14]

Alerted parents used the information they gleaned from closely observing their children to help their children stay in school. In contrast, because Out of Touch parents were not attentive to their children's lives, they did not have a basis either for evaluating their children's school status or for taking action on behalf of their children's education.

It seems likely that the cultural and educational backgrounds of parents influenced their response to the "at risk" letter. Parents who could not read English or who had little education could not understand the significance of the "at risk" letter. They were more likely to fall into the Out of Touch or Unable categories. However, we were unable to use our data to test these ideas statistically for two reasons. First, our sample was small, and second, our sample was limited in range to the pool of students who were both "at risk" and of Mexican origin. Our qualitative data suggested, however, that factors other than the educational and cultural backgrounds of the parents also influenced whether the students graduated. These factors are described below in terms of the effective strategies used by parents of graduates.

EFFECTIVE STRATEGIES

The parents of graduates used seven strategies to keep their children in school long enough to graduate.

1. Parent in Charge

Parents of graduates took charge of their adolescent-age children. When challenged, the parents never abandoned their authority. In contrast, the parents of dropouts typically had no control over their children. It was common for such parents to have no idea of the whereabouts of their children when we called to schedule our interviews. They would go for days without hearing from them.

When youths believed that their parents had authority over them, then the actions of their parents had more meaning for them. For example, because of his father's influence, Robert took Algebra in summer school so that he would be able to graduate on time. Richard enrolled himself in night school because he believed what his mother had told him about the importance of a high school diploma. In response to the strong advice of her mother and sisters, Ramona chose to act like a model student so that she would be selected to get into the special program that helped her to graduate. Despite numerous arguments over curfews, Linda came home from parties when her parents wanted.

When parents were not in charge, their children easily ignored their parents' efforts aimed at keeping them in school. Losing authority over adolescent-age children was easy. One mother explained how she almost lost control of her daughter: "It's not only my daughter, though, and I guess I can't blame her always for being like that, because it's all of them that are like that. . . . None of those people go to school and they have no rules. Everybody meets somewhere, probably on the street and they have a party. So, to me I guess I can't really say it's my fault I've lost control 'cause it's not really, it's all the kids are doing it, and you try to control one of them, your own child, and she looks at me like, you know, I'm boring, I'm strict, 'nobody else is like that,' you know."

2. Two-Way Influence

Having a parent in charge was not enough to bring about a successful outcome. In order to succeed, parents had to share power with their teenaged children. Parents of graduates asserted their authority in ways that were respectful of the youths. The youths felt comfortable telling their parents about school and social events because they knew that their parents would respond reasonably to them.

During our interviews with families of graduates, the parent and teen both recounted episodes of negotiating with each other in order to arrive at a decision. While the youths acknowledged that their parents were in charge, the parents still listened to the youths and attempted to give them what they wanted when the youth made a good case for it. In this way, the parents trained their children in making decisions for themselves.

Furthermore, the parents taught their children effective ways of influencing others. They did this several ways. One common way was for the parents to let themselves be influenced when the youth used "good" strategies, such as cleaning up the kitchen so that the parent would give the youth permission to spend the night at a friend's house. Effective parents made it clear to the youths that if the youths did what the parents wanted, then the parents would do what the youths wanted. Another way involved imitation. The student would observe the parent succeed in influencing school personnel on his or her behalf. This would inspire the student to attempt to influence school personnel, using similar types of positive social strategies. Generally, these parents tried to influence their children with strategies that were direct, cooperative, and rational. Their children responded by trying to influence their parents and other adults with similar types of strategies.

Two mothers gave us their perspective on this type of two-way influence. One said, "I'm more of a guidance to him. I am his teacher and I teach him. But my method of teaching is to help guide him and not to tell him what to do."

Another said, "We really didn't lay down the law. Like I said, we tried to explain to him why he shouldn't have done it or why what he did was wrong, even though we could have just knocked the heck out of him when we found out he was doing it [skipping school, not doing his schoolwork, and hiding his failing grades from his parents], you know. It wouldn't have been the right thing to do. We felt that by talking to him he would understand a lot more."

3. Set Limits

The youths who graduated knew that there were some things that their parents regarded as nonnegotiable. These included completing their schoolwork and staying out too late. The teens knew that their parents set limits and stuck to them. Teens who graduated from high school accepted these limits, even if they complained about them.

One mother described her method of setting limits while still respecting her son's independence: "He is very independent. There are certain activities that I don't like and the only thing I can do, because of what age group he is in, is tell him the decision is his to make. He knows his limits and I still don't hesitate to restrict him if he oversteps his bounds. . . . While he's young and while he's still semidependent on me, he'll have to go by my rules, some of my rules, and I'll respect him. It's a two-way thing."

A father described it this way: "His work goes first. Schoolwork, that is. He doesn't get to watch TV. He doesn't get to eat. And he's hungry all the time. But I tell him he has to do his homework. Doesn't get his allowance. I don't let him use my camera."

Similarly, when we asked how she got her children to do what she wanted them to do, a mother told us, "I just tell 'em that they need to do their homework first. And I ask them, 'Have you done your homework first? Have you done your homework already? Have you done it?' And I just bug 'em. I bug 'em until they want me to stop."

Speaking of her daughter, she continued, "I went through a period where we were having a lot of problems, you know. She wanted to go out a lot and I couldn't allow that. And I told her, 'There are rules here. You're going to have rules at work. You'll have rules. Your whole life is made up of rules.' I said, 'God made the Ten Commandments, you know.'"

4. Monitor Student

The teens who graduated knew that their parents "kept an eye on them." Although they were irked by this surveillance, they appreciated that their parents spent their time and energy keeping track of them. Parents of graduates paid attention to their children and were able to determine when something bothered them or when they appeared to have a school problem. They were sensitive to body language, tone of voice, and other signs that suggested that the adolescent wanted to talk about something, but did not know how to start talking about it.

One mother explained her monitoring of her son: "He approaches me in a way. I know from his actions and some of his words that he is approaching me for help. He doesn't want to talk about it. He doesn't come to me right on 'Mom, this happened,' you know. So, I know what his signs are: bossy language, certain words. Things like that. So I take a certain step, and bring it out. And we talk."

Another mother explained how easy it was for her to miss the signs of trouble: "I was just blind, you know, I just didn't catch on, but uh, I think a lot of things that happen with these girls these days and anybody in school, so much can get past a parent, you know, that I'll say even after a few months, after so much gets by them and the kids get by with it, it's hard to get them changed back the way you had them. It's hard to explain, but it's really hard for them to get by with so much and then all of a sudden tell them this is wrong, what you are doing. You have to come home at a certain time and stuff like that, you know."

This mother was able to regain control over her daughter because she was persistent. She explained, "I get on her nerves so bad 'cause I'm the type of person, you know, and kids like to go to their room and be by themselves and I'm constantly going in. I open the door and I go in and try to talk to her."

5. Draw the Line with Peers

Parents of graduates took many actions to make certain that their children were not influenced by peers who did not attend school or take their schoolwork seriously. Youths who graduated understood that their parents did not approve of such peers. The parents clearly communicated to their children the types of people and social activities that the parents thought were good for them. The youths knew that the parent would not approve of their bringing "bad" friends home or their socializing with "bad" friends.

Parents of graduates talked to their children's friends to get to know them better. For example, one mother told us, "Her friends, well, I like them. I try to do everything for them. I try to keep a close . . . you know, I talk to them and everything."

Sometimes the parents approved of their children's friends. One mother told us that her son's friends made good grades and did a better job of turning in their schoolwork than her son did. She told us, "I've met all of his friends. I know who he hangs around with. I know their parents. Uh, I think they're a great bunch of kids. They're not into drugs, they're not into alcohol. They're not in the streets all hours of the night. And I think they're really good kids."

Parents who monitored their children's friends and activities had to contend with the experience of being told they were too strict and old-fashioned. This name-calling did not deter the graduates' parents, who stood their ground and fulfilled their responsibilities as parents. One mother of a graduate described her dilemma when her daughter's girlfriend began skipping school with a boyfriend: "I did tell her that I wish that one friend wouldn't come around as often as she had because I thought that what she was doing was not right, and as a parent, it is my responsibility to take care of my daughter. And if the other girl's parents didn't want her to go to school—it's fine with them, but not me."

Similarly, one mother, who knew that her son had some gang friends, let him know why she did not approve of the friends: "And I tell him why I don't like his friends. 'I don't like your friend because he's a gang member' or because 'I feel that maybe he puts a lot of pressure on you, the drug situation, or whatever the reason might be.' But he respects me, I mean, we have to meet halfway somewhere, and if I don't want them in my house, he just doesn't bring them."

One father who lived in a neighborhood with many gangs explained how he dealt with the problem of gang friends. He and his son had an understanding. He explained, "He doesn't judge my friends. I don't judge his friends. Unless they get him in trouble."

6. Continuous Message

Youths who graduated got the same message from all family members, and they got the message often: "Stay in school." Parents worked as a team, or parents and siblings acted as a team to reinforce the message. These family teams would also give frequent pep talks to encourage failing students to keep trying.

In the words of one of the fathers of our graduates, "I just been poundin' it into him that he needed to, you know, go to school."

Another father told us, "I have always tried to stress to them, 'Look, you need the education. Look, I don't have to tell you. You know what it is like out there, in order for you to succeed and have a good job. Look at me. I have a good job and that's because I graduated. You don't want to work at McDonald's the rest of your life. You don't want to work sacking groceries.' So I stressed to them, you know, having an education."

A mother described her inspirational messages this way: "We keep pushing him and telling him that, uh, 'Hey, you know, this year didn't go as well or this class didn't go as well as you expected, but we know you can do it, you know, next time just try a little bit harder.' And we show him examples of people that really try to do well, and that really try to achieve . . . the people in our family, this person went to school, this person didn't. Look where this person is, and look where this person is now. And I think he sees it."

Another mother confided in us: "I use myself as an example, and I'll say things like 'OK, you know there's two different kinds of people in this world— those that give orders, those that take. What do you want to be? Do you want to go to college and get a good education and give orders? Or do you want to be like me, who takes orders?'"

This mother continued, "I guess just letting her know that she's capable. That she is smart, that she is not stupid, and that she's got a lot in her. And wonderful things can happen to her by finishing school, by going to college. I keep telling her that her college years are going to be the best years of her life. I mean, I could have gone to college and I didn't go and it's one of my biggest regrets."

7. Involved in School

Youths who graduated knew that their parents were involved in their schooling. These parents scrutinized report cards, talked to teachers and counselors, and even talked to principals, if necessary. The youths knew that their parents had an independent source of information about their school performance, and therefore they knew they could not fool them.

The parents who succeeded in keeping their children in school were aggressive in making contacts with the schools. They asserted their right to be adequately informed about their children's educational progress and did not hesitate to demand that school staff meet with them and provide accurate information. These parents had the social skills to keep the interactions with school staff positive, despite the fact that their teenagers had serious school problems. Their attitude and their presence at the school encouraged school staff to try to help them resolve the student's problems.

One mother told us, "I think I have a good relationship [with teachers and school administrators]. Because they know where I'm coming from. They know that I feel comfortable enough to tell them how I feel. If I hear something from my son, I won't hesitate to call the next day, or ask the teacher about it. They know I feel comfortable enough to go to them. And I know that a lot of parents for many reasons don't do that. But he is my son, then I have my right. I'm his first teacher and his mama, and I have a right to ask what I need to know."

We listened as a mother thought through her need for more involvement in her daughter's summer school program. She said, "Usually, I don't find out till I get a report card through the mail. . . . I don't know how that works, how you get the grades from summer school. I guess that since she's going to summer school—and now this made me realize I should have more contact with the teachers. I should find out who to talk to and see how she is doing in summer school—and not six weeks from now and find out she flunked."

THE CASE STUDIES

To illustrate the effectiveness of these seven strategies, we will examine the 14 case studies from the earlier chapters and evaluate the parents in terms of the actions they took to keep their children in school. Table 9.2 presents the data on the actions of the parents of graduates in terms of which of the seven strategies they employed. Graduates had parents who used most of the seven.

Parents of Graduates

Three of the five parents of graduates used all of the strategies listed in Table 9.2. Maria Elena, Roland, and George were parents who recognized the many vulnerabilities of their children and took purposeful action daily to make certain that their children attended school regularly, did their homework, stayed out of trouble, and stayed in school. All three parents took charge of their children. They also listened to their children and were sympathetic to their perspectives. They set limits on the children's social life by preventing them from staying out too late. They drew the line when it came to "bad" peers. All three parents repeatedly lectured their children about the necessity of going to school. They gave their children frequent pep talks promoting the belief that they could succeed in school.

Maria Elena was the most involved in her son's school. She was a good model of school involvement. She spent time working with the school staff making certain that her son got into every program that might help him.

TABLE 9.2. Strategies Used by the Parents of Graduates

Student (Parent)	Parent in Charge	Two-Way Influence	Set Limits	Monitor Student	Draw Line with Peers	Continuous Message	Involved in School
Chapter 2—Tracking Robert (Roland)	Yes	Yes	Yes	Yes	Yes	Yes	Yes
Chapter 3—Grade Retention Richard (Maria Elena)	Yes	Yes	Yes	Yes	Yes	Yes	Yes
Chapter 4—Gangs Ramona (Paula)	Yes	Yes	Yes	Yes	Yes	Yes	No
Chapter 5—Teen Motherhood Norma (Alfredo)	No	Yes	No	Yes	No	Yes	Yes
Chapter 6—Immigrants Linda (George)	Yes	Yes	Yes	Yes	Yes	Yes	Yes

When her son left home and became independent, he was able to enroll himself in the programs he needed to graduate. Maria Elena had taught her son how to make the school system work for him.

Roland was less involved in his son's school. Roland had attempted to change his son's status in middle school by asking that his son be moved up to the college-preparatory track in math. When Roland was rebuffed by a teacher, he gave up advocating for his son's academic placement. Still, Roland was a sponsor of his son's soccer team and, therefore, a parent known to at least some of the high school personnel. He knew when to expect report cards and studied them closely when they arrived. He did not hesitate to contact teachers if he needed to.

George, along with his wife Estella, had avoided contact with the school until their daughter attempted suicide and was threatened with a knife at school. Perceiving that Linda's life was on the line, they mustered their courage and met with the high school principal to advocate for her. Their intervention succeeded in reducing the disciplinary actions against her. Linda was grateful and she stayed in school to graduate.

The two other parents of graduates employed most, but not all, of the seven strategies, which suggests that it is not essential that parents take all seven actions in order to bring about the graduation of their children.

One of the two was Alfredo. He lacked authority over his daughter. Norma was a headstrong teenager, and she did not perceive her father as in charge of her school or social life. However, Alfredo did take other actions that were critical in keeping his daughter in school long enough to graduate. He listened to her, monitored her schoolwork, and communicated regularly with school personnel. However, his lack of authority with Norma and his inability to draw the line with peers resulted in the birth of her two children.

Alfredo succeeded in instilling in Norma a belief in the importance of getting a high school diploma so that when Norma became a teen mother, she was motivated to study hard and stay in school. Alfredo also worked hard to take care of Norma's baby so that she could continue in school and graduate on time. Watching her father make many personal sacrifices so that she could stay in school made Norma aware of the strength of his commitment to her education. She graduated from high school on time.

The other parent, Paula, was unable to involve herself in the school of her daughter, Ramona. Paula did not feel comfortable going to the school, and she did not have a telephone. She was obese; she had dropped out of school in the sixth grade; she was extremely poor. Given her own limitations, Paula was forced to rely on her children to advocate for themselves within the school.

The fact that Ramona did advocate for herself is a testament to the persuasiveness of her mother who continuously preached to Ramona about the value of a high school diploma. Working as a team with their mother, Paula's older sisters who had dropped out gave Ramona the same message as their mother, *"Don't be like me. Stay in school."*

Paula also drew the line about Ramona's gang friends and drug-addicted boyfriend. This message, combined with some careful advice from a drug counselor, helped Ramona pull back from the group that would have made her high school graduation unlikely.

Parents of Dropouts

Table 9.3 presents the actions taken—or not taken—by the parents of dropouts. As you can see, it was rare for such parents to use any of the seven strategies described earlier in this chapter. Three of the parents, Suzanna, Petra, and the Garcías, used none of the strategies. Specifically, these parents did not take charge of their children, they did not engage in two-way influence with their children, they did not set limits on their children's school and social life, they did not closely monitor their children, they did not draw the line between good and bad peers, they did not continuously lecture their children about the value of an education, and they were not involved in their children's school.

Suzanna had never been highly involved with her son Salvador. Salvador was the second child born to her as an unmarried teen. She sent Salvador to live with a relative. Salvador returned to live with Suzanna only after he became a young adolescent and an active gang member. Petra had been more involved with her son James, who was the youngest of her six children. Yet Petra and her husband had little education, and they felt unable to do much to help him get what he needed. Especially after James began working part-time and driving his own car, Petra and her husband lost what little contact they had with him. Finally, the Garcías were overwhelmed with the needs of their large family and did not perceive themselves as having the resources to take the actions that might have encouraged Pedro to stay in school. To their credit, they prevented him from further involvement in gang activities, but they were unable to promote a proschool peer group for him.

Three of the parents of dropouts attempted to employ a few of the seven strategies. The mothers of the teen mothers each attempted one of the seven parental strategies. Caroline did listen to her daughter and tried to negotiate with her to get her back in school. However, because Caroline worked long

TABLE 9.3. Strategies Used by the Parents of Dropouts

| | Parent Strategies | | | | | | |
Student (Parent)	Parent in Charge	Two-Way Influence	Set Limits	Monitor Student	Draw Line with Peers	Continuous Message	Involved in School
Chapter 2—Tracking James (Petra)	No	No	No	No	No	No	No
Chapter 4—Gangs Salvador (Suzanna)	No	No	No	No	No	No	No
Chapter 5—Teen Motherhood Kathy (Caroline) Lupe (Graciela)	No Yes	Yes No	No No	No No	No No	No No	No No
Chapter 6—Immigrants Enrique (Antonio)	No	Yes	No	No	No	No	No
Chapter 8—Bureaucratic Glitches Pedro (the Garcías)	No	No	No	No	No	No	No

hours, Kathy had many opportunities to avoid school. Caroline attempted to assume command of the household many times, but her long work hours made it impossible for her to monitor her daughter's school attendance or social life or set limits on her. Although Caroline criticized her daughter's "bad" friends, her frequent absence from home made it impossible for her to promote a healthy peer group for her daughter. Caroline gave her daughter inconsistent messages about the value of a high school diploma. She told us that her own high school degree had not helped her get a decent job. Caroline had little comprehension of the school system and never could get the school to untangle the administrative snarls caused by her daughter's frequent absences.

Graciela also worked long hours, and this prevented her from taking most of the parental actions associated with graduation. In fact, Graciela relied on her daughter to act like a surrogate mother to take care of her many younger siblings while her parents worked. Because Graciela expected obedience, she felt that all she needed to do was tell her daughter what to do. Graciela had no appreciation of the value of listening to her daughter, or of establishing a relationship with her based on mutual respect. She assumed that because she had told her daughter to go to school and stay out of trouble, that her daughter would do this. But since Graciela was unable to monitor her daughter's social or school life, or set limits on her schoolwork, or draw the line with peers, it was easy for her daughter, Lupe, to stop attending school. Graciela did not directly involve herself in her daughter's school because, as an undocumented immigrant with little education, she did not feel comfortable visiting her school or talking to school personnel. Indeed, Graciela's expectation that her daughter stay home from school to take care of younger siblings when they became sick meant that Lupe was expected to be a caretaker first and a student second. These priorities undercut the power of Graciela's message to Lupe to go to school.

Enrique also came from a large Mexican family that expected him to give up school to work for the family. When we first met Enrique, he was living with his brother Antonio. Perhaps because Antonio and Enrique were brothers, they naturally engaged in mutual influence. However, because Antonio and his wife viewed Enrique as a young adult, they did not take charge of him or take any of the other actions that parents of graduates took. Antonio and his wife were not involved in his schooling, and they did not constantly lecture him about staying in school. Enrique had no friends outside of school because his family forced him to come home directly after school. While they did not monitor his schoolwork or social life, Antonio, his wife, and Enrique did have talks about their desires; and when we began the study, Enrique's desire to continue in school was listened to. But then the family situation changed, and

Enrique was pressured to give up school and work to support his parents. Enrique became a dropout to satisfy his family's needs.

Parents of Students with Ambiguous Outcomes

In our sample, there were many students who neither graduated nor dropped out. We consider their outcomes to be ambiguous. Some of these students got a GED; some left school without a diploma because they could not pass the standardized test required by the state; others were still in high school when we ended our study. In Table 9.4 we present three examples of such outcomes from our case studies.

We consider the GED an ambiguous outcome because it is a certificate of completion, but one that has less value than a high school diploma. In Chapter 7, we described two students who left school with a GED. When we examined their parents' actions, we could see no consistent pattern.

Martin, Sr.'s actions resemble those of the parents of dropouts. Martin, Sr. had little authority over his son. Apparently, Martin, Sr. had not paid much attention to his son in elementary school, assuming that he was a "chip off the ol' block" and doing fine. When Martin, Jr. started having problems in middle school, all Martin, Sr. could think of was bossing his son around, an action that his son reacted very strongly against. Compounding the problem, the mother reacted emotionally to her son's failures, and this only isolated Martin, Jr. further from the family. Consequently, there was little communication between the son and his parents.

Martin, Sr. was totally ineffective in promoting a positive peer group for his son. The father did set limits on his son, making him do his schoolwork before he went out with his friends. This resulted in his son spending hours in his room alone, dabbling in his homework and talking to his friends on the telephone. The parents engaged in constant propagandizing about the value of a high school diploma, but their message—"Stay in school. Don't become a bum"—probably produced more anxiety in Martin, Jr. than motivation to stay in school. Martin, Sr. became discouraged by the lack of resources within the school to solve his son's problem and essentially gave up working with the school personnel.

In contrast, the father of Felipe, Juan Felipe, took most of the actions typical of a parent of a graduate, despite the fact that his son chose to get the GED. In bringing up his son, this father had two major difficulties. First, his son had marked learning disabilities, and second, he had to get custody of his son from his ex-wife and then integrate him into his new family. Juan Felipe handled

TABLE 9.4. Strategies Used by the Parents of Students with Ambiguous Outcomes

Student (Parent)	Parent in Charge	Two-Way Influence	Set Limits	Monitor Student	Draw Line with Peers	Continuous Message	Involved in School
				Parent Strategies			
Chapter 3—Grade Retention							
Alice (Jesse)	Yes	Yes	Yes	Yes	Yes	Yes	Yes
Chapter 7—The GED							
Martin, Jr. (Martin, Sr.)	No	No	Yes	No	No	Yes	No
Felipe (Juan Felipe)	Yes	Yes	Yes	Yes	Yes	Yes	No

these difficulties and kept his son in school until he was 18. Then he encouraged him to get his GED and go to the local community college.

Juan Felipe and his second wife took charge of Felipe when he was in sixth grade. Felipe recognized that his parents had specific expectations regarding his conduct, and Felipe had to comply or face the consequences. In his new family, his parents monitored his behavior closely and routinely promoted the value of trying hard in school to all the children in the family. They encouraged Felipe to make friends with the academically successful students in school.

The only weakness in Juan Felipe's behavior was his failure to become involved in his son's school. This caused problems at two critical points: first, when Felipe repeated the sixth grade, and second, when the father neglected to get special education services for Felipe upon entering high school.

In addition to the two students who got the GED, we considered the case of Alice, who had accumulated enough credits to graduate but was unable, after four tries, to pass the standardized test required for graduation. Her father Jesse, a widower who brought up nine daughters, took all seven of the parental actions associated with a graduation outcome. Specifically, he had authority over Alice. Yet, he listened to her and gave her opportunities to get her way. He set strong limits, particularly on her social life. He monitored her schoolwork closely and communicated regularly with school personnel. He was a motivational expert, constantly giving Alice pep talks. He called on all her older sisters to help Alice stay in school and get jobs.

Alice would have graduated if the school district had educated her to meet the academic standards required for graduation. Because the schools failed her, she was left without a diploma.

POLICY RECOMMENDATIONS

Cultural differences between homes and schools do not inevitably become educational barriers unless school policies make them so. Indeed, schools and families must become allies to overcome the negative peer cultures that discourage school achievement and encourage self-destructive behavior among youth. Most of the Mexican-origin parents we studied were willing to communicate with school personnel and to do whatever they could to help their children graduate from high school. But the schools treated them in ways that made their participation in their children's education almost impossible.

If school districts are going to reduce their dropout rates, school personnel will have to assume greater responsibility for keeping all students in school and on the path toward graduation. They cannot expect all parents to take the primary responsibility for solving their children's school problems. Many parents are like those in our sample. They are keenly aware of their own limitations and are surprised that the school personnel expect them to take the responsibility for motivating students to go to school. These parents believe that school personnel, as the experts in education, should know how to motivate students to stay in school, do their schoolwork, and graduate. These parents believe that they themselves have done all they know how to do, and in our view, they are correct.

Our ethnographic information told us clearly that an inability to understand English and a lack of understanding of the American educational system were barriers for many of the parents in our study. One of the reasons that our statistical results indicated that these cultural variables were unrelated to graduation was that the schools discouraged the participation of all parents, regardless of their ability to understand English or the educational system. Even the parents who spoke English and were born and educated in the United States encountered resistance when they tried to intervene in course planning for their children. We met many parents who had enough education to understand what was happening to their "at risk" children, but who were unable to prevent their children from dropping out of school.

We recommend that all parents use the seven effective strategies to guide their children toward high school graduation. But we recognize that these strategies only keep the student in school. School attendance will result in improved outcomes for students only if the schools do a better job educating them. Because of the importance of improving schools, our last chapter is dedicated to the kinds of changes schools need to make so that all students can graduate from high school with skills that allow them to either continue their education or get a good job.

TEN

"What
would I
change?
Everything."

What Schools Must Do to Improve Graduation Rates

This chapter describes the changes schools must make in order to improve the graduation rates of Mexican-origin youth. Our recommendations for change are derived from our observations of the disparity between what the students in our study needed and what schools provided them. For the most part, the schools blamed the parents for the low achievement, bad attitudes, and scholastic gaps of the students. We argue that the schools must accept the students and their families as they are, assess the academic skills of students, and meet their academic needs promptly and effectively.

Our recommendations for change are based on the premise that *schools* have the primary responsibility for educating students. Parents and communities have a part to play in the formal educational process, but schools must assume the leading role in assuring that our youth have the scholastic skills they will need to be productive adults and good citizens.

Overall, the recommendations we make in this chapter will improve the graduation rates for all students, not just "at risk" students of Mexican origin. These recommendations involve changing many of our basic assumptions about education, and they will require a major restructuring of our schools. It is not enough that a few individuals in schools try hard to solve the school problems of individual "at risk" students. The entire educational system must be overhauled so that schools can meet the needs of all students.

Our recommendations for change are not original. In fact, since the time of our study, parts of these recommendations have been tried, in piecemeal fashion, in a few schools within the school district we studied. What is unique about our recommendations is that we put all the pieces together to define a coherent package of revisions that will improve greatly the chances that all youth will graduate from high school. Furthermore, we explain why these revisions will help students stay in school.

Our recommendations for change can be clustered into seven broad areas. They are:

- putting the learning of students first
- clarifying scholastic standards
- preventing student failure
- making participation in schoolwork rewarding
- emphasizing hard work
- making schools accessible
- creating clear pathways to good outcomes

In the following sections of this chapter we will elaborate on these areas and make specific recommendations for change.

PUTTING THE LEARNING OF STUDENTS FIRST

Most of the school personnel who worked in the school district we studied did not focus their attention on student learning. They were doing their jobs as defined by tradition. Administrators responded to the demands of higher authorities, and teachers covered the course material.

Administrators

During our study, we observed administrators doing everything but participating in the learning of students. Each of the district's four superintendents was focused on meeting the demands of the school board. The superintendents' time, and the time of most district-level administrators, was devoted largely to compliance with state laws, accreditation requirements, federal laws, and court mandates.[1] School principals spent much of their time meeting with their supervisors, trying to meet the demands of the higher administrators as they tried to meet the demands of state-level administrators. Assistant and vice principals spent their time on discipline and administrative tasks, most of which added little to the academic skills of individual students. The attention of these administrators was focused on their own career promotion or their own career protection. They took actions to free themselves from blame for the failures of students and schools.

We recommend that all administrators become instructional leaders and part-time teachers. If administrators spent more of their time teaching, helping students learn, then administrators would be more likely to identify learning problems earlier than they do now. By working in the classroom, administrators would have firsthand knowledge of the many problems facing teachers. They could see the empty seats in the classroom and the number of students who do not complete their schoolwork. By taking their turn as teachers, they, too, would see that the traditional teaching techniques and the content of most courses do not motivate students.

The point of having administrators spend more time engaged in the process of educating students is that this experience helps administrators identify problems early so that they can be solved early. During our study, administrators took actions to solve problems only after they had become so widespread and severe that state politicians and educational bureaucracies demanded change. If administrators had spent their time in school classrooms, observing student performance, they could have seen that a high proportion of students were not meeting the necessary scholastic standards. This observation could have provided them the opportunity to take action quickly to enhance the learning of these students before they failed standardized tests, became alienated from school, and dropped out.

Continuing work in classrooms would give administrators the kind of experience they need to find realistic solutions to school problems. Because teaching administrators would have direct experience with the problems, they would be more likely to understand what needs to be done to solve them. Such administrators could look to two sources for solutions—one inside, the other outside the school itself. Most schools have some teachers who are able to teach in ways that enhance the skills of students who are having various academic problems. Working with these teachers would inform administrators about what less effective teachers need to be doing to bring about positive results. Administrators should also seek help from teachers and teaching experts outside their school and be responsible for the dissemination of information on effective techniques to all teachers.

Teachers

Teachers have the lowest status of all the professionals in the school system. Yet, they are the ones with the most direct influence on the learning of students. *Before student achievement can become the first priority of the school system, teachers and teaching must be seen as more important than administrators and the work they do.* The job of administrators should not be to serve the interests of those higher in the hierarchy, but to serve the needs of teachers and students as they work together to promote learning.

Even though we advocate greater authority and respect for teachers, we must acknowledge that not all the teachers our students encountered were effective. Partly this is the result of basing school administration on scientific management, an orientation to organizational structure that puts teachers on the bottom of the hierarchy and discourages them from thinking and taking responsibility for the outcomes of their students. Like assembly line workers, they are supposed to do what they are told to do. Teachers have been trained to create lesson plans that cover the course material or the essential elements of the grade-level content assigned to them. It was assumed that if teachers followed the script laid out in their lesson plans, then all students would learn.[2] The inability of relatively high proportions of students to meet scholastic standards after the enactment of these lesson plans suggests that the "essential elements" approach to teaching does not work. These methods of teaching do not induce all students to learn what they need to learn in order to meet scholastic standards.

All the students and parents in our study differentiated good teachers from bad ones. They saw good teachers as people who bent over backward to help students learn. Bad teachers were ones who didn't try to help all students learn. When we asked one mother what she would change about the schools to meet the needs of her son, she answered, *"What would I change? I mean I would probably change everything.* I would get teachers in there that I felt were really concerned about their students, that were really wanting to see the students achieve and were willing to take the time."

Rather than continuing to do what they have always done, teachers need to rearrange their priorities so that the scholastic gains of all of their students are their measure of success, not the quality of their lesson plans or the merit of their bulletin boards. The best teachers will be those who are able to bring all students up to meeting the standards.

Before all teachers can become good teachers, they must be trained and re-trained to have the teaching skills necessary to promote learning in all students. Only after they have mastered a wide and deep range of teaching techniques can we expect all teachers to believe that all their students can learn. As long as some teachers believe that some students can never meet the scholastic standards, then teachers will give up on some students, and students will give up on themselves.

We found that teachers gave up on many of the students we studied. For example, Salvador, from Chapter 4 (Gangs), was allowed to spend his entire elementary school years in bilingual classrooms, pretending not to know how to speak English. He was able to fool his teachers because they believed that not all Mexican-origin students could learn English. Obviously, his teachers had given up on him. His learning was not a priority to them.

Some teachers teach the same way year after year regardless of whether their approach has been effective in bringing all students up to standard.[3] They blame the students' lack of ability and/or their parents' deficiencies when students do not learn. Typically, these teachers do not attempt to change the way they are teaching so that failing students can succeed.

This resistance to change must be eliminated if student learning is to become the first priority of schools. When everyone in the school believes that all students can meet high academic standards, then it is more likely that all students will meet these standards. Teachers should not give up trying to get students to learn. They must try one approach, assess its effect on the student's learning, and if the student still is not learning, then they must try another approach, and on and on, until the student demonstrates understanding and is performing up to specific scholastic standards. Teachers need to use a wide variety of teaching techniques and understand better what is interesting and meaningful to their students. They need to be open to innovation and help from other teachers and administrators. They should never be allowed to give up on a student.

Social Services

Mexican-origin students are less likely than others to have their basic needs met, because of the high and increasing rates of poverty for this segment of society.[4] Given this, schools serving Mexican-origin students will need to take actions that allow the basic needs of all students to be met. In particular, schools must allow social workers and other health professionals to work within schools to assist poor families in meeting the basic needs of students. We are not recommending that the school district pay for these additional services, but that schools allow social workers and other health professionals, paid from other sources, to work within the school.

School districts have been reluctant to allow social workers and other health professionals to work within the schools. They have preferred that poor families seek their services outside of the school. But many poor families avoid contact with social service agencies, even if their children need help.[5] These families, however, are more willing to receive services if they are offered within the school, as a part of their children's educational program. Because students have difficulty learning when their basic needs are not met, teachers are often stymied in their efforts to enhance the learning of these students. Thus, in order to bring the scholastic performance of all students up to desired standards, schools must facilitate the work of social workers and other health professionals by allowing them into the school.

For example, in Chapter 5 (Teen Motherhood), Caroline's children stayed out of school for one week because the school district would not enroll them until they had the appropriate immunizations. Similarly, when Caroline's daughter Kathy developed a sore throat, Caroline let her stay home from school for two weeks. She could not afford a doctor. Apparently, the school district assumed that all families have quick and easy access to health care. This is not a reasonable assumption for any low-income family.[6] For Caroline's children, the lost time from school made it difficult for them to start school with the other students and feel accepted by teachers and classmates. If there had been a health clinic in the school, then Caroline's children would have lost no days of school for these health reasons. They would have been able to adjust to the school environment and understand their coursework more easily because they could have begun the school year with everyone else.

CLARIFYING SCHOLASTIC STANDARDS

Caroline, like most of the parents we studied, did not realize the importance of each day of classroom attendance. She had no understanding of the high graduation standards her children would have to meet. She did not understand that they would have to take advantage of every learning opportunity available to them to be able to meet these standards. This was true because the schools had not communicated these standards to her in a meaningful way.

School Personnel

Not only have parents been left in the dark about academic standards, but also most school personnel as well have lacked a clear understanding of these standards. *We recommend that all teachers, administrators, and school board members be able to describe in detail the type and level of skills all students need to graduate from high school.* Even those teaching kindergarten and other elementary grades should know what standards their students will have to meet to graduate.

There has been no shared understanding among all teachers within a district of how their own personal or grade-level standards fit into those used to evaluate students for graduation. It was not uncommon for each teacher to use her or his own unique set of standards when teaching and evaluating students. Teachers were not trained to calibrate their standards so that the students completing their course or grade level were prepared to meet the standards at the next level. Indeed, teachers within a grade level across schools were not required to have the same standards of evaluation for students.

One of the problems we identified in our research was the misalignment between the standards used by elementary school teachers and those used by secondary school teachers. Many of our students arrived in middle school without the skills they needed to succeed in the middle school classroom. Clearly, many of the elementary school teachers had not brought the students we interviewed up to the scholastic skills standards required to continue on the pathway to graduate from high school.

There are several reasons why this happened. One reason was ignorance. Teachers in most elementary schools are organized by grade level. Kindergarten teachers talk to kindergarten teachers, first grade teachers talk to first grade teachers, and so on. Rarely do teachers compare evaluation standards across grade levels, even within the same school. During the time of our study, middle school teachers never talked to elementary school teachers about the type and level of skills that elementary school graduates should have. Consequently, elementary school teachers never knew that many of the students they had passed on to middle school were not able to function in middle school classrooms. They did not have the benefit of feedback giving them the information they needed to change their teaching.

Another reason is prejudice. Many teachers do not believe that all students can learn.[7] In particular, they are quick to conclude that Mexican-origin students, especially those from lower socioeconomic backgrounds, are unable to meet the standards. Consequently, they give up on these students, even as early as kindergarten. They expect little from them and, given the nature of self-fulfilling prophecies, their expectations are confirmed. Take, for example, Lupe, the teen mom from Chapter 5. She attended eight years of bilingual education within the district and still did not feel capable of talking to us in English. When she stopped attending school, at age 18, she had a fourth-grade reading level in English. Clearly, no one knew what standards to use in educating Lupe, and given that she was from an illiterate Mexican family, no one bothered to teach her English or bring her up to an acceptable academic level.

The problem of academic standards does not reside exclusively in elementary schools. As the example of Alice from Chapter 3 (Grade Retention) clearly demonstrated, there were many students who were able to accumulate enough credits to graduate from high school, but in the process, did not acquire the skills necessary to pass the standardized exit-level exam, even after four tries! High schools have offered classes with standards so low that they fail to give the students the skills they will need to graduate and get a job with the potential of generating income above the poverty level.

High Standards That Are Well Known

To prevent this misalignment between skill levels taught and skill levels needed, we recommend that secondary teachers use standards in their courses that are linked to those required for graduation. Students should not be allowed to take four years of English and mathematics courses that are taught at such low levels that students are not prepared to meet the standards for graduation. Taxpayers should not allow schools to waste money by offering such English and math courses.

We recommend that graduation standards be high enough so that high school graduates are qualified to get good jobs or to enroll in postsecondary education immediately after graduation. Many of the students in our sample were trained to meet such low standards that by the time they graduated, they had no chance to succeed in college or in a job with a future. Even the graduates within our sample were not trained to have the skills they would need to get a good job in the local high-tech industries. Instead, they had been prepared to work in minimum-wage jobs the rest of their lives. As taxpayers, we should not allow this to happen. Schools should exist to give all students the skills they need to get jobs that pay above poverty-level wages.

The only way that high standards can be understood by all parents, school personnel, and taxpayers is through open and public discussion of the content and level of these standards. This discussion will need to occur in the newspapers and on television and radio shows as well as in public meetings at schools, churches, recreational centers, and so on. Currently, the citizens who pay for the school system generally have no idea what standards the schools are using when they produce high school graduates. Standards are rarely discussed in the news media, and when they are, the content of the standards is not described, only the percentages who are passing or failing.[8]

In Germany, students seeking entry to college must pass the Arbitur, an examination created by teachers and graded by teachers. These examinations involve extensive essay writing. On some topics, such as art or technology, students are expected to demonstrate their skill by performing the skill for a group of evaluators. Because the content of the examination and the quality of performance required to pass the test are known to teachers, they know what to teach their students. They know which skills and what level of skills their students must have. Because teachers understand the standards for passing the Arbitur, they communicate this information to students, who, in turn, learn what will be expected of them. To fulfill these expectations, German students intending to get bachelor's degrees take challenging courses that prepare them to meet the standards.[9]

German students seeking apprenticeships in any of about 370 separate occupations can also learn what is expected of them in order to enter and graduate from these programs with a certified skill. The contents of these standards are created and evaluated by committees composed primarily of industry representatives, both workers and management, working with teachers. In this way, the public has access to the graduation standards used by schools and can judge if they are high enough and appropriate for success in the real world of employment. Taxpayers in Germany have direct knowledge that public monies spent on education are well spent. They have direct knowledge that the schools are training students to have the skills they will need to be successful adults.[10]

Standardized Tests

Open discussions by a diverse group of Americans about the substance and level of graduation standards have not happened in the U.S., in part because we have relied on standardized tests to evaluate our students. These tests have been created by corporations to be sold to schools, school districts, and state boards of education so that the administrators in charge of the schools can demonstrate to taxpayers that the schools are performing well. Instead of relying on the evaluations of teachers, American schools have evaluated their students by means of these standardized tests. This reliance on external evaluation of students originated in the early 20th century when school administrators and political leaders began to doubt that teachers could do an objective job of evaluating students.[11]

The educational testing industry has flourished in the U.S. The industry produced affordable products—that is, standardized tests—that offered quick and easy assessments of student achievement. The use of multiple-choice items and the optically scannable answer sheet has made it possible for thousands of these tests to be "graded" in a short time by the use of computers.

The testing industry preferred using the same test questions over and over again. They explained that this was necessary in order to preserve the reliability of the tests. By using the same items year after year, test makers claimed the tests could gauge whether student performance was improving, declining, or staying the same.

The test makers argued that if the test questions were made public, teachers would simply teach the students the answers to these multiple-choice questions so that their students would look good. This would jeopardize the validity of the evaluation. The items were copyrighted by the testing corporations. School personnel were prevented by education codes from allowing parents and teachers to view the questions. In so doing, they also prevented the public from learning what students were expected to know. The net result has been that parents and teachers are blind to academic standards and are unable to help children meet them.

The problem with keeping the items secret became apparent after passing the TAAS test became a requirement for graduation. Thousands of students flunked the TAAS exit test and were denied their diplomas. A body of disgruntled parents began questioning the value of such standardized tests. Other parents did not approve of the control that the test had over the curriculum. Almost all school districts in the state had responded to the pressure created by the TAAS test by aligning their curriculum to the content of the test.

Since the TAAS test began driving the curriculum and the consequences for failing were severe, parents realized that they needed to know what questions were on the test. Parents had to resort to legal challenges in order to gain access to the TAAS test questions. A district court ruled that keeping the test questions from the public infringed on the fundamental right of parents to direct the education of their children. (See Endnote 8 for information about the case.) Therefore, the Texas Education Agency agreed to make public the TAAS test questions after the tests had been administered and graded in the spring of 1995.

Accountability

In this book, we described briefly the evolution of the TAAS test in Texas, a criterion-referenced test that has been used to evaluate students and schools. Texas enacted legislation requiring that individual students be able to pass the TAAS test in order to receive a high school diploma. Only later did the Legislature begin the effort to hold the schools accountable for the success of their students in passing the TAAS test. Meanwhile, students like Alice were left out, having to suffer the consequences of taking a series of low-level courses and of school neglect, to bear the burden alone of being unable to get a high school diploma.

We recommend that schools and school districts be the first entity to be held accountable for educating students up to the desired standard. This may involve decentralizing school administration and encouraging school-based decision making. If schools or school districts continue to fail, then they need to be taken over by other entities, such as state- or national-level ones. This might involve replacing school administrators with educators more active in producing scholastic results. It might also involve retraining teachers so that they will have the skills and resources they need to bring about the desired learning in the failing students. The families of failing children may need additional services to help them do their part of the work involved in bringing all students up to acceptable levels of scholastic skills. The state or national entities taking over the schools would have to generate the resources to provide these services.

While individual students should be held accountable for attending school and participating fully in the educational process, they should not be held accountable for meeting the standards for graduation if their school or school district has been ineffective.

To hold schools accountable, students, their parents, and school personnel need to have reliable information about the scholastic progress of schools, classrooms, and individual students. The parents and students in our study got their most frequent indicator of scholastic progress in the form of grades, and yet the standards used by teachers to give grades varied so extremely that they were almost meaningless. Teachers of low-income Mexican-origin students were often overly generous to elementary school students, giving the students and their parents no reason to suspect that the students might be unprepared for middle school. Similarly, many middle and high schools have offered so many courses at such low levels that it was easy for students to pass these courses with good grades and still not acquire the skills they needed to get a decent job or succeed in college.

We recommend that parents and students receive frequent and meaningful feedback about the scholastic progress of students. Students should be "graded" on their proximity to the next higher skill level. We recommend that fourth-grade, eighth-grade, and exit-level standards in reading comprehension, writing, and mathematics be clearly defined. They should also be calibrated so that the standards used at the exit level are related to standards used at eighth grade, and the standards used at eighth grade are related to standards used at fourth grade. Beginning in the first grade, each student's performance in reading, writing, and mathematics should be evaluated frequently to determine how far each individual student is from meeting the fourth-grade standards. Once the student has met these standards, the student should be evaluated in terms of progress toward meeting the eighth-grade standard. Having met the eighth-grade standard, the student should be evaluated in terms of progress toward meeting the exit-level standard. These assessments should be shared with parents so that both parents and teachers know how far a student needs to go to meet the next standard.

Such feedback was not given to the students or parents in our study. Information about each student's percentile scores on norm-referenced tests was mailed home, but these computer-generated sheets had little or no meaning for the students or the parents in our sample. They were couched in educational jargon. The local newspaper published the percentage of students passing the state's required standardized tests at three grade levels, but few of the parents in our sample read the newspaper, and even if they did, the articles did not explain the content of the tests.

What we are recommending may seem like grade equivalents. The problem with grade equivalents is that they are norm referenced and inform us more about how the student's skills stack up compared to others than about how their skills compare to an absolute standard. Instead of grade equivalents, we recommend that students' performance be scored in terms of their proximity toward the skills they will need to pass the next level of criterion-referenced tests. We assume that students will make steady progress towards meeting the standards. If some students are not progressing at a rate that will allow them to pass the exit-level test by the age of 18 years, then teachers and parents will know early so that efforts can be made to increase these students' rates of progress.

Similarly, some high schools in our study distributed information at Back-to-School Nights listing the competencies that students were supposed to possess at specific grade levels. This information was not useful for parents because it was couched in educational jargon, not plain English, and the information did not indicate the extent to which each student demonstrated specific competencies. Administrators must stop giving parents meaningless information about standards and instead begin giving them useful information about each student's progress.

We recommend that criterion-referenced evaluations be substituted for the norm-referenced multiple-choice tests that have been used so that the students will not be overburdened with continuous testing. While we believe that the introduction of criterion-referenced tests like the TAAS is a step forward in making the standards high and clear, we do not endorse all aspects of the TAAS test, nor do we endorse an evaluation system that relies largely on multiple-choice tests. Indeed, we recommend that states substitute performance-based assessments for multiple-choice tests, particularly at the exit level and in some specific content areas, such as social studies, science, and writing. Rather than pass a multiple-choice test in social studies, science, or writing, we prefer that students demonstrate mastery by producing an acceptable social studies, science, or writing project.

Furthermore, all standards should be evaluated continuously to determine if they are relevant to success after graduation, defined broadly. If there are skills needed for success that we have not selected as graduation standards, then we should add those skills to the requirements for graduation; likewise, if there are required skills that have no bearing on success at employment, citizenship, or general well-being, then we should delete them from graduation standards.

Finally, we recommend that states incorporate national standards into their own state standards. This infusion of national standards into those used by each state to evaluate students for graduation would help each state evaluate the success of its schools. Moreover, if the schools become successful at bringing all students up to national standards, this will attract more industries into the state. For example, if 90% of Texas high school students met national standards in math and English, industries that bring with them high-paying jobs would be excited about expanding in Texas. Such industries would be guaranteed an ample supply of easy-to-train workers. More importantly, when schools become successful at bringing all students up to national standards, existing industries will be able to upgrade their production processes faster because their employees will have the necessary skills to make this transition quicker.

PREVENTING SCHOOL FAILURE

We believe that most of the students we studied could have graduated if the schools had been organized so that no students were allowed to fail. *We recommend that when a student is not making enough progress toward meeting academic standards, teachers and other school personnel should mobilize to change the way they have been delivering the student's education.* School personnel should identify the cause of the slow pace of progress quickly and take action immediately to increase the student's pace of learning. Students would not be passed on unprepared to the next grade level. Promotion would be based on performance, not on time served in class. Students would move up by mastering a task, skill, or topic, not by completing a course or passing a grade level. Each student would receive the appropriate instruction until the task or skill was mastered. Students should never be allowed to flunk a course or a whole grade level.

Good Teachers

The measure of a good teacher should be how many students they turn around, not how many students they flunk. It has been assumed that teachers who flunk students are good teachers because they have high standards. This will change when the absolute standards, described above, are used by all teachers. Then, an excellent teacher will be one who has brought students from making little or no progress to making average or above-average progress in meeting standards. All students should be in classrooms where instruction is at a high level. The school and the teacher should be responsible to make certain that support services and additional resources are made available so that no students fail. This approach has been used in San Diego with remarkable success.[12] In the instructional setting we envision, a poor teacher is someone who ends a course or school year with a high proportion of students who have made little progress. In the past, teachers who failed many students were thought to be keeping high standards. No one questioned the quality of their teaching. In our opinion, the very best teachers ought to be those who can teach heterogeneous groups of students and make them all learn enough to meet high standards.

This will require giving some students more time than we give others to learn the skills they need to meet the standards. In the case of learning to speak, read, and write the English language, students who speak other languages will generally need more time than native speakers of English to meet the standards. This means that such students will probably need longer school days, more school days per year, after-school tutoring and Saturday Morning School in order to meet the graduation standards by the time they are 18 years old.[13] This extension of their learning time should begin the moment that students get off the pace needed to lead to high school graduation at age 18.

More Time Devoted to Learning

Our experience suggests that middle-class Mexican American parents will support the idea of more time spent learning. Juan Felipe, the father of Felipe, who got his GED, is a good example. He thought his son should go to summer school and have more homework, particularly on the weekends. He said, "I think it's something wrong with the school system. Nothing on the weekends, so when they leave Friday, they don't have to do anything until Monday. And it seems to me that the weekends are times when some students can put in an hour or two on Saturday and Sunday."

It may be harder to persuade parents who are extremely poor and need the income from the labor of their adolescent children to support an extension of students' learning time. There were several students in our study who left school to work so that their families could have the income from their full-time employment. If these students and their parents had been convinced that the schoolwork the students were doing would lead them directly to a better future, most of the students would have stayed in school, and worked only part-time.

Such extra time was not available to the students in our study on a daily or weekly basis. When these students did not make the standard for promotion to the next grade level, they were simply recycled through the school year again. This added to the time that it took them to graduate, and many of the dropouts gave up going to school rather than attend classes with younger students.

The extension of a student's learning time should begin at the moment their difficulties first appear, not later, when the students have flunked an entire grade level. With more and better learning experiences, some students will pick up their pace and begin to learn at an average or above-average pace. But others will need more time and assistance to learn throughout their educational career. For them, schools need to provide learning on a 12-month-a-year basis, giving them the amount and type of learning experiences they need to be able to graduate by the time they are 18.[14]

Schools have operated on the assumption that parents are primarily responsible for keeping their children on track academically in school. When a child is having academic difficulties, teachers and school administrators assume that it is the parents' responsibility to mobilize the school's resources on behalf of the child. When parents do not visit the school frequently to demand help for their child, schools ignore the student and assume that the parents do not care.

Jesse, the father of Alice from Chapter 3, was especially exasperated by the inaction of teachers. He made contact with the schools and told them that he wanted his daughter to succeed, but Alice still did not receive the type of help she needed. Jesse explained, "I always tell the teacher, 'I can't teach her, 'cause I don't know the subject.' If she needs more work in so and so, I want her to get that help. . . . Maybe the teachers are waiting for me to go up to them and say, 'Is she doing bad in this, this deal here? Can you teach her about it?' Maybe we're supposed to go up to the teachers and tell them that they should get that kind of attention. I mean, it looks to me that the teacher ought to tell her or me, 'Look here, we're going to have to do that with Alice because she's not doing too good. And we want to try to help her out twice a week, after school when she gets out.' Instead of going home, she'd want her to come there for 30 minutes or an hour, you know. But they never tell me that. Probably it's like, they're not supposed to tell me that. I'm supposed to go out there and tell them about it." But when he told teachers to help his daughter, nothing happened.

Schools failed to appreciate the fact that because many of the parents in our study had little education, they were slow to recognize that their child was having academic difficulties. Even when it became clear to the parents that there was a problem, they did not know how to solve it. These parents rarely approached the school because their work schedules, lack of transportation, or inability to speak English prevented them from interacting with school personnel. Many of the parents we interviewed told us that when they attempted to communicate with school personnel, the school personnel either blamed them for their children's problems or had no useful suggestions for solving the student's academic difficulties. Consequently, these parents gave up trying to communicate with school personnel.

One parent told us, "The teachers don't know, you go in and talk to them and they can't tell you anything useful. They tell you that you need to talk to your kid and ask them how they're doing. Well, we ask them how they're doing and they say they're doing fine."

We recommend that teachers and other school personnel learn how to give parents useful advice about how to keep their children in school and on the pathway toward graduation. Such advice could come in the form of explaining the seven strategies described in Chapter 9. Or the teacher could recommend that the parent contact a parent support group in their neighborhood and give the parent the telephone number and name of a contact person. This useful advice could also encompass recommending home visits by social workers. School administrators should provide such information to all teachers so that they have specific recommendations to give parents when the parents ask for help.

Only if the student is absent from school frequently or shows signs of abuse or neglect should school personnel blame the child's parents for his or her slow pace of academic progress. A student's poverty, inability to speak English, or lack of parents who are highly involved in the school should not be used as an excuse for ignoring the education of that student.

MAKING PARTICIPATION IN SCHOOLWORK REWARDING

One of the common reasons that the students in our study failed was that they skipped classes. Skipping, or leaving school without permission, was a popular activity among the students in our sample. As one student put it, "'Cause English . . . it wasn't fun, and it's your easiest class to skip because you can't get caught . . . there's other students in the halls. And I cut that class a couple of times. I shouldn't have, but I'm a kid. I'm still young. I'm experiencing things . . . it's hard to stop. You're there and you're bored . . . all you hear is the teacher talking. Your friends are bored. And you gotta do somethin'."

Admittedly, this student was partially responsible for his own skipping. He knew he was supposed to be in class and yet he rationalized his skipping in terms of his adolescent status. Parents have little control over skipping once the child is at school. Consequently, the school was also responsible. School personnel had given up on keeping students in classrooms. It was easy to skip because school policies made it virtually impossible for school personnel to determine who was skipping and who had permission to be in the halls. Skipping was so common that it became a central part of the peer culture. Furthermore, the teacher of this student did not seem attentive to the problem. The teacher did not assume authority for class attendance by attempting to engage the interest of all students in the content of the course. Skipping was a problem because students missed the learning experiences present in the classroom and because skipping students often became involved in risky behavior, such as sexual intercourse or drug use. When students skipped too much, they could not complete the work needed to earn credit for the course. Without the credit, they were less likely to be promoted. Yet neither the students nor the school staff seemed to link skipping directly to school failure.

We found that school personnel blamed students and their parents for skipping and did not perceive it as a problem that school practices facilitated.[15] We disagree with the explanation for skipping that solely blames students and parents and recommend that schools and the police take action to discourage skipping.

Discourage Skipping

We recommend that schools make the act of skipping difficult. The temptation to skip was especially pronounced for middle school students. To make skipping harder, schools should be organized so that students spend less time in hallways, walking to various classrooms. This can be accomplished by scheduling the same group of students to have several classes in the same classroom and by grouping classrooms together by grade level, not academic topic. Grouping classrooms together by grade level means that students within each grade level don't need to walk to far-flung parts of the building at the end of each period, but rather they move the short distance from one nearby classroom to another.

Eventually, however, students will need to walk to labs, gymnasiums, rest rooms, and so on, and this will give them the opportunity to slip out an exit. To discourage this, we recommend that official monitors be stationed at all exits during the time when students make these moves. We recommend that these monitors be parents. Their job would be to talk to students as they leave the building, advising them that they are losing out on their education as they leave. Exiting students would have to face a parent as they leave the building, and the prospect of being confronted by an adult would discourage skipping.

We recommend that when official monitors identify skipping students, a uniformed police officer should notify their parents within 24 hours.[16] Involving more uniformed police officers in truancy work will be expensive for the county or city, but given that this work helps to prevent juvenile crime, this investment in prevention would be worthwhile in the long run. The students in our study told us that members of gangs would meet in school and then skip together. While skipping they would engage in vandalism and burglary, as well as alcohol abuse and violence. Preventing skipping would give gang members fewer opportunities to engage in delinquency, at least during school hours.

During the time of our study, students were able to skip and could do so for long periods before any serious efforts were made by the schools to inform parents. When efforts were made to inform parents, the information came in the form of computerized telephone calls or forms known as "Progress Reports." However, by intercepting phone calls and mail before their parents came home from work, skipping students could prevent their being notified. Preventing parents from knowing about their skipping was particularly easy for the students with illiterate Spanish-speaking parents. Most of the telephone messages about skipping were spoken in English, and written notices would have been unreadable by illiterate parents, even if written in Spanish.

Then, there is the issue of lunchtime. For the past few decades, secondary schools have allowed students to leave the campus for lunch. It is not uncommon for students to become so involved with their peers at lunch that they do not come back. Since the parents of students often work during the day, skipping students have the opportunity to go to another student's home where they can do whatever they want, without adult supervision. We recommend that the privilege of leaving campus for lunch should be given only to students who have demonstrated a long record of classroom attendance. Leaving campus for lunch should not be regarded as a right, but as a privilege that is earned. One way of keeping students at school during lunch is improving the quality of the food provided in the school cafeteria. For example, student-run enterprises could make and sell lunches in the cafeteria or work with popular fast-food franchises to make pizzas, eggrolls, and tacos available. Similarly, lunchtime recreation within the schools could help make in-school lunches fun and refreshing. Some American high schools sponsor recreational sports during the lunch hour and social events, such as music competitions and dancing in the gym. Giving the students a reason to enjoy lunch in school would make staying in school a more rewarding experience.

Encourage Attendance

We also recommend that schools make attending class more rewarding than skipping class. For most of the students we studied, attending classes was not a rewarding experience. For example, one graduate told us, "In eighth grade, school was pretty fun. I wasn't doing the best I could do, but I was doing pretty good. I was, like, making at least a 70. But then high school came around and everything changed. Everything became so quick paced and so complex that it just became dull. Ever since ninth grade, I've been doing terrible in school." This student recommended that courses consist of "more class activities instead of just the teacher talking up there. You sit down, take out a paper, write down everything that he says. That's not fun. School's got to be fun at least. I mean if you're going to spend eight hours a day there, it's got to have some fun besides lunch and gym. Gotta have some excitement."

Another student who graduated on time told us of how she dreaded going to school: "I just didn't want to go. I just, I had no interest in school. I just didn't want to go. I just hated school. I had no interest in it at all. I thought it was so boring, you know, I hated going to school. I hated it. I'm serious. I hated the thought of getting up and going to school. I just hated it. . . . I'd go to school, but I'd end up leaving half the day and going home, or I'd, like, go and then I didn't feel like being there."

Students are not born with this attitude toward school, and few of them learn it at home. Almost all of the parents we interviewed wanted their children to succeed, and they respected the educational process. Students acquire these negative attitudes by having multiple, negative experiences in school. Obviously, a student with this type of attitude is difficult to teach. Therefore, it is important that school personnel behave in a respectful and nurturing manner toward students so that students maintain positive attitudes toward school.

Ramona, in Chapter 4, graduated on time, but her overall impression of what she experienced in her classrooms was negative. She told us, "School, it wasn't really nothing for me. You know, it was like you go to school, you learn, you forget about it. You know, you go back to school, you learn again, and during the summer you forget about everything you learned. It's a waste of time."

Like most students, Ramona went to school to be with her friends. Describing them, she said: "It's, like, they go to school for the fun of it. They don't go to school to learn, really. They go to school to have fun, meet friends, talk around to their friends. That's what school is to me, to other people I see."

Peer relationships are important for adolescents, and being with friends is one of the major reasons why students go to school. This general statement applies not just to those "at risk" of dropping out of school, but to all students. Schools should make use of this normal desire of adolescents, to promote learning. Schools can do this by changing the ways students are grouped together and changing the ways that students are taught.

Create Schools within Schools

We recommend that secondary students be grouped into "schools within schools" and that these students spend the three years of middle school or the four years of high school together. We also recommend that the same team of teachers follow the same group of students throughout their years in the "school." In this way, the teachers can get to know the students and the students can get to know their teachers. This familiarity will also aid parents in getting to know the teachers. Few of the parents in our sample could even name one member of the staff at their child's school.

These "schools" should be heterogeneous in terms of the students' abilities and ethnic backgrounds, in order for both high- and low-achieving students to acquire the kinds of skills they will need to become good citizens and good employees. Subgroups of these "schools" would take courses together so that the same students are together most of the day. In this way, schools would be creating peer networks that are integrated into the school structure. This would make it easier for low-achieving students to develop friendships with students who are successful and who participate in school, while discouraging their participation in gangs. When schools are organized this way, "being with your friends" will require "going to class." Interacting with friends would involve participating in classroom learning.

A few school programs were dedicated to "at risk" students during the time of our study. Some of these programs block-scheduled groups of students. The difference between what was done then and what we recommend here is that we recommend that all students be part of a "school within a school" and that the students in each "school" be heterogeneous in terms of scholastic abilities and ethnicity. The programs for "at risk" students usually had long waiting lists, and many students became frustrated when they were denied access to these programs. What we are recommending eliminates the need for waiting lists. All students will be part of "the program," because all students would be part of a smaller school within the larger school.[17]

Create Teams within Classrooms

The students in our study were educated as isolated individuals. Instruction was focused on the actions of the teacher. In the general and vocational tracks, students worked individually on their worksheets; they were rarely given the opportunity to work together or become actively engaged in a class project. In order to interact with a peer, a student had to do things like hang out in the hallway between classes or sit through two lunch periods. When the bell rang and these students found themselves stranded in the hallway or cafeteria, they preferred to exit the building rather than face teachers who might berate them for being tardy.

To solve this problem, we recommend that teachers make use of teaching techniques that make it possible for students to work in teams. With this type of classroom organization, students can practice new concepts and develop the teamwork skills that major American employers say will be required for success in the workplace of the 21st century. These skills involve "knowing how to work in teams, teach others, negotiate, and work well with people from culturally diverse backgrounds."[18] These skills can only be learned if students have numerous classroom experiences working as teams.

To make the process of learning in teams more exciting, teachers can organize competitions between teams of students within the classroom. Instead of pitting individual students against each other, classroom competitions would pit teams of students against other teams of students. Teachers who know how to use team teaching techniques can create groups of students who, collectively, have comparable skills, thereby enhancing the competitiveness of the field within each classroom. Teams can be reorganized periodically within the same classroom or course in order to allow all students in a classroom to work together and give all students the experience of winning and losing together.

Similarly, competitions between the "schools within the school" for grades, the number of books read, attendance, reports written, biology samples taken, etc., can be conducted throughout the course of a school year. At a central location in the high school, the scores of the "schools" could be posted and updated weekly. At the end of each grading period and school year, awards can be given to the "schools" with the best scores. This would encourage students within each "school" to apply peer pressure so that all students would come to school, study for exams, turn in homework, and generally participate in schoolwork.

Since student grades will be determined by the degree of progress that each student makes toward meeting the fixed, not relative, standard, there is no benefit in competing against other students in the same classroom or "school." All students are competing against an absolute standard, and all students can meet the standard. Teachers and students are on the same side, both striving to have the student meet the absolute standards.

With schools and classrooms organized this way, students will not have to leave the classroom in order to interact with peers. Their friends will be on their team, in their "school within a school," learning with them most of the school day. Such changes allow schools to use the adolescents' desire to be together to make school and classroom attendance rewarding experiences.

Make Content Relevant

In addition to creating teams of students, teachers need to make the content of their teaching more relevant to the lives of students. This will involve teachers providing more active and engaging class exercises relevant to the goals and interests of students from a broad range of backgrounds. In our observations, students in the regular and low tracks were rarely given the opportunity to engage in the kinds of learning experiences that might motivate them to work hard. Alice, the student who was unable to pass the exit-level test and get her diploma, told us of one teacher who gave her a project that involved studying the background of Mexican-origin people and her family in particular. She told us that the project motivated her to learn: "I really understand the stuff and I really get into it and I wanna learn more about it." Such projects were common in honors-level courses, but rare in the lower tracks.

Teachers should seek to link the academic content and skills they are teaching with the student's language and cultural identity. When students can relate their own background and experiences to what they are supposed to learn, they will be much more motivated to do the work necessary to learn it.[19]

EMPHASIZING HARD WORK AND PERSISTENCE

One of the reasons why classroom attendance was not rewarding for the students in our study was that in the traditional classroom, teachers assign grades "on the curve," giving the best-performing students the best grades, the second-best students the second-best grades, and so on. This type of classroom competition discouraged many of the students in our study because they had little chance of getting the best grades. At the same time, those students with strong academic abilities were not necessarily rewarded for working hard, because most could get good grades without much effort.

Hard Work and Ability

Historically, American education has rewarded ability much more than hard work.[20] The highest awards have been given to high-ability students who compete against other students and outscore them. Students who have exceptional athletic or musical ability are also honored by our schools. But the overwhelming majority of students never receive such recognition, regardless of how hard they try.

Indeed, highly intelligent students, those scoring at the 90th percentile or higher on norm-referenced tests, have little need to work hard in school. Given that the assessment instruments used by the schools repeatedly placed them at the 90th percentile, school counselors group them with other bright students and assign them to teachers who try to challenge them, arouse their curiosity, and urge them to "live up to their potential." The schools devote most of their resources to high-scoring students even if they do not work hard.[21]

The consequence of valuing ability more than effort is that even our best and brightest are not inspired to achieve more. American college professors are frequently disappointed by the lack of skills and the ignorance of first-year students, even those who are at the top of their high school classes.[22] Professors complain that these freshmen don't know enough about history, science, and foreign languages; they cannot write good term papers or coherent essay exams. What these critics don't understand is that because the schools value ability over hard work, high-ability students don't need to work hard in order to reap the benefits of public education.

In order to motivate students of high ability, we need an educational system that values hard work more than ability. Then, high-ability students will have more reason to work hard and will acquire more knowledge and skills.

Precisely the same argument can be made for students of middle and low ability. Only when the schools reward hard work more than ability will students of average and below average ability "live up to their potential." Teachers haven't been eager to challenge students of low or middle ability to learn more. Students who can't "get it" quickly are quietly placed at the edge of the classroom or in the lower tracks where their need to spend more time learning is ignored. Rather than spend more time teaching these students the skills they will need to meet scholastic standards, teachers spend less time engaging them in learning. The results are disastrous. Year after year, the gap between the talented and gifted few and the rest of the student body grows. In the district we studied, less than 2% of the students taking honors courses dropped out every year, compared to the district average of about 10%.

English and Mathematics

For Mexican-origin students, the acquisition of English reading and writing skills has been daunting. For example, in our sample, the percentage of students who were two or more years below grade level in reading (45%) was twice as high as the percentage of students who were two or more years below grade level in mathematics (22%).

Part of the reason for the difficulty of these students in acquiring adequate English language skills is that many parents spoke Spanish only and were unable to help their children acquire English language skills. The school district did not provide the support these students needed to become proficient in English. If students had some oral English language skills, they were plunged into English-only classrooms where their inexperience with English was ignored. Students who received Limited English Proficiency services at the secondary level were not given the training they needed to succeed in English-only classrooms. Too often these services did not integrate all aspects of language acquisition with academic content, such as the study of geography or science. The bilingual programs were expected to serve any child who had limited English proficiency, whether they had ever attended school or not. Thus, it is not surprising that students who participated in the district's LEP program were much more likely to drop out (20%) than those who were not in those classes (10%).[23] Overall, these efforts at improving the English language skills of such students were ineffective in helping students earn a diploma.

For Americans in general, the acquisition of mathematics skills has been more difficult. Some Americans think that math skills are genetically determined and that some people just can't do math. As a result, mathematics in the U.S. has been taught as a sort of speed game, with those who have the "natural" talent shouting the answers and the rest remaining quiet in the classroom. Students are rushed to get the right answers in math. They are not encouraged to enjoy math and savor the experience of solving math problems in the same way they are encouraged, for example, to write and rewrite poems. More importantly, students who don't get math quickly are left to learn nothing. Rather than arranging the learning time during the school day so that such students have more opportunity to learn math, no extra time is set aside for them because they are assumed to be unable to learn it.[24] This is exactly the opposite of what should be happening.

In Japanese elementary schools, the students earning the most praise and admiration from their teachers and classmates are those who work the longest on their schoolwork.[25] Students who have difficulty mastering a skill are assigned more homework, and teachers spend more time with them during the school day. Students in Japan go to school 220 days a year, compared to the 180 in Texas and most of the U.S. It is estimated that about 60% of Japanese students go to cram schools at the end of the school day and on Saturday to improve their scholastic performance. Average and slightly below average

Japanese students are still expected to work hard and acquire strong language and mathematics skills. Their schoolwork is challenging, and the students know that doing well in school will make a difference in terms of the kinds of jobs that they will get. The net result of all this time learning is that the average Japanese 16-year-old has attended three years more school than the average American of the same age. We can hardly be surprised that Japanese youth outscore American youth on most standardized tests.[26]

Persistence

We recommend that schools create honors for students who persist at working hard on their schoolwork over whole school terms and school years. Honor societies should be created that reward students who make major gains in their mastery of skills and who have persisted in elaborating and extending various projects, such as science or community projects. Currently, honor societies are limited to a small, elite group of students who teachers think have leadership potential. While such honor societies will no doubt continue into the future, the creation of new honor societies that are open to any hardworking student, regardless of his or her academic abilities, will help provide the kinds of incentives needed in American schools.

Age at Graduation

It is likely that the changes we recommend will result in some students meeting the scholastic standards for graduation before they are 18 years old. In fact, one of the groups attempting to establish national standards for U.S. schools, the New Standards Project, has defined their version of a high school diploma, the Certificate of Initial Mastery, as one that can be achieved by students as young as 14.[27] In our plan and theirs, students will graduate from high school whenever they meet the requirements. For students who graduate before the age of 18, we recommend that programs be established by their schools to continue their education. These programs can take the form of providing challenging courses that prepare early graduates to pass advanced-placement tests for college credit in the high school building or sending early graduates to nearby colleges to take courses.

Students who work at more average paces will graduate from high school around the age of 18. The skills that they will have mastered in order to meet the exit standards for graduation will qualify them for jobs with a promising future, ones paying above the poverty level. These skills will also allow graduates to gain admission to a variety of postsecondary educational institutions, including technical colleges and universities.

It will be difficult to keep students in school after the age of 18 unless their schooling takes place in community colleges and/or at worksites. The students in our sample resisted staying in high school until they were 20 years old or older. James, in Chapter 2 (Tracking), was allowed to flunk the seventh grade twice, then was accelerated out of middle school, only to be put in a regularly paced vocational program in high school. He stopped attending school when it became clear to him that he was much older than all the others in his classes. He explained, "I'm already 18, I should have been graduated!" Similarly, Felipe, from Chapter 7 (GED), was retained twice in elementary school. He left high school at age 18, after getting a GED, and enrolled in community college because, as he said, "I was just too old for it. You're supposed to outgrow high school and I didn't want to be 20 when I graduated."

MAKING SCHOOLS ACCESSIBLE

One of the most significant changes that schools need to make is to reach out to parents in order to get their help in educating their children. In general, the secondary schools we studied had not made enough effort to form partnerships with the parents of "at risk" youth. They expected parents to come to the school when the school summoned them, always during regular school hours, to work out the problems with school staff—at times convenient to the staff and in the language of the staff.

But many parents were like Paula, the mother of Ramona in Chapter 4, who had many young children at home and could not leave home to travel to school. When we began our study, Ramona was often late to school, even though she lived only a few blocks from the high school. The counselor had sent letters to inform Paula that Ramona arrived to school tardy. Paula tried responding by letter since she had no telephone. Paula explained, "They wanted to know how come she gets there late. I said, 'I don't know how come she gets there late.' I said, 'She leaves home with plenty of time. School starts at 9:00 and she leaves here at 8:15 or 8:20, so that's plenty of time to get there. It's just right there, the school, it's just right there.' And I don't know why she gets there late. . . . The counselor, I can't remember her name, but she's the counselor, they sent me letters for signing, telling me if I knew the problem. I mean, how come she's getting there late? And then, I just answer on the back of the letter, that I tell them that I don't know why, and that maybe they can find out themselves what the problem is, 'cause I sure don't know. I gave them permission. I said, 'You all take her to the counselor's office and talk to her and see if you can come out with an answer, 'cause I can't.' They never answered me back. They never sent me anything back."

Other parents tried going to the school about a problem and got no response. Caroline, the mother of Kathy, a teen mom, told us of her efforts to get help: "I have tried. In the morning I dropped the kids off at school. I came home, got dressed, and I went twice up there. And I sat there and then I thought it was going to be time for the kids to come out for lunch, so I just went back to the car and sat there and waited. And I tried to talk to her counselor and be sensible about it. There was nobody there. Well, they weren't in the office. And like I said, I had limited time to sit there and wait for them. So what can you do if you can't get ahold of them?"

Some parents were able to make contact with teachers or counselors only to discover that they could give no suggestions to them on how to solve the child's problem. One mother of a dropout described her disappointment with counselors and teachers this way: "They wouldn't really tell me what I could do as a parent. They would say, 'Well, he needs to study harder, and he needs to turn in his work.' Which I knew. But they never really said what I could do as a parent on my own. They told me what he could do as a student to help bring up his grades, and that was it. . . . I didn't know who to turn to, who could help me find the answers that I was looking for as a parent. I figured if anyone should know, the school should know, the teachers should know."

We found that school personnel often looked down on parents of "at risk" students, blaming them for the student's academic problem. This is consistent with previous research indicating that educators assume parents who don't get involved in the school do not value education.[28] We heard many stories from parents who went to the school to attempt to solve their child's problems, only to be lectured at, scolded, ignored, or rebuffed by school personnel. Such actions did not encourage parents to return to the student's school. This comment from the mother of a dropout is typical: "I couldn't really say they gave me the answers. So, I'm going, 'If the teachers don't know, who does? Who can tell me what to do?'" She gave up.

Schools and Parents as Partners

Before schools can build partnerships with parents, they will have to learn how to communicate with parents in respectful and meaningful ways. The failure of teachers and other school personnel to treat parents with respect convinced many parents that the schools were prejudiced against people of Mexican origin. Parents interpreted the bad treatment that they and their children received as instances of discrimination. This perception of discrimination aroused anger in the parents and their children, and they decided to avoid school personnel altogether.

George, the father of Linda, the athlete in Chapter 6 (Immigrants), saw discrimination against people of Mexican origin everywhere in the school. He gave an example: "She signed up for a class, and then this counselor tells me that it was already full and so she put her in study hall. And you don't get any credit for study hall. Linda said, 'Well, if I tell them they won't listen to me, Daddy. You need to call them yourself.' So I called her a few times. Well, I think that's unfair. You know what I mean? I wonder about this, but I can't go in there and break through the walls and see what's going on. I won't play detective. And I say how come all these people were able to get in that [class]? A lot of problems with the Hispanics, they don't go to the principal and ask him, 'How come all this, only the Whites got the classes they want and the Hispanics have to settle for what they give them?' There should be an equal opportunity for everybody, I think."

We recommend that teachers, counselors, and all other school personnel learn how to behave in a respectful manner to all parents and learn how to give helpful advice to parents on how to solve their children's problems. Teachers and other school personnel ought to be able to suggest solutions for the child's problem, by referring the parents to counselors, social workers, or other parents who have solved similar problems in the past.

Speaking Spanish

A major problem for some parents in our sample was their inability to find someone at the school who spoke Spanish. One parent explained it this way: "Busco quien hable español. Porque solamente así me puedo comunicar y expresar. Porque muchas veces les digo yo a mis hijos, 'Díganles esto.' Pero no dicen lo que yo les digo. Dicen otra cosa, quizás les da pena, lo que yo digo. Pero, busco quien hable español, y es como yo puedo, lo mismo que por teléfono. Luego, luego busco quien hable español, para comunicarme y preguntar qué es lo que está pasando." (I look for someone who speaks Spanish. Because that's the only way I can communicate and express myself. Because lots of times I tell my children, 'Tell them this.' But they don't tell them what I told them to say. They say something else. Who knows? Perhaps it embarrasses them, what I said. But I look for someone who speaks Spanish, and that's how I can, myself, the same by telephone. Then, then, I look for someone who speaks Spanish, so I can communicate and ask what is happening.)

In the school district we studied, there was only one major alternative language, Spanish, and yet most of the schools did not have staff members who could speak Spanish well enough to deal with sensitive issues such as school failure. Often parents were forced to rely on their own children to translate for them, resulting in poor communication between parent and school. Many of the children who were stuck in the role of translator simply were too immature to do the appropriate translation. Other children, when put in the role of translator, intentionally misled both their parents and school personnel in order to avoid blame, punishment, or embarrassment. *We recommend that schools have staff members trained to facilitate the communication between non-English-speaking parents and school personnel.*

Parent Information Centers

Most of the parents in our sample had difficulty communicating with the school because they could not get to the specific person they needed to talk to when the parents had the time to communicate. To avoid this problem, school districts need to invest in both the staff and the technology to facilitate communication between parents and school personnel. To do this, schools will need to create parent information centers in each school—plainly marked, like checkout counters—near the major entrance of the school. Ideally, there should be personnel at each school who continuously staff these parent information centers during regular working hours, Monday through Friday, 12 months a year, to enhance communication between parents and schools. These parent information centers should be equipped with computers connected to networks that link all the necessary information about all the students enrolled in the school district. These centers should be staffed 12 hours a day and on Saturdays during critical times, such as the beginning and ending of the school year, and they should be equipped with answering machines so that parents or other adults can leave messages for school personnel on a 24-hour-a-day basis.

It would be the responsibility of these staff members to resolve any problems that students have and to work with both teachers and parents to enhance communication. In order to fulfill this responsibility, these staff members would have to have access via the computer network to information from each teacher about the student's schoolwork problems. Similarly, the staff should be able to relay information from the parents to the teacher and help students and their parents resolve disagreements with teachers. These staff members should have the power to authorize specific educational services for students and teachers. They should have the authority to arrange for the provision of transportation and baby-sitting for parents who need this form of help in order to communicate with the school. Similarly, they should have the job of contacting employers to request time off for parents so that they can participate in the partnership with the school.

School counselors should work at these parent information centers part of every day. When the counselors are not at the centers, parents should be able to leave messages for them on answering machines, and the counselors should get back to these parents within 24 hours of their message. Counselors should be trained so that they know how to establish rapport with parents from all social classes and ethnicities, listen to their concerns, and explain to them what they should do to help the student overcome his or her school problems. Successful counselors are able to give parents insights into how to solve their child's problem. And this can be done in several ways, including by the counselor's making suggestions for change within the parent-and-child relationship or by the counselor's intervening directly with teachers as an advocate for the student.

By creating, nurturing, and maintaining partnerships between parents and school personnel, schools will be able to keep more students on the pathway toward graduation.

CREATING PATHWAYS TO GOOD OUTCOMES

Partnerships between schools and families will facilitate communication so that students can do what they need to do in order to graduate. But before "at risk" students will stay in school long enough to graduate, they and their parents will need to be persuaded that spending more time in school will make a difference for their futures. This will be a hard sell to many students, particularly those who have had academic difficulties. For example, 76% of the students in our study told us, when they were 15, that they did not feel that school was "going to do anything" for them.

The Value of a High School Diploma

Among the students in our sample, even those who graduated, few believed that the high school diploma would really make a difference in the kinds of jobs they would get. The opinion of Richard, who graduated on time despite having been retained once, was typical. When we asked him whether getting a high school diploma had really helped him get a good job, he answered, "No, not really. It didn't. Actually, it didn't. A lot of people say when you graduate and you get a diploma it's going to help you find a better job and it's going to make a difference, but it doesn't. I don't see where they think that. You know, these days you have to go to college and go four or five years or something to make good money. And still that's probably not enough."

Richard was not misinformed. For the average student, working hard and long in school is not necessarily rewarded by better outcomes after high school. Several studies have documented that grades in high school for average students have no bearing on a student's later occupational success.[29] The real distinction in terms of annual earnings is between graduates of four-year colleges and those who have a high school diploma or less.[30] If we want all of our youth to work hard in high school, then we need to reward hard work in high school with better jobs or other postsecondary opportunities for all students immediately after high school graduation.

We found that the jobs available to high school graduates immediately after graduation were not different from the jobs available to high school students. Almost all of the students who participated in the half-time school and half-time work vocational program in high school ended up with the same minimum-wage, part-time jobs after graduation. Consider Ramona, who graduated and then earned less than Salvador, who dropped out but got a state job. Ramona had relatively strong mathematics skills, and yet she was tracked into clerical work by school administrators. Similarly, Linda, after graduating, worked at the same part-time, dead-end job she had before graduation, checking groceries. Ironically, her first-generation counterpart, Enrique, did not graduate and yet made more money working in a restaurant than Linda did. While women who enter traditionally female occupations are paid less than men who enter traditionally male occupations, this fact is not the whole story. Part of the reason for the differences in pay experienced by these youth is that the high school diploma does little for non-college-bound youth within the first five years after graduation.[31]

The U.S. is the only industrialized nation where hard work and achievement in school by average students is not rewarded by access to good jobs soon if not immediately after graduation. In Japan and Germany, average students, especially those who work hard and accomplish more in school, are given better jobs at better companies after high school graduation.

If American students are to be motivated to meet high scholastic standards, then they will need incentives. This might be the most difficult aspect of the changes we recommend, because these changes require the cooperation of employers outside the school and strong linkages between high schools and postsecondary training schools. It requires that communities structure job and training opportunities so that the hard work of all students will pay off in jobs with bright futures.

New Models of High School

We recommend that all high school students become members of industrial cluster schools. These cluster schools fit the "school-within-a-school" model in that each "school" can become an industrial cluster school. The buildings we now call high schools can house several cluster schools. Industrial cluster schools provide explicit coursework pathways that lead to related careers. They "untrack" high schools because students with a wide range of academic abilities participate in these clusters. Cluster programs integrate the industry theme into the content of basic academic courses and promote learning by hands-on experience.

For example, a health cluster school within a high school would focus on medical occupations ranging from nurse's aides to brain surgeons. Students would choose to be in this "school" if they were interested in working in health-related occupations. The local hospitals, laboratories, nursing homes, veterinary clinics, and so on would work with the teachers in this "school" to develop course content and learning experiences that integrate the scholastic skills (reading, writing, and mathematics) with the industrial theme. Teachers, students, and industry professionals would devise and complete projects together. Some of the students in the health "school" might go on to universities and then medical, dental, nursing, or veterinary schools. Others might go on to community colleges or private training schools to become physical therapists, nurse's aides, and so on.

The value of these "schools" is that they motivate students to work hard at acquiring scholastic skills while simultaneously giving them occupational guidance. Yet the skills they acquire are not so narrow as to leave students with few career options to develop throughout their lives.

We recommend that a wide variety of cluster schools be present in large school districts. For example, within an urban school district, one high school could house cluster schools focused on electronics, financial services, ecology, and the performing arts. Another high school in the same district could house cluster schools focusing on construction (including architecture and engineering), manufacturing (ranging from assembly to design), and hospitality (e.g., food service and tourism). Another choice for those interested in the liberal arts would be a liberal arts cluster. This cluster school could focus on foreign language programs and traditional humanities programs, leading to enrollment in liberal arts colleges. With the guidance of parents, school counselors, and teachers, students would select a "school" that captured the student's interests, regardless of the academic abilities of the student. The school would use these interests to build strong academic skills.

Some of the industrial cluster schools can be modeled along the lines of California Academies. These academies have been built on partnerships between local businesses and high schools. They involve the grouping of 100–120 students together with the same team of teachers for several years. These teachers work together to integrate the English and math curriculum with vocational knowledge and skills.[32]

The value of a liberal arts education as well as the value of education as an end in itself would not be diminished in this cluster approach. Students entering the work force in the future will need higher order thinking skills and facility in a second language in order to thrive in the 21st century. Mastering the basics will not be enough. Strong reading, writing, and math skills along with motivation to continue learning must be a part of that training.

These new models of education create supportive environments that make students feel cared for by teachers and other students. They also provide a context for learning high-level English and mathematics skills. Students in academies or cluster schools work through exercises that are real-life applications of language and/or math skills to the industry or business theme. Cluster schools and academies require that teachers work in interdisciplinary teams, integrating English, math, social studies and science curricula around the specific theme of each cluster school. Finally, these new educational models create a platform for industry and school cooperation, and thus a basis for high school teachers and industry representatives to work together. In this way, teachers can come to understand the high level of skills American businesses and industries need in high school graduates, and in turn, industries and businesses can give teachers the assistance they need to bring students up to these high standards.

Occupational Knowledge for Teachers and Counselors

Most teachers and school counselors have some understanding of occupations that require four-year college degrees or graduate education, but they often are ignorant of other occupations and the skills needed to get and keep jobs that do not require at least a four-year degree. This ignorance has negative consequences for our society because only about 25% of secondary students nationwide will complete their bachelor's degrees.[33] Most jobs in the future will not require a bachelor's degree.[34] That teachers and school counselors typically do not know much about the new jobs being created or about the kinds of skills that these occupations require suggests that our school personnel cannot be preparing most of our students for their journey along the pathway from kindergarten to a good job.

Before high school, students and all of their teachers should be educated regularly about the kinds of good jobs that exist *in their state and communities* and the types of skills people need to get these jobs. The information about these jobs and the training needed to get them should be provided to teachers by industry representatives who talk to them about the kinds of skills and personal characteristics that employers are looking for in their employees. In this way, teachers and counselors can remain current about the kinds of skills needed for good jobs within their state and community.

The ignorance of school personnel about labor market realities has particularly negative consequences for children whose parents have little education. While better-educated parents can learn about the skills their children need and prepare them for good jobs, poorly educated parents have no way of knowing what these skills are or how their children should acquire them. Since neither their parents nor their schools know how to prepare them adequately for good jobs, the occupational success of children whose parents have little education is limited.

Most of the students in our sample had no knowledge of the full range of good jobs available in their community or of how to acquire the needed skills to get those jobs. Only 26% of them told us when they were 15 that they expected to attend at least two years of college; however, during the same interview, the jobs that 78% of them said they wanted required between two and four years of college. The students in our sample aspired to such jobs as electrical engineer, teacher, or commercial artist. But the linkages between what they were doing in their classrooms and what they wanted to be when they grew up was not clear to them. Since most of the students in our sample did not complete high school, let alone attend a few years of college, this means that the schools did not assist them in realizing their goals. Given this lack of connection between their goals and their everyday experiences in school, we cannot be surprised that most of the students we studied did not complete high school.

Communities and Schools as Partners

Schools need to change, but so do the communities they serve. In particular, industries within communities need to build institutions that work with schools to educate youth so that the youth will become the workers that industries will want to hire and develop. In many European countries, such institutions have worked with schools for several decades by helping teachers and others develop curricula, setting skills standards, and participating in the process of evaluating students for graduation. European educators have welcomed this participation by industry because such involvement in the secondary education of students helps to assure that the students will acquire the kinds and level of skills they will need to be employable.[35]

Most American industries have limited their investment in schools to "adopt-a-school" programs. They do not perceive themselves as responsible for the development of the youth who will become their future workers. American firms do not want to become more involved in the schools because they prefer that the schools do their work for them—that is, provide personnel who have all the skills that industries need. But by avoiding involvement in the education of youth, American industries are missing the opportunity to guide the development of their own future employees and consumers.

In fact, instead of being a positive force in the development of youth, some employers take advantage of youth by hiring them to work late on school nights, reducing the energy they have for their schoolwork.[36] We observed many students dropping out because they could not meet at the same time both the demands of work and the demands of school. *We recommend that employers be allowed to hire workers under the age of 18 only if the employer can prove that the worker is enrolled in school or has already graduated.*[37] This will require that employers not only benefit from the youthful energy of student workers, but also take some responsibility for keeping them in school.

As citizens in the community, employers should take some responsibility for the education of the youth in their community. Texas law requires teens to present proof of school attendance to get automobile insurance. It is not unreasonable to require that school-aged employees do the same in order to continue their employment.

While some students we studied benefited from working part-time while going to school part-time, only students in their last two years of high school were eligible for these programs. Because many of our students from low-income families needed to work before they attained that level in high school, they dropped out of school in order to work full-time. *We recommend that schools become more flexible in allowing students from low-income families to work part-time and go to school part-time as early as in middle school.* Young adolescents should not have to choose between serving the needs of their family or going to school.

We argue that the lack of involvement by industry in schools has not helped American industrial competitiveness or student motivation to work hard in school. American industries complain about the high cost of training and retraining employees; students give up going to school because their schoolwork appears to lead them nowhere. Industry involvement in secondary education has strengthened the economies of Germany, Denmark, Switzerland, and Japan, and we recommend that such involvement begin in the U.S.[38]

CONCLUSION

Our analysis has convinced us that the chief cause of the high dropout rate of Hispanic youth lies not with Hispanics but within schools and communities. All the students and their families we studied embraced the ideology that education was essential for getting a good job and for having a better life. The students wanted to earn a high school diploma, but they saw no way to fulfill their aspirations within their own schools.

Many students in our study made a reasonable decision when they decided to drop out. They were correct when they realized that school was wasting their time. They recognized that they were gaining few marketable skills in school. They felt demeaned and demoralized by the way teachers and other school personnel treated them. Getting pregnant, working dead-end jobs, and even staying home and watching TV offered more satisfying alternatives than school.

As citizens, we must all take responsibility for the education of our youth. We must demand that the schools implement these reforms in partnership with parents and the community. Schools must take responsibility for educating all students to have the skills that will qualify them for success at post-secondary training or good jobs soon after graduation. To maintain the status quo will result in more dropouts, more juveniles incarcerated, more teen mothers, and the growth of an underclass of citizens who are alienated from the rest of society.

We have the opportunity to make a difference for the children of the students we studied. Their children began arriving in kindergarten in the fall of 1995.

Parent Questionnaire

Parent's Name: _____

Child's Name: _____ Date of Birth: _____

1. Describe the "parent's" relationship to the child: (Check One)

___ I am the child's mother.
___ I am the child's father.
___ I am the child's stepmother.
___ I am the child's stepfather.
___ I am the child's grandparent.
___ I am the child's aunt or uncle.
___ I am the child's legal guardian.
___ I am the child's brother or sister.
___ Other

2. Parent's Ethnicity: (Check One)

___ Mexican American
___ Puerto Rican
___ Cuban American
___ Mexican
___ Other Latino (Describe) _____
___ Other (Describe) _____

3. Why was your child designated as "at risk" of dropping out?
   (Check All That Apply)

___ I don't remember.

___ was not promoted one or more times in elementary school and has been unable to master the course requirements in grades 7 through 12.

___ was two or more years below grade level in reading or mathematics.

___ failed at least two courses in one or more semesters and is not expected to graduate within four years of the time he/she entered the ninth grade.

___ failed one or more of the reading, writing, or mathematics sections of the most recent TEAMS test beginning with the seventh grade.

4. For the last grading period, what kinds of grades did your child get?

___ Mostly As
___ As and Bs
___ Mostly Bs
___ Bs and Cs
___ Mostly Cs
___ Cs and Ds
___ Mostly Ds
___ Ds and Fs
___ Mostly Fs

5. Did your child fail any of his/her courses?   ___ Yes   ___ No

6. How many people live in the home now (typically, and if nothing is typical, then ask about today)? _____

7. Please let us know more about the people living in your home. The interviewer should read each category below and ask the parent if one of these types of persons lives in the home now. Place checks in front of each category that the parent indicates there are examples of in the home now.

___ Husband or Wife
___ Children
___ Stepchildren
___ Other Adult Relatives, such as your parents or sisters
___ Other Child Relatives, such as your nieces, nephews.
___ Boarder(s)
___ Other Adults, such as your friends.

8. What language do your speak at home? (Check One)

___ Only Spanish   ___ Mostly Spanish   ___ Mostly English
___ Only English   ___ Other

9. What language do other adults speak at home? (Check One)

___ Only Spanish   ___ Mostly Spanish   ___ Mostly English
___ Only English   ___ Other

10. What language does the 15-year-old child speak most often at home? (Check One)

___ Only Spanish   ___ Mostly Spanish   ___ Mostly English
___ Only English   ___ Other

11. Within the last year, I came back to or joined the family.

___ Yes   ___ No

12. Within the last year, I left our household for an extended period.

___ Yes   ___ No

13. Where was the 15-year-old child born? (Check One)

___ In U.S.
___ In Mexico
___ Other.

14. I was born (Check One)

___ In U.S.
___ In Mexico
___ Other.

15. Educational Attainment of Parent Interviewed:

What is the highest education attained?
    Number of years _____

He/she graduated from high school	___ Yes	___ No
He/she got a GED	___ Yes	___ No
He/she took vocational classes after high school, but did not graduate.	___ Yes	___ No
He/she graduated from vocational school.	___ Yes	___ No
He/she took classes at community college.	___ Yes	___ No
He/she graduated from community college.	___ Yes	___ No
He/she took classes at a four-year college.	___ Yes	___ No
He/she graduated from college.	___ Yes	___ No

16. Ideally, what would the parent like the child to do during the next three years?

(Read each to the parent and check the category if the parent indicates that he/she would like the child to do this.)

___ Help the family financially
___ Get a good-paying job
___ Get married
___ Start a family
___ Obtain a GED
___ Graduate from high school
___ Go to vocational school
___ Make plans to go to college

17. Realistically, how much education do you think the child will get before he/she is 21 years old? (Check All That Apply)

___ Obtain a high school diploma
___ Obtain a GED
___ Get training in a skilled trade
___ Complete vocational training
___ Get training in the military
___ Attend at least 2 years of college
___ Graduate from a 2-year college
___ Attend classes at a 4-year college
___ Graduate from a 4-year college

18. In your opinion, what has given the child problems in school? (Check All That Apply)

___ Schoolwork
___ Language problems
___ Other students
___ Fighting/Violence
___ Teachers
___ Discipline
___ Absences
___ Lack of money
___ Health Problems
___ Alcohol/Drugs

19. Whom do you talk to about the child's schoolwork?
    (Check All That Apply)

    ___ No One
    ___ Friends
    ___ Other Mothers/Fathers
    ___ Relatives
    ___ Neighbors
    ___ Spouse
    ___ The School Principal
    ___ School Counselors
    ___ Teachers
    ___ Others (Describe)

20. If the parent is employed, what kind of work does he/she do?
    (Describe On Line Below)

    _____

21. How many hours a week does the parent generally work outside the home? _____

22. Regardless of where the children now live or their age, how many children and stepchildren does the parent have? _____

23. How many older siblings does the child have? _____

24. Of these older siblings, how many:
    have completed high school? _____
    are still in school? _____

25. How many younger siblings does the child have? _____

26. Of these how many are still in school? _____

THE CHILD'S FRIENDS

We are interested in knowing more about the 15-year-old child's best friends. Listen to each statement and tell us your opinion. Say

   Yes, if the statement is *True*
                or
   No, if the statement is *Not True*, in your opinion.

27. My child's best friends are interested in school.   ___ Yes   ___ No

28. My child's best friends attend classes regularly.   ___ Yes   ___ No

29. My child's best friends expect to graduate from
high school.   ___ Yes   ___ No

30. My child's best friends expect to go to college.   ___ Yes   ___ No

31. At least one of my child's best friends has
dropped out of high school.   ___ Yes   ___ No

32. Most of my child's friends are Mexican
American or Mexican.   ___ Yes   ___ No

33. My child's best friends often get in trouble.   ___ Yes   ___ No

THE PARENT-CHILD RELATIONSHIP

Now tell us about you and the child (name him/her). Listen to each statement
and tell us your opinion. Say

> Yes, if the statement is *True*
>   or
> No, if the statement is *Not True*

34. I talk to the child about school.   ___ Yes   ___ No

35. I usually help the child with his/her homework.   ___ Yes   ___ No

36. I keep close track of how well the child is doing
in school.   ___ Yes   ___ No

37. I always know where the child is and what
he/she is doing.   ___ Yes   ___ No

38. I want the child to stay in school.   ___ Yes   ___ No

39. I want the child to get good grades in school.   ___ Yes   ___ No

40. The child talks to me about school.   ___ Yes   ___ No

41. I have always lived with this child.   ___ Yes   ___ No

42. I have visited my child's school this fall
(for any reason, sports event, pick up
students, teacher conference).   ___ Yes   ___ No

43. I expect my child to get married in the next
three years.   ___ Yes   ___ No

44. I expect my child to drop out of high school. ___ Yes   ___ No

45. My child's teachers want him/her to do well
    in school. ___ Yes   ___ No

46. I expect my child to start a family in the next
    three years. ___ Yes   ___ No

47. I talked to at least one of the child's teachers
    this fall. ___ Yes   ___ No

THE CHILD

Now tell us about your child. Listen to each statement and tell us your opinion. Say

   Yes, if the statement is *True*
                  or
   No, if the statement is *Not True,* in your opinion.

48. My child is deeply religious. ___ Yes   ___ No

49. My child expects to attend at least 2 years
    of college. ___ Yes   ___ No

50. My child has had disciplinary problems this fall. ___ Yes   ___ No

51. My child cuts classes every once in a while. ___ Yes   ___ No

52. My child expects to go to college sometime in
    the future. ___ Yes   ___ No

53. My child has never been expelled or suspended
    from school. ___ Yes   ___ No

54. My child makes good grades in school. ___ Yes   ___ No

55. In my opinion, my child is "at risk" of dropping
    out of school. ___ Yes   ___ No

56. My child feels that school is not for him/her. ___ Yes   ___ No

57. My child likes school. ___ Yes   ___ No

58. My child is afraid when at school. ___ Yes   ___ No

59. My child expects to graduate from high school. ___ Yes   ___ No

60. My child doesn't get along with the teachers. ___ Yes   ___ No

61. My child has a quiet place at home to study and
    do homework.   ___Yes   ___No

62. My child finds some of the classes to be dull
    or boring.   ___Yes   ___No

63. Staying in school will make a difference for
    my child.   ___Yes   ___No

64. My child participates in school-sponsored
    activities, such as sports or clubs.   ___Yes   ___No

65. This fall, my child participated in organized
    sports, outside of school.   ___Yes   ___No

66. This fall, my child participated in organized
    dance/music classes, sponsored by groups
    outside the school.   ___Yes   ___No

67. This fall, my child participated in church-
    sponsored activities.   ___Yes   ___No

68. My child expects to be married within the
    next three years.   ___Yes   ___No

69. My child expects to start a family within the
    next three years.   ___Yes   ___No

70. My child could start a family and still stay
    in school.   ___Yes   ___No

71. My child doesn't have many friends at school.   ___Yes   ___No

72. My child has a job.   ___Yes   ___No

    If yes, complete the following questions.

        How many hours a week does this child work? _____

        Does the parent think that this work interferes
        with schoolwork?   ___Yes   ___No

73. My child has been absent from school a lot lately
    due to sickness.   ___Yes   ___No

74. My child likes most of the students in his/her
    classes.   ___Yes   ___No

75. My child wants to enlist in the military as soon
as possible. ___Yes ___No

76. My child feels that teachers want him/her to
do well. ___Yes ___No

77. My child's teachers listen to what he/she has
to say. ___Yes ___No

78. My child expects to drop out of high school. ___Yes ___No

79. My child's grades prevent him/her from participating
in after-school activities, like sports and clubs. ___Yes ___No

80. My child feels that the teachers expect him/her
to drop out. ___Yes ___No

81. Compared to other students in his/her classroom,
my child's schoolwork is about average. ___Yes ___No

82. My child knows many people who have dropped
out of high school. ___Yes ___No

83. At least one of my child's brothers or sisters has
dropped out of high school. ___Yes ___No

84. My child's brothers and sisters encourage
him/her to stay in schools. ___Yes ___No

85. My child's absences from school cause problems. ___Yes ___No

86. My child works on his/her homework until
it is finished. ___Yes ___No

87. My child works on his/her homework in
school only. ___Yes ___No

MY CHILD'S SCHOOLWORK

Tell us about your child's schoolwork. Listen to each statement and tell us
your opinion. Say

Yes, if the statement is *True*

or

No, if the statement is *Not True*, in your opinion.

88. Most of the courses my child is taking will
prepare him/her for college. ___Yes ___No ___Don't Know

89. My child's schools have provided him/her with
    special classes or tutoring to help him/her with
    schoolwork.   ___Yes ___No ___Don't Know

90. The teachers expect my child to
    drop out of school.   ___Yes ___No ___Don't Know

91. Someone in the family usually helps the child
    with his/her schoolwork.   ___Yes ___No ___Don't Know

92. The child's English and/or math classes are
    too hard for him/her.   ___Yes ___No ___Don't Know

93. My child is enrolled in honors courses.
                                   ___Yes ___No ___Don't Know

94. During the fall, a teacher or counselor from
    the school contacted me about my child's
    school problems.   ___Yes ___No ___Don't Know

95. On the average, how many hours does the child
    spend each night on homework? (Fill in the blank)_____

96. How many times has the child changed schools
    in the last five years? _____

WHAT IS MORE IMPORTANT?

We all know that doing schoolwork is important, but sometimes, things get in
our way and the child can't get his/her schoolwork done. Please let me know
which of these activities sometimes is more important than doing schoolwork.

97. Check A or B: ___A. Buying a car, or
                       ___B. Doing schoolwork.

98. Check A or B: ___A. Doing schoolwork, or
                       ___B. Wearing stylish clothes.

99. Check A or B: ___A. Helping the family, or
                       ___B. Doing schoolwork.

100. Check A or B: ___A. Doing schoolwork, or
                       ___B. Making money now.

101. Check A or B: ___A. Spending time with friends, or
                       ___B. Doing schoolwork.

102. Check A or B: ___ A. Doing schoolwork, or
                      ___ B. Starting a family.

103. Check A or B: ___ A. Talking on the telephone, or
                      ___ B. Doing schoolwork.

104. Check A or B: ___ A. Watching television, or
                      ___ B. Doing schoolwork.

THE OTHER PARENT

When we use the term "other parent," we are expecting the interviewed parent to describe one other adult caregiver in the child's immediate family. For example, if the interviewed parent is the child's mother, then it is likely that the other parent will be the child's father. Pay attention to the response of the interviewed parent to question number 1. If the interviewed parent is anyone other than the child's mother or father, then you need to determine if there is another "parent" and what relation this person may have to the child. If there is no "other parent," leave this section blank. After determining that there is another parent to describe, ask the interviewed parent to read the following questions about this person. Ask them to respond

Yes, if the statement is *True*
   or
No, if the statement is *Not True,*
   or
Don't Know, if the interviewed parent doesn't know.

105. The other parent is:

___ the biological parent, such as father
___ a grandparent or other relative
___ an adoptive or custodial parent
___ other (please describe)

106. The other parent is:

___ male   ___ female

107. Educational Attainment of the Other Parent:

What is the highest education attained?
Number of years _____
He/she graduated from high school.   ___ Yes   ___ No
He/she got a GED.   ___ Yes   ___ No

He/she took vocational classes after high school,
but did not graduate.   ___ Yes   ___ No

He/she graduated from vocational school.   ___ Yes   ___ No

He/she took classes at community college.   ___ Yes   ___ No

He/she graduated from community college.   ___ Yes   ___ No

He/she took classes at a four-year college.   ___ Yes   ___ No

He/she graduated from college.   ___ Yes   ___ No

108. The "other parent" wants the
child to stay in school.   ___ Yes   ___ No   ___ Don't Know

109. Within the last year, the other parent came
back to or joined the household.   ___ Yes   ___ No   ___ Don't Know

110. Within the last year, the other parent
left the household for an extended
period.   ___ Yes   ___ No   ___ Don't Know

111. The other parent spends time
with the child.   ___ Yes   ___ No   ___ Don't Know

112. The other parent was born in Mexico.
   ___ Yes   ___ No   ___ Don't Know

113. The other parent is Mexican American.
   ___ Yes   ___ No   ___ Don't Know

114. The other parent speaks predominantly
Spanish at home.   ___ Yes   ___ No   ___ Don't Know

115. The other parent has worked in
many places.   ___ Yes   ___ No   ___ Don't Know

116. What kind of work does the child's "other parent" do?
(If no other parent, skip this.)

_____

117. Since receiving notification that your child has been designated as "at risk"
of dropping out, what actions have you taken to keep your child in school?

_____

_____

_____

_____

Student Questionnaire

Name: _____   Date of Birth: _____

Sex: ___ Male   ___ Female

1. Ethnicity: (Check One)

___ Mexican American
___ Puerto Rican
___ Cuban American
___ Mexican
___ Other Latino (Describe) _____
___ Other (Describe) _____

MYSELF

First we'd like you to tell us about you. Listen to each statement and say

Yes, if the statement is *True*
          or
No, if the statement is *Not True*, in your opinion.

2. I was born in Mexico.	___ Yes	___ No
3. I am deeply religious.	___ Yes	___ No
4. I expect to attend at least 2 years of college.	___ Yes	___ No
5. I have had disciplinary problems this fall.	___ Yes	___ No
6. I cut classes every once in a while.	___ Yes	___ No

7. I expect to go to college sometime in the future. ___ Yes   ___No

8. I speak mostly Spanish at home. ___ Yes   ___No

9. I have been expelled or suspended from school. ___ Yes   ___No

10. I make good grades in school. ___ Yes   ___No

11. I feel that school is not going to do anything
    for me. ___ Yes   ___No

12. I cannot relate to the stuff I learned in school. ___ Yes   ___No

13. I expect to graduate from high school. ___ Yes   ___No

14. My teachers and I don't get along. ___ Yes   ___No

15. I have a quiet place at home to study and do
    my homework. ___ Yes   ___No

16. I find some of my classes to be dull or boring. ___ Yes   ___No

17. Staying in school will make a difference for me. ___ Yes   ___No

18. I participate in school-sponsored activities,
    such as sports or clubs. ___ Yes   ___No

19. This fall, I participated in organized sports,
    not sponsored by my school. ___ Yes   ___No

20. This fall, I participated in organized
    dance/music/art classes, sponsored by
    groups outside my school. ___ Yes   ___No

21. This fall, I participated in church-sponsored
    activities. ___ Yes   ___No

22. I expect to be married within the next
    three years. ___ Yes   ___No

23. I expect to start a family within the next
    three years. ___ Yes   ___No

24. I could start my family and still stay in school. ___ Yes   ___No

25. I don't have many friends at school. ___ Yes   ___No

26. I have been absent a lot lately due to sickness. ___ Yes   ___No

27. I like most of the students in my classes. ___ Yes   ___No

28. I want to enlist in the military as soon as I can.   ___ Yes   ___ No

29. I feel that my teachers want me to do well.   ___ Yes   ___ No

30. My teachers listen to what I have to say.   ___ Yes   ___ No

31. I expect to drop out of high school.   ___ Yes   ___ No

32. My grades prevent me from participating in after-school activities, like sports and clubs.   ___ Yes   ___ No

33. I feel that my teachers expect me to drop out.   ___ Yes   ___ No

34. Compared to other students in my classroom, my schoolwork is about average.   ___ Yes   ___ No

35. I know many people who have dropped out of high school.   ___ Yes   ___ No

36. At least one of my brothers or sisters has dropped out of high school.   ___ Yes   ___ No

37. My absences from school cause me problems.   ___ Yes   ___ No

38. When I grow up, I want to be a: (i.e., what job do you want?) (Describe on Line Below)

_____

39. Do you have a job now?   ___ Yes   ___ No

If yes, how many hours a week do you work? _____

What kind of job is it? _____

MY FAMILY

Now tell us about your family. Listen to each statement and say

Yes, if the statement is *True*

or

No, if the statement is *Not True*, in your opinion.

When we say "mother," we are referring to the woman who lives with you and acts as your guardian. She may be your mother, stepmother, other relative, or other adult. Likewise, when we say "father," we are referring to the man who lives with you and acts as your guardian. He may be your father, stepfather, other relative, or other adult. If you do not know the information about your parents, say you don't know. (Also, if they do not have "a mother" or "father," you should leave the item blank.)

40. My mother or father talks to me about school.   ___ Yes   ___ No

41. My mother or father usually helps me with my homework.   ___ Yes   ___ No

42. My mother or father keeps close track of how well I am doing in school.   ___ Yes   ___ No

43. Within the last year, my mother came back to or joined our household.   ___ Yes   ___ No

44. Within the last year, my mother left our household for an extended period.   ___ Yes   ___ No

45. Within the last year, my father came back to or joined our household.   ___ Yes   ___ No

46. Within the last year, my father left our household for an extended period.   ___ Yes   ___ No

47. Within the last year, I moved away from my parents.   ___ Yes   ___ No

48. I have always lived with my mother and/or father.   ___ Yes   ___ No

49. My mother or father always knows where I am and what I am doing.   ___ Yes   ___ No   ___ Don't Know

50. My mother wants me to stay in school.   ___ Yes   ___ No   ___ Don't Know

51. My father wants me to stay in school.   ___ Yes   ___ No   ___ Don't Know

52. My mother or father wants me to get good grades in school.   ___ Yes   ___ No   ___ Don't Know

53. My mother graduated from high school.   ___ Yes   ___ No   ___ Don't Know

54. My father graduated from high school.

___ Yes   ___ No   ___ Don't Know

55. My mother has taken some college courses.

___ Yes   ___ No   ___ Don't Know

56. My father has taken some college courses.

___ Yes   ___ No   ___ Don't Know

57. My mother graduated from college.

___ Yes   ___ No   ___ Don't Know

58. My father graduated from college.

___ Yes   ___ No   ___ Don't Know

59. My mother or father has visited my school this fall
(for any reason, e.g., sports event, teacher conference).

___ Yes   ___ No   ___ Don't Know

Now tell us about the people who live with you now:

60. How many people live in your home now (e.g., today)? _____

61. Regardless of where they now live, how many brothers
and sisters, stepbrothers and stepsisters do you have? _____

62. Do you have any older brothers or sisters?   ___ Yes   ___ No
If yes,
Has at least one of your older (siblings)
gone to college?   ___ Yes   ___ No   ___ Don't Know

63. Please let us know more about the people living in your home.
Do you live with

___ Mother
___ Father
___ Sister(s), stepsister(s), cousin(s)
___ Brother(s), stepbrother(s), cousin(s)
___ Stepmother
___ Stepfather
___ Grandparents
___ Other Relative/Adults

64. Whom do you talk to about school?
    Do you talk to:

___ Friends
___ Mother or stepmother
___ Father or stepfather
___ Sister(s) or stepsister(s)
___ Brother(s) or stepbrother(s)
___ Grandparent(s)
___ Other Relatives
___ Other Adults
___ Counselors/Teachers
___ No One

65. What language does your mother speak at home? (Check One)

___ Only Spanish   ___ Mostly Spanish   ___ Mostly English
___ Only English   ___ Other

66. What language does your father speak at home? (Check One)

___ Only Spanish   ___ Mostly Spanish   ___ Mostly English
___ Only English   ___ Other

67. What language do you speak at home? (Check One)

___ Only Spanish   ___ Mostly Spanish   ___ Mostly English
___ Only English   ___ Other

MY FRIENDS

We are interested in knowing more about your best friends. Listen to each statement and say

Yes, if the statement is *True*
        or
No, if the statement is *Not True*, in your opinion.

68. My best friends are interested in school.   ___ Yes   ___ No

69. My best friends attend classes regularly.   ___ Yes   ___ No

70. My best friends expect to graduate from
    high school.   ___ Yes   ___ No

71. My best friends expect to go to college.   ___ Yes   ___ No

72. At least one of my best friends has dropped
out of high school.   ___ Yes   ___ No

72. Most of my friends are Mexican American
or Mexican.   ___ Yes   ___ No

73. At least one of my friends is involved
with gangs.   ___ Yes   ___ No

75. My friends sometimes help me with
my schoolwork.   ___ Yes   ___ No

MY SCHOOLWORK

Tell us about your schoolwork. Listen to each statement and say

> *Yes*, if the statement is *True*
>   or
> *No*, if the statement is *Not True*, in your opinion.

76. Are there courses you need to take in high school
in order to qualify for training in skilled trades,
such as typist or electrician?   ___ Yes   ___ No

77. Are there courses you need to take in high
school in order to go to college?   ___ Yes   ___ No

78. I work on my homework until it is finished.   ___ Yes   ___ No

79. I work on my homework in school only.   ___ Yes   ___ No

80. Most of the courses I am taking will prepare
me for college.   ___ Yes   ___ No

81. My school has provided me with special classes
and/or tutoring to help me with my schoolwork.   ___ Yes   ___ No

82. Someone in my family usually helped me
with my schoolwork.   ___ Yes   ___ No

83. My English and math classes are too hard
for me.   ___ Yes   ___ No

84. How many times have you changed schools in the last five years? _____

85. On the average, how many hours do you spend each night on homework?
(Fill in The Blank)_____

HOW HARD I TRY TO GET GOOD GRADES

Now we are interested in finding out how hard you try to get good grades in various subjects. For each type of class, please tell me whether you try

Very Much, Some, or Very Little

in that subject. If you don't take any of these types of classes, tell me.

How hard do you try in

86. your math classes?   ___ Very Much   ___ Some   ___ Very Little

87. your English classes?   ___ Very Much   ___ Some   ___ Very Little

88. your social studies classes?
                              ___ Very Much   ___ Some   ___ Very Little

89. your vocational/business classes?
                              ___ Very Much   ___ Some   ___ Very Little

90. your fine arts (e.g., music, drama) classes?
                              ___ Very Much   ___ Some   ___ Very Little

91. your foreign language classes?
                              ___ Very Much   ___ Some   ___ Very Little

92. your physical education classes?
                              ___ Very Much   ___ Some   ___ Very Little

WHAT IS MORE IMPORTANT?

We all know that doing our schoolwork is important, but sometimes, things get in our way and we can't get our schoolwork done. Please let us know which of these activities sometimes is more important than doing your schoolwork.

93. Select A or B: ___ A. Buying a car, or
                          ___ B. Doing my schoolwork.

94. Select A or B: ___ A. Doing my schoolwork, or
                          ___ B. Wearing stylish clothes.

95. Select A or B: ___ A. Helping my family, or
                          ___ B. Doing my schoolwork.

96. Select A or B: ___ A. Doing my schoolwork, or
                          ___ B. Making money now.

97. Select A or B: ___ A. Spending time with my friends, or
                        ___ B. Doing my schoolwork.

98. Select A or B: ___ A. Doing my schoolwork, or
                        ___ B. Starting a family.

99. Select A or B: ___ A. Talking on the telephone, or
                        ___ B. Doing my schoolwork.

100. Select A or B: ___ A. Watching television, or
                        ___ B. Doing my schoolwork.

Ethnographic Interview #1—Parent

I. BEING "AT RISK"

1. Why do some students stay in school and others drop out?

2. Do you think your child is "at risk" of dropping out of high school? Why/Why not?

3. Why do you think the school identified your child as "at risk" of dropping out?

4. What did you do when you found out the school considered your child "at risk" of dropping out?
   A) How do you try to help your child with schoolwork?
   B) Who do you turn to for help with school problems?

5. What would you change to make your child more successful in school?

II. SCHOOL

6. What problems does your child have at school?

7. What has the school done to help your child stay in school? What would you like for the school to do?

8. What is your relationship with your child's teachers/administrators?

9. How do you find out how your child is doing in school? How often do you go to school? For what purposes?

10. What things interfere with your child's schoolwork? How do you deal with those interferences?

11. What things help him/her stay in school?

III. ASPIRATIONS/GOALS

12. What are your goals for this child? How do you let the child know these goals?

13. How well do you expect this child to do in school? How do you decide what to expect of this child in school?

14. What goals does this child have? How do you know?

IV. FRIENDS/SIBLINGS

15. How do your child's friends affect his/her schoolwork?

16. How do you feel about his/her friends? How do you deal with that?

17. How do brothers/sisters affect attitudes about school or staying in school?

V. COMMUNICATION/DISCIPLINE

18. How are decisions regarding your child's activities made? What happens when you and the child disagree?

19. What are the rules in your house? How are the rules decided? What happens if they are broken? How does your child react? How do you react?

20. How do you get him/her to do what you want him/her to do?

21. How often do you talk with your child about school? What are the conversations like? Who initiates/talks? What do you talk about?

22. What does the other parent do to help this child in school?

23. If you could change things in your family, what would you change?

Ethnographic Interview #1—Student

I. BEING "AT RISK"

1. Why do some students stay in school and others drop out?

2. Do you think you are "at risk" of dropping out of school?

3. Why do you think the school identified you as someone who might drop out?

4. How do you feel when someone thinks you might drop out of school?

5. Who do you turn to for help with school problems?

6. What did you do when you found out the school considered you "at risk" of dropping out?

II. SCHOOL

7. How do you feel about school? What do you like/dislike? How do you feel about your schoolwork?

8. What are your biggest problems in school? How do you deal with them?

9. What would it take for you to do really well in school?

10. How hard do you try to do well in school? Why? Give some examples.

11. What have you done to try to stay in school?

12. What do people in the school do to help you stay in school? (i.e., teachers, counselors) How do your teachers treat you?

13. How do your parents help you do your schoolwork?

14. What things interfere with attending school? with doing your school-work? How do you handle those things?

15. How well are you doing in school? How do you know? How do your parents feel about that?

III. ASPIRATIONS/GOALS

16. What plans do you have for the future? How did you decide on those plans? Will school help you?

17. Do you talk to your parents about those plans? Why or why not?

18. What are your parents' goals for you? Do you think you will achieve those goals?

19. What are your goals for the future? What do you want to be when you grow up?

20. What obstacles do you think you might have in reaching those goals?

IV. FRIENDS/SIBLINGS

21. How do your friends feel about school? Do they do well in school? Explain.

22. What do you do when you spend time with your friends?

23. What kinds of "groups" are there at your school? Are you a part of one of those groups? Explain.

24. Do friends help you or hurt you in your schoolwork? Explain.

25. Do your brothers or sisters help you with your schoolwork? Do they want you to stay in school?

V. COMMUNICATION/DISCIPLINE

26. How are decisions made in your family about you? What happens when you disagree with your parents? when you disobey?

27. What are the rules in your house? Who sets them? How do you feel about those rules?

28. How often do you talk to your parents about school? What are those conversations like?

29. How do you get your parents to do what you want them to do?

30. If you could change things in your family, what would you change?

Ethnographic Interview #2—Parent

SOCIAL SUPPORT/NETWORKS/RESOURCES

What do you think is the key thing that made your son/daughter stay in school? How has that decision worked out for him/her? Were there key people who helped him/her try to stay in school? What did they do? Other than the school, where would you go to get information or help when you have school problems?

COURSE TAKING/PREPARATION FOR JOB OR COLLEGE

Tell me about the courses your son/daughter took in high school. How did the courses prepare him/her for what he/she wants to do in the future (college/job)? How do you find out about schedules and courses? How did he/she decide to take these courses? How much say did you have in the courses he/she took? (Refer to transcript for specific questions.)

How have you helped him/her with a job? planning for college?

FUTURE PLANS

What was school like for your son/daughter? What is he/she doing now? (Refer to previous responses for specific questions.)

Compare school with the other things in his/her life now (school versus work, school versus being at home, school versus parenthood).

What are your son's/daughter's plans for the future? What does he/she plan to be doing at this time next year? five years from now? What are your plans for him/her?

[*If planning to go to college*, where does he/she plan to go? What made him/her think about going there? What does he/she need to get in there? (the courses needed, the cost) What steps have you taken to help him/her go?

If looking for a job, what kind of job is he/she looking for? What kinds of skills does he/she need for that job?]

PHILOSOPHY OF LIFE

What do you think are the most important things for your son/daughter to achieve in life?

SELF-CONCEPT

Who is (parent's name)?

Ethnographic Interview #2—Student

SOCIAL SUPPORT/NETWORKS/RESOURCES

What do you think is the key thing that made you stay in school? How has that decision worked out for you? Were there key people who helped you stay in school? What did they do? Other than the school, where would you go to get information or help when you have school problems? How have your friends influenced you?

COURSE TAKING/PREPARATION FOR JOB OR COLLEGE

Tell me about the courses you took in high school. How did the courses prepare you for what you want to do in the future (college/job)? How do you find out about schedules and courses? How did you decide to take these courses? How much say do your parents have in what courses you take? (Refer to transcript for specific questions.)

FUTURE PLANS

What was school like for you? What are you doing now? (Refer to previous responses for specific questions.)

Compare school with the other things in your life now. (school versus work, school versus being at home, school versus parenthood)

What are your plans for the future? What do you plan to be doing at this time next year? five years from now?
[*If planning to go to college*, where do you plan to go? What made you think about going there? What do you need to get in there? (the courses needed, the cost) What steps have you taken to try to go?
If looking for a job, what kind of job are you looking for? What kinds of skills do you need for that job?]

PHILOSOPHY OF LIFE

What do you think are the most important things for you to achieve in life?

SELF-CONCEPT

Who is (student's name)?

Telephone Interview—Parent

Date _____ Interviewer _____

1. Name and Address of Parent interviewed

   _____ Phone numbers _____

   _____ _____

   _____

2. Did the student (interviewer should make sure that the parent understands which student we are talking about; use the student's name) return to school this fall?   ___ Yes   ___ No

3. *If yes,* does the student like school better or worse this year compared to last year?   ___ better   ___ worse   ___ the same
   Why?

4. *If yes,* what have you done to help your child stay in school?

5. *If yes,* is your child in any special programs or classes at school?

6. *If no,* how was the decision to leave made?

7. *If no*, how do you feel about the child's decision to leave school?

8. *If no*, what is the student doing now?

Is he/she in any special programs?

9. What did the student do this summer? (Get an open-ended response and then ask about the following specific activities, if they were not mentioned.)

Some students have told us they did things like work at a job. We have created a list, and I will read each activity to you. You tell me if your child engaged in this activity this summer.
Did he/she:
___ go to summer school?
___ work at a job?
___ travel?
___ spend time on Sixth Street?
___ visit malls and/or video arcades?
___ baby-sit or help around the house?
___ participate in a sports or recreation program, such as swimming or softball?
___ participate in other organized activities, such as camp or volunteer work?

10. Did anything else important happen this summer?

11. Since we contacted you last, has anything else important happened that has affected the student?

12. Since we contacted you last, has your relationship with your child changed?

13. Since we contacted you last, have there been any changes in the family or household, such as new people joining or leaving the family?

14. How are your child's friends doing in school?

15. Does he/she still have the same friends as last year?

16. Do you think your child has been treated fairly by the school?

17. Who or what do/did you rely on in order to know if your child is/was doing OK at school?

18. Who do you talk to about the child's schoolwork or school issues? Some other parents have mentioned various persons. I'm going to go through a list, and let's see if any of these people have been helpful to you.

___ child
___ coworkers
___ no one
___ friends
___ other mothers and fathers
___ relatives, for example, other sons/daughters
___ neighbors
___ husband/wife
___ the school principal
___ school counselors
___ teachers
___ school secretary

___ other school person

___ people at church

___ any one else you can think of?

19. How often do/did you talk to someone *at school* about any issue concerning your child? (Interviewer, do not read the options below. You must interpret the parent's response and put it into a category. If you cannot do this, ask the parent, for example, "Do you mean you rarely or occasionally talk to your child?")

___ never

___ rarely (less than twice per year)

___ occasionally (3–6 times a year)

___ frequently (more than 6 times a year)

___ monthly or more

20. Whom have you contacted at the school?

21. What is the above-named person's (use his/her name) position at the school?

___ teacher

___ counselor

___ principal

___ secretary

___ other, specify _____

___ don't know

22. Has the school provided any more information since we first talked to you about your child's school progress? If so, what?

    Are there any special programs the school has provided?

23. If student is no longer in school, what have you done to get your child to return to school or get a GED?

For Interviewer, immediately after interview

1. How much in touch with the child's emotional state does the parent seem to be?
   ___ very much in touch
   ___ somewhat in touch
   ___ neutral
   ___ somewhat out of touch
   ___ very out of touch

2. How much does the parent seem to know about the child's day-to-day activities?
   ___ very much in touch
   ___ somewhat in touch
   ___ neutral
   ___ somewhat out of touch
   ___ very out of touch

Telephone Interview— Student

Date _____ Interviewer _____

1. Name and Address of student interviewed

   _____ Phone numbers _____

   _____ _____

   _____

2. Did you return to school this fall? ___Yes ___No

3. *If yes,* do you like school better or worse this year compared to last year?
   ___ better ___worse ___the same

   Why?

4. *If yes,* what has helped you stay in school?

   Have you participated in any special programs or classes?

5. *If no,* why did you stop attending school?

6. *If no,* how do you feel about your decision to stop attending school?

7. *If no*, what are you doing now?

Are you participating in any special programs or classes?

8. What did you do this summer? (Get an open-ended response and then ask about the following specific activities, if they were not mentioned.)

Some students have told us they did things like work at a job. We have created a list, and I will read each activity to you. You tell me if you engaged in this activity this summer.
Did you:
___ go to summer school?
___ work at a job?
___ travel?
___ spend time on Sixth Street?
___ visit malls and/or video arcades?
___ baby-sit or help around the house?
___ participate in a sports or recreation program, such as swimming or softball?
___ participate in other organized activities, such as camp or volunteer work?

9. What is the best and worst thing that happened to you since we last contacted you?

10. Did anything else important happen?

11. Since we contacted you last, has your relationship with your parents changed?

12. Since we contacted you last, have there been any changes in your family or household, such as new people joining or leaving the family?

13. How are your friends doing in school?

14. Do you still have the same friends as last year?

15. Do you know people who have dropped out?
    If yes, what are they doing now? What kind of job do they have?

16. Do you know people who have graduated from high school?
    If yes, what are they doing now? What kind of job do they have?

17. Do you think you have been treated fairly by the school?

18. Who or what do you rely on (or did you rely on) in order to know if you are doing OK at school?

19. Whom do you talk to about schoolwork or school issues? Some other students have mentioned various persons, and we have made this into a list. I'm going to go through this list, and tell me if you have talked to any of these people in the last year about your schoolwork or school issues.
    ___ no one
    ___ friends
    ___ parents
    ___ relatives
    ___ neighbors
    ___ the school principal

___ school counselors
___ teachers
___ school secretary
___ people at work
___ people at church
___ any one else you can think of?

20. How often do (or did, for dropouts) you talk to your parents about school? (Interviewer, do not read the options below. You must interpret the student's response and put it into a category. If you cannot do this, ask the student, for example, "Do you mean you rarely or occasionally talk to your parents?")
___ never
___ rarely
___ occasionally
___ frequently
___ daily

21. If the student indicates "never" to "occasionally," then ask the following question: "Why do/did you (never/rarely/occasionally) talk to your parents about school?"

22. If student indicates "frequently" to "daily," then ask the following question: "I talk to a lot of kids and they don't/didn't talk to their parents very often at all about school. What makes you and your parents different?"

23. If student is no longer in school, ask "What have you done to get back in school or get a GED?"

For Interviewer, immediately after interview
How open did you find the student?
___ not at all
___ less than average
___ average
___ more than average
___ very open

NOTES

1. THE GOALS AND METHODS OF THIS BOOK

1. U.S. Department of Education. (1992). *Dropout rates in the United States: 1991*. Washington, D.C.: U.S. Government Printing Office.

2. Levine, M. F., Taylor, J. C., & Davis, E. (1984). Defining quality of working life. *Human Relations, 37*, 81–104.

3. U.S. Bureau of the Census. (1992). School enrollment—social and economic characteristics of students. *Current Population Reports, October 1990* (Series P-20, No. 460). Washington, D.C.: U.S. Government Printing Office. (See table D.)

4. Rumberger, R. W., Ghatak, R., Poulos, G., Ritter, P. L., & Dornbusch, S. M. (1988, April). Family influences on dropout behavior: An exploratory study of a single high school. Paper presented at the American Educational Research Association meeting, New Orleans.

   U.S. Department of Education, National Center for Education Statistics. (1987). *School dropouts in the United States: Issue paper*. Washington, D.C.: U.S. Government Printing Office.

   U.S. Department of Labor, Bureau of Labor Statistics. *News Release*. (Document #90-326). Tuesday, June 26, 1990.

5. Fernandez, R., Paulsen, M. R., & Hirano-Nakanishi, M. (1989). Dropping out among Hispanic youth. *Social Science Research, 18*, 21–52.

6. Frazer, L. H. (1992). The use of school-maintained and school-related variables to differentiate between students who stay in and students who drop out of high school. Unpublished doctoral dissertation, University of Texas at Austin.

7. Dornbusch, S., Ritter, P., Liederman, H., Roberts, D., & Fraleigh, M. (1987). The relation of parenting style to adolescent school performance. *Child Development, 58*, 1244–1257.

8. Hodgkinson, H. L. (1986). *Texas: The state and its educational system*. Washington, D.C.: The Institute for Educational Leadership.

9. Bureau of Business Research Texas. (1991). *Texas fact book supplement*. Austin: The University of Texas.

   The biggest employer in Austin in 1989 and 1990 was state and local government with 107,000 employees, including those working for the University of Texas, the

City of Austin, and AISD. The second biggest employers were service industries with 96,500 employees. Wholesale and retail trade (77,000) and manufacturing (48,000) were ranked third and fourth, respectively.

10. Texas Employment Commission. (No Date). *Texas work force 2000*. Austin: Economic Research and Analysis Department, Texas Employment Commission.

11. Ibid.

12. Ibid.

13. These average expenditures per pupil were calculated by dividing the total amount in the district's general fund by the enrollment. For the 1988–89 school year, the average expenditure was $3,641; for 1989–90, $3,844; for 1990–91, $3,952; and for 1991–92, $3,982.

14. Ligon, G. (Personal communication, May 1, 1992).

15. Texas Education Agency. (1992). *Report on 1990–91 public school dropouts*. Austin.

16. Frazer, L. H. (1990). *1989–90 dropout report*. (Publication No. 90.12). Austin: Austin Independent School District, Office of Research and Evaluation.

17. Frazer, L. H., & Nichols, T. (1991). *1990–91 at risk report*. (Publication No. 90.41). Austin: Austin Independent School District, Office of Research and Evaluation.

18. U.S. Bureau of the Census. (1991). The Hispanic population in the United States: March 1990. *Current Population Reports*. (Series P-20, No. 449). Washington, D.C.: U.S. Government Printing Office. (See figure 1, p. 2.)

19. The 70th Legislative Regular Session defined "at risk of dropping out of school" in House Bill 1010 in 1987. The definition was amended in 1989, 1991, and 1993 and remains as part of the Texas Education Code, Section 21-557, Section F.

20. Frazer & Nichols. (1991). *1990–91 at risk report*.

21. Sanchez, M. (1993). *1992–93 dropout report*. (Publication No. 93.17). Austin: Austin Independent School District, Office of Research and Evaluation.

22. Sanchez, R. (1983). *Chicano discourse: Socio-historic perspectives*. Rowley, Mass.: Newbury House.

23. Bureau of the Census. Hispanic population in the United States: March 1990. (See table A, p. 4)

24. Coleman, J. S., Campbell, E., Hobson, C., McPartland, J., Mood, A., Weinfeld, F. D., & York, R. (1966). *Equality of educational opportunity*. Washington, D.C.: U.S. Government Printing Office.

 Hauser, R. M., & Featherman, D. (1976). Equality of schooling: Trends and prospects. *Sociology of Education, 49*, 99–119.

25. Bowles, S., & Gintis, H. (1976). *Schooling in capitalist America: Educational reform and the contradiction of economic life*. New York: Basic Books.

 Foley, D. E. (1990). *Learning capitalist culture: Deep in the heart of Tejas*. Philadelphia: University of Pennsylvania Press.

 Willis, P. (1977). *Learning to labor: How working class kids get working class jobs*. New York: Columbia University Press.

26. Blau, P. M., & Duncan, O. D. (1967). *The American occupational structure*. New York: Wiley.

 Featherman, D., & Hauser, R. M. (1978). *Opportunity and change*. New York: Academic Press.

 McClendon, M. J. (1978). The occupational status attainment processes of males and females. *American Sociological Review, 31*, 52–64.

Rosenfeld, R. (1978). Women's intergenerational occupational mobility. *American Sociological Review, 43*, 36–46.

Treiman, D. J., & Kermit, T. (1975). Sex and the process of status attainment: A comparison of working women and men. *American Sociological Review, 40*, 174–200.

27. Carter, T. P., & Segura, R. D. (1979). *Mexican Americans in school: A decade of change.* Princeton: College Entrance Examination Board.

28. The "no pass, no play" section of the education reform legislation was approved on July 13, 1984, to become effective in the 1984–85 school year, beginning in the spring semester of 1985. The Texas governor called a second session of the 68th Legislature, which passed Chapter 28, House Bill No. 72 enacting extensive school reform. Part F of that act addressed extracurricular activities. The act amended the Texas Education Code to say: "any student, other than a mentally retarded student, enrolled in a school district in the state shall be suspended from participation in any extracurricular activity sponsored or sanctioned by a school district during the grade reporting period after a grade reporting period in which a student received a grade lower than the equivalent of 70 on a scale of 100 in any academic class."

2. THE TRACKING OF HISPANIC STUDENTS

1. Kinney, D. A. (1993). From nerds to normals: The recovery of identity among adolescents from middle school to high school. *Sociology of Education, 66*, 21–40.

2. National Center for Education Statistics. (1988). *The condition of education: Elementary and secondary education.* Washington, D.C.: U.S. Government Printing Office.

    Alexander, K. L., Cook, M. A., & McDill, E. L. (1978). Curriculum tracking and educational stratification: Some further evidence. *American Sociological Review, 43*, 47–66.

3. According to Eva Baron, an administrator in the Austin Independent School District, the Zenith Program that James tried to enroll in selects students who lack only a few credits to qualify for graduation. The program was not designed to help students like James who lacked a large number of credits and would take several years to graduate. Students were recommended for the Zenith Program by teachers or counselors. The director of the program interviewed candidates and selected those who were perceived to be motivated to graduate. The program was already filled to capacity and had a waiting list when we inquired about it in October of the school year.

4. The distribution of 15-year-old students from one- and two-parent homes by their graduation status four years later is represented in the table below.

| Number | Graduation Status | |
of Parents	Dropout	Graduate
Two	42	21
One	17	6

Although it may appear that graduation was associated more with having two parents than having one parent, a statistical test of these frequencies indicated that no significant association existed here. This is due to the fact that dropping out was the most common outcome for all students we studied regardless of the number of parents they had when they were 15. Keep in mind that the number of parents a given student had often changed during the course of this study, with some parents getting divorced and others getting remarried during the four years we studied the families. The results of our study suggest that the marital status of parents was less important in determining whether the student graduated or dropped out than were other factors, such as the educational attainment of the parents and whether they monitored the student closely.

5. The correlation between the combined educational attainment of parents and whether their child graduated from high school was $r(89) = .29, p < .05$. This indicates that children with better-educated parents were more likely to graduate.

6. The literature demonstrating that American schools function largely to perpetuate inequality is voluminous. The following articles represent the evidence most frequently cited in this literature:

Bowles, S., & Gintis, H. (1976). *Schooling in capitalist America*. New York: Basic Books.

Coleman, J. S., Campbell, E., Hobson, C., McPartland, J., Mood, A., Weinfeld, F. D., & York, R. (1966). *Equality of educational opportunity*. Washington, D.C.: U.S. Government Printing Office.

Featherman, D. L., & Hauser, R. M. (1978). *Opportunity and change*. New York: Academic Press.

Jencks, C. S., Smith, M., Ackland, H., Bane, M. J., Cohen, D., Gintis, H., Heyns, B., & Michelson, S. (1972). *Inequality*. New York: Basic Books.

7. Mehan, H. (1992). Understanding inequality in schools: The contribution of interpretive studies. *Sociology of Education, 65*, 1–20.

8. Useem, E. L. (1992). Middle schools and math groups: Parents' involvement in children's placement. *Sociology of Education, 65*, 263–279.

9. Oakes, J. (1985). *Keeping track: How schools structure inequality*. New Haven: Yale University Press.

Gamoran, A., & Berends, M. (1987). The effects of stratification in secondary schools: Synthesis of survey and ethnographic research. *Review of Educational Research, 57*, 415–435.

Braddock, J. H. (1989). National education longitudinal study of 1988. Washington, D.C.: U.S. Department of Education, National Center for Educational Statistics.

10. Useem, E. L. (1992). Getting on the fast track in mathematics: School organizational influences on math track assignment. *American Journal of Education, 100*, 325–353.

11. Hill, D., & Suttles, A. (1991). *Setting sail for the future: The high school information guide*. Austin: Austin Independent School District.

This guide was given out by counselors to students for their course planning. It explained what standardized test scores students needed in order to take specific courses.

12. Dornbusch, S., Wood, K., & Romo, H. (1990). Course-taking patterns of Anglo, African American, Hispanic, and Asian students. Paper presented at the annual meeting of the American Educational Research Association, Boston.

13. This strategy was suggested by a school counselor at Bowie High School, Austin Independent School District, during a telephone conversation on April 9, 1993.

14. The Texas law pertaining to the identification of Gifted and Talented students can be found in Texas Education Code Section 21.651 and 21.655, available from the Texas Education Agency in Austin.

15. There is a long and extensive literature about the effects of labeling, which the following list of references represents:

> Rosenthal, R. (1968). *Pygmalion in the classroom*. New York: Holt, Rinehart and Winston.

> Cooper, H., & Good, T. (1983). *Pygmalion grows up: Studies in the expectation communication process*. New York: Longman.

> Harris, M. J., & Rosenthal, R. (1985). Mediation of interpersonal expectancy effects. *Psychological Bulletin, 97*, 363–386.

> Jussim, L. (1986). Self-fulfilling prophecies: A theoretical and integrative view. *Psychological Review, 93*, 429–445.

> Rosenthal, R. (1985). From unconscious experimenter bias to teacher expectancy effects. In J. B. Dusek, V. C. Hall, & W. J. Meyer, eds. *Teachers' expectancies*, 37–65. Hillsdale, N.J.: Erlbaum.

> Snyder, M. (1984). When beliefs create reality. In L. Berkowitz, ed. *Advances in experimental social psychology*, vol. 18, 247–305. New York: Academic Press.

16. Oakes. (1985). *Keeping track*.

17. Finley, M. K. (1984). Teachers and tracking in a comprehensive high school. *Sociology of Education, 57*, 233–243.

18. Commission on Chapter 1. (1992, December 10). *Making schools work for children in poverty*.

19. Hieronymus, A. N., & Hoover, H. D. (1986). *Manual for school administrators*, levels 5–14, 77. Iowa City: University of Iowa.

20. Scannell, D. P. (1958). *Differential prediction of academic success from achievement test scores*. Unpublished doctoral dissertation, University of Iowa.

21. Hieronymus & Hoover. (1986). *Manual for school administrators*, levels 5–14, 106.

22. Ibid., 1.

23. Ibid., 106.

24. In response to the widespread perception that many low-level courses were not preparing students to have the skills they would need to be successful adults, the Texas State Board of Education decided to eliminate the Correlated Language, Pre-Biology, and Pre-Algebra courses that James and Robert took. This action is described in the following newspaper article: Education board to halt low-level classes. (1992, June 13). *Austin American-Statesman*, B4.

> A debate between M. T. Hallinan and Jeannie Oakes about tracking appeared in a special issue of *Sociology of Education* (1994), 67(2), 79–91.

25. Oakes. (1985). *Keeping track*.

26. Wheelock, A. (1992). *Crossing the tracks: How "untracking" can save America's schools*, 77, 149–190. New York: The New Press.

27. Marshall, R., & Tucker, M. (1992). *Thinking for a living: Education and the wealth of nations*. New York: Basic Books.

28. Secretary's Commission on Achieving Necessary Skills (SCANS). (1991). *What

work requires of schools: A SCANS report for America 2000. Washington, D.C.: U.S. Department of Labor.

29. Slavin, R. E. (1979). Effects of biracial learning teams on cross-racial friendships. *Journal of Educational Psychology, 71,* 381–387.

Slavin, R. E. (1980). Cooperative learning. *Review of Educational Research, 50,* 315–342.

Slavin, R. E. (1983). When does cooperative learning increase student achievement? *Psychological Bulletin, 94,* 429–445.

Slavin, R. E. (1990). *Cooperative learning: Theory, research, and practice.* Englewood Cliffs: Prentice Hall.

30. Shepperd, J. A. (1993). Productivity loss in performance groups: A motivation analysis. *Psychological Bulletin, 113,* 67–81.

31. Most opposition to doing away with tracking has come from the parents of high-achieving students. The advantages of advanced coursework are well known to high-status parents, and these parents often act to ensure the placement of their children in these courses, even if their children have only average ability.

Stevenson, D. L., & Baker, D. P. (1987). The family-school relation and the child's school performance. *Child Development, 58,* 1348–1357.

Baker, D. P., & Stevenson, D. L. (1986). Mothers' strategies for children's school achievement: Managing the transition to high school. *Sociology of Education, 59,* 156–166.

Lareau, A. (1987). Social class differences in family-school relationships: The importance of cultural capital. *Sociology of Education, 60,* 73–85.

32. Oakes, J. (1987). Tracking in secondary schools: A contextual perspective. *Educational Psychologist, 22,* 129–154.

Oakes, J. (1990). *Multiplying inequalities: The effects of race, social class, and tracking on opportunities to learn mathematics and science.* Santa Monica, Calif.: The RAND Corporation.

33. A basic textbook covering the differences of criterion-referenced and norm-referenced tests is:

Sax, G. (1989). *Principles of educational and psychological measurement and evaluation.* 3d ed. Belmont, Calif.: Wadsworth.

3. CAUGHT IN THE WEB OF SCHOOL POLICIES

1. Lesley, B. (1992). [Grade 11 TAAS, All Tests Taken, by Ethnicity]. Unpublished raw data.

2. de la Rosa, B. (1992, September). A sociodemographic overview of the middle school student population cohort. Paper presented at the Eighth Robert Lee Sutherland Seminar, Austin.

3. Nazario, S. L. (1992, June 16). Move grows to promote failing pupils. *Wall Street Journal,* B1.

4. Triscari, R. S. (Personal communication, August 28, 1992).

5. Lesley. (1992). [Grade 11 TAAS].

6. Frazer, L., & Nichols, T. (1991). *1990–91 at risk report.* (Publication No. 90.41). Austin: Austin Independent School District, Office of Research and Evaluation.

7. Shepard, L. A., & Smith, M. L., eds. (1989). *Flunking grades: Research and policies on retention.* Bristol, PA: The Falmer Press.

8. The correlations between being overage (ranging from 0 to -2) and the following variables were:

   sex: $r(89) = .24$

   1989–90 ITBS mathematics percentile: $r(89) = .36$

   1989–90 ITBS reading percentile: $r(89) = .24$

   All of these correlations are significant at $p < .05$.

9. The correlations between being overage and the students' responses to the following items on the initial questionnaire were:

   I feel that school is not going to do anything for me.

   $r(89) = .07$

   My English and math classes are too hard for me.

   $r(89) = -.04$

   To what extent do you speak Spanish?

   $r(89) = .04$

   The correlation between being overage and the low-income status of the parents was: $r(89) = -.18$

   None of these correlations was significant.

10. Dr. Harriett Romo accompanied Alice to her half-day vocational program at her high school.

11. Dawson, D. A. (1991). Family structure and children's health and well-being. *Journal of Marriage and the Family, 53,* 573–584.

12. This conclusion has been drawn from several studies, including those done in the Austin school district, according to the presentation of Dr. Linda Frazer, AISD research analyst, on September 21, 1992, to a meeting of school and community leaders. At the state level, this conclusion was drawn by the following publication:

    Texas Education Agency. (1991). Older is better, right? Not really. *Research Briefs.* (Issue 91.1). Austin.

    At the national level, this conclusion has been drawn by research presented in the following chapter:

    Holmes, C. T. (1989). Grade level retention effects: A meta-analysis of research studies. In Shepard & Smith. *Flunking grades..*

13. Texas Education Agency. (1991). Older is better, right? Not really.

14. Ibid.

15. Dryfoos, J. G. (1990). *Adolescents at risk: Prevalence and prevention,* 84. New York: Oxford University Press.

16. Nazario. (1992, June 16). Move grows to promote failing pupils. B1.

17. Triscari. (Personal communication, August 28, 1992).

18. McDill, E. L., Natriello, G., & Pallas, A. M. (1986). A population at risk: Potential consequences of tougher school standards for student dropouts. In G. Natriello, ed. *School dropouts: Patterns and policies,* 106–147. New York: Teacher's College Press.

19. Stevenson, H. W., & Stigler, J. W. (1992). *The learning gap: Why our schools are failing and what we can learn from Japanese and Chinese education.* New York: Summit Books.

4. GANG INVOLVEMENT AND EDUCATIONAL ATTAINMENT

1. Analyses of our survey data indicate that the female students with gang-involved best friends were more likely than other girls to report cutting classes—$r(47) = .27$, $p < .04$.

2. In our study, the students with gang-involved friends were also more likely to say that they had friends and siblings who had dropped out of school—$r(88) = .61$, $p < .0001$—than were students without gang-involved friends.

3. In our sample, the girls who lived in smaller households were less likely to have best friends in gangs—$r(47) = .31, p < .02$. Ramona lived in one of the bigger households.

4. Salvador's experience was common among the students in our sample. During our first follow-up telephone interviews, students who had indicated in our questionnaire that they had gang-involved best friends were more likely to tell the interviewer that the family had undergone a recent crisis, including such events as divorce, unemployment, or death—$r(74) = .35, p < .001$.

5. Our findings show that the effects of having at least one sister with gang participation varied depending on the youth's sex. For girls, having sisters was associated with being less involved in gangs—$r(47) = .20, p < .08$. In contrast, boys who were living with at least one sister were more likely to have best friends in gangs—$r(42) = .29, p < .03$.

6. Moore, J. W. (1991). *Going down to the barrio: Homeboys and homegirls in change.* Philadelphia: Temple University Press.

   Moore, J. W. (1978). *Homeboys: Gangs, drugs, and prison in the barrios of Los Angeles.* Philadelphia: Temple University Press.

7. Ekstrom, R. B., Goertz, J. M., Pollack, J. M., & Rock, D. A. (1986). Who drops out of high school and why? Findings from a national study. *Teachers College Record, 87,* 356–373.

   Valverde, S. A. (1987). A comparative study of Hispanic high school dropouts and graduates: Why do some leave school early and some finish? *Education and Urban Society, 19* (3), 320–329.

   Moore, J. W., & Vigil, J. D. (1989). Chicano gangs: Group norms and individual factors related to adult criminality. *Aztlan, 18* (2), 27–43.

8. Kaplan, H., & Pokorny, A. D. (1971). Self derogation and childhood broken home. *Journal of Marriage and the Family, 33,* 328–337.

   Moore (1991). *Going down to the barrio,* 81–103.

9. We found no significant correlation between having parents who were born in Mexico and having gang-involved best friends. Previous studies of gang life, such as the ones listed below, have portrayed gang participation as part of the assimilation process:

   Cloward, R. A., & Ohlin, L. B. (1960). *Delinquency and opportunity: A theory of delinquent gangs.* New York: Free Press.

   Moore, J. W. (1978). *Homeboys.*

   Short, J. F., Jr., & Strodtbeck, F. L. (1965). *Group process and gang delinquency.* Chicago: University of Chicago Press.

   Vigil, J. D. (1988). *Barrio gangs: Street life and identity in southern California.* Austin: University of Texas Press.

Whyte, W. (1943). *Street corner society*. Chicago: University of Chicago Press.

10. This interview between Dr. Harriett Romo and Officers Gil and Martinez took place on June 4, 1992.

11. In our study, we found that male students who reported having best friends in gangs were more likely than other boys to say that schoolwork was not important—r (42) = .40, $p < .005$.

12. This information is from a memo, dated February 5, 1992, and written by Dr. Linda Frazer to Dr. Glynn Ligon, both of the Austin Independent School District.

13. Moore. (1991). *Going down to the barrio*.

14. Epstein, J. L. (1992). Decade sees progress in research on school and family. (Research and Development Report, No. 2, 12–14). Boston: Center on Families, Communities, Schools, and Children's Learning.

15. The remarkable impact of creating a school community. (1988, Spring). *American Educator*, pp. 10–43.

16. Dayton, C., Raby, M., Stern, D., & Weisberg, A. (1992, March). The California partnership academies: Remembering the "forgotten half." *Phi Delta Kappan*, 539–545.

17. Dayton, C., Weisberg, A., & Stern, D. (1989). *Graduate follow-up survey of the June 1988 and June 1989 graduates of the California Partnership Academies*. Berkeley: University of California, Policy Analysis for California Education.

5. TEEN MOTHERHOOD

1. The issue of sex education in Texas textbooks and school course content is quite controversial and complex. The Texas Education Agency and local school boards have refused to allow the adoption of texts that deal with issues of contraception, sexuality, and the consequences of teen parenthood. Norma was experiencing typical teen desires to "experiment" with sex with very little factual knowledge of the consequences.

2. 71st Legislature, Regular Session, Chapter 658, Senate Bill No. 1668, effective September 1, 1989. In *General and Special Laws, Texas*. Bk 2, 71st Legislature, Regular Session, 1989, Chapters 498–773, p. 2166.

3. In psychological research about the White middle-class population in the U.S., authoritarian parenting style is associated with lower educational outcomes. However, these results are not consistent for Asian American parents, who also tend to use authoritarian parenting style, but their children tend to do well in school. Among the Mexican-origin population, respect for parents and their authority is still highly valued and was evident in the case of Lupe's family, but not Norma's or Kathy's. The following reference represents a recent review of the psychological literature about authoritarian, authoritative, and permissive parenting styles:

Darling, N., & Steinberg, L. (1993). Parenting style as context: An integrative model. *Psychological Bulletin, 113*, 487–496.

4. Generally, undocumented immigrants are ineligible for social welfare. They can receive free emergency health care, WIC, and public education, including Head Start and free school lunches. In order to apply for social welfare, all family members must be listed, and many undocumented immigrants are fearful of exposing them-

selves in the process of obtaining benefits for eligible family members (typically, children born in the U.S.). Those who were trying to qualify under amnesty for citizenship could not apply for benefits for a five-year period. One immigrant whom Harriett Romo helped fill out a Food Stamp application was told that only her U.S.-born child was eligible and, furthermore, that her application would be reported to the INS.

5. When we applied a statistical analysis to our data about teen motherhood and graduation, we were not able to find a statistically significant association between these two variables. The chi-square probability = .29, $p < .06$. This result was just shy of statistical significance and could be called borderline in its significance. The results in the table below indicate that few (3) mothers were able to graduate while more nonmothers were able to graduate (11). There are two likely reasons why our results were not statistically significant. First, the sample size in general was very small, with only three cases in one of the cells (e.g., the mothers who graduated). The second reason was many students who did not become mothers still dropped out (13). Thus, dropping out was not associated solely with motherhood, but with other factors as well. The few teen mothers who were able to graduate were like Norma. They had strong academic abilities, a network of adults and peers for support, financial resources to support the mother and child, and teachers and administrators who encouraged their continuation in school; and their school had a program that helped them care for their children and stay in school.

| | Graduation Status | |
Motherhood Status	Dropout	Graduate
No baby	13	14
Baby	11	3

6. Fennelly Darabi, K., & Ortiz, V. (1987). Childbearing among young Latino women in the United States. *American Journal of Public Health,* 77 (1), 25–28.
7. Grant, C. A., & Sleeter, C. E. (1993). Race, class, gender, and disability in the classroom. In J. A. Banks & C. A. M. Banks, eds. *Multicultural education: Issues and perspectives.* Needham Heights, Mass.: Allyn & Bacon.
8. Several reports have discussed the elements of programs successful at preventing teen motherhood:

    Children's Defense Fund. (1986). *Preventing adolescent pregnancy: What schools can do.* Washington, D.C.: Children's Defense Fund.

    National Guidelines Task Force (1993). *Guidelines for comprehensive sexuality education: Kindergarten through 12th grade.* Washington, D.C.: Sex Information and Education Council of the U.S., third printing.

    Sylvester, K. (1994). *Preventable calamity: Rolling back teen pregnancy.* Washington, D.C.: Progressive Policy Institute, Policy Report No. 22.
9. Jones, E., Forrest, J., Goldman, N., Henshaw, S., Lincoln, R., Rosoff, J., Westoff, C., & Wulf, D. (1985). Teenage pregnancy in developed countries: Determinants and policy implications. *Family Planning Perspectives,* 17, 53–63.

10. Miller, B. C., & Paikoff, R. L. (1992). Comparing adolescent pregnancy prevention programs: Methods and results. In B. C. Miller, J. J. Card, R. L. Paikoff, & J. L. Peterson, eds. *Preventing adolescent pregnancy*, 265–284. Newbury Park, Calif.: Sage.

11. Miller, B. C., & Moore, K. A. (1990). Adolescent sexual behavior, pregnancy, and parenting: Research through the 1980s. *Journal of Marriage and the Family, 52*, 1025–1044.

12. Ibid.

13. Ibid.

14. Horowitz, R. (1981). Passion, submission, and motherhood: The negotiation of identity by unmarried innercity Chicanas. *Sociological Quarterly, 22*, 241–253.

15. Polit, D. F., & Kahn, J. R. (1986). Early subsequent pregnancy among economically disadvantaged teenage mothers. *American Journal of Public Health, 76* (2), 167–171.

16. Nightingale, E. O., & Wolverton, L. (1993). Adolescent rolelessness in modern society. *Teacher's College Record, 94*, 472–486.

17. Reich, R. B. (1991). *The work of nations: Preparing ourselves for 21st century capitalism.* New York: Knopf.

18. Glover, R. W., & Marshall, R. (1993). Improving the school-to-work transition of American adolescents. *Teachers College Record, 94* (3), 588–610.

19. Adolescent Pregnancy and Parenthood Advisory Council. (1993, January). *Report to the 73rd Texas Legislature.* Austin: Texas Department of Human Resources.

20. U.S. Bureau of the Census. (1985–1989). Fertility of American women. *Current Population Reports* (Series P-20, Nos. 406, 427, 436). Washington, D.C.: U.S. Government Printing Office.

21. Fennelly, K. (1993). Sexual activity and childbearing among Hispanic adolescents in the United States. In R. Lerner, ed. *Early adolescence: Perspectives on research, policy, and intervention*, 335–352. Hillsdale, N.J.: Erlbaum Press.

22. Center for Social Work Research. (1992, August). *Teen birth data and statistics in 254 Texas counties.* Austin: School-Age Pregnancy and Prevention Clearinghouse, University of Texas.

23. The correlation between the teen reporting at least one pregnancy and also reporting she had been disciplined in school was r (43) = .49, $p < .05$. Because few female students, relative to male students, were disciplined at school, this finding suggests that the motherhood of some of our students may be part of a larger pattern of deviance.

24. The correlation between the teen reporting at least one pregnancy and reporting knowing many people who had dropped out of school was r (43) = .36, $p < .05$. This finding indicates that teen mothers in our sample knew more dropouts than female students who did not get pregnant. Knowing many people who had dropped out was associated with dropping out among our female students—Pearson chi-square = 5.04, $p < .02$.

25. The correlation between the teen reporting at least one pregnancy and reporting that her teachers expected her to drop out was r (43) = .43, $p < .05$. We also found that none of the girls who graduated thought that their teachers expected them to drop out, while most (80%) of the girls who dropped out thought that their teachers expected them to drop out.

26. The correlation between the teen reporting at least one pregnancy and the expectation at age 15 of attending at least two years of college was r (43) = −.32, $p < .05$.

The correlation between the teen reporting at least one pregnancy and the taking of college-preparatory courses at age 15 was $r(43) = -.32, p < .05$. These results suggest that pregnant teens had lower educational expectations than teens who did not become pregnant.

27. Harris, L., & Associates. (1986). *American teens speak: Sex, myths, TV, and birth control.* New York: Louis Harris & Associates.
28. Miller & Paikoff. (1992). Comparing adolescent pregnancy prevention programs.
29. Forrest, J. D., & Singh, S. (1990). The sexual and reproductive behavior of American women, 1982–1988. *Family Planning Perspectives, 22* (5), 206–214.

6. IMMIGRANT AND SECOND-GENERATION STUDENTS

1. When we applied a statistical analysis to our data about immigrant children and graduation, we were not able to find a statistically significant association between these two variables. The results in the table below indicate that few children of Mexican-born parents (7) were able to graduate while many more children of these parents dropped out (25). Similarly, our results indicate that few Mexican-born students were able to graduate (4); they were more likely to drop out (11). Although this difference suggests that immigrant students were disproportionately likely to drop out, statistical analyses of both tables take into consideration the fact that dropping out was the most common outcome for all students in our sample. This was true regardless of the students' birthplace or the parents' birthplace. In fact, in our sample, graduation was relatively unlikely, regardless of the national origin of the students or their parents. Another reason why our results were not statistically significant is that the sample size in general was very small, with only a few cases in one of the cells (the 7 or 4). Thus, dropping out was not associated solely with having foreign-born parents, but with other factors as well. The few children of foreign-born parents who were able to graduate were like Linda. They had families with at least a middle-class income, and their foreign-born parents had more than a primary education.

	Not Graduate	Graduate
U.S.-born parent(s)	35	20
Mexican-born parent(s)	25	7

	Not Graduate	Graduate
U.S.-born student	48	23
Mexican-born student	11	4

In both cases, the total adds up to less than 100 due to missing data. Both U.S.-born and Mexican-born students had high rates of dropping out, but often the reasons for dropping out were different for the two groups.

2. Advocates for Mexican families who come to the U.S. to make a better life for themselves without official immigration papers refer to these individuals as "undocumented" rather than illegal immigrants. Before the Immigration Reform and Control Act (IRCA) in 1986, immigrants without visas or work permits could work in the U.S. legally, but could be deported for not having immigration documents. After IRCA, immigrants without such documents could not legally work or reside permanently in the U.S.

3. We found a statistically significant association between not graduating from high school and coming from a low-income family—Pearson chi-square probability = 9.75, $p < .002$. Our data on income are derived from the school district's files regarding the eligibility for a free or reduced-price lunch. The school district used USDA guidelines to determine who was eligible for a free or reduced-price lunch at school. Any student who was eligible was considered as low income in our study. Below is a table showing the cross-tabulation of income status by graduation status.

	Not Graduate	Graduate
Low-income	40	8
Not low-income	21	19

4. The Office of Research and Evaluation of the Austin Independent School District generated many reports about correlates of dropping out of school. During the 1990–91 school year, the senior year of most of our graduates, the annual dropout rate for students who came from a low-income family was 14.5%; for students not from low-income families, the rate was 8.2%. This information comes from the following document:

Frazer, L. H. (1991). *1990–1991 dropout report: Executive summary.* (Publication No. 91.12). Austin: Austin Independent School District, Office of Research and Evaluation.

Information about the relationship between low-income status and dropping out in the Austin Independent School District is also provided in the following dissertation:

Frazer, L. H. (1992, May). The use of school-maintained and school-related variables to differentiate between students who stay in and students who drop out of high school. Unpublished doctoral dissertation, University of Texas at Austin.

The significant relationship between low-income status and dropping out of school has been found nationally. The following publication documents this association at the national level:

Ekstrom, R. B., Goertz, M. E., Pollack, J. M., & Rock, D. A. (1986). Who drops out of high school and why? Findings from a national study. *Teachers College Record, 87,* 356–373.

5. Hakuta, K. (1986). *Mirror of language: The debate on bilingualism.* New York: Basic Books.

6. Bean, F. D., & Tienda, M. (1987). *The Hispanic population of the United States.* New York: Russell Sage Foundation.

In 1848, when the Treaty of Guadalupe Hidalgo was signed, about 100,000 Mexicans living in California and other parts of the Southwest became Mexican Americans. Their descendants are also part of the U.S. Mexican-origin population. One consequence of the influx of Mexicans to the U.S. in the 1920s and again in the 1970s and 1980s was that this resident population of Mexican-origin people became outnumbered by the more recent arrivals from Mexico.

7. The support for this can be found in Bean & Tienda (1987), cited above, and by the following publications:

Bean, F. D., Chapa, J., Berg, R., & Sowards, K. (1994). Educational and sociodemographic incorporation among Hispanic immigrants to the United States. In B. Edmonston & J. S. Passel, eds. *Immigration and ethnicity: The integration of America's newest immigrants*, 73–100. Washington, D.C.: The Urban Institute Press.

Dinnerstein, L., & Reimers, D. M. (1988). *Ethnic Americans: A history of immigration*. New York: Harper & Row.

8. Bean et al. (1994). Educational and sociodemographic incorporation among Hispanic immigrants to the United States.

Portes, A., & Rumbaut, R. G. (1990). *Immigrant America: A portrait*. Berkeley: University of California Press.

9. Bean, F. D., Edmonston, B., & Passel, J. S. (1990). *Undocumented migration to the United States*. Santa Monica, Calif.: The RAND Corporation.

10. Gordon, M. (1964). *Assimilation in American life: The role of race, religion, and national origins*. New York: Oxford University Press.

Gordon, M. (1978). *Human nature, class, and ethnicity*. New York: Oxford University Press.

11. Chapa, J. (1990). The myth of Hispanic progress. *Journal of Hispanic Policy, 4*, 3–18.

Chapa, J. (1991). Special focus: Hispanic demographic and educational trends. In D. J. Carter & R. Wilson, eds. *Ninth annual status report on minorities in higher education*. Washington, D.C.: American Council of Education.

12. Portes, A., & Zhou, M. (1993). *The new second generation: Segmented assimilation and its variants among post-1965 immigrant youth*. (Paper No. 34). New York: Russell Sage Foundation.

13. San Miguel, G. (1987). *Let all of them take heed: Mexican Americans and the campaign for educational equality in Texas, 1910–1981*. Austin: University of Texas Press.

Acuna, R. (1981). *Occupied America: A history of Chicanos*. 2d ed. New York: Harper & Row.

Valdievieso, R., & Dains, C. (1988, December). U.S. Hispanics: Challenging issues for the 1990s. *Population Trends and Public Policy*, 1–16.

14. Marshall, R., & Tucker, M. (1992). *Thinking for a living: Education and the wealth of nations*. New York: Basic Books.

15. LeCompte, M. D., & Anthony, G. D. (1991). *Giving up on school: Student dropouts and teacher burnouts*. Newbury Park, Calif.: Corwin Press.

16. *Plyler v. Doe*, 457 U.S. 202. (1982). The *Plyler* case involved a Texas statute which denied local school districts funds for education of illegal-alien children and allowed school districts to deny free public education to such children. Texas argued that because Congress did not admit these children legally to the U.S., it gave the state authority to treat them less favorably than citizens and resident aliens. Texas

contended that its statute might help "stem the flood of illegal immigrants" and that "illegal-alien children" imposed an especially heavy burden on the state's ability to provide high-quality public education. Texas also claimed that "illegal-alien" children were less likely than other children to remain within the state and therefore less likely to put their education to use there. The Supreme Court argued that preservation of scarce resources (state educational funds) was never a sufficient reason for denying those resources to one particular group. The Court also argued that public education, while not a "right" guaranteed by the Constitution, was certainly more important than other social welfare "benefits." Denying these children an education would render them illiterate, and would thus prevent them from advancing based on their individual merit and from becoming useful members of society.

This controversy resurfaced with the campaign for Proposition 187 in California. Sixty percent of California voters approved this initiative on November 8, 1994. Proposition 187 bars public schooling, social services, and nonemergency health care to illegal immigrants. School districts are required to verify the legal status of students to assure that they are citizens, legal immigrants, or permanent residents. Beginning in 1996, the status of each child and that of his or her guardian will have to be verified. In addition, school administrators are required to report any student or parent who they suspect has illegal status. The passage of this proposition immediately triggered lawsuits charging that Proposition 187 unlawfully intrudes on federal jurisdiction on immigration. The suits also claimed that the proposition would encourage discrimination against people who appear or sound foreign.

Ferrell, D., & Lopez, R. J. (1994, November 10). State waits to see what prop. 187 will really mean. *Los Angeles Times,* A1, A21.

We obtained a copy of a U.S. Department of Education draft report from Dr. Eugene Garcia of the Bilingual Education Office. The report (dated December 2, 1994) described the impact of 187 on education. This report argued that Proposition 187 is contrary to the *Plyler* v. *Doe* ruling. The report also suggested that implementation of 187 would violate the due process clause of the 14th Amendment since neither children nor their parents are given any notice or right to contest being reported as "suspected" illegal aliens. The report argued that 187 violates the Federal Educational Rights and Privacy Act because student records might be used to disclose the immigration status of a pupil or his or her parents without prior consent of the parent. This report concludes that 187 will require school personnel to become law enforcers and this role will adversely affect the learning environment of all students. The report concluded that it is unlikely that 187 will cause undocumented immigrant children to return to their countries of origin. Instead, they will become further marginalized from participation in U.S. society.

17. These numbers were provided to Toni Falbo by Bill Perry of the Austin Independent School District in October 1993. Called "abusive conduct," the types of fighting included in this count were acts of rude or profane language or gestures, harassment, extortion, threats of violence, coercion, physical contact of a violent nature, and assault. The numbers in this chapter do not include the above behaviors with an adult, such as a teacher, and also exclude weapon possession.

18. These numbers were provided to Toni Falbo by Bill Perry of the Austin Independent School District in October 1993. The types of fighting included in this count

are called "abusive conduct" among students and include the same types of behaviors listed in note 17. For both male and female students, the most frequent type of abusive conduct was physical contact of a violent nature.

19. This information comes from the Austin Independent School District's student discipline policy, which was originally adopted on November 10, 1986.

20. This information is from a memorandum (dated September 28, 1993) from David Wilkinson to Dan Robertson, both employed by the Austin Independent School District. The Office of Research and Evaluation of the Austin Independent School District conducted a survey of the LEP students to determine the different types of languages spoken by the district's students.

21. It is common to find a wide range of languages as well as needs and abilities in ESL classrooms. Enrique's sister-in-law attended a few ESL classes for adults and commented on the inability of these classes to meet the needs of a wide range of students. Teachers often have students who are well educated and only lack English skills in the same classroom with students who are completely illiterate. She described the ESL classes thus: "Por ahí en, en esa escuela pienso que no, no tenían todo en orden, porque tenían personas que no sabían ni leer ni escribir en español. Y ahí estábamos los que sí sabíamos leer y escribir en español. Entonces, algo para escribir lo hacíamos más fácil nosotros que los que no sabían ni el abecedario ni en español siquiera. Y por eso ya, ya no fui, porque no, no tenían todo en regla, digo." (Over there in that school, I think that they don't, they don't have everything in order because they had people who did not know how to read or write in Spanish. And there were also those of us that knew how to read and write in Spanish. Then, to write something it would be easier for us who knew how than for those who did not even know the alphabet in Spanish. And because of that, now I don't go, because they don't have everything in order, I said.)

22. Carter, T., & Chatfield, M. L. (1986). Effective bilingual schools: Implications for policy and practice. *American Journal of Education, 95*, 200–232.

23. Hakuta. (1986). *Mirror of language.*

24. Frazer. (1991). *1990–1991 dropout report.*

25. Kirsch, I. S., Jungeblut, A., Jenkins, L., & Kolstad, A. (1993). *Adult literacy in America.* (Table 1.1B, p. 114). Office of Educational Research and Improvement, U.S. Department of Education. Washington, D.C.: U.S. Government Printing Office.

26. Lucas, T., Rosemary, H., & Ruben, D. (1990). Promoting the success of Latino language-minority students: An exploratory study of six high schools. *Harvard Educational Review, 60* (3), 315–339.

27. First, J. M., & Carrera, J. W. (1988). *New voices: Immigrant students in U.S. public schools. An NCAS research and policy report,* 99. Boston: The National Coalition of Advocates for Students.

28. Romo, H. D. (1985). The Mexican origin population's differing perceptions of their children's schooling. In R. O. de la Garza, F. D. Bean, C. Bonjean, R. Romo, and R. Alvarez, eds. *The Mexican American experience: An interdisciplinary anthology.* Austin: University of Texas Press.

29. Delgado-Gaitan, C., & Trueba, H. (1991). *Crossing cultural borders: Education for immigrant families in America.* London: The Falmer Press.

30. Information provided to us by Dr. Eugene Garcia (U.S. Department of Education,

Draft Report, 12/2/94) indicated that the 1994 federal share of total education spending—including funds from all departments and agencies—was only about 6–8%. State and local governments and private organizations provided the remaining money needed to educate students in U.S. schools. The U.S. Constitution limits the federal role in education, allocating that responsibility to state and local governments. The argument was that local government could best determine local needs. However, federal policies, in areas such as immigration, can have a serious impact on local school districts.

7. GOING FOR THE GED

1. Cameron, S., & Heckman, J. (1993). Nonequivalence of high school equivalents. *The Journal of Labor Economics*, *11* (1): 1–47.
   The *New York Times* published the following articles discussing the merit of the GED:
   Peterson, I. (1992, October 21). More get equivalency diploma amid questions about its value. *The New York Times*, A1, B8.
   Marriott, M. (1993, June 15). Value of GED diplomas to high school dropouts questioned. *The New York Times*, A18.
   Celis, W., III. (1994, January 5). High school equivalency test poses a new question: Will taking it matter? *The New York Times*, B8.
2. Cameron & Heckman. (1993). Nonequivalence of high school equivalents.
3. Ibid., 21.
4. Ibid., 1–47.
5. Texas Education Agency. (1993). Closing the gap: Acceleration vs. remediation and the impact of retention in grade on student achievement. *The Commissioner's Critical Issue Analysis Series*, 1.
   Grissom, J. B., & Shepard, L. A. (1989). Repeating and dropping out of school. In L. A. Shepard and M. L. Smith, eds. *Flunking Grades: Research and Policies on Retention*. Bristol, Penn.: The Falmer Press.
   Frazer, L. H., & Nichols, T. (1991). *1990–91 at risk report*. (Publication No. 90.41). Austin: Austin Independent School District.
6. Cameron & Heckman. (1993). Nonequivalence of high school equivalents, figure 1.
7. During the fall of 1991, 12,179 high school students in the Austin Independent School District were surveyed about a variety of issues, including their perceptions of the dropout problem. Not all students received the same questions. The results about the reasons for dropping out are based on the responses of 2,073 high school students, and the results about the factors that would motivate students to achieve or stay in school are based on the responses of 2,084 high school students. These results currently exist as unpublished documents in the Office of Research and Evaluation of the Austin Independent School District.
8. Frazer, L. H. (1991). *1990–1991 dropout report: Executive summary*. (Publication No. 91.12). Austin: Austin Independent School District: Office of Research and Evaluation.
   According to this report, students who received fewer than three hours of ser-

vices a day were less likely to drop out than were students in general. However, students who needed more than three hours of services a day were more likely to drop out.

9. Cameron & Heckman. (1993). Nonequivalence of high school equivalents, 36–43.

10. Although the specifics of medical insurance vary from policy to policy, it is common for any neurological problem diagnosed as a "learning disability" to be excluded from medical coverage. Thus, if a parent sought treatment for the child's learning disabilities outside of school, such as in the summer when the schools do not provide services, then most medical insurance policies would not cover it.

8. BUREAUCRATIC GLITCHES

1. Frazer, L. H. (1991). *1990–1991 dropout report: Executive summary.* (Publication No. 91.12). Austin: Austin Independent School District, Office of Research and Evaluation.

2. An analysis of variance was conducted with glitch as the independent variable (coded: yes or no) and graduation status in the fall of 1992 as the dependent variable (coded: 1 = graduate, 2 = still enrolled, 3 = GED, 4 = dropped out). The analysis yielded a nonsignificant F (1, 90) = .93, n.s.

3. The correlation between having an administrative glitch and the number of siblings the target student had was r (89) = .32, $p < .01$.

4. Hill, P. T., & Bonan, J. (1991). Decentralization and accountability in public education. (R-4066-MCF/IET). *Selected Rand Monographs.* Santa Monica, Calif.: RAND Corporation.

5. Callahan, R. E. (1962). *Education and the cult of efficiency.* Chicago: University of Chicago Press.

   Taylor, F. W. (1916). *The principles of scientific management.* New York: Harper & Brothers.

6. Marshall, R., & Tucker, M. (1992). *Thinking for a living: Education and the wealth of nations.* New York: Basic Books.

7. Officially, in the U.S. Census Index of Industries and Occupations, elementary and secondary teachers are coded as managerial and professional specialty occupations. The coding is based on "kind of work" and "most important activities or duties." But in the unofficial hierarchical organization of education in the United States, teachers have become the "laborers and operators" in the public education system. These terms are based on the classifications described below:

   U.S. Department of Commerce, Economics and Statistics Administration, Bureau of the Census. (1990). *Census of Population and Housing, Alphabetical Index of Industries and Occupations.* Washington, D.C.: U.S. Government Printing Office. (See p. xvii.)

8. Marshall & Tucker. (1992).

9. Ibid.

10. Following are the percentages of registered voters within the Austin Independent School District boundaries who voted for school board elections between April 7, 1984, and January 15, 1994:

Date of Election	Percentage of Voters
April 7, 1984	12.0
April 5, 1986	6.1
April 26, 1986	4.8
January 16, 1988	8.1
February 13, 1988	6.8
January 20, 1990	8.7
February 17, 1990	5.4
January 18, 1992	9.2
February 15, 1992	6.1
January 15, 1994	11.1

11. According to the Texas Association of School Administrators, the most common tenure for a superintendent in Texas school districts with 5,000 or more students is 3–5 years.

12. Paredes, V. (1991). *Caution: Hazardous grade*. (Publication No. 90.26). Austin: Austin Independent School District, Office of Research and Evaluation.

13. Tomlinson, T. (1992). *Hard work and high expectations: Motivating students to learn*. Washington, D.C.: U.S. Government Printing Office.

14. American Association of School Administrators. (1992). *Creating quality schools*. Arlington, Va.: The American Association of School Administrators.

Deming, W. E. (1982). *Quality, productivity, and competitive position*. Cambridge, Mass.: MIT.

Dobyns, L., & Crawford-Mason, C. (1991). *Quality or else: The revolution in world business*. Boston: Houghton Mifflin.

9. CULTURAL BOUNDARIES, FAMILY RESOURCES, AND PARENTAL ACTIONS

1. Delgado-Gaitan, C., & Trueba, H. (1991). *Crossing cultural borders: Education for immigrant families in America*. London: The Falmer Press.

Eccles, J. S., Midgley, C., Wigfield, A., Buchanan, C. M., Reuman, D., Flanagan, C., & MacIver, D. (1993). Development during adolescence: The impact of stage environment fit on young adolescents' experiences in schools and in families. *American Psychologist, 48*, 90–101.

Garcia, E. E. (1992). "Hispanic" children: Theoretical, empirical, and related policy issues. *Educational Psychology Review, 4* (1), 69–93.

Swap, S. M. (1990). Comparing three philosophies of home-school collaboration. *Equity and Choice, 7*, 9–19.

Violand-Sanchez, E., Sutton, C. P., & Ware, H. W. (1991). *Fostering home-school cooperation: Involving language minority families as partners in education*. Washington, D.C.: National Clearinghouse for Bilingual Education.

2. We conducted two kinds of analyses to determine if cultural variables influenced the graduation outcome of the students we studied. In Chapter 6, we reported (in note

1), the results of chi-square tests to determine if immigration status was related to graduation status. We found that neither a student's birth in Mexico nor his or her parent's birth in Mexico was related to whether the student graduated.

In the second kind of analysis, an analysis of variance, we used the parent's reported frequency of speaking English as the dependent variable (0 = speak English only, 1 = speak mostly English, 2 = speak mostly Spanish, 3 = speak Spanish only) and graduation status (graduate/dropout) as the independent variable. The results indicated that graduation status was unrelated to frequency of speaking English.

3. To test the possibilities that parental education or income influenced the graduation outcomes of students, we conducted two types of analyses of variance. In one type, parental education was the dependent variable; in the other, the breadwinner's earnings was the dependent variable. All three analyses of variance had the same independent variable, graduation status (graduate/dropout).

In one of the analyses about education, the dependent variable was the educational attainment of the mothers. In the second, the dependent variable was the educational attainment of the fathers. Graduation status yielded a statistically significant effect when the dependent variable was mother's education—$F(1, 59) = 7.27$, $p < .009$. For father's education, the effect for graduation status was of borderline significance—$F(1, 51) = 3.70, p < .06$. An examination of the means indicates that in both cases, graduates had parents who had completed more years of education than the parents of dropouts had completed.

In the analyses about income, the dependent variable was the estimated hourly wage of the chief breadwinner in the family. We estimated the hourly wage of the breadwinner by taking the occupation reported for the chief breadwinner and comparing it against a table of mean wages for that occupation in Texas as reported by the Texas Employment Commission for 1986, the closest year for which wage information was available when we began our study. Breadwinners who were unemployed were assigned a zero monthly wage. We found that the breadwinners for graduates made about \$8.99 an hour, while the breadwinners for dropouts made about \$5.67 an hour. This difference was statistically significant—$F(1, 64) = 7.28, p < .009$.

These findings are consistent with that of previous studies of Hispanic parents.

Valenzuela, A., & Dornbusch, S. M. (1994). Familism and social capital in the academic achievement of Mexican origin and Anglo adolescents. *Social Science Quarterly, 75* (1), 18–36.

4. U.S. Bureau of the Census. (1991). The Hispanic population in the United States: March 1990. *Current Population Reports.* (Series P-20, No. 449). Washington D.C.: U.S. Government Printing Office. (See table A, p. 4.)

5. We found that the mother's education was strongly correlated with the reading—$r(62) = .51, p < .01$—but not the mathematics—$r(63) = .19$, n.s.—percentile scores of their students in our study. Similarly, the father's education was strongly correlated with the reading—$r(54) = .48, p < .01$—but not the mathematics—$r(55) = .18$, n.s.—percentile scores of their students in our study. The percentile scores were based on the students' performance on the Iowa Test of Basic Skills.

6. The relationship between the qualities of the home environment and the educational levels of parents has been investigated by many researchers over the years. One of the leaders in this field is Bettye Caldwell, who has quantified the qualities of the home environment in terms of the experiences that promote intellectual de-

velopment. With her colleagues, she has found that better-educated people provide homes that promote intellectual development more than do less-educated people. Following are two of her publications:

Bradley, R., Caldwell, B., & Elardo, R. (1977). Home environment, social status, and mental test performance. *Journal of Educational Psychology*,*69*, 697–701.

Caldwell, B., & Bradley, R. (1984). *Home observation for measurement of the environment*. Little Rock, Ark.: University of Arkansas.

7. Delgado-Gaitan, C. (1990). *Literacy for empowerment: The role of parents in children's education*. New York: The Falmer Press.

Philips, S. (1983). *The invisible culture: Communication in classroom and community on the Warm Springs Indian Reservation*. New York: Longman.

8. We found that the father's education was strongly and negatively correlated with the number of children he had—r (70) = $-.57, p < .01$. That is, the more education a man had, the fewer children he had. In our sample, the correlation between the mother's educational level and the number of children she had was not significant.

9. At the beginning of our study, when our students were 15 years old, we asked them to make eight choices between two alternatives. They were asked to tell us which of the two was more important to them. In each paired comparison, one of the choices was "doing schoolwork." We found that only when "helping my family" was pitted against "doing schoolwork" did the schoolwork choice *not* beat out the competition. Below are the results.

Percentage of students selecting each option in the eight paired comparisons:

34% Buying a car, or
64% Doing my schoolwork.

64% Doing my schoolwork, or
34% Wearing stylish clothes.

66% Helping my family, or
27% Doing my schoolwork.

71% Doing my schoolwork, or
25% Making money now.

37% Spending time with my friends, or
61% Doing my schoolwork.

91% Doing my schoolwork, or
5% Starting a family.

24% Talking on the telephone, or
73% Doing my schoolwork.

26% Watching television, or
71% Doing my schoolwork.

10. In 1986, the Texas Legislature passed a law, House Bill 1010, dealing with school dropouts, which required parental notification of a student being designated as "at risk" of dropping out.

11. The Austin Independent School District had an annual dropout rate of around 10%. That is, each year, almost 10% of the secondary-level students dropped out. And yet, every year, almost 50% of the secondary students were designated by state criteria as "at risk" of dropping out. The state criteria were based on research taking a longitudinal perspective. That is, the research indicated, for example, that a student who had been retained more than once was very likely to drop out some time during his or her secondary school experience. But the student could stop attending during any school year. Of those who dropped out each year, about two thirds had been designated as "at risk." The other third, however, had not been designated as "at risk." Given all of this ambiguity, the school district decided not to use the words—"at risk of dropping out," for fear of needlessly alarming some parents.

12. We found a statistical connection between parents' not being able to remember why their child had been designated as "at risk" and parents' not believing that the child was truly "at risk." Only 15% of the parents who did not know why their child had been designated as "at risk" also told us that their child was "at risk" of dropping out. The remaining 85% who did not remember also told us that they did not believe that their child was "at risk." The chi-square $(1, 89)$ between these two responses on our first questionnaire was $9.86, p < .002$.

13. The chi-square $(1, 67)$ between the parents' belief that the student was "at risk" at Year One and their graduation status at Year Four was $6.83, p < .01$. This relationship is statistically significant and indicates that parents who recognized that their children were "at risk" were more likely to have their children drop out.

14. After each telephone interview with the parents, the interviewers rated how much "in touch" with the child's emotional state the parents seemed to be during the interview. The interviewers rated the parents as a 1 if they seemed out of touch completely, 2 if they seemed only a little in touch, 3 if they were somewhat in touch, and 4 if they seemed very much in touch. The mean scores of these ratings for the four categories of parents are given in the table below.

| | | Year One: Recognized "At Risk"? | |
		Recognized Risk	Did Not Recognize Risk
Year Four:	Graduate	3.20	2.53
Graduation Status	Dropout	2.33	1.87

We conducted an analysis of variance on these "in touch" means, as dependent variables. In this analysis, the Recognized "At Risk" at Year One variable (coded: Recognized/Not Recognized) was one of the independent variables and Graduation Status at Year Four (coded: Graduate/Dropout) was the other independent variable. The results of this analysis indicated that the "At Risk" at Year One variable was not significantly related to being "in touch." However, the Graduation Status at Year Four variable was significantly related to being "in touch"—$F(1, 53) = 5.54, p < .02$.

The parents of graduates were more in touch with their children than were the parents of dropouts.

More importantly, the two independent variables yielded a significant statistical interaction—$F (1, 53) = 5.17, p < .03$. As shown in the table, the parents who recognized the risk and yet their children were able to graduate (we called them Alerted in table 9.1) were much more "in touch" with their children than any of the other three categories of parents (named in table 9.1: Denied, Unable, and Out of Touch). Conversely, parents who did not recognize the risk and their children dropped out (we called them Out of Touch) were the least "in touch" with the feelings and concerns of their children.

10. WHAT SCHOOLS MUST DO TO IMPROVE GRADUATION RATES

1. Hill, P. T., & Bonan, J. (1991). Decentralization and accountability in public education. *Selected Rand Monographs* (R-4066-MCF/IET). Santa Monica, Calif.: The RAND Corporation.

2. The fundamental problem in American education is that school administrations took the management theories developed at the end of the last century for industrial production and applied them to public schools. In line with this mass production, industrial model, school administrators regarded their job as one of directing the production of graduates, not facilitating the learning of children and youth. An excellent description of the application of "scientific management" to American public schools is provided by the following book:

    Callahan, R. E. (1962). *Education and the cult of efficiency*. Chicago: University of Chicago Press.

3. Fullan, M. (1982). *The meaning of educational change*. New York: Teachers College Press, Columbia University.

    Waugh, R. F., & Punch, K. F. (1987). Teacher receptivity to systemwide change in the implementation stage. *Review of Educational Research, 57* (3), 237–254.

4. According to the Bureau of the Census, 26.4% of Hispanic men and 36.6% of Hispanic women were low earners in 1992. Low earners were defined as those who earned less than $13,091 from year-round, full-time work. For comparison, among Whites, 11.6% of men and 21.1% of women were low earners. In 1979, 13.4% of Hispanic men and 32.3% of Hispanic women were low earners, while 7.2% of White men and 19.8% of White women were low earners. This information is found in the following report:

    U.S. Bureau of the Census. (1994). The earnings ladder: Who's at the bottom? Who's at the top? *Statistical Brief* (SB/94-4). Washington, D.C.: U.S. Department of Commerce.

5. Estrada, A. L., Trevino, F. M., & Ray, L. A. (1990). Health care utilization barriers among Mexican Americans: Evidence from HHANES 1982–84. *American Journal of Public Health, 80,* 27–31.

6. Trevino, F. M., Moss, A. J. (1984). Health indicators for Hispanic, Black, and White Americans. *Vital and Health Statistics*, Series 10, No. 148. (DHHS Pub. No. PHS-84-1576). Washington, D.C.: Public Health Service, National Center for Health Statistics.

Trevino, F. M., & Moss, A. J. (1983). Health insurance coverage and physician visits among Hispanic and non-Hispanic people. *Health — United States, 1983*, 45–48. (DHHS Pub. No. PHS-84-1232). Washington, D.C.: Public Health Service, National Center for Health Statistics.

7. In 1992, Austin Independent School District conducted a survey of teachers. One of the items on the survey was: "All students can function at or beyond age-appropriate grade level." Teachers were asked to rate the degree of their agreement with this statement on a 5-point scale. Among elementary school teachers, only 38.4% agreed or strongly agreed with the statement, 17% were neutral, and 44.6% disagreed or strongly disagreed. Among secondary teachers, only 26.1% agreed or strongly agreed, 13.2% were neutral, and 60.7% disagreed or strongly disagreed. Overall, these results suggest that most of the teachers in the district did not believe that all students were able to acquire grade-level skills. More information about this survey is contained in the following document:

Spano, S. G. (1992). *Shedding light on district issues, 1991–92: Survey of students, staff, and graduates.* (Publication No. 91-21). Austin: Austin Independent School District, Office of Research and Evaluation.

8. As we were in the process of finalizing this book, a court ruling gave parents the opportunity to see the TAAS questions within 30 days after the test had been administered and graded. On December 29, 1994, Judge Dan Downey, presiding in the District Court of Harris County, Texas, determined that parents have a fundamental right "to direct the upbringing and education of their children." He ruled that refusing to allow parents to view the TAAS test after it had been administered and graded violated that right. The Pasadena, Texas, school district and the Texas Education Code had prohibited parents from viewing the tests, claiming that the confidentiality of the questions had to be maintained to preserve the validity and reliability of the test. The court ruled that there was "no rational and reasonable basis" for refusing to permit parents to view the test after it has been administered and graded. The judge argued that "prohibiting parents from viewing the test after it had been administered and graded unconstitutionally infringed upon the fundamental right of parents to direct the upbringing and education of their children."

Larry Maxwell et al. v. *Pasadena ISD et al.*, No. 92-017184, District Court of Harris County, Texas, 29th Judicial District, December 29, 1994.

9. National Education Commission on Time and Learning. (1994). *Prisoners of time.* Washington, D.C.: U.S. Government Printing Office.

Cheney, L. V. (1991). *National tests: What other countries expect their students to know.* Washington, D.C.: National Endowment for the Humanities.

10. Glover, R. W., & Weisberg, A. (1994). *School-to-work transition in the U.S.: The case of missing social partners.* College Park: Center for Learning and Competitiveness, University of Maryland.

11. Callahan, R. E. (1962). *Education and the cult of efficiency.* Chicago: The University of Chicago Press.

12. Mehan, H., Hubbard, L., & Villanueva, I. (1994). Forming academic identities: Accommodation without assimilation among involuntary minorities. *Anthropology and Education Quarterly, 25* (2), 91–117.

Mehan, H., Hubbard, L., Okamoto, D., & Villanueva, I. (1994). Untracking high school students in preparation for college: Implications for Latino students. In A.

Hurtado & E. E. Garcia, eds. *The educational achievement of Latinos: Barriers and successes.* Santa Cruz: Regents of the University of California.

Swanson, M. C., Mehan, H., & Hubbard, L. (1994). The AVID classroom: Academic and social support for low-achieving students. In J. Oakes & K. H. Quartz, eds. *Creating new educational communities.* Chicago: National Society for de Sheiyl Education. 94th Yearbook.

13. National Education Commission on Time and Learning. (1994). *Prisoners of time.*
14. Ibid.
15. Zane, N. (1994). When discipline problems recede: Democracy and intimacy in urban charters. In M. Fine, ed. *Chartering urban school reform,* 122–135. New York: Teachers College Press, Columbia University.
16. After our study was completed, several cities began crackdowns on truancy by devoting more uniformed officers to finding and arresting truants. In 1994, Austin began such a program. Truants were arrested by police and sent to collection centers in high schools where their reasons for not being in school were heard and acted upon.
17. McMullen, B. J. (1994). Charters and restructuring. In Fine. *Chartering urban school reform,* 63–78.
18. Secretary's Commission on Achieving Necessary Skills (SCANS). (1991). *What work requires of schools: A SCANS report for America 2000.* Washington, D.C.: U.S. Department of Labor.
19. Ferdman, B. M. (1990). Literacy and cultural identity. *Harvard Educational Review,* 60 (2), 181–204.
20. Stevenson, H. W., & Stigler, J. W. (1992). *The learning gap: Why our schools are failing and what we can learn from Japanese and Chinese education.* New York: Summit Books.
21. "The average public expenditure for college youths is more than seven times larger than the average post–high school investment for the noncollege population." The U.S. invests about $20,000 for each college youth and about $9,000 for each noncollege youth ($9,000 being the average cost of a high school education). This information is from the following document:

U.S. General Accounting Office. (1990). *Training strategies: Preparing noncollege youth for employment in the U.S.,* 3. Washington, D.C.
22. Carnegie Foundation for the Advancement of Teaching. (1994). *The academic profession: An international perspective.* Ewing, N.J.: California/Princeton Fulfillment Services.
23. Frazer, L. H. (1990). *1989–90 dropout report.* (Publication No. 90.12). Austin: Austin Independent School District, Office of Research and Evaluation.
24. Stevenson & Stigler. (1992). *The learning gap.*
25. Ibid.
26. Berliner, D. C. (1993). International comparisons of student achievement: A false guide for reform. *National Forum: Phi Kappa Phi Journal,* 73 (4), 25–29.
27. The New Standards Project is one of several endeavors that aim to establish national standards for American high school graduates. The New Standards Project is sponsored by the Center on Education and the Economy in Rochester, New York, and will establish "world class" standards that will be assessed by a variety of methods, including performance-based methods.

28. Lareau, A. (1989). *Home advantage: Social class and parental intervention in elementary education.* New York: The Falmer Press.

29. Bishop, J. (1989). Why the apathy in American high school? *Educational Researcher, 18* (1), 6–10, 42.

30. Berlin, G., & Sum, A. (1988). *Toward a more perfect union: Basic skills, poor families, and our economic future.* Occasional Paper 3. New York: Ford Foundation.

 Reich, R. B. (1991). *The work of nations: Preparing ourselves for 21st century capitalism.* New York: Knopf.

31. Glover, R. W., & Marshall, F. R. (1993). Improving the school-to-work transition of American adolescents. *Teachers College Record, 94,* 588–609.

32. Dayton, C., Raby, M., Stern, D., & Weisberg, A. (1992, March). The California partnership academies: Remembering the "forgotten half." *Phi Delta Kappan,* 539–545.

 Dayton, C., Weisberg, A., & Stern, D. (1989). *Graduate follow-up survey of the June 1988 and June 1989 graduates of the California partnership academies.* Berkeley, Calif.: University of California, Policy Analysis for California Education.

 Stern, D. (1992). *Career academies: Partnerships for reconstructing American high schools.* San Francisco: Jossey Bass.

33. The Austin Independent School District estimates that about 20% of their graduates complete a bachelor's degree within 5 years after graduation.

34. Texas Education Agency & Texas Department of Commerce. (1993). *School-to-work transition: A Texas perspective.* (GE4-301-01). Austin.

 A national study of the high-performance workplace of the future estimated that 70% of the jobs available in the 21st century will not require a bachelor's degree. This national study is described in the following document:

 National Center on Education and the Economy's Commission on the Skills of the American Workforce. (1990). *America's choice: High skills or low wages!* Rochester, N.Y.

35. Glover, R. W., & Weisberg, A. (1994, March 23). America's school-to-work transition: The case of the missing social partners. *Education Week,* 1.

36. Greenberger, E., & Steinberg, L. D. (1986). *When teenagers work: The psychological and social costs of adolescent employment.* New York: Basic Books.

37. National Center on Education and the Economy's Commission on the Skills of the American Workforce. (1990). *America's choice,* 73.

38. Texas Education Agency & Texas Department of Commerce. (1993). *School-to-work transition.*

INDEX